THE VOICE
OF THE NARRATOR
IN CHILDREN'S LITERATURE

Recent Titles In
Contributions to the Study of World Literature

THE VOICE
OF THE NARRATOR
IN CHILDREN'S
LITERATURE

Insights from Writers and Critics

Edited by
CHARLOTTE F. OTTEN
and
GARY D. SCHMIDT

Contributions to the Study of World Literature, Number 28

GREENWOOD PRESS
New York • Westport, Connecticut • London

Library of Congress Cataloging-in-Publication Data

The Voice of the narrator in children's literature : insights from
   writers and critics / edited by Charlotte F. Otten and Gary D.
   Schmidt.
      p. cm. — (Contributions to the study of world literature,
   ISSN 0738–9345 ; no. 28)
      Bibliography: p.
      Includes index.
      ISBN 0–313–26370–1 (lib. bdg. : alk. paper)
      1. Children's literature—History and criticism.   2. Children's
   literature—Authorship.   3. Narration (Rhetoric)   4. Point of view
   (Literature)   I. Otten, Charlotte F.   II. Schmidt, Gary D.
   III. Series.
   PN1009.A1V65   1989
   809'.89282—dc19   88–7709

British Library Cataloguing in Publication Data is available.

Copyright © 1989 by Charlotte F. Otten and Gary D. Schmidt

All rights reserved. No portion of this book may be
reproduced, by any process or technique, without the
express written consent of the publisher.

Library of Congress Catalog Card Number: 88–7709
ISBN: 0–313–26370–1
ISSN: 0738–9345

First published in 1989

Greenwood Press, Inc.
88 Post Road West, Westport, Connecticut   06881

Printed in the United States of America

The paper used in this book complies with the
Permanent Paper Standard issued by the National
Information Standards Organization (Z39.48–1984).

10 9 8 7 6 5 4 3 2 1

Contents

Illustrations

Preface

With the growth of literary theory in the study of English literature has come an increasing awareness of the complexities of narration. What once seemed a simple matter of identification—naming the narrator—is now as elusive as it is important. No longer can the familiar categories of narration (first person; second person; third person, omniscient or limited) explain the role of the narrator, let alone define the voice of the narrator. The word *voice* itself is undergoing changes: it has moved from being a strictly descriptive term into the realm of metaphor that now includes more than point of view and that encompasses all that identity itself connotes.

For us, two teachers of children's literature (one a medievalist, the other a Renaissance scholar), the narrators of the Arthurian cycle are now as resistant to categorization as is the narrator of *Paradise Lost*. Our discussion of the narrators in our specialized areas did not extend to children's literature. Gradually, however, the voice of the narrator entered our conversations by way, first of all, of Maurice Sendak's illustrations, when we realized that the visual narrator has a voice distinct from that of the textural narrator, and when we next identified the narrator of *Winnie-the-Pooh* and found him dual. The more we looked at the voice of the narrator in children's literature, the more we realized that the voice of the narrator is as unique there as is the voice of each human being in life, and that to identify the voice of the narrator is to burrow into the creative process of narration.

Our next step was to try out our discovery on illustrators, on authors, and on critics. We hoped not to impose a theory of narration upon them but to act as a stimulus to inquiry and discovery. We wrote to more than forty authors and critics, inviting them to engage in a critical discussion with us (and eventually with a larger audience) on what was turning out to be no longer merely a topic for discussion but the focus of a book. The response was corroborative: They agreed that whether the literature was written for adults or for children, whether it was written recently or centuries ago, who tells the story makes all the difference. And the question they tackled was, Who is the *who*?

They began the difficult but exhilarating task of attempting to identify the voice of the narrator in their own books (in the case of illustrators and authors) and in the books of others (in the case of critics). We selected the areas of inquiry: eight genres along traditional lines in the study of children's literature, and each genre divided into the authorial voice and the critical voice. The literature they chose to write about ranged from Old Testament stories to realistic stories about nuclear war, from illustrated book to poetry to nonfiction. The essays came from various geographic areas: the United States, Canada, Great Britain, and Australia. The critical theories on which they drew included not only the contemporary theory of a Bakhtin, but the classical narrative theory of a Henry James. As the essays arrived we were delighted with the paradox: the voice of the narrator in children's literature was unique in each instance, but the essays were united by their concern with voice. Our introductions to each section, although expository, continue the exploration of these "harmonious" paradoxes.

The pleasant task of thanking our contributors confronts us. The truth is obvious—without them the book could not have been written. There are others to thank: Calvin College for summer Faculty Research Grants; the Calvin College Alumni Association for a research grant; Conrad Bult and Jo Duyst, Calvin College librarians, for assistance in tracing bibliographic entries; the staff of the English Department for typing the manuscript in various stages—Alma Walhout, Keri Bruggink, Michelle DeRose, and Kathleen Struck; student research assistants—Danette Thomas, Cindi Monte, and Elizabeth Doornbos; Ellen Alderink, audio-visual technician; and our spouses, Robert T. Otten and Anne Stickney Schmidt, whose voices of support were clearly audible, even when the din of the word processor printer drowned out all other sounds.

PART I

The Illustrated Book

Introduction

CHARLOTTE F. OTTEN

At first glance there seems to be an implied contradiction (or at least syn-aesthesia) in the phrase "the voice of the illustrator." Voice is aural, illus-tration is visual; voice is heard, illustration is seen. In contemporary literary criticism, however, voice has come to mean the act of narrating, with a teller and an audience; the unique qualities of a story; the aspects of the story that help to identify the narrator. It has become, in short, what the French critics call "identity." Identity is defined to include the narrator's point of view, perspective, focus, and stance. Voice is more than aural, more than verbal.

In the case of illustrator and illustration, voice is complicated by the fact that the illustrator is mandated by the text to discover not only the unique qualities of the text but also the identity of the narrator (even when the book is authored by the illustrator). The illustrator, however, also has a voice, which, though nonverbal, embraces all the aspects of voice described above. Identity defines the voice of the illustrator as much as it does the voice of the verbal narrator, with the linguistic tools of verbal narration being aug-mented by the artistic tools of visual narration. Although the illustrator cannot ignore the voice of the verbal narrator or subvert the text, the illus-trator cannot suppress his or her own voice. The illustrated book then is a collaboration—or, better, a polyphony—of voices.

Maurice Sendak, whose voice is unmistakable (no less in someone else's text than in his own), suggests, in an interview with Charlotte F. Otten, that his narrative images in Randall Jarrell's *Fly by Night* and *The Juniper Tree and Other Tales from Grimm* and in his own *Outside Over There* are more than his own subjective experience and more than an elaboration of the connected discourse of the text. His images, whether of a flying, luminous boy; the maternal lapse and the mother owl; death, the devil, and a "phoenix" bird; maternal children and absent fathers, are thick with the passionate needs of a child, including those of the child Sendak, the child Jarrell, the child Grimm, and the child reader. His narrative voice catches the child's involvement in retribution and forgiveness, and the child's recognition of the complexities and contradictions of love's demands. Sendak's narrative voice defies predictability, searches for and finds subtexts (even in his own texts), identifies personal and universal experience, and calls reader and illustrator to experiences that transcend the narrow autobiographies of illustrator, teller, and reader.

Barbara Cooney's voice is multiple yet single. She hears the voices of Chaucer, Lumiansky, Grimm, Hall, and Cooney, and incorporates them into her illustrations, where they blend into one voice. The resonances of *Miss Rumphius* are magnified by Cooney's own voice, which climbs "tall mountains where the snow never melted," catches the "steeple of the Second Congregational church just over the hill" in Damariscotta, Maine, and watches her grandchild eating a cookie during the cycle of New England seasons. Her narrators not only tell the story but are part of the meaning. Cooney's self-conscious choices of elements are, paradoxically, her way of linking the consciousness of her readers to her own.

For Leonard Everett Fisher, the changes in his voice are essential to his identity. Both an artist and a writer, he describes himself as "an artist who writes." His artistic tools and articulation of them create a new voice. Whether illustrating fiction or nonfiction, Fisher's voice chooses the medium, and the medium forms the voice. Trained in every aspect of the graphic arts, Fisher can use egg tempera or acrylic, scratchboard or otherwise, black and white or color, and turn them into dramatically resolved form. When communicating information, he has the same commitment—to the writing and the illustration—as he has for all the genres in which he works. Form and voice become one.

Ruth MacDonald shows that Beatrix Potter puts herself and her child reader into her voice: Potter views the collaboration of artist, animals, and readers as a delightful conspiracy. Potter's voice, if viewed by modern critical theory, is a unique blend of all three—and all three create the meaning. Her illustrations of animals, fictionalized by the voice, interpret human behavior in ways that are comic despite the potential for tragedy.

Patricia Morley's William Kurelek emerges as an illustrator who read his own identity in terms of faith in God: his lifelong quest was to get editors and readers to recognize the religious voice in his illustrations. His voice is complicated by his awareness of readers' hostility, ambivalence, resistance to and sometimes acceptance, of its religious distinctiveness. Autobiography and art were for Kurelek one inseparable religious voice.

THE AUTHORIAL VOICE

1

Maurice Sendak's Narrative Images

MAURICE SENDAK

Maurice Sendak in an Interview with Charlotte F. Otten
October 6, 1987, Ridgefield, Connecticut

OTTEN: When we talk about the role of the illustrator for someone else's text, we usually expect the illustrations to enlarge or enhance the text: The artist encounters the language of the story and in illustration makes the language come alive. It seems to me, however, that in your encounters with the text of Randall Jarrell's *Fly by Night* (1976) and *The Juniper Tree and Other Tales from Grimm* (1973) you made discoveries about your own personal experiences of childhood and linked them to the universal experiences of childhood. Beneath the surface of the text lurk powerful images—images that you transformed into an artistic narrative that deepens (even mythologizes) the text and that transcends the merely autobiographical. Let's take a look at your illustrations of Randall Jarrell's *Fly by Night*.

Randall Jarrell starts *Fly by Night* with unusual specificity to convince the reader that this is a credible story. A boy named David lives on a specific road, a mile and a half north; then Jarrell says, "You come to a lake on a farm," and beyond is a house. "A big red chow walks along by you on the inside," and a little boy lives there "sitting in a tree house in the willow." Then, crucially, "At night David can fly. In the daytime he can't. In the daytime he doesn't even remember that he can." Now comes the artist-narrator Maurice Sendak in the frontispiece of *Fly by Night*. I have a list here of the ways in which I think that you not only enhance and enlarge the text, but that you create narrative images of your own that do fascinating things to or with the text. For example, David is not a *little* boy, he dominates the scene, he's almost as large as the house, he rides the tree like he's flying,

1. Illustration by Maurice Sendak from *Fly By Night* by Randall Jarrell. Illustration copyright © by Maurice Sendak 1976. Reprinted by permission of Farrar, Straus & Giroux and The Bodley Head, London.

he's not wearing identifiably little boy's clothing or night clothing, and his face seems to indicate that he remembers, although Jarrell tells us that he does not. I suspect, however, that Maurice Sendak is telling us that David may have dim memories of flying and that images of freedom are floating about in his subconscious. You have frequently traveled the road back into childhood where the Wild Things dance and a boy named Mickey flies. My question is this: When you met Jarrell's David in the text, did you identify with him? Did the surface description of him push you into remembering dreams of flying and discovering something about your own mythic past?

SENDAK: In the case of Jarrell, hearing it again read by you, that wonderful commonplace lead into "At night David can fly," that's a perfect example of how only Randall could throw you on your side. There's the clue: In the "ordinariness" is the "extraordinary." Randall as a poet and writer does that so well. What, then, was there for me to do? This was always a problem between me and Randall; it was a discussion that came up very frequently. Much as I loved his work and wanted to illustrate it, really, what could I accomplish when I thought he served the purpose of both writer and illustrator? I had to find a particular and unique way of discovering myself in his book.

I don't identify with David, and I don't identify with flying (or at least not consciously). What I was trying to do was burrow myself into the text, or into Randall's mind, because when one is illustrating a great book it isn't so much to find the self in the book (ultimately that is what you do), but one's conscious effort is to find the writer in the text, or to find the subtext—the routes to what the author was trying to achieve. It isn't anything you can do consciously. You cannot take a class in reading the subtext, or a class to teach you how to serve the purpose of the book. It is an instinctual capacity, and you either have it or you don't. For this reason there are many books that I cannot illustrate. That is why I illustrate just those books that I can nose in on. We could name a dozen wonderful books that I couldn't handle. With Randall there was a peculiar sensibility, knowing where he was, or at least thinking I knew where he was. We never spoke of it, we never verified it or checked it out. But with *Fly by Night* I found—it's almost too private to discuss actually and I don't want to discuss it in literal terms—but I found such a wealth of "personalness." It was like entering a very vivid world, alive, intense, a world that I could inhabit during the time that I illustrated Jarrell that I felt was perfectly my own. Once I smell out the world of the writer, things that seem a bit arbitrary to most people don't concern me at all because I know I'm there.

On the surface there is no similarity between the kind of child I was or the man I am, or the kind of man Randall was, or the kind of boy David is. He's a midwestern, middle-America boy; I have no identification with such a child—none. I even have difficulty drawing such children since I'm used to drawing big-headed immigrant children. He's a blondish-looking boy, and that's a problem. But once I sniffed out the subtext, I didn't much care what he looked like. I mean, he symbolized something. He became emblematic of something else. I figured out how to draw him good enough (drawing has never been a major concern of mine, as critics will tell you). Once I'm there, then the surface is only surface. If you're not there, then you shouldn't be bothering anyway. So I found myself entering Jarrell's world, as I have in all the books I've done, and finding my own mother there, and finding my own childhood there; again, not in the obvious autobiographical sense, at all. If my mother's there it's not because of conceit, not because it would be charming to get my mother in there, it's because the book is so, on one level, passionately about mothers, passionately about the owl's maternal song. Even what isn't said is about the hungry attention demanded from mothers. Once you know that, once you feel that, then, of course, you can attach yourself to your own mama in ways that you remember from your own childhood. It's a perfectly natural thing to have my own mama there.

And so all these echoes, all these calls, all these signals you get from a great text, is all the meat and potatoes that an illustrator needs. Without them, it's like scratching on the wall. You have to get to that central place. You know, there's an argument against that, the one that says that illustrations are purely decorative. But that isn't my particular role, that isn't my concern. There are many others that achieve that. Mine always will be to burrow in like a tick and to find the necessary blood to eat off until I'm satisfied.

OTTEN: And that's what comes out in *Fly by Night*. I personally could not read Jarrell without you.

SENDAK: That's a lovely compliment. I think it's almost to say too much because I've always felt not exactly intimidated by Randall, but just a bit uneasy. Randall's work was unquestionably the most difficult to cope with because I respected him so much, I loved him so much. My own ethic in terms of what is to be illustrated and what is not to be illustrated came into conflict in his books. Randall and I had a difference of opinion over *The Animal Family*. We ended up with "Decorations by Maurice Sendak," and I couldn't have done more discreet pictures. He was like a locomotive barreling down the tracks, and I didn't want to get in his way. But, alas, in the end there were only three books from Jarrell, and I could wish for a dozen more. For me there has not been a contemporary writer since Jarrell's death who could match him.

OTTEN: The images in the illustrations suggest more than subjective experience and do not reflect the connected discourse of the text. Like surrealism, you give the simultaneity of experience, which is intensely dramatic without movement. In *Fly by Night*, there is not a great deal of movement, as there is in *Wild Things* and *Night Kitchen*. *Fly by Night* is a quieter, more static experience; it doesn't have all that dancing about, though it has the word "fly" in it. Your symbols are doing the narrating. For example, although the mice talk about "that great black thing in the sky," actually David—your illustration of him—is luminous: He sheds light on the mice and the cat (11). There again, you are pulling from the subtext what the surface text does not give. David is light (he's not lit by the moon), and there's a physical radiance in your David which shows inner delight in freedom without ever having him move. It's interesting that we usually associate darkness with nightmare, and instead you have given us David in a night state, lighting up everything in his presence. Did you intend to show that the dream state of a child is perhaps a freer state than the conscious state?

SENDAK: There's something always interesting in the paradox of contradiction. I mean, if the text is about action, the pictures might be about nonaction. It's not to contradict arbitrarily, but just to make a point. As I said earlier, Jarrell doesn't need me to show mice scurrying about and the movement that they would obviously make. To me the book is the landscape of something still, something frozen in time. I don't want to see David moving; I want to see frozen images of him, because in dreamscapes, and in my own dreams, if there's any movement, it might be of falling off a cliff, but I don't move. It's that excruciating sense of hanging in space, and that's what I wanted to get into David's dream—the sense of excruciating non-movement, but also the incredible (we spoke of the mother image, allied to that) sensuality of the story. It's so thick with the passionate need of a child for his mother, and the pleasurable sense that a child has of his own naked body. And there's nothing more erotic than a dream, even without Freud's intervention.

This luminosity you were talking about—he is giving off a kind of electrical light because he's giving it off to himself. He's giving himself tremendous pleasure in this dream. That is a very important aspect of life to me—that the body plays some part in the esoteric rhythms of living. And so to a child there is this exquisite pleasure in the flesh and bones of our lives, until he or she learns otherwise. This is an erotic dream: he's stark naked in balmy air. Let's imagine how wonderful that must feel.

OTTEN: And that kind of ecstasy comes out in the light you use.

SENDAK: *Ecstasy* is a good word.

OTTEN: Going on with *Fly by Night*. It is interesting to note that Jarrell has a set pattern of storytelling: David floats off, has a series of encounters, meets an owl who tells a story-within-a-story where the mother is the essence of maternity, and then there is the return to orange juice and pancakes. You seem, however, as the artist-narrator almost to have destroyed the formal, predictable patterns, and created new ones. For example, in that final scene, the sparrow is larger than a sparrow, the cat is menacing on the table; and, although David is larger than life size in all the illustrations, he is absent from the final illustration. While Jarrell's text predicts this wonderful reunion with his mother and orange juice and pancakes, what we have in the closing scene from you is an illustration where the cat is menacing, the sparrow is as large as a hawk, David is absent. All this seems to indicate that there is some order of reality here that you've established to finish *your* story (31).

Your images have an artist's autonomy, an integrity that comes from an artist's construction of the text.

SENDAK: You see, I don't buy the pancakes and orange juice. Randall was dead already when I was doing the pictures, so there obviously wasn't any way of conferring with him on this point. But I felt that although this was not a totally ironical ending, it was a somewhat ironical ending. To me, safety lay in the nightmare-like landscape of that dream. The reality of that kitchen was much more terrifying. And when you are a little boy everything is potentially treacherous: the cat and the sparrow, even maybe real-life mama. The dream is much safer. And that's how I take that ending. After what's gone on in that place, who can buy orange juice and pancakes? It's not a flaw on Jarrell's part. My own feeling is that that is just what he intended.

OTTEN: Also, you have broken into the linear story that Jarrell tells with what appears to be an interlocking three-line spread on pages 25 and 26. On the top line are the owl and the moon. The owl is a kind of benevolent deity; underneath her is David protected by her. She seems to "feather" him: David has been a substitute owling. The mother owl, however, is not looking at David nor at the reader. Her eyes draw the reader in, who wishes that the mother owl would look at him or her. I don't know how you feel when you go back to it, but I keep wanting to say, "Look at me, please." She keeps looking past me. And like the mother in the bottom line of the page, she's maternal but detached. The mother in the corner of the bottom line is your mother holding you; there are sheep next to your mother (those sibling rivals transformed into sheep); there is the shepherdess in the opposite corner next to the suckling lamb. So there are both those mother figures: they are both looking off into space, not at David underneath nor at the child in the arms. And then there's that static middle line with what seems to be David's house—it's illumined—and there are the fence and the sheep. Time is obliterated, and space has no ordinary dimensions.

What we have is a classic pastoral scene—the kind we usually associate with pastoral poetry or pastoral music, and with tranquillity. Does it seem to you, as it does to me, that the maternal is unmoved by events and that tranquillity is only on the surface?

SENDAK: I don't know whether I can answer all of that. All I can say is that there would almost be no need to dream so passionately if your mama were satisfactory in real life. Without saying more than that, there is something omnipresent about the mother, but there is also something detached about her, which doesn't make her unloving or uninterested. It makes you know that there will be another dream and another and another to attach her more and more and more. It's a kind of lure into the dream world that she's there, but she's not looking at you. She is provocative, which means that you will dream about her again. This is not a portrait of my mother or

2. Illustration by Maurice Sendak from *Fly By Night* by Randall Jarrell. Illustration copyright © by Maurice Sendak 1976.
Reprinted by permission of Farrar, Straus & Giroux, and The Bodley Head, London.

of Randall's mother or of David's mother. It is a portrait that comes together from discussions Randall and I had about mothers and the roles they play in our work. And this was not a conscious—it was an unconscious—juxtaposing of images—the ones you describe—that came out of an old sense of how things stood between me and Randall and our mamas, and I can't explain them, nor do I have any wish to. You described it well: the look of the owl, she is both feathering and caring; she's also threatening. And I think what I said to you earlier about the mama and the orange juice and pancakes—I find that a much more threatening mama than I do the owl staring straight out without giving the loving blink that one would like her to give.

OTTEN: That one keeps asking for.

SENDAK: One keeps asking for that all one's life.

OTTEN: As a mother myself I find those maternal lapses in your illustration very reassuring.

SENDAK: Well, you know that image of the maternal lapse is a very crucial one throughout all my work, not just in the book we're describing now. The maternal lapse in *Outside Over There* (1981) pushes, galvanizes the dramatic action. It's the maternal lapse in *Wild Things* that drives Max bonkers; his mother doesn't respond in the way he wishes. It's taking those normal moments when a mother eases back, or more vulgarly said, "poohs out," isn't as attentive as the child wishes twenty-four hours at a time for his or her needs—at that moment the child is unforgiving. And that's also when the child notices the lapse and will interpret it in ways based entirely on what has happened previous to this moment. And so one doesn't know how the child will respond. In point of fact, the lapse is normal; the mother has a right to avert her gaze once in a while. Except that I run into a problem with that. Apparently things like that get me in trouble in my work because it's almost as though it were an insult to motherhood to allow that the poor dame should just knock it off for a minute and make believe that she's living in Zanzibar, and doesn't have four kids and a boring husband (or even a nice one) who's coming home for the night. Strange thing that mothers must always be alert and vigilant; they can't be, so why do we pretend that they are?

OTTEN: Yes, there's that painful honesty in your illustration. Another question. Did Jarrell's death influence your approach to the text?

SENDAK: I'm sure it did, but that would be almost impossible to analyze.

OTTEN: Was it a hard thing to take the text up after his death?

SENDAK: I didn't illustrate the book for I don't know how many years. It may be five, not more than seven years. I didn't want to do it. It was only pressure from my publisher and my own love for Mary, Randall's wife—the feeling that I was letting her down in some way—and my own love for the story, that made me take it up. I had never had to do a story without him. And I couldn't imagine doing it without those particular conversations and insights and pleasures between us as friends and artists. It was a very hard book to do. As it turns out, paradoxically, it's almost my favorite. It has something of everything that I was suffering from his loss in it without it being obvious or apparent.

OTTEN: And it keeps hinting at things that all of us have thought but can't quite articulate.

SENDAK: That's good. That's what it's supposed to do. You see, as I said earlier, it's all there in the story. Randall really tells more than what you call a surface story. He's telling one story, but he's actually telling any number of stories, and he does that all at the same time. There are many great writers—one of my favorites is Herman Melville, and I don't think I'd ever illustrate any of his stories; that would be yielding to a bad impulse; it's belaboring a point; he's already written all the subtexts: everything is there. There's nothing for an illustrator to do except for the vanity of attaching his name to that of the author. *Pierre*, the title of one of my books, is as close as I've gotten to Melville. I chose the name for just that reason, so that I could have a book with the same title as one by Herman Melville. It's as fatuous as that. And I rhymed something with Pierre, and that was "I don't care." And thus is born a book.

OTTEN: Let's leave *Fly by Night* and go on to Grimm. This is appropriate because in *Fly by Night* and the tales from Grimm (which appeared under the title *The Juniper Tree*) you do not create meaning in terms of artistic equivalences to the text but you create meaning by means of narrative images. There are startling things in Grimm that the text doesn't tell us immediately but that your narrative images clue us into: We recognize them when we go back to the text. The illustration that I like very much is, oddly enough, your illustration of Death. It reminds me of Max Ernst and his illustrations of Death; "Death," he said, "is something like Cousin Cynthia." The text of the Grimm story tells us, when the doctor is bargaining with Death, that Death has an ice-cold hand and is angry. But your illustration (233) gives us the story that lies beneath this spare description. You show death as more luminous than the doctor; Death as rather friendly and smiling; Death with hair; Death with his arm around the doctor (the arm is a little longer than normal, or so it seems); the instrument of Death, the sickle, as luminous; the candle lights as reassuring. Your view of Death in this illustration—is it something like this—remembering Sir Thomas Browne, who said, "Thank God, I can die"? Or another way of putting it, how awful it would be to live forever?

SENDAK: I think that as a fifty-nine-year-old man, obviously I've thought a good deal about dying. I was only in my forties when I illustrated Grimm, but I think in a sense I agree with that quote—there is something reassuring about Death. Maybe in the simple sense that "God knows, that there is an

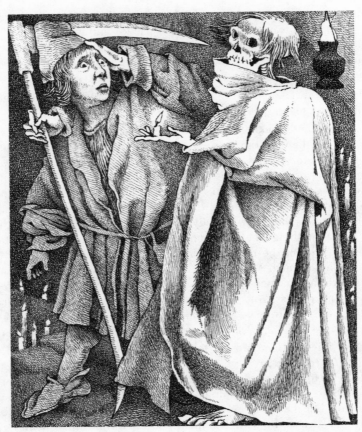

3. Illustration by Maurice Sendak from "Godfather Death" from *The Juniper Tree and Other Tales from Grimm*, translated by Lore Segal and Randall Jarrell. Illustration copyright © by Maurice Sendak 1973. Reprinted by permission of Farrar, Straus & Giroux and The Bodley Head, London.

end." I find no fear in any of that. I find only a kind of comfort. It's curious if that illustration conveys that to you because in doing that picture that was not at all in my conscious mind. I frankly don't remember what I was trying to say. It would be interesting if you were right and that that were some aspect of it. The doctor, as I recollect, was quite fearful—traditional fearful. If you have ever had to put dogs down, as I recently did, along with the misery and the pain comes the astonishment of relief. You feel released. Beyond that, I have no imaginings except to get out of what I think of as a broken jalopy, I mean a body which is brutalizing the spirit. I'd be crazy to be afraid of that. To be hopeful for something else is just as crazy, but that's another story. I don't know whether that had anything to do with your question.

OTTEN: You know, there are so many illustrations of Death, but I keep coming back to yours. Death is almost chummy, and he isn't angry or rude. Your sickle is more luminous than any sickle in art that I can think of. Usually Death scenes are menacing, formidable, and dark (we think of Shakespeare's sonnets with Time as the scythe and sickle).

SENDAK: I have him all traipsed out in the traditional paraphernalia—but he's really just holding the sickle, he isn't conveying anything more than that.

OTTEN: I'm saying that your images are conveying something to us that is also a part of Death. We were just talking about contradictions. In your illustrations we find those contradictions. Yes, Death is going to take the doctor, BUT . . .

SENDAK: Ah—BUT . . .

OTTEN: Next, I'd like to talk about goblins. I've been looking at your goblins in Grimm and, of course, in your own book *Outside Over There*. The goblins in Grimm (frontispiece) are bringing home a very large baby. Most of us as children thought goblins were large and we were small. You've revised that. You've got this enormous baby and these little goblins who seem benevolent, even bewildered, don't they?

SENDAK: They also seem weary from *schlepping* that huge bulk.

OTTEN: They strike me as elders from the synagogue.

SENDAK: They look very irritated, as though this job of dragging babies about is very tiring and vexing.

OTTEN: And one goblin is almost nestled under the baby's arm as though he's seeking protection. The goblins in *Outside Over There* are quite different. The goblins there are the size of babies and turn into babies. They're faceless at first, are hooded like monks, and then they are indistinguishable from Ida's baby. We surely have a different kind of myth here. In the Grimm, we were just saying that they're solemn, and they're tired, and they're frustrated . . .

SENDAK: And they may be Jewish . . .

OTTEN: And in *Outside Over There*, they're funny. Don't you think they are humorous?

SENDAK: Oh, I think so. That's why I was so amazed when people didn't find them charming. They were taken aback by them. They are threatening, too, of course; they're meant to be threatening. I was just remembering a little girl's letter about how she wished their clothes fit them better. That's why their heads didn't show, because their clothes didn't fit them better—so she thought.

There is a difference between the goblins in Grimm and *Outside*. I see the Grimm goblins as being really workaday creatures, who have to go through this ritualized business of stealing babies and bringing them back. It's like anybody going to work, punching a clock. And there's something pedantic, tiresome about their job. Couldn't they move out of state and get another job? It's that kind of look they have about them.

Also, there's something else about the baby. A man wrote and said how much the picture amused him. Could I answer a question, Was this the goblin baby being brought to the house or was this the baby being taken—it looks so idiotic that we cannot tell which it is. And I thought, that's very funny because normal babies do dribble and drool and roll their eyes. And in fact, I don't know which baby that is either. Is it the peasant woman's baby or is it the goblin changeling? It could be either one. She cannot tell the difference between one imbecilic looking baby and another.

The *Outside* goblins are a younger bunch. They are babies, and there's a flashing purposeful character to their efforts. They come at Ida's call. They are her henchmen. They are her dark insides acting out for her. They also have the impish, uncontrollable movements of infants. I tried hard to get that sense of broken movement that babies have—collapsing and colliding into everything.

OTTEN: Moving from goblins to the devil—in the Grimm tales we meet the devil at a couple of points. Does the devil appear in the new Grimm story, the one you are illustrating, *Dear Mili*?

SENDAK: No. We have a saint in this one. Death appears in this story quite grimly, but the devil does not make his dire appearance. Saint Joseph appears in it.

OTTEN: The devil in Grimm is referred to as a monster. In the story of the young man and the avaricious king titled "The Devil and His Three Golden Hairs," the devil "yells in a fury." Your illustration (89) shows the devil as a type of peasant fool: he thinks he is being nurtured, but he is actually being deceived. He is nonthreatening. His old grandmother, however, is serene and wise, and a collaborator with the foundling boy and with the reader. Later on the devil appears in the Bearskin story (225) where he is a barber—squat, ugly, tailed and hoofed (a kind of joke?). My question focuses on your illustrations of the devil in Grimm. Are your images hooking into the iconography of a devil in medieval cathedrals (not so much ominous as ludicrous); into the contradictory aspect where he appears grotesque, rather than diabolical, to a human being?

SENDAK: You see I don't have, being Jewish, a sense of the devil. I never grew up with an image of the devil. That was not a part of my mythology at all. The devil was a kind of literary idea which was imposed upon me, and I think my reaction to him is based on that literary idea or, better yet, musical idea. The devil that most impressed me years ago is the one in *Mephistopheles*, an opera by Boito. (Based on Goethe, of course, but very much angled to look at the devil with a raked eye.) There's a wonderful section in the prologue where the devil shakes his fist at God, and he's very vulgar. The aria ends with him whistling, and the whistling is as tasteless as you can get. Now that is the very devil of a devil, and he perhaps may have posed for my Grimm devil, and almost certainly for my I. B. Singer devil in *Zlateh the Goat*. But, in fact, I'm not attached to the devil. He's too silly even to think of. If a story demands one, then you must simply reach for him wherever you can.

OTTEN: We're still in Grimm, "The Poor Miller's Boy." He looks to me like an older version of David in *Fly by Night*. John and David have dreams for themselves; they seem oblivious to what is going on around them. The Grimm text, however, tells us that John is a dull boy. Your John has a face that shows intelligence and sensitivity, and he is loved by those cats (181). It seems to me that you see more in John than the text does, or that the text hints at—and even more than John understands about himself. You've put hopes and visions in the face of one who dreams about himself and his future.

SENDAK: The young man who posed for that illustration is a particular person, a friend, in my life, and it was very important that he be in that picture. I had great sympathy for that poor miller's boy. You mustn't believe Grimm when he says people are dull; very often that's a hint that they are people who are most canny—or I take it to be that. If I want to focus on the boy (and in this case I particularly did), I will ignore *dull, stupid*, whatever the adjectives are that put the character down because I feel the liveness of his personality.

OTTEN: Another question on Grimm. We have "Frederick and his Katelizabeth." Freddy in the text, is angry, and he says, "The devil take it." But in your illustration, we have Katelizabeth: large and squat, somewhat bewildered, but not stupid, not even self-conscious. She's stepping on the heads of the thieves, when she's perched up there in the tree. Her husband, beside her, is tolerant and amused; both of them are amused by the whole human predicament (197). And so when I look at them, I say, "Maurice Sendak is telling us a story that Grimm isn't telling us—or a story that he found beneath the surface in Grimm." You take these people that in the surface text are humorless and stupid (and the Grimms have a lot of stupid people) and redeem them in what you reveal about them in your illustration.

SENDAK: Well, you could look at that as a sign that I am either an extraordinary illustrator or a bad one—or not a proper illustrator—i.e., one that does not fly in the face of or contradict what the story is saying. You see, I think all good stories tell many stories.

OTTEN: What we're saying is that really good texts give us more than a surface meaning. There's always a great deal there, and it's a question whether we know how to decode that.

4. Illustration by Maurice Sendak from "The Juniper Tree" from *The Juniper Tree and Other Tales from Grimm*, translated by Lore Segal and Randall Jarrell. Illustration copyright © by Maurice Sendak 1973. Reprinted by permission of Farrar, Straus & Giroux and The Bodley Head, London.

SENDAK: It's something that you and I have throughout this discussion automatically taken for granted in any great work of art. We'd never imagine reading Jane Austen as a tiresome, meddling woman who's busy arranging marriages for young girls; and yet there are people, including Charlotte Brontë, who didn't see any more in Jane Austen than that. We assume that the genius lies in simply telling a tale. There are those who think that thickness and density of purpose do not occur in books for children. That we should be surprised that a Grimm tale should have anything more to say than it seems to say only confirms our low opinion of children and what they read. In other words, treat children like imbeciles. Of course, the real purpose of any great story—whether for children or for adults—is to create

5. Illustration by Maurice Sendak from *Outside Over There* by Maurice Sendak.
Copyright © by Maurice Sendak 1981. All rights reserved. Used with permission.
Reprinted by permission of Harper & Row.

many levels; otherwise, why would we remember it twenty years later and
go back to that old copy of the book? I'm making a very unoriginal point
here by saying that all works of art have this in common. A book without
these qualities, in my opinion, is not worth a second reading, unless you
like the category of popcorn fiction that's just for the fun of it, or whatever.
I could never object to that. But I also do not approve of that—there is just
not enough to eat. I can think of nothing more delightful than reading
Austen's *Emma* over and over again. It's the easiest book to read in the
superficial sense, and yet each time you are getting every bit of nourishment
that you could possibly need.

The same, of course, holds true for children's books, which is why I keep
going back to Grimm. These dualities, these contradictions (this woman
Katelizabeth is supposed to be stupid—she isn't—you just have to read the
story very carefully to see that she isn't) make for entertaining and invigor-
ating picture-making. It's another one of those marriages where the wife
plays stupid to protect the husband—and yet I don't want him entirely stupid
either. I want him to recognize her gifts and to seem to say, "Look what
I've got." Under the guise of being a moron, she's got her feet on those
men's heads. That's lovely, and so I set them there because people play
roles. People in Grimm play roles too, and the fun of illustrating Grimm is
to see if you can figure out what they're doing. The story has so much to

6. Illustration by Maurice Sendak from *Outside Over There* by Maurice Sendak. Copyright © by Maurice Sendak 1981. All rights reserved. Used with permission. Reprinted by permission of Harper & Row.

tell. The story is intact. You have to justify your purpose for why you are intruding on the story, and the only possible purpose is that you see other things and that you point over the side of the mountain and over the moon and say "Look. Listen. Over there. Don't take so literally what you're reading." See something else in the meaning. It might not be what you like. It might not even be what you agree with. You might prefer the other illustrator who tells you just what the story on the surface says. You know, there are options.

OTTEN: Finishing Grimm, *The Juniper Tree*. The text describes the bird as "this lovely bird that sang oh, so gloriously sweet" (320). Your bird (321; cover) tells us the full story: He looks like a phoenix, rather terrifying, risen out of the fire of suffering. You seem to be alerting your readers to the bird's quest for justice and retribution. The text describes Ann Marie as a little child. Your Ann Marie is a "maternal" child akin to Ida in *Outside Over There*. This girl is a mother-sister who is guarding the bones of her child-brother. The image of Ann Marie recalls for me the Old Testament story of Rizpah whose two sons were torn from her and crucified for Saul's bloodguilt; she spread herself on the rock to guard the bones of her sons from predators, the birds of the air and the wild beasts of the field.

SENDAK: I don't know that story.

OTTEN: It's in II Samuel 21. I think of Antigone also and the body of her brother, Polynices. In *The Juniper Tree* illustration (which also is the cover of the collection), you have the child-mother, and the phoenix-bird of retribution. Do you have any comments on this?

SENDAK: No. Sorry. You've done a very nice description of it. I suppose out of the whole collection that was the most frustrating. I was determined to do one illustration summing up emotionally what was going on in the stories. I think I succeeded in most of them, I don't feel as happy about *The Juniper Tree*. Maybe because it's for me one of the great stories of all time. I feel that even if I had done a dozen pictures, I wouldn't have been satisfied.

Her similarity to Ida is something I hadn't thought of, but there definitely is that motherly quality to her. The bird is like Jehovah, a kind of vengeance bird. She's a much more human, long-suffering creature. I love that little girl. I just love that little girl.

OTTEN: I do too. Going from the maternal little girl to what you call the Jehovah-like bird, that bird is vengeful, isn't he?

SENDAK: Well, look what that bird has to do. He's going to "blow the brains out" of the mother that butchered him. It's what some of the children in Grimm have to do. I think of *Hansel and Gretel*. They are children who have to get rid of the evil of stepmothers. The father is usually a very passive person. Papa in *Hansel and Gretel* is truly one of the most unforgivable creatures in all literature in that he weakly yields to the stepmother's atrocious demands. That's not unlike the father in *The Juniper Tree* who eats his son's flesh. Really there's a kind of "dumbness" which lets these pathological stepmothers run the house, and yet what is heartbreaking and wonderful is that children forgive. They can't forgive pathology because pathology is beyond redemption or hope; they get rid of the stepmother. But there's the father who enjoys the wealth that they find in the witch's house; they join him; they forgive him; they love him. *The Juniper Tree* father is forgiven too, by Ann Marie, and even by the son. You can say, "Well, he didn't do it," but yes, he did do it. He was there. He should have known what he was living with. I find him so unbearable that I didn't want to depict him

The father in *Outside Over There* is definitely an afterglow of these fathers. "When Papa was away at sea" is saying it all because most papas are away at sea—or they're at sea. In terms of making a living, dealing with children, dealing with wives—"Papa ain't there." And I think in these Grimm stories papa isn't there. Well, I remember somebody saying that she was annoyed with the ending of *Outside Over There* because it is peaceful and tranquil, and Daddy loves Ida, and how could I make such an ending? I said, "How silly you are for thinking I had." That Papa-letter is meant to be ironical. Here's this great pompous ass, the father, sending his love from across the sea and dumping this huge burden on this little girl and claiming that his love for her is sufficient reason. And that has to suffice: she has to take care of mama, she has to take care of the baby, she has to take care of herself, and she has to be content with that. And she is. She truly loves her Mama and her Papa.

OTTEN: And so we finish with the impossible task imposed by a father on a young girl. Like Ann Marie, the depth of her love helps us as readers to forgive the father that she has already forgiven. The narrative images in the final illustration, however, tell us to notice that, although the goblin of the first scene is absent, the stones that replace the goblin can metamorphose at any time, and that the sunflowers are larger and are creeping up. In the end, the images alert us to the complexities and contradictions of love's demands.

REFERENCES

Grimm, Wilhelm. *Dear Mili*. Illustrated by Maurice Sendak. Translated by Ralph Manheim. New York: Farrar, Straus and Giroux, 1988.

Jarrell, Randall. *Fly by Night*. Illustrated by Maurice Sendak. New York: Farrar, Straus and Giroux, 1976.

Segal, Lore, and Randall Jarrell, trans. *The Juniper Tree and Other Tales from Grimm*. Illustrated by Maurice Sendak. New York: Farrar, Straus and Giroux, 1973.

Sendak, Maurice. *Outside Over There*. New York: Harper and Row, 1981.

2

Narrating Chaucer, Grimm, New England, and Cooney

BARBARA COONEY[1]

"In the beginning was the word." Picture books are like strings of beads, the story the string, and the pictures the beads, each one individual in itself, but also part of the whole. I start with the story itself.

Chanticleer and the Fox (1958) began with a reading of Chaucer's "The Nun's Priest's Tale." I did have some pictures in mind that would go into this work: an open barn door seen on a walk in Massachusetts where the afternoon sun was golden on the chickens and roosters, and Oriental embroideries of roosters and chickens. But I needed a story to provide a string for these pictures, as well as a narrator.

The text is Chaucer's; the narrator is his character, the Nun's Priest. I used the Lumiansky translation because of its clarity. It is bad to delete material from a classic, but it needed to be done in order to make a picture book from this tale. Since all I wanted was a simple story line, I omitted Chaucer's material on dreams, astrology, mutability, the classics, the Greek gods, the Church fathers.

When I came to adapt Grimms' tale of *Little Brother and Little Sister* (1982), I worked with the original German text. *Little Brother and Little Sister* is a fairy tale, full of poetry and magic. Fairy tales were my meat and drink when I was little, and though many of the tales are being freshly edited and illustrated today, this particular tale had been neglected. Each writer who tells a folk or fairy tale is a reteller, but the reteller has the responsibility to remain true to the original tale. My narrator is the same as the narrator of the Grimm fairy tale—somewhat detached, somewhat restrained. The narrator never questions anything that goes on, for this is a fairy tale: no questions are asked about the house that Little Brother and Little Sister find, the transformations of humans into animals, the unlikely substitution of a one-eyed woman who looked like a weasel for a beautiful queen. Instead, the narrator simply tells what does happen. That is all that is required of the narrator of a fairy tale.

Ox-Cart Man (1979) is a different kind of project. Here the narrator of Donald Hall's text is represented pictorially in the illustrations. Since pictures of this period were often painted on wood, to make the pictures appropriate to the period, I coated the illustration board with a raw umber wash, making the background look grainy, like wood, and painted over this surface.

The date of this period was determined by research into the early New Hampshire turnpikes, into Portsmouth and the seaboard markets of New England, even into hairstyles to determine when beards were in fashion. I finally settled on the date of 1832. The backgrounds and the settings are all from New England, still there despite the encroachment of modernization.

Ox-Cart Man is a hymn to the seasons, not to any one particular person. The ox-cart man and his family are not individual characters but are symbols of those who work on a farm. The book is really an almanac, celebrating the simple beauties of each month, and I tried to capture that in the pictures. Toward the end of the book, the family pauses from its work in the field and looks at May and its blossoms. The tailpiece shows the geese who drop feathers "as soft as clouds." And summer comes before the cycle begins again in October.

The pictures of Portsmouth come from my research into the town and into the market that burned down from time to time. It is not unlike Boston's Faneuil Hall market. The beautiful Octobers I have seen in both Massachusetts and Maine. The sunsets I watch over the Damariscotta River. All of the buildings that the ox-cart man passes on his way to Portsmouth are familiar to me: one is my house and barn in Pepperell, Massachusetts. The two children are my two youngest. The kitchen is that of the Pepperell House, which had pewter plates on the fireplace mantle. The ox-cart man's beard is that of Leon, one of the carpenters who built my house in Damariscotta. So while the illustrations tell of the journey of the ox-cart man and the changing seasons, they also come from my own experience.

The narrator of *Miss Rumphius* (1982) combines many of the elements of the narrators of *Chanticleer and the Fox*, *Little Brother and Little Sister*, and *Ox-Cart Man*. In some ways, Miss Rumphius is a fairy tale. There are the three tests that are passed on to her and that she, in turn, passes on to the narrator. There is the journey that she undertakes. There is the acceptance of what happens. It is not necessary to know, for example, how Miss Rumphius paid for all of her travels, for this is a fairy tale.

But this narrator is not outside the plot like the narrator of *Little Brother and Little Sister*, and the tale the narrator tells is not a traditional fairy tale. It is a mixture of stories. There is the story of Hilda Hamlin, the real lupine lady, who actually did sow lupine seeds behind churches and by stone walls

7. Illustration by Barbara Cooney from *Ox-Cart Man* by Donald Hall. Illustration copyright © 1979 by Barbara Cooney Porter. Reprinted by permission of Viking Penguin, Inc., and Julia MacRae Books, London.

all around Christmas Cove in Maine. There is the story of Maria Dermoût, who wrote about the Molucca Islands between the Philippines and Java, and who wrote specifically of a seventeenth-century Dutch naturalist named Rumphius who lived in those islands. And there is the story of my own family, who lived in Manhattan and in Brooklyn, the two places pictured on the first page of *Miss Rumphius*. Alice's grandfather was my great-grandfather, a German immigrant who painted pictures, sometimes by the yard, and carved cigar-store Indians. My grandmother, Philipina Krippendorf, did at times paint in the skies for his pictures, just as Alice does in *Miss Rumphius*. We still have a painting, "Cleopatra's Barge," by him. Alice's grandfather's parlor, though somewhat smaller, is that of my own grandparents who lived in Brooklyn. The girl in the pink dress in the library scene is my mother, while the Edwardian lady in the stacks is my grandmother.

As in *Ox-Cart Man*, many of the illustrations come from my own life. The book is autobiographical in a sense. The library where Miss Rumphius works is the Lawrence Memorial Library in Pepperell, Massachusetts, where I was a trustee for some fifteen years. The conservatory in the middle of the park is modeled after the one at Smith College, which I attended. I too, following the footsteps of the naturalist Rumphius and Maria Dermout, went to Kate2 of the Molucca Islands, and though I was dressed in a sarong, not in the clothes of an Edwardian lady, I was surrounded by children, like Miss Rumphius. The Bapa Raja did give me a shell on which was written, in Indonesian and in English, "You will always remain in my heart." I have climbed tall mountains where the snow never melted and traveled to Djerba, the land of the lotus eaters, in Tunisia. Miss Rumphius' bedroom is patterned after one in Pepperell, and her kimono and shawl and slippers and blankets are all my own. She sows seeds along the roads around Damariscotta, Maine. The steeple of the Second Congregational church is visible just over the hill. In the far background on the bank of the Damariscotta River, I have painted the house built while I was doing the illustrations for *Ox-Cart Man*. The cape she wears is my favorite green cape, and the brick building she bicycles by is a school in Waldoboro, just east of Damariscotta. The figure on the mantlepiece of Miss Rumphius' living room is one of two I picked up in the South Seas, the pillows are made from the sarongs I wore in Indonesia, and the boy eating a cookie and sitting on the pillow is my grandson.

I am not exactly Miss Rumphius, nor am I the young Alice who tells the story. Actually Miss Rumphius is a character made up of Hilda Hamlin, my grandmother, Marie Dermoût, and myself. All of these make up Alice the narrator, who will, like Miss Rumphius and me, move away from the sea for a time, travel to distant places, come home to live by the sea, and try to do the third thing: to make the world more beautiful.

The book is about the life cycle of Miss Rumphius and young Alice just as *Ox-Cart Man* is about the cycle of the seasons. Young Alice not only tells

8. Illustration by Barbara Cooney from *Miss Rumphius* by Barbara Cooney. Copyright © by Barbara Cooney 1982. Reprinted by permission of Viking Penguin, Inc., and Julia MacRae Books, London.

9. Illustration by Barbara Cooney from *Miss Rumphius* by Barbara Cooney. Copyright © by Barbara Cooney 1982. Reprinted by permission of Viking Penguin, Inc., and Julia MacRae Books, London.

the story; she is part of its meaning, for she will carry on her life cycle just as Miss Rumphius did. I am doing a similar kind of thing in my newest book, *Island Boy* (1988), which ends with the death of Matthias, the hero, but promises the continuation of a good life to his grandson, young Matthias.

Miss Rumphius ends with the narrator running down the path from Miss Rumphius' house carrying an armful of lupines, and wondering what she will do to make the world more beautiful. And the reader knows, though the narrator does not, that Alice will continue the cycle, that she will find some way to make the world more beautiful. Thus the narrator becomes the central character in a tale yet to be told, but told already in the life of Miss Rumphius.

NOTE

1. Based on an interview with Gary D. Schmidt, Damariscotta, Maine, August 25, 1987.

REFERENCES

Cooney, Barbara. *Chanticleer and the Fox*. New York: Harper and Row, 1958.
———. *Island Boy*. New York: Viking Penguin, 1988.
———. *Little Brother and Little Sister*. New York: Doubleday, 1982.
———. *Miss Rumphius*. New York: Viking Penguin, 1982.
———. *Ox-Cart Man*. New York: Viking Penguin, 1979.

3

Finding the Narrative Voice through Dramatically Resolved Form

LEONARD EVERETT FISHER

From time to time I am asked to explain some aspect of my creative self. How do I do this? Is it possible that the work cannot speak for itself? I have created a large and diverse body of art and literature over a long and continuous period of time. I hardly remember the rationale for half of it. In recent years my artistic and literary outcome has been as much a product of instinct as reason. I am neither a one-dimensional painter of a singular motif nor an author-illustrator of books for young readers cast solely in the text of history or nonfiction as seen through the black and white of scratchboard. I am not a writer who illustrates or paints. I am not a writer's writer, as it were. I am an artist who writes.

But on second thought, I usually decide to give it a try—to explain. Perhaps, in the process, I can explain myself to myself. That would be a learning experience. It usually is. So much so, that the exercise usually turns me to new artistic realms. Take for example my work of the 1970s—I had then been at it tooth and nail some forty to fifty years—since the age of two. My paintings of the 1970s were large, brightly colored acrylic *trompe l'oeil* interiors of boxes. "His concept of still life . . . focuses not so much on arrangements of related . . . objects . . . isolated in space. It is the space . . . that is the true subject of a Fisher still-life," wrote Charles M. Daugherty in *Six Artists Paint a Still Life*. My book illustrations of the 1970s, like those of the late 1950s and 1960s, on the other hand, were often stark black and white scratchboard drawings. They did not deal with the still life of a defined space. They communicated objective ideas quickly and dramatically. Sometimes I used ordinary line with or without a halftone. My writing during the 1970s dealt with survival, however—*A Russian Farewell* (1980), *Across the Sea from Galway* (1975), *The Death of Evening Star* (1972), *The Warlock of Westfall* (1974), *The Hospitals* (1981)—immigration, whaling, sorcery, nineteenth-century America. Even books like *Alphabet Art* (1978) and *The Art Experience: Oil Painting 15th–19th Century* (1973) were related to survival inasmuch as they involved the continuum of written language and visual art.

At the end of that decade—1979—I accepted an award in Hattiesburg from the University of Southern Mississippi with a ten minute talk. I explained myself to the audience and in the process grew tired of myself. "In most instances," I told my Mississippi audience, "my visual imagery is not aimed solely at eye entertainment. In its muscularity, it surely is not an imagery of despair or escape but rather of pride and courage." I think this is still true, for the most part. Nevertheless, at the conclusion, I was overcome with the urgency to change my artistic presence. And I did. I made a new start in 1980 with a fitting book, *The Seven Days of Creation*, in which I returned to the mode of broad strokes that I had used in the 1940s while in the army and later as a Yale student. That youthful art was pure genre—Coney Island themes, a troopship, a prizefighter, and so forth. I talked myself out of that style and concept in 1950 (with the help of a concerned mentor) after listening to myself sermonize my artistic *raison d'être* while teaching design theory at Yale. For the next ten years I pursued the sharply focused calligraphic image of egg tempera. It was a near faultless medieval technique that I maneuvered into a modern imagery that leaned toward allegory and fantasy. "His craftsmanship is of the best," said *The New York Times* (February 16, 1952), " . . . remarkable is the rhythm that controls his groups . . . galvanized by the artist's hand and imagination into paroxysms of movement. . . ." The whole process required careful application underwritten by skillful drawing. Book illustration had no clear meaning for me during the 1950s. It was a mixed bag of fiction and nonfiction appearing in trade books, textbooks, and learning materials.

I gave up egg tempera in 1960 following several lectures I gave in which again I fell out of favor with myself. Now I became interested in gray theosophical gelatine temperas—an instinctive response to the stressful 1960s. These works evolved from the type of drawings I had been doing for egg temperas called "form drawings." The technique was ancient and exacting. Meanwhile, I began to illustrate more and more books and to write the *Colonial Americans*, a nineteen-volume series that would take fourteen years in the making.

As I said in the 1960s about colonial Americans and say again now, I know of no other time in our history when the aspirations of the people were so clearly expressed by their extraordinary craftsmanship. Their skill was a matter of profound and lengthy training. They applied themselves with

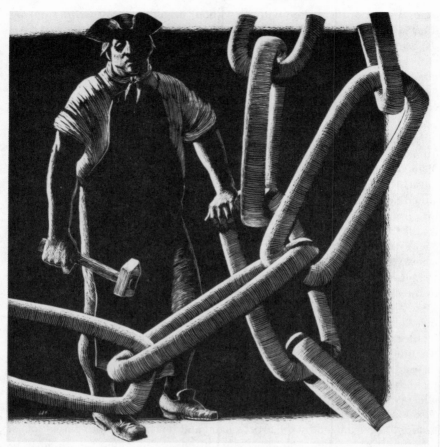

10. Illustration by Leonard Everett Fisher from *The Blacksmiths* by Leonard Everett Fisher. Copyright © 1976 by Leonard Everett Fisher. Reproduced by permission of Franklin Watts, Inc.

energy and care. Their attitude was always one of pride in their singular ability and individualism. The craftsman was master of his creations.

Much of what I did in books during the 1960s seems to have been black and white scratchboard. There were, nevertheless, a number of bright two, three, and four color picture books—some fiction, some nonfiction (*Pumpers, Boilers, Hooks and Ladders* [1961]; *A Head Full of Hats* [1962]; *The Golden Frog* [1963]; *The Burning Mountain* [1965])—all hinting of color in my soul.

At the end of that stretch I turned away from gray paintings and gelatine to the fierce brightness of acrylic. At first the paintings were tight but romantic. Little by little they became sharply focused and less romantic. The illustrations were still the black and white, stark and demanding scratchboard. What few people realized was that there was a definite connection between what I had been doing for years in painting and drawing, much of it sharply linear—especially those form drawings—and the linear nature of scratchboard. I simply exchanged a fine sable brush for a sharp knife. It was easy. Moreover, my drawing skills were old fashioned and highly disciplined. I knew a great deal about the play of light on a form. And this is the thread that binds all of my art in or out of books, tight or loose, egg tempera or acrylic, scratchboard or otherwise, black and white or color—dramatically resolved form.

In the end the paintings of the 1980s became more relaxed in appearance and contained more fluid movement. It would not take long for this change to surface in my books. The best examples of these would be *A Circle of Seasons*; *Sky Songs, Sea Songs, Earth Songs, Space Songs*; *Celebrations*; *Storm at the Jetty*; *The Great Wall of China*; and *The Tower of London*— all published in the 1980s. Books like *Boxes! Boxes!* and *Look Around*, also published in the 1980s, echoed the sharply focused acrylic box paintings I had created during the 1970s. Whether sharply focused or fluid, the essential unifying element of my creations is my longstanding interest in form as opposed to shape—in the solidness of a rendered object rather than the flatness of an object and the application of that interest to informational books. This view alone may remove me from the ranks of the obvious decorators and modish designers but surely not from the realms of information and art. The earth itself is a form in space. Not a flat shape!

I have been a witness to historical events. Sometimes a participant. My books are rife with history. Why? Because without history I feel disconnected. That is the information I narrate in my books—history—nonfiction and fiction alike. And I do not rewrite history except to revise history as warranted by data heretofore undisclosed or forgotten. I need history to give me clues to who I am and why I am here. So does everyone else whether or not they recognize that fact. There is continuity in history. Therein, in that continuity, lies our humanity.

My nonfiction is as spare and as stark in some ways as the scratchboard illustrations. Note, too, that the scratchboard illustrations are not always printed in black. Sometimes they appear in a color and seem softer. There are two reasons for this. When I want to dramatize the text, I prefer black, and when the text is a bit more ornamental and the illustrations serve more as a design element with respect to the overall appearance of the book, I prefer color. Of course there are marketing, pricing, and budgetary considerations that influence how the book is treated. One's aesthetic parameters are defined by such pedestrian matters. These considerations can be found in a host of books I have written over the past twenty-five years, including

11. Illustration by Leonard Everett Fisher from *The Great Wall of China* by Leonard Everett Fisher. Copyright © 1986 by Leonard Everett Fisher. Reproduced by permission of Macmillan Publishing Company, and John Hawkins and Associates, New York.

The Railroads (1979), *The Unions* (1982), *The Statue of Liberty* (1985), *Ellis Island* (1986), *The Alamo* (1987), and *Pyramid of the Sun, Pyramid of the Moon* (1988).

The sparing quality of my nonfiction is aimed at leaving a memory of what has been said while at the same time creating a time and place—an atmosphere—for the events depicted. There is a little less ornament to the writing and illustration and a little more directness. The two are similar because they not only reflect me and my persona but the thrust of my intent—to make dramatic and memorable the stretch of humanity in us all and from which we are derived. Our continuity is uppermost in my mind. There is an energy and dynamic to people and events that simply will not dissolve. That is what I seek to inject into the reader's or viewer's stream of consciousness, and I have been determined to state this in as simple a manner as possible.

That is not to say that the visual effect—the design—of the book—or any work of art—is not important to me. Obviously, it is. I view the book as a whole concept: words, pictures, size, proportion, color, and the relationships between these seemingly separate elements on a given page, on facing pages, and as the book unfolds from cover to cover. The visual and literary atmosphere thus conceived must serve the intellect and express the information contained therein however simply formed. What is then delivered with respect to the visual and literary nature of the book is art, and it should make no difference to either the creator or to the audience whether it is fact or fiction. Art is art.

Intellect not moistened by appropriate style—style designed to express content (vis à vis information)—is as dry as dust and usually forgettable. In my view content must supersede appearance in a civilized society. But content without appearance is artless and gone is the joy of life—and the content—and maybe the society as well. This is the essence of *Alphabet Art* (1978), *Number Art* (1982), *Symbol Art* (1985), and *Calendar Art* (1987). Appearance without content flirts with mindlessness. A civilization bent on appearance at the expense of mindless disinformation at the expense of an historical presence puts itself at risk. It seems to me that in our time and place, the "Age of Information," we should communicate information and ideas (i.e., nonfiction) with the same artistic commitment we reserve for our fantasies (i.e., fiction).

I am reminded of my wartime military experiences (1942–46) when I was a young topographic specialist assigned to a sensitive overseas mapping unit. I was one of a group entrusted with the responsibility of initiating, editing, and coordinating the production of tactical maps for some of the major invasions and battles of Europe and the Pacific Ocean area. A number of us were artists with other appropriate qualifications. Most of these maps were prepared and printed in five colors from gathered intelligence and photographic information. I soon learned what was important and what was not.

The planning of these sheets was a lesson in understanding the immediacy of getting to the heart of the matter and finding ways for its precise communication. The intent of these maps was absolutely pragmatic. No one thought about graphic cosmetics. The resulting maps were handsome in their simplicity and craftsmanship. They were amazingly clear in the presentation of extremely complex information. A reader of such a map knew exactly where he was in relation to where everything else was, and how to get from here to there without ornamental obstacles. These maps were graphic entities delivering an aesthetic message, at least to me, that was visually and verbally unforgettable. Perhaps that is where it all began with me, this taste I have in a muddled world for clear statements delivered with style. The only other influences on my illustrative and literary offerings are the works of Michelangelo, Abraham Lincoln's "Gettysburg Address," and the language of Loren Eiseley, deceptively simple but powerful renderings of complex ideas and events from muddled worlds that leave the audience with indelible connections to life and art.

REFERENCES

Daugherty, Charles M. *Six Artists Paint a Still Life*. Cincinnati, Ohio: North Light, 1977.

Fisher, Leonard Everett. *Across the Sea from Galway*. New York: Four Winds, 1975.

———. *The Alamo*. New York: Holiday House, 1987.

———. *Alphabet Art*. New York: Four Winds, 1978.

———. *The Art Experience: Oil Painting 15th–19th Century*. Danbury, Conn.: Franklin Watts, 1973.

———. *Boxes! Boxes!* New York: Viking, 1984.

———. *The Burning Mountain*. New York: Holiday House, 1965.

———. *Calendar Art*. New York: Four Winds, 1987.

———. *Celebrations*. New York: Holiday House, 1985.

———. *A Circle of Seasons*. New York: Holiday House, 1982.

———. *Colonial Americans*. 19 vols. Danbury, Conn.: Franklin Watts, 1966–1986.

———. *The Death of Evening Star*. Garden City, N.Y.: Doubleday, 1972.

———. *Ellis Island*. New York: Holiday House, 1986.

———. *The Golden Frog*. New York: Putnam, 1963.

———. *The Great Wall of China*. New York: Macmillan, 1986.

———. *A Head Full of Hats*. Garden City, N.Y.: Dial, 1962.

———. *The Hospitals*. New York: Holiday House, 1980.

———. *Look Around*. New York: Viking, 1987.

———. *Number Art*. New York: Four Winds, 1982.

———. *Pumpers, Boilers, Hooks and Ladders*. New York: Dial, 1961.

———. *Pyramid of the Sun, Pyramid of the Moon*. New York: Macmillan, 1988.

———. *The Railroads*. New York: Holiday House, 1979.

———. *A Russian Farewell*. New York: Four Winds, 1980.

———. *The Seven Days of Creation*. New York: Holiday House, 1981.

———. *The Statue of Liberty*. New York: Holiday House, 1985.

————. *Storm at the Jetty*. New York: Viking, 1981.

————. *Symbol Art*. New York: Four Winds, 1985.

————. *The Tower of London*. New York: Macmillan, 1987.

————. *The Unions*. New York: Holiday House, 1982.

————. *The Warlock of Westfall*. Garden City, N.Y.: Doubleday, 1974.

Fisher, Leonard Everett and Myra Cohn Livingston. *Earth Songs*. New York: Holiday House, 1986.

————. *Sea Songs*. New York: Holiday House, 1986.

————. *Sky Songs*. New York: Holiday House, 1984.

————. *Space Songs*. New York: Holiday House, 1988.

THE CRITICAL VOICE

4

William Kurelek's Persona

PATRICIA MORLEY

The period when William Kurelek was creating his beautiful children's books, text and paintings, covers the last five years of his relatively brief life (1927–77). Like the others that flowed from his pen and brush during the same period, those books were part of a grand design, a calculated plan to call public attention to the evangelistic witness prompted by his religious faith. The three that are best known—*A Prairie Boy's Winter* (1973), *Lumberjack* (1974), and *A Prairie Boy's Summer* (1975)—are not overtly religious. Only a dedication in one and a closing scene in another alert the careful reader to that faith. When his children's books are seen, however, in the context of his life and published autobiography, their narrative voice is inseparable from the face that Kurelek himself presented to the world.

That face, or persona, is revealed in *Someone with Me* (1973, 1980), the autobiography that the artist wrote and rewrote throughout his adult life. Like Kurelek, the young narrator in the prairie-boy books grew up on a farm on the Canadian prairies during the depression of the 1930s, was fearful of parental criticism, felt inadequate and incompetent with machinery and in athletic competitions, and—most importantly—was imaginative and artistic. Like any shy child, he dreamed of recognition and success; the ugly duckling wanted to become a swan. The dream of success, a minor motif in the books for children, becomes a major theme for the adult artist.

Kurelek's first book for children is *A Prairie Boy's Winter*. Its third person narrative voice is practical, almost literal, yet quietly engaging. The characters are William, his siblings, and their parents. John and Winnie are slightly younger than William, a boy of eleven or twelve. Nancy, the beloved little sister, is just old enough to be helpful. The book is also peopled by William's schoolmates and the farm animals whom the children serve and tease. Despite the distancing in the introduction by the use of the third person, the reader is led to identify with William. It is his emotions, his hopes, fears, and thrills that stand at the center.

The artist's actual siblings have the same names and ages, if we take the date for the action in both *Winter* and *Summer* as 1939. This date is introduced into the latter book in episode 16, where William is "drafted" into harvesting by the advent of World War II, which removed his father's hired hands.

Kurelek's private name for a painting entitled *Tobogganers in High Park* (1970) was "the thrill of terror." The phrase is relevant to the narrative voice in the prairie-boy books, where two themes encourage the reader to identify with William. One is his ineptitude, his dread of argument and criticism, his fear of failure; the other, stronger voice is William's zest for life, his ability to turn farm chores into play, his relish for danger, and his love of challenge.

In *Winter*, the first snow of the season makes William "giddy with excitement" (episode 2). Skating on the bog ditch (episode 12) appeals to his exploring instinct. A winter blizzard, the kind in which children have been known to freeze to death, challenges the children to test their strength against it and investigate its fearsome beauty (episode 14). A painful mistake—bare hands on sub-zero metal—is accepted stoically and put down to experience (episode 15). Snowdrifts generate euphoria, exhilaration (episode 16). Testing the depth of the water in ditches in early spring is another challenge accepted: "He never knew from day to day how deep it was, so he had to test it—just as mountains have to be climbed" (episode 19). (That same love of challenge led the adult Kurelek to try, and succeed, in numerous new fields.)

These same complementary themes dominate *Summer*, published two years later. William has mixed feelings about school ending (episode 1). He enjoys school work, but dreads the athletic competitions that mark the year's end (episode 4). He is simply not as quick and strong as other boys. His fantasies include making a sensational catch in a softball game, being a cowboy in frontier days, and telling stories of farm "adventures" to an admiring audience of city high school students: "How mistaken his daydreams turned out to be! . . . Many years would pass before William found a way to get people interested."

Meanwhile, he works at turning farm chores into play. Milking allows him to squirt the waiting cats with milk (episode 12). By "riling up" the cows, William and John hope to make them do their droppings outside the barn (episode 5). Burning quack grass becomes a game with fire (episode 8). Haying is exhausting but challenging, like the water in the ditches in spring (episode 9); the entire family turns out one night to save an unfinished stack: "Tired and sleepy and looking like drowned rats they got back to the house

12. Illustration by William Kurelek from *A Prairie Boy's Winter* by William Kurelek. Copyright © 1973 by William Kurelek. Published by Tundra Books (except in the U.S. by Houghton Mifflin). Reprinted by permission of Tundra Books.

at dawn." Physical discomforts are eased by love and attention from Nancy, and by philosophical reflections: bullying goes on among animals as among humans. The horses shoulder the cows aside to take for themselves the best places in the smudge against mosquitoes.

In some chores, the farm animals are adversaries with whom William matches wits. Pigs, for example, are perennial "escapees" who contemplate fresh breaks as John and William repair the fence (episode 18). Gophers are hunted by the boys for the municipality's bounty of one cent per tail. Their desperate efforts to evade the youthful posse raises a twinge of pity in William, but "a pest is a pest" (episode 19). Whether at work or play, William is always ready to test his abilities to the limit.

In all of Kurelek's books, the narrator stands in awe of nature's beauty.

13. Illustration by William Kurelek from *A Prairie Boy's Summer* by William Kurelek. Copyright © 1975 by William Kurelek. Published by Tundra Books (except in the U.S. by Houghton Mifflin). Reprinted by permission of Tundra Books.

This attitude, along with the narrator's zest for life and determination to succeed, helps to account for the books' perennial appeal. In a foreword to *Lumberjack*, memories of Kurelek's "magical" first days and weeks in the bush move him deeply: "I shall never forget them: the wraiths of mist rising from our lily-padded lake in the morning; the laugh of the loon echoing over the water in the moonlight; rainy days when the hillsides covered with dark green forest stretched up into the clouds." Nature is also an adversary, a fearsome one worthy of respect as well as admiration. Similarly, the narrator of *Summer* mirrors Kurelek's own vision of the natural world. "Catching Baby Killdeer" (episode 6), for example, shows William holding a baby bird with reverence and love, "darling fluffy little bits of life" that he "wouldn't dream of harming."

Summer closes with the note of aspiration that forms such an attractive element in the narrative voice. Using equipment he has carved himself, William excels in archery. He shares his expertise with his schoolmates: "It seemed the boys were conquering the awesomeness of the prairie expanses at last." William anticipates leaving his one-room rural school for a secondary school in the city nearby. The shot arrow, venturing boldly into the sky, suggests both the widening lives of the children and the artist's imagination— a perennial quest, and a very personal one.

Correspondence between Kurelek and May Ebbitt Cutler, his editor at Tundra Books and his major publisher, provides a fascinating background to the union of artist, author, and narrator in the eleven books that he published between 1973 and 1976. His passion to publish and the pace at which he drove himself could not be guessed from his books, with the possible exception of the autobiography. He wanted money, mostly for charitable projects in Third World countries. More importantly, he wanted greater public exposure, believing that an audience gained initially through pleasant paintings and books would remain to hear his serious pleas on behalf of God and man. The need to evangelize was central to his life after his conversion to the Roman Catholic faith in the 1950s in England.

Cutler had been following Kurelek's work for several years and was hoping to make a book from one of his series of paintings. The two were introduced by gallery owner Mira Godard at the Montreal exhibition of Kurelek's apocalyptic series, "The Last Days" (June 1971). When Cutler asked Kurelek if he would do a children's book for her, the artist replied that he had always wanted to do such a project.[1] Cutler was impressed, at the time and in years to come, by the strength of the painter's desire to publish.

Winter took shape rapidly following this meeting, as correspondence reveals. Cutler suggested a winter setting for the first book, since harsh winters are exotic to those who live in gentler climates. She urged Kurelek to keep the story autobiographical and to focus on a single character with whom a child reader could identify. One month later Kurelek had planned the twenty scenes and was working on the sketches. The paintings were done in the late summer. Cutler, surprised and delighted, felt that she had played God. Kurelek would later credit her with discovering him as an author. The book was simultaneously published in Montreal and Boston, and the paintings sold promptly.

Kurelek's confession to his publisher in 1973 illustrates the kind of transformation that some of his autobiographical material underwent in order to become lighthearted tales and illustrations for children. Cutler loves to tell of an exchange that originally struck terror into her heart at the time of the book's launching: "Bill shyly confided that he had a confession to make: 'That book is not honest.' I was nearly dying. I said, 'What do you mean?' Bill said, 'I gave all the children bright clothes, but we had navy blue, brown or dark grey.' My heart fell back into place and I told him, 'I think that that is artistic license.' "[2]

That license included the exorcism from the prairie books of the schoolyard bullying that had made his young life miserable, the sharp criticism that fostered fear and hate for the father he continued to revere, and the fighting and bullying that one assumes would be part of life in a lumber camp but which is hinted at only once in *Lumberjack*, when Kurelek is teased for being "skinny" (episode 15). Schoolyard bullying and unfair paternal criticism loom large in *Someone with Me* but play no part in Kurelek's books for children.

Awards for *Winter* included "Best Illustrated Children's Book" in both Canada and the United States. Following this success, Cutler sought sequels. He had forwarded a rough text for *Lumberjack*, written in moments stolen from numerous other projects. In long, detailed letters Cutler urged Kurelek to rewrite this text, adding human interest and an individual focus.[3] She disliked his titles, "William's Winter" and "The Student Lumberjack." As an author and editor, Cutler has a feeling for language that Kurelek lacked. His gifts lay in storytelling and illustration. He cared little for words save as a medium to convey meaning. He spoke as he wrote and wrote as he talked, in a colloquial idiom that reflects his rural background and the haste with which his words were set down. Dates and facts were often inaccurate. He was cavalier with regard to such data, since he was unwilling to spend the time required to check.[4] Cutler's sensitive editing and reshaping of Kurelek's rough original texts formed no small part of the success of his books for children. When Kurelek generously suggested co-authorship ("something like 'story by William Kurelek as told to May Cutler' "),[5] Cutler refused; she would admit only to playing "midwife" to the publications.

In *Lumberjack*, Kurelek employs a first person voice in the text proper as in the foreword. There is really very little difference between these sections. The text tends to shorter sentences and more tactile descriptions. The feeling is rather *less* personal there than in the foreword, despite various personal anecdotes. The voice of the student lumberjack surfaces from time to time, but much of the text (as Cutler shrewdly noted) is purely descriptive of life in the lumber camp and of methods of working and coping on the site.

The foreword allows more of the simmering and long-standing conflict with Kurelek's father to surface, although the depths of this antagonism are revealed only in the autobiography and in some short texts to individual paintings. In the foreword, the artist states that he went into the bush to prove to his father and himself that he could make it on his own: "Physically, I could do a man's work for, after all, I had been raised on a family farm. But emotionally I felt very immature and dependent on my parents." His second stint in lumbering, four years later, was undertaken in order to earn a two thousand dollar stake to take him to Europe. In proving that he could endure and survive, Kurelek was working out some of the concerns the narrator had expressed in *Summer*.

Near the beginning of *Lumberjack*, Kurelek expresses his gratitude for having experienced traditional lumber camp living before it disappeared forever. Curiously, as the artist's luck would have it, lumbering had changed very little for two centuries prior to his double exposure. In the following two decades, those ways of working and living were altered beyond recognition. The epilogue celebrates the "mechanical marvels" that have revolutionized the industry, one of them invented by Kurelek's own brother, John.

The foreword of *Lumberjack* establishes that this lumberjack is an artist. His gift enabled him to preserve and celebrate this passing way of life. Only a single painting was actually done in the bush. Sketches, photographs, and his memory—"fortunately vivid"—allowed him to recreate the experiences later. The final scene speaks of the frosted windows as having been done by a better artist than himself, "He who gave me such talent as I have."

The motif of ineptitude in the lumberjack book takes different forms. Here Kurelek is not the physically disadvantaged youth of school competitions but a hard worker who can hold his own in a very tough world where other young men fail. He is not, however, particularly good with tools. He declares himself to be too impatient to keep them in good working condition, having therefore to work all the harder to compensate. Sharpening he terms one of his failures and something he particularly hates (sections 8, 16, 17). He also very readily admits to being a novice, a stance that allows him to introduce suspense and the fascination of the new. "Would the bridge hold?" he wonders, watching the driver of a Caterpillar tractor move supplies.

The narrative voice employs questions to involve the reader ("Does anyone know how delicious cold baked beans are in a sandwich?") and often expresses tactile pleasures and sensations. Children love the notion of squashing hard boiled eggs into the corners of a metal lunch box ("round or flat, they tasted good"), of trudging back to camp in squishing wet boots, of steaming bodies in a sauna whose tired benches rise "much like a chicken roost." Homey details such as laundering bring the daily routines to life.

Lumberjack is also a how-to manual, as the prairie books are not. The narrator tells us how to notch and fell and stack, how to sharpen a saw or grind an axe. Meticulous and detailed instructions are leavened by occasional personal comments: "I never figured out the physics of it, I just did as I was told," and " . . . it's really the best way, once you're used to it." Cutler kept pressing for personal and tactile additions. Did he recall stepping knee-deep in swamps? Did he come across rabbit holes, or other animal nests? Just how did the black flies and mosquitoes cluster, and what kind of weather encouraged them?[6]

The unobtrusive voice in *Lumberjack* conveys a gentle personality who survives on the fringes of the lumbermen's society as a silent observer, a watcher. He is pleased and touched by personal attention from the foreman. When the latter, a Lithuanian, addresses him in Ukrainian, Kurelek is "thrilled" and worked all the harder (section 6). Culture in the camp is hard to come by and is represented largely by an old radio that picks up one station: "Sputtering with static one evening, it still gave me my most memorable cultural experience of camp life, a reading of T. S. Eliot's *Murder in the Cathedral.*" "Starved for art and music," the narrator orders a hand-wound record player by mail. This is really an extraordinary expenditure for one whose frugality was notorious, who worked on rainy days when others stayed in camp, and who wore cast-off clothing rather than buy workshirts in the camp store. Lumberjack culture centered in hard work and erotic fantasies, followed by a few days or weeks of women and drink in a nearby frontier town. The narrator's "sheltered upbringing" makes sexual innuendo and stories a source of embarrassment (section 20).

The narrator, the student lumberjack, is absolutely autobiographical. Kurelek's work habits were, by his own admission, obsessive. His sexual morality remained extremely conservative. He loved music. He was always an introvert and watcher, blessed with the gift of being able to translate a lifetime of careful observation into thousands of paintings that record ways of human living, thinking, and reacting. His related gift of storytelling shines in his anecdotal paintings just as it does in his texts.

The impatience that made Kurelek unwilling to care for his tools also made him unwilling or unable to refine his words. Strangely, many of his paintings are finely detailed, the product of long hours of patient craftsmanship. This is especially true of his *trompe l'oeil*, a type of still life by which he earned a living for a few years in Britain in the 1950s.

In the medium of language, however, an editor was essential. Kurelek was fortunate to have Cutler act in that capacity. His basic gratitude alternated with feelings of irritation that his texts were being changed. When one stops to reflect on the situation and on human nature, this is hardly surprising. Lacking sensitivity toward language, Kurelek tended to ignore improvements to his basic text ("my not-so-brilliant text"), while focusing on details of particular significance to himself.

The dedication to *Winter* became a sore point between Kurelek and his editor. Back in 1971, when Cutler requested a dedication, Kurelek responded by saying that a dedication to his wife and children would not be true, since they belonged to a different culture and simply did not see the value of endurance and effort.[7] The passage makes painful reading. Kurelek seems so alone. Since he believed that a dedication should be to someone who understands, he considered that the only suitable party would be God. He opted for a dedicatory prayer, while telling Cutler that it was entirely at her discretion whether it went in or not.[8] When she later substituted (without consultation) her own simple dedication ("For everyone who ever spent a winter on the prairie—and for all the others who wonder what it was like"), Kurelek was deeply offended. "Even some small prayer-like dedication," he wrote, "would be better than nothing in the secular subjects I do."[9] In the same letter he returned to his favorite theme, that without God's mercy and love he would not be producing either paintings or books.

Later letters to Cutler continue to display the ambivalence that marked Kurelek's feelings toward her editorial work. He saw the changes as being merely grammatical or factual and was at pains to emphasize that "moral references" were far more important to him. Relenting, he added "It's a beautiful book [Lumberjack] and Canada owes you a pat on the back for doing it."[10] With all his publishers, Kurelek insisted that the religious content of his work be left untouched.

One result of this small fracas would be the religious dedication to Summer. Written by novelist W. O. Mitchell, the dedication delighted Kurelek since it expressed his feelings so well. The painter had met the novelist late in 1973, when Mitchell was working in Toronto as writer-in-residence at the university. Kurelek approached Mitchell and sought help with his writing. Mitchell subsequently did some editing of Summer. He warned the painter that writing was an art and a craft, as subtle as painting and as slow to learn; this was wisdom that the painter was very reluctant to accept. Mitchell found Kurelek "strangely innocent about the craft and work involved in another art."[11] Kurelek did spend time on the manuscript of his autobiography in his last years, but he continued to believe that it required cosmetic rather than major surgery. In the "proper publication" that he sought, his text would be "corrected and polished."[12]

He remained suspicious that every editor was hostile to his religious message. The manuscript of Someone With Me, originally written in England during the 1950s and published unedited in 1973 by photographing a lengthy typescript, was eventually taken out of his hands by fate. It was edited posthumously by Max Layton, who cut it to approximately a third of its original length for the 1980 edition.

Kurelek's naive hope of learning to write like Mitchell was never realized, but their friendship led to a beautiful edition of Who Has Seen the Wind (1976). To illustrate Mitchell's classic prairie novel (1947), Kurelek created eight paintings and thirty-two black and white sketches, one per chapter. Sparkling with humor and vitality, artwork and text are wonderfully complementary. A delighted Mitchell called it one of the most beautiful marriages between two arts that he had ever seen. He remains convinced that Kurelek believed the two men to be very similar: both rural, both from the prairies, both religious. Feeling that his religious humanism was very different from Kurelek's conservative Catholicism, Mitchell countered Kurelek's idea about them but could not dissuade the painter. Who Has Seen the Wind had apparently convinced Kurelek that Mitchell was devout, a reaction that suggests a broadening of Kurelek's religious attitudes in the last years of his life.

The would-be friendship, however, remained blocked. Kurelek found it surprising that someone would help him without expecting a painting as payment. Mitchell became convinced that Kurelek "didn't think he [Kurelek] was lovable." In a recent interview, Mitchell wrestled with the word "suspicious," temporarily rejecting it as being perhaps harsh and unfair but returning to it in the end to describe Kurelek's attitude toward people who were kind to him. Ironically, Kurelek had observed this same cast of mind in his father and had disliked it. Mitchell found that Kurelek tended to think in terms of adversary relationships. The novelist's strongest impression of Kurelek would be of his suspicion of the motives of those who helped him.[13]

Mercifully, *Lumberjack* and the two prairie books for children contain no trace of Kurelek's suspicions and relatively few of his anxieties. Here, as in the face with which Kurelek met the public and lived his daily life, the tonic note evokes a strong but gentle personality, one with imagination and courage. Difficulties are met with humor and patience, which seems surprising in the youth who declares his impatience with tools.

The narrative voice in these three books is charitable and forward-looking. In life, a conservative and traditional religious faith led Kurelek to expect a future heaven for believers. In his books for children, metaphors soften and expand these expectations into an all-inclusive hope. *Winter* ends with the cyclic return of spring and the promise of renewed life. *Summer* anticipates a widening world of learning and adventure for the rural youths who will go to city high schools. *Lumberjack* ends with gratitude to the divine artist who gave Kurelek his talent and for the good life in which he had been permitted to share. Its foreword ends with sunshine and song: "It seemed as if everyone on the train was going somewhere great."

In Kurelek's books for children, wonder and joy are made tangible. They interest not only those who would like to know what rural life was once like but also all who have dared to hope, venture, attempt some difficult task. Kurelek's voice defeats many of its dragons, including his father and his fear of failure. He suggests that readers may do the same. Kurelek considered these books to be among his secular works. Perhaps they are more religious than he realized.

NOTES

1. See Morley, *Kurelek. A Biography*, Chapter 14, *passim*.
2. May Cutler interview with Patricia Morley, 22 November 1982.
3. Letter by Cutler to W. K., 14 December 1973.
4. Contrary to data given in the Foreword, Kurelek went to the camp at Neys, Ontario, in the summer of 1947 (not 1946), when he was twenty, not nineteen. He was indeed nineteen in 1946 but that was not the summer when he worked as a lumberjack. He had completed his first year at the university and would begin his second in the fall after his lumber camp work.
5. Letter by W. K. to Cutler, 25 February 1974.
6. See letter by Cutler to W. K., 21 February 1974.
7. Letter by W. K. to Cutler, 30 October 1971.
8. Letter by W. K. to Cutler, 18 October 1971.
9. Letter by W. K. to Cutler, 7 December 1973.

10. Letter by W. K. to Cutler, 6 June 1974.
11. W. O. Mitchell interview with Patricia Morley, 23 June 1983.
12. Letter by W. K. to Cutler, 7 December 1973.
13. Mitchell interview with Morley, 23 June 1983.

REFERENCES

Kurelek, William. *Lumberjack*. Montreal: Tundra Books, 1974.

———. *A Prairie Boy's Summer*. Boston: Houghton Mifflin; Montreal: Tundra Books, 1975.

———. *A Prairie Boy's Winter*. Boston: Houghton Mifflin; Montreal: Tundra Books, 1973.

———. *Someone With Me*. Ithaca: Cornell University Press, 1973; Toronto: McClelland and Steward, 1980 [abridged].

Mitchell, W. O. *Who Has Seen the Wind*. Toronto: Macmillan of Canada, 1947.

Morley, Patricia. *Kurelek. A Biography*. Toronto: Macmillan of Canada, 1986.

5

Narrative Voice and Narrative View in Beatrix Potter's Books

RUTH MACDONALD

Beatrix Potter's narrative intrusions have received much commentary from critics. Enid and Leslie Linder's careful cataloging of her artwork and writings lists the arguments with her editors over her individual choices of words, ones that were frequently unusual and polysyllabic. Rumer Godden's "Imaginary Correspondence" between Potter and a hypothetical editor interested in bringing out a new, revised edition of *The Tale of Peter Rabbit* has Potter arguing against changing the "fine" words that she insisted her child readers would appreciate. Potter's style of narration attracts commentary from such critics as Graham Greene, Roger Sale, and Marcus Crouch. The lack of condescension, the high level of diction, and Potter's confidence in her child reader's ability to handle this complex vocabulary all point to a writer who respected her readers, her story, and the power and variety of the English language.

Potter's unflinching use of the word "soporific" on the first page of *The Tale of the Flopsy Bunnies* (1909) is characteristic of the level of diction that Potter uses when she presents herself in her books. Through her refusal to compromise on levels of diction, she shows her respect for children in not talking down to them. She assumes that children will gather the meaning of these adult locutions, and indeed, is careful to supply contexts that will help children define those meanings, as with the word "soporific":

It is said that the effect of eating too much lettuce is "soporific."
I have never felt sleepy after eating lettuces; but then *I* am not a rabbit.
They certainly had a very soporific effect upon the Flopsy Bunnies! (9)

The accompanying picture of the bunnies flopped in sleep around the base of a lettuce plant reinforces the sleep-inducing effect of the greens, at least upon bunnies. Thus, Potter sets up a verbal as well as a visual environment that helps to define the meaning of her adult diction in her books.

Furthermore, in this passage Potter's articulation of her non-rabbithood might seem to make her an unbelievable narrator. She disclaims knowledge of the effect of lettuce because she is not a rabbit. But the picture confirms the old adage, and Potter's knowledge of it gives her the status of a narrator who is both reliable and knowledgeable about rabbit affairs. Throughout her books, she uses the technique of first-person narration to do just the opposite of what first-person narratives are supposed to do; instead of limiting the perspective to what one person, a human, can know, it has the effect of becoming omniscient narration, based on Potter's assertion of her knowledge about the intimate conduct of animal lives. By claiming such inside knowledge, Potter creates a credible animal universe that exists side by side with the human.

By placing herself both in the illustration and in the narrative of her books, Potter solidifies the fantasy world of her animals. Though it would seem more likely that a human presence would destroy the fantasy, especially when the human appears in the illustration, the opposite is true with Potter. Her voice is part of the seamlessness of the animal world as it converges with the human world. In fact, her intrusions are hardly intrusions; instead, they are simply part of the telling of the story. Frequently, she uses her own voice in an aside to supply details that otherwise interrupt the flow of the narrative, as in *The Tale of Benjamin Bunny* (1904). In this story, she explains how Mrs. Rabbit supports her family: "Old Mrs. Rabbit was a widow; she earned her living by knitting rabbit-wool mittens and muffettes (I once bought a pair at a bazaar). She also sold herbs, and rosemary tea, and rabbit-tobacco (which is what *we* call lavender)" (13). Here Potter supplies the details of rabbit life with which humans would be unfamiliar. She asserts personal knowledge of Mrs. Rabbit's wares by her purchase of them and shows her familiarity with herbal lore in the aside about lavender. Instead of betraying herself as a human, she demonstrates her ability to see things from an animal point of view. Once again, she establishes herself as more animal than human, thus creating credibility for the fantasy.

Potter most frequently appears at the beginnings and endings of her stories. In her endings, she appears to interpret the story for the reader and sometimes to prejudice the meanings of the story according to her own predilections. At the end of *The Tale of Johnny Town-Mouse* (1918), her retelling of Aesop's fable of the town mouse and the country mouse, Potter concludes evenhandedly: "One place suits one person, another place suits another person." But throughout the story, she has shown that the country mouse Timmy Willie's situation is much more desirable and pleasant. So she concludes with less equanimity: "For my part I prefer to live in the country, like Timmy Willie" (59). Here, because Potter does not trust her child reader to come to the conclusion to which her story elsewhere tends, is one of her least successful uses of her own presence in the narrative.

Potter's most aggressive use of her voice appears at the beginning of *The Tale of Mr. Tod* (1912), one of her darkest, most menacing books. The story continues the Peter Rabbit family saga. Her fatigue with the cute animals that the public clamored to see long after her interest in rabbits had failed is clear from her opening: "I have made many books about well-behaved people. Now, for a change, I am going to make a story about two disagreeable people, called Tommy Brock and Mr. Tod" (7). These two villains are some of the blackest, most recalcitrant in all of Potter's books. They threaten rabbit babies and battle each other in cutthroat fashion. They smell bad and have low standards of household cleanliness, which Potter, the fastidious housekeeper, found particularly repugnant. Potter's sense of her audience's willingness to read almost any book she wrote allowed her this assertive beginning.

Potter's most remarkable use of her own voice is in *The Roly-Poly Pudding* (1908). In this book, Potter not only appears in the narrative, she also appears in the illustration, and clearly calls attention to herself as Miss Potter, the author of the book. Furthermore, she makes authorial commentary as early as the title page and carries on in this personal mode in the dedication. She also appears both in the narrative and in the illustration in *The Tale of Pigling Bland* (1913). The story begins with Potter narrating in first person as an unidentified "I." She is clearly the voice of a farmer, one who knows the economic realities of raising pigs. She seems particularly heartless in sending young Pigling Bland off to market, when he is so young and still feeling the need for his mother. She appears in a faceless sketch slipping a piece of paper into Pigling Bland's pocket as he takes leave of the farm. After the pig sets off, the story reverts to third-person narration, and Potter the farmer disappears, in favor of a narrator who is much more sympathetic to the young pig's plight.

In *The Roly-Poly Pudding*, Potter is present throughout the story. In fact, the entire book is a response to a personal comment to an earlier book, *The Tale of Tom Kitten* (1907): "And I think that some day I shall have to make another, larger, book, to tell you more about Tom Kitten!" (54). Potter clearly enjoyed the antics of the kittens in the story and knew that there was more to be made of the mischief of which they were capable. Tom is clearly a character of whom she approves.

But Tom's next book is more the story of a rat, about whom Potter is more ambivalent. The first indication of her feelings toward Samuel Whiskers is his picture on the cover of the book. She portrays him making eye contact with the viewer through his sharp, animated eyes. But his body is so rotund as to border on the grotesque. Though humorous in his rotundity, he is also disgusting. Potter makes clear her ambivalence in the dedication to another rat of her personal acquaintance:

IN REMEMBERANCE OF
"SAMMY,"
THE INTELLIGENT PINK-EYED REPRESENTATIVE
OF
A PERSECUTED (BUT IRREPRESSIBLE) RACE
AN AFFECTIONATE LITTLE FRIEND,
AND MOST ACCOMPLISHED
THIEF

This is Potter's own voice unedited. There is nothing in the conventions of the dedication page that keeps an author from using her own voice, even when that voice might otherwise need editing to conform to the capabilities of the audience for which she wrote. Sammy's miniature picture, a simple pen sketch, sits pleasantly atop the dedication and resembles Samuel's on the cover. The remarkable words here are "persecuted," "irrepressible," and "thief." The enmity of rats and humans has been a fact of life ever since the two races have lived in close proximity, but that humans persecute rats accuses humanity of racism. The fact that rats are "irrepressible" suggests not only their ability to survive, but also their droll appearance to humans. The rest of the dedication loads compliments on Sammy, but the final word interrupts the flow with an unexpected accusation. The word is a small one, emphasized by the gradual diminution of line length as the dedication progresses. The word is all the more emphatic for being the last word in the dedication and being set off on a line by itself. Potter is clearly a human here, on the one hand with an appreciation of rat humor and on the other hand, an acute realization of rat rapaciousness.

Potter intrudes again in the illustration on the title page with a pictorial aside indicating her feeling about the fame of her rabbit characters. It was the usual practice in her books to note that she was also "Author of 'The Tale of Peter Rabbit,' &c. .'" On the title page of *The Roly-Poly Pudding*, the ampersand is followed by a line of four identical rabbits hopping across the page. Potter noted in her correspondence at this point in her career that she was tired of the rabbits and pleased to turn her attention to another kind of animal. Tom Kitten and Samuel Whiskers were her clear choice. Samuel and his rolling pin are clearly triumphant on this page, sitting victoriously over the title, with two playful kittens below and six rats with long tails gracefully arranged as part of the decorative border. Lowest on the page is a kitten bundled up like a sausage. The reader will later find that this is Tom Kitten. The title page clearly foreshadows the eventual outcome of the story: Samuel Whiskers and his race will trounce the cats.

In the story itself, Potter resorts to her own voice at three points in the narrative. The first occasion is signaled first by a break in the text, marked by six spaced ellipsis points at the bottom of the preceding page. Thus, the reader is prepared for some kind of break in the story; in this case, it is the flow of time. Potter steps in at this point with a parental tone, to deliver the moral of the story before it is told: "Now this is what had been happening to Tom Kitten, and it shows how very unwise it is to go up a chimney in a very old house, where a person does not know his way, and where there are enormous rats" (29). The narrative up to this point concerns Tom's siblings and Tom's mysterious disappearance. Tom is now located and the story resumes. But Potter signals clearly to the reader that Tom is about to find himself in trouble. Her tone of voice almost shakes a warning finger at children. But the moral itself is unlikely to apply to most children, who are unlikely to go up chimneys in old houses and who are even more unlikely to find a rat as sizeable as Samuel Whiskers. It is therefore difficult to take the moral seriously. The complications that follow seem to be Tom's fault. But the picture on this page shows an innocent-looking Tom peering almost apprehensively around the corner of a doorframe. He seems more victim than perpetrator. Once again, Potter uses her own voice to maintain the ambivalence in the story. She also changes the direction of its flow in a manner typical of a traditional storyteller.

Potter intrudes again, this time simultaneously in illustration and in text, to point out where the action of the story is taking place. Tom has been crawling into the mysterious, unfamiliar passageways in the chimney and along the walls. Potter narrates objectively and then intrudes: "He groped his way carefully for several yards; he was at the back of the skirting-board in the attic, where there is a little mark * in the picture" (41). Just as Potter promises, there is an asterisk on the baseboard in the picture. The picture itself is unusual in the story, since it shows the room not from animal perspective, close to the ground, but rather from a human vantage point, looking at one corner of the room from another. The open door suggests the human passageways more familiar to the reader; the asterisk juxtaposes the animal passageways that exist otherwise unnoticed in everyday life. By this juxtaposition, Potter lends credibility to the fantasy and emphasizes the coexistence of the animal and human worlds, with stories in each that take place unknown to the other, except as a go-between like Potter can tell them.

This shift to human perspective foreshadows Potter's last appearance in the story, near the end. Her entrance, in full sight of the viewer, though in the background, is signaled on the preceding page. John Joiner, the carpenter-dog whom Tom's mother summons to extricate him from beneath the floorboards, excuses himself from staying to dinner with the cats. "He regretted that he had not time to stay to dinner, because he had just finished making a wheel-barrow for Miss Potter, and she had ordered two hen-coops" (65). John's logic is not clear here. If the wheel-barrow is done, that is no reason to excuse himself; presumably the work on the hen-coops calls him.

The wheel-barrow must have been finished in order for it to be used on the next page, when both Potter and the fleeing rats appear. Potter's business transactions with John Joiner signal her presence in the community as a local resident, like the cats, and as a farm woman who needs such practical items as a wheel-barrow and hen coops. Thus, when she appears on the next page, she is not an intruder, but simply a neighbor.

In this case, Potter points to herself as the narrator of the story. The page turn reveals Potter, talking about herself in the first person, as if she had been present all along. For some children, especially the young ones for whom Potter designed her books, the idea that books are written by actual people is a difficult one to comprehend. But Potter assumes that children can comprehend, and she places herself as herself in the background of the following picture, seen in the late afternoon sunlight, with the runaway rats in the front. She appeals to the accuracy of her own eyes to lend credence to the sight of two rats running down the street, pushing a wheelbarrow full of their treasures. She makes clear that the sight of them is not a deliberate one, but rather occurs by happenstance, in the course of her other ordinary activities: "And when I was going to the post late in the afternoon—I looked up the lane from the corner, and I saw Mr Samuel Whiskers and his wife on the run, with big bundles on a little wheel-barrow, which looked very like mine" (66). Potter's figure is present, but small and definitely subordinate. It is so small that any facial features are too minuscule to see, though her posture, simply standing upright, with no particular emotion to be implied from it, is obvious enough. Samuel Whiskers and his wife are clearly the subjects of the illustration, and they run away not only from the house where they have been discovered, but away from Potter too.

At this point, the thievery of the rats receives clear denunciation, for though the rats have elsewhere labeled their thefts as "borrowing," Potter implies that her "loans" to the rats might not be so innocuous: "I am sure I never gave her leave to borrow my wheel-barrow!" (66). In fact, all the bundles that the rats transport are "borrowings," as the rats would call it, or "thefts," as Potter and human readers would more likely label them. Samuel Whiskers is so fat in the picture, he hardly looks fleet; his obesity is also the result of "borrowings" from Potter and other humans. But it is hard to evaluate the rats as felons; after all, their thievery is simply part of rat nature. The idea that rats are such hoarders of human possessions that they cannot run away without their gleanings is a humorous one, and it is difficult to point an accusatory finger at them, though Samuel seems to have overdone his borrowing, as suggested by his size. But Potter does not step in and punish the rats. Their posterity is threatened by the rat-catching capabilities of Tom Kitten's siblings, yet they thrive.

The only one who truly suffers in this story is Tom Kitten, who is so scarred by his experience as a pudding that he is no longer capable of catching rats. Thus, Potter delivers on her promise to show a moralistic tale and to show the moral in action. But Tom's punishment is more endearing than truly punitive. That "he never durst face anything that is bigger than—A Mouse" (75) is more laughable than vengeful. Tom is punished, it is true, but Potter's narrative intrusions suggest her ambivalence about cats and rats. The final effect is comic rather than tragic.

REFERENCES

Crouch, Marcus. *Beatrix Potter: A Walck Monograph*. New York: Henry Z. Walck, 1961.

Godden, Rumer. "An Imaginary Correspondence." *Horn Book* 39 (1963): 369–75.

Greene, Graham. "Beatrix Potter." In *Collected Essays*. New York: Viking, 1969.

Linder, Leslie, ed. *A History of the Writings of Beatrix Potter: Including Unpublished Works*. London and New York: Frederick Warne, 1972.

Linder, Leslie and Enid Linder, eds. *The Art of Beatrix Potter: With an Appreciation by Anne Carroll Moore and Notes to each Section by Enid and Leslie Linder*. Rev. ed. London and New York: Frederick Warne, 1972.

Potter, Beatrix. *The Roly-Poly Pudding*. New York: Frederick Warne, 1908.

———. *The Tale of Benjamin Bunny*. New York: Frederick Warne, 1904.

———. *The Tale of the Flopsy Bunnies*. New York: Frederick Warne, 1909.

———. *The Tale of Johnny Town-Mouse*. New York: Frederick Warne, 1918.

———. *The Tale of Mr. Tod*. New York: Frederick Warne, 1912.

———. *The Tale of Peter Rabbit*. New York: Frederick Warne, 1902.

———. *The Tale of Pigling Bland*. New York: Frederick Warne, 1913.

———. *The Tale of Tom Kitten*. New York: Frederick Warne, 1907.

Sale, Roger. "Beatrix Potter." In *Fairy Tales and After: From Snow White to E. B. White*. Cambridge and London: Harvard University Press, 1978.

PART II

Folk Literature and Myth

Introduction

GARY D. SCHMIDT

It is axiomatic that folk literature comes out of an oral culture. Shaped by generations of storytellers, the mythology and folklore of a culture are constantly revised by the voices that take up their telling. As new narrators come to the stories, the tales are reordered, details deleted and added, endings changed, emphases shifted, and points of view reconstructed as the narrator appraises the audience and evaluates its receptivity, its background, its assumptions, its needs. The elasticity of the stories presupposes their orality.

Writers who transpose words meant for the ear into words meant for the eye are faced with a set of paradoxes. Is it possible for the literary form to replicate the effects of an oral form? Is it possible—is it even legitimate—for one culture to reproduce the tales of another culture by attempting to capture its modes of plot structures, characterization, and language? Can tales that have come from a specific culture be removed from that culture and allowed to stand simply as items of story? Is it the work of either the storyteller or the historian to record the tales? Is it possible to remove the elasticity and tendency toward variation from the oral tales and still maintain their artistic integrity?

The writers in this section argue that the answers to these questions come through a consideration of the narrator's voice. Each considers the meaning of a tale as it is removed from the boundaries of its own culture and exposed to a larger community, which is part of the process of moving from the oral to the printed mode of transmission, from elasticity to, perhaps, permanence. The writers conclude that the success of this transmission depends upon the author's successful creation or re-creation of a narrator who can reinterpret old forms.

When Julius Lester came to rewrite Joel Chandler Harris' tales of *Uncle Remus*, he faced the tension of the permanence of the written page. Deciding that since each story is in some measure newly made with each telling, he perceived the written page only as the means for the transmission of the story. The tales' elasticity would be preserved by the flesh and blood narrator that he created. So he decided not to recast Uncle Remus, or even to use him as a character. Instead, Lester's narrator would be a collective voice, the voice of all black people—past and present—who were affected in some way by the tales. In this way the stories retain their vitality, by interacting with their changing culture.

Through such a narrator, Lester was able to maintain the elasticity of the tales, varying details by including contemporary references. Malcolm Jones, co-editor of *Jump! The Adventures of Brer Rabbit* with Van Dyke Parks, similarly felt the tensions of dealing with Harris' narrator. Jones and Parks decided to eliminate Uncle Remus, but not particularly because of problems with his voice. Jones acknowledges that any story removed from its specific culture faces loss, despite the ability of a tale to stand on its own. But at the least, the recorder has contributed to the preservation of the tale. For Jones, the narrator of the Uncle Remus tales is engaged not because that narrator participates in the culture from which the stories sprang, but because the narrator's culture shares the world view of the culture of the tales. Both Lester and Jones are concerned with retelling stories to readers who may not recognize many of the culturally based elements of these stories.

For Peter Dickinson, the problem in retelling ancient stories was quite different: he had to deal with the deadening effect of overfamiliarity. Dickinson begins with the premise that the stories of the Old Testament are, in their essence, narratives in an oral tradition; they were kept alive by retellings across generations. In *City of Gold*, Dickinson reconstructed an oral tradition. He approached the retellings through the voices of thirty-three distinct narrators. A Hebrew servant tells the story of the fall to a Babylonian nobleman during an open-air feast in a garden. A shepherd in Canaan tells the story of the burning bush. Saul's bodyguard tells of the king's death to Saul's rival, the new King David. In each case, a new, strong voice would overcome the familiarity of the tales by establishing fresh approaches and fresh points of view.

Dickinson acknowledges the difficulty of capturing the oral tradition in written form; the contemporary writer can only hope to imitate the oral voice of folklore and myth. The voices, however, are more than bardic echoes. Tuning his readers in to voices of the past, he helps them hear the cultural cadences of the original. In each voice readers hear, as though for the first time, the conflicts, struggles, triumphs, warnings, mistakes, foibles, doubts, and faith found by the oral reteller. The cultural affiliation rids the literary version of its familiarity. Nevertheless, Dickinson recognizes with

Lester that the oral voice, is, paradoxically, also the written voice. By blending the two voices, oral and literary, Dickinson captures, in an ancient cultural voice, the truth of the stories for our contemporary world; and the truth is heard all the more clearly for its ancient cultural setting.

Alice Mills also deals with the question of familiarity when she takes up Norse myths. Here the reteller is faced not with the familiar, but with the strange, the obscure, and the arcane. The result, Mills claims, is that the narrator of the Norse myths must begin by establishing a stance similar to that of a bard to an audience but must extend that stance so that the contemporary audience can be made familiar with the Norse pantheon. This stance determines such aspects as the tense of the stories, decisions on the translation of names, treatment of the sexuality in the tales, ordering of the myths, and even how myth itself is to be understood.

Emrys Evans explores the role of the narrator in dealing with myth not as one who is concerned with transmitting a body of lore, but as one who explores how myth is adapted and integrated into story. Arguing that the discourse of myth needs to be mediated if it is to fit into a plot structure, Evans identifies four narrative stances. The "implied author" moves the plot along, while the "close observer"—the closest stance to the actual author— comments through personal knowledge on such things as the setting and the context of the action. The characters' voices also represent a facet of the narration, revealing characterization, motive, and bias through language. The narrative stance closest to the mythic elements of the novel is that which employs what Evans calls "high language," a stance that breaks into the other narratives to announce the presence of mythic discourse. In the works of Susan Cooper and Alan Garner, such mythic discourse is tied to its culture principally through setting and language; it is mediated through a complex narrator who is aware of its assumptions and its effects on a work of fantasy.

Will James' *Smoky* is also tied to a specific culture through its discourse: here, the culture is the American West. As Lester, Evans, Dickinson, and Mills tie folklore to a culture, so James Higgins suggests that this novel is informed by the bunkhouses of the frontier, and its language, settings, plot situations, imagery, and narrative stance all emerge from a folk tradition fostered by the storytellers of these bunkhouses. Will James—himself a descendent of that tradition—creates a narrator who incarnates the bunkhouse storyteller, who speaks with that storyteller's language, who holds that storyteller's assumptions: the fear of the outsider, the belief in the melodrama of western story, a recognition of the special relationship between horse and cowboy. For James, the experience of the reader is to match the experience of the listening audience.

Whether two such different experiences can ever be matched is unlikely; certainly most of the writers of this section would argue that it cannot. At the same time, however, retellers of folk literature try in some basic sense to move the literary into juxtaposition with the oral and to move the visual into juxtaposition with the aural. One measure of the success of any retelling is whether the author can bridge those gaps, so that the narrator's voice can speak out of the past to a contemporary audience with the same sense of immediacy and import with which it spoke generations ago.

THE AUTHORIAL VOICE

6

The Storyteller's Voice: Reflections on the Rewriting of Uncle Remus

JULIUS LESTER

There is a paradox: Stories from the oral tradition are not meant for the page. Once confined there they become literature and are responded to and judged as literature. They are not.

Literature is the product of a single mind; it is the product of one person's skill with words and silence. A story comes from a community and is told by any member of the community, shaped and reshaped by all who tell the story and hear it. A detail in one person's telling is deleted and a new one added in the telling by someone else; a detail is omitted for one audience and new details improvised for another.

Literature exists on the page. Once it takes that form, it cannot be changed.

A story is elastic; it is recreated by the tongue of each teller and with each telling. Though its basic plot with its characters will not change, how much life is infused into the story depends on how much the storyteller infuses it with his or her life.

The nature of our society obviates against storytelling. We no longer live in cohesive communities. We no longer entertain each other with stories in which our own joys and sorrows are sublimated and refashioned into an art that serves as a mirror for the entire community. And yet, the story retains its appeal, its importance, its vitality through books.

But how can one fit the marvelous elasticity of a story onto the page without injuring it? It is possible only if one refuses to regard the page seriously, if one knows that the page is merely the necessary means and not an exalted end.

Most stories from the oral tradition that become books are written in a disembodied voice, using a language of literary images. The story is transmitted but it is not told. A story can only be told by a person, and that is what voice is, a flesh and blood human being whose voice is the embodiment of the community's past. When the story is being presented by someone called an author, the author writes words because that is what authors do.

A storyteller who uses the book as his vehicle writes *down* words. Some of them are the storyteller's own. Most of them have no owners but belong to all those whose mouths and lips shaped and polished the story until it became a gem worthy of being treasured and passed on.

When I began the project of retelling the Uncle Remus stories of Joel Chandler Harris, my task was to do what Harris himself had done, namely, to write embodied tales so that the reader (listener) would feel as if he or she were being called into a relationship of warmth and intimacy with another human body. The story is not separate from the teller. Only in this way will the listener not be separate from the story.

My first important decision was not to refashion Harris' Uncle Remus. Though I would've enjoyed transforming the old plantation "darkie" into something more appealing, this could only distract from what was important—the stories.

Instead, the personality of my storyteller would be communicated entirely through voice, through his asides, imagery, and allusions. Perhaps because I had grown up during the Golden Age of Radio, perhaps because I had had a live radio show for eight years, I knew the power of the voice and all that can be conveyed through the sound of it. However, I was not aware that anyone had attempted to put on paper that atmosphere created by the unseen human voice, to recreate the sound and feeling of what it was like to sit on the porch late at night and hear voices coming from the darkness as the old people told tales. This is how the slaves had told and heard the tales, and this is how I had heard tales as a child.

When my editor and I met to discuss the manuscript of the first volume of my retelling of the Uncle Remus stories, *The Tales of Uncles Remus: The Adventures of Brer Rabbit* (1987), it was evident immediately that we had conflicting conceptions of what a tale on the page should be.

She objected to many of the contemporary references, the changes in verb tense from past to present and past again, sometimes in the same paragraph. She especially objected to what she considered sexism in some of the stories.

In the story, "Brer Rabbit and the Mosquitoes," Brer Rabbit courts Brer Wolf's daughter: "Brer Wolf's daughter, who had always thought Brer Rabbit kind of cute, put on her mascara and eyeliner and whatever else it is that the women put on their face. She squeezed herself into a pair of jeans four sizes too small. Have mercy! And she put on a pink halter top! When Brer Rabbit saw her, he thought he'd died and gone to heaven." My editor found this especially objectionable and exploitative of women.

It proved to be a long and arduous afternoon, and for me, an exceptionally lonely one. I sat in her tiny office and we went through the manuscript, page by page, and I found myself having to defend each of her queries regarding voice and language. In 1969 I had published *Black Folktales* (1970) and the same publisher had refused the book because of the contemporary references I had put into the mouths of the animals and others. I saw nothing incongruous with God reading *TV Guide*, for example, but that was because I had grown up in a culture in which God did all kinds of extraordinary things that had not made their way into the Bible. So I had taken the book to another publisher. It has been in print continuously since 1969.

My editor continued to argue, however. If not for the acceptance *Black Folktales* had had, I might have acceded to her pressure, but doing so would have been a betrayal of all those black people from whose lives the stories had come, all those blacks whose stories these were. My responsibility was to them as their descendant.

Yet I could not arrogantly dismiss my editor's concerns. She feared that the contemporary references would make the book outdated very quickly and pointed to Italo Calvino's recent *Italian Folktales* as the model for what my book *could* be.

But I was not interested in creating a work of literature. Folktales exist in time and the Uncle Remus tales as told by Joel Chandler Harris are replete with references that are scarcely understood now. Only because of my southern roots did I understand that when Uncle Remus says "branch," he is not referring to a tree but a creek. (Up north people drink bourbon and water; down south they drink bourbon and branch.) Other references had left me baffled, however. In one of the Harris tales the social setting is a "candy pulling." I'd heard them referred to but never in such detail that my storyteller would have been comfortable in recounting it. So I omitted it.

Harris' use of references contemporary to his time did not injure the stories. Quite the contrary. They communicated something of the lives of the storytellers, and even though a story is told by one person only, the story being told is not one person's story.

In the story "Brer Rabbit Finally Gets Beaten," my editor did not like the following paragraph: "Brer Rabbit went into training. He bought a red jogging suit, a green sweatband, and some yellow Adidas sneakers, and he jogged ten miles every day. Then he'd come home and do a whole mess of push-ups, sit-ups, and skip rope to his records. Some folks wondered if he was training for a race or 'Soul Train.' " She suggested that I delete "Soul Train." To do so would take away my narrator's voice, and the story resides as much in the voice as it does the plot.

Without the voice, there would be only summaries of stories, and a story is not merely plot. The Uncle Remus stories scarcely vary in plot. They are trickster stories in which one animal tricks another. It is the voice of the storyteller that maintains our interest as readers (listeners).

The heart of storytelling is the human encounter between teller and listener. The goal of the teller is to make the listener more alive to him or herself. Especially in tales from the oral tradition, it is the voice of the teller that softens and humanizes the horrors and violence with which these tales abound.

I have had many manuscript conferences with editors over the past twenty years and sixteen books but never one as difficult and bitter as the one about *The Adventures of Brer Rabbit.*

My editor did not think that the inconsistencies in grammatical usage would communicate to white readers. I told her they weren't supposed to. But there was no harm in asking whites to read stories written in language with which they were not intimately familiar. The stories would communicate to anyone. That the language carried nuances and evoked memories that would be available primarily to blacks merely gave the stories an added dimension.

As for the references my editor considered sexist, I could only laugh. My Uncle Remus could not refer to "halter tops" if women did not wear them. Of course, my editor considered women who wore halter tops to be "unliberated." To rewrite a history and culture to satisfy white feminism was too ridiculous to even consider. My editor's inability to relinquish certain cultural assumptions pained me deeply.

She assumed she knew what stories in a book were supposed to be. Worse, she assumed that her assumptions were correct and was unwilling to be taught that, in this instance, they were not.

For her, folk tales were historical artifacts. For me they are a breathing, pulsating reality, and they are in no way incompatible with shopping malls and halter tops. My Uncle Remus is as much a man of his time as his predecessor was of that time.

I never describe Uncle Remus. I couldn't because I don't know what he looks like. He sounds like he is an old man, but I don't think he's so. However, he's not young. Even though I refer to him as "he," I'm not wholly convinced that that is so. As I wrote, the images of old women I'd known in the south came to me more frequently than those of old men.

The voice is more that of a presence, the presence of all black people whose lives were shaped by the tales. It is a collective voice, which is why it moves so easily backward and forward in time, referring at one moment to "the haslett" and at the next to Adidas sneakers. It is a voice that is as much at ease at a hog killing during slavery as it is eating Chicken McNuggets. It is a voice that stands simultaneously outside history while being at the very heart of history.

To tell the stories with any other voice is to think that the stories exist apart from their telling. They cannot because, ultimately, the stories are about our lives, all of us. If they were not, the stories would not be the source of joy that they are for whites and blacks. That is the paradox: The universality of the stories is only revealed if the voice in the stories is specific, if it is immersed in the blackness of yesterday and today. The way to the universal is through the particular.

Uncle Remus would have said to my editor, "Lord, child, how come you worrying so much about how I tell these stories? Ain't nothing that ever come out of my mouth ever done nobody no harm. Leastways not when I done brushed my teeth good and jiggled the Listerine around in my mouth. That stuff tastes worser than hog's breath. Don't you be trying to tell these stories without using my voice. Folks done tried that and you know what happened? Them stories had to go to the hospital. That's the truth! Them stories had to have highway bypass operations. Then they had to have bad grammar transplanted into them and take all kinds of pills to keep 'em from getting infections from literature. Then they had to take baths every day for about forty-eleven months. So, you leave these stories be. They don't be needing no clean clothes or grease for their hair and please don't come shining they shoes. What you got to understand is that the story is me. If you can't accept the story the way it rides on my voice, then that mean you can't accept me."

Voice is who I am.

Voice is who you are.

If I listen deeply to your voice, I am the recipient of a wonderful and irreplaceable gift—you.

If you listen deeply to mine, you will receive something very rare and precious—me.

REFERENCES

Lester, Julius. *Black Folktales*. New York: Grove, 1970.
———. *The Tales of Uncle Remus: The Adventures of Brer Rabbit*. Vol. 1. New York: Dial, 1987.

7

The Talespinner's Mind

MALCOLM JONES

It would be nice to say that it's all voice, wouldn't it? In an oral tradition, that is, what else is there? The storyteller is pitchman, barker, emcee, preacher, stump speaker, barber over your shoulder, and beautician in your ear, mother and father murmuring while you lay you down to sleep, tucking you in with a tale. Pure, disembodied voice.

Would that it were so simple. Instead, we have something more complicated. Voices belong to somebodies. Tales get told for a reason. So, we have to know who is doing the telling. And why.

We say we are held prisoner by a good storyteller, but I wonder. In the cases of the two most famous storytellers I know, Scheherazade and Uncle Remus, one told stories to save her life, while the other was an ex-slave who in the presence of even a little white boy had to mind every word, watch every step. They were the prisoners.

Something goes on in the tale-teller's mind besides the story. Or rather, circumstances outside the story dictate certain things to the person spinning the tale. These are tale-tellers under pressure.

Scheherazade's circumstances are all part of the frame tale that surrounds the other stories. In the case of Uncle Remus, it gets a little trickier. You aren't supposed to be worrying about Remus getting lynched if he puts a foot wrong. He's just this harmless old man telling stories to Miss Sally's little boy, isn't he?

I'm not too sure about that. Joel Chandler Harris invented Uncle Remus out of necessity. To publish the slave tales he had collected, he needed a context, a mouthpiece to answer those questions mentioned above. Where was the voice coming from? Who was telling these old slave tales and Indian legends? Uncle Remus, that's who.

For his trouble, Harris would in time be accused of, first, purloining stories that rightfully belonged to black Americans, and second, of saddling those stories with this obsequious, wooly headed fiction.

I fear these charges are leveled most often by the same people who complain that the heavy dialect makes the stories unreadable, for certainly they could not make such charges if they had read the tales.

You don't have to read far in Uncle Remus to see that not only was Harris one of the all-time great folktale collectors, but a subtle fiction maker as well. Remus emerges no more or less subservient than a black man had to be in rural nineteenth-century Georgia, but more important he turns out to be witty, sardonic, subtle, and kind. In other words, he is not only admirable, he is interesting. Likewise, his animal stories, endless variations on the theme of the weak triumphing over brutish oppressors through guile, pluck, and a fairly flexible sense of fair play, first appear to be high-grade Aesopian imitation but prove on further examination to be nothing less than an elaborately symbolic vision of the relations between blacks and whites. Remus—which is to say, Harris—makes it clear many times that he realizes the importance of the stories. Harris seems to have been content to let those who would understand what he had uncovered do so without any prodding; what an astonishing thing for a white man to do in a society where segregation was viewed as not only excusable but condign.

So, naturally enough, when my partner and I sat down to retell the Brer Rabbit stories, the first thing we did was get rid of Uncle Remus. He served an important function for Joel Chandler Harris, but great creation though he is, that function is not intrinsic to the tales. They predate Remus, and with any luck they will outlive our grandchildren.

Nonetheless, Harris' problem was our problem. The question is still, who is telling these stories about rabbits and foxes and bears? If not Uncle Remus, then who?

A couple of southern white guys sitting out in Hollywood? The great ur-memory of us all? Again, a question without much of an answer. A better question, or at least one I have an answer for is, why tell the stories again?

Two reasons: Harris' dialect is impenetrable for a lot of people (not as impenetrable as you might think, but the perception is the reality in this case) and the vitality of the stories is obvious to anyone who reads or hears them. They speak to something in the human heart that never goes out of date. They are as close to the bone of myth as tales can get.

At the same time—and this is what continually attracts me—there is something distinctively southern about them. As a southerner, I am hard put to say exactly what this something is, but I know it has to do with the humor found in fatalism and the ironies found in almost every angle of existence. It has a lot to do with ease, not working when you don't have to, the coolness of the con (Brer Rabbit has the proper dream of a house for himself and his family, but he cons his chums into building it), and the importance of keeping square with reality. Brer Rabbit suffers at the hands of those more powerful than he, and so he is forever on the defensive, getting in a lick when he can, even when it is the first lick. He is not above a pre-emptive strike, because he knows that in the ultimate analysis, it is all he can do to stay alive, forget about staying even.

This is not a very cuddly, or polite philosophy, but it is honest, and therein lies its constant appeal. Brer Rabbit's tongue is coated with honey but he never lies to himself, and these stories don't lie either. They paint a world pretty and ugly by turns, but a world we never fail to recognize.

Without meaning to get fancy, and speaking only for myself, I have to say that I am possessed by these stories. I am their prisoner. Their world view is one that I grew up on. I read them unquestioningly, and given the chance, I retell them without an iota of self-consciousness. Their voice is my voice.

As for the practical aspects of retelling folktales, it would be simplistic to pretend that traditionally black, originally African stories are not changed when white people tell them, but how much and in what way, is hard to say, and besides the deed was accomplished long ago. Brer Rabbit now lives in everybody's neighborhood. Then there is the equally tough question, What happens when oral storytelling makes the transition to the printed page? The hard answer is, Something is lost. The writer, even a great writer such as Harris, can only approximate what the storyteller says. A real voice becomes a literary device. This is lamentable, but it is not tragic. On the contrary, there is something salutary in it. The writer is, in many cases, saving something that would otherwise be lost, and if reading pales beside hearing them, it is a sight better than not knowing them at all.

At any rate, when it came time to dismantle Harris' carefully constructed dialect, the decision as to how to rebuild was easy. The stories are southern and rural and should sound that way. We ended up with a mildly oracular vernacular, a voice that liked its own sound and didn't mind running on a bit.

There was nothing arbitrary about this, though. The stories themselves are so strong, their trajectories so direct, that you never need to worry about where you're headed. The rhythm and speed built into their structure dictate the rhythm and speed in the words used to tell them. These stories have been across so many tongues that they tell themselves. All you have to do is get out of the way.

Which brings me to the one thing I learned from this exercise, which was a lesson in humility. Never again will I set so great a store by the totems of originality or individual creation, and I think it might be a blessing for every creative writing student or anyone who fancies the writing trade to spend time retelling folk tales. A great good can be done by keeping traditional stories alive. At the very least, you learn a lot about how a story is put together.

I shouldn't preach. After all, I did my share of tampering, too. I think this is an irresistible part of storytelling. So, buried now in one of the stories is a fragment of a blues lyric by Willie Dixon that just seemed to fit a hollow corner. If it's apt, it will stay. If not, nothing is lost. For this is the way that stories go, I think, picking up a phrase here, a plot twist there, and so they thrive, like a stew pot that never leaves the heat and never goes empty, but dipped from and added to constantly, nourishes us right along.

REFERENCES

Parks, Van Dyke and Malcolm Jones. *Jump! The Adventures of Brer Rabbit*. New York: Harcourt Brace Jovanovich, 1986.

8

The Oral Voices of *City of Gold*

PETER DICKINSON

When my publisher telephoned and asked me to do a retelling of stories from the Old Testament, I refused with all the emphasis I could muster. She wanted it, she said, to continue a series that had begun with Hans Andersen and Grimm. I told her, first, that there was no way in which the Bible stories could now be retold; and second, that there was no way in which they belonged in that series. I put the phone down. Twenty minutes later I called her and said I would take the job on. I had an idea.

Thinking about it since writing the book I have realized that both of my objections were to do with "voice." All books, even the telephone directory, have voices. When I first responded to my publisher I was assuming that there were only two possible voices in which to tell Bible stories: low style and high style. "Low style" is as-told-to-the-children, bland, simple, homogenized, describing a world in which very clean shepherds look after very white and woolly lambs in a sunny but strangely hazed place called The Holy Land. "High style" doesn't even *see* that much. It is all sound, words lovingly deployed, language as it was never spoken and was written only for the purpose of translating Homer and retelling Bible stories. In a culture awed by pomp and superior education the high-style voice may have had a semblance of life in it, but that is no longer the case. The low-style voice lives on, just, in its jejune fashion.

My second objection, that the stories do not belong with Andersen and Grimm, was instinctive, but right. I have since realized that it too is a matter of "voice." Fairy stories and folk tales have become almost detached from their origins; they are told in the voice of someone whose primary purpose is to entertain, though they may have other functions. In our culture, despite the rush toward unbelief, we are still historically bound by the feeling that the Bible stories are different. Remote though they too are from their origins, they do not exist in order to entertain. They need to be written or spoken in the voice of someone who is trying to tell you something important, to instruct or persuade or explain.

I can illustrate this at its simplest by the tale of Elisha and the bears (II Kings 2: 23 ff.), which tells how some children mocked the prophet for his baldness, and in response he called a couple of bears from the woods who tore the children to bits. Naturally this episode has worried commentators. It is both nasty and trivial. What on earth is it doing in the tremendous account of the traffickings of the Omnipotent with His people? Even in the Bible the story is already in the wrong voice, especially if read aloud from the King James version, with the parsonic syllables reverberating among gothic arches. But anyone who has had much dealings with children (unlike the commentators) will recognize it at once for what it is—a frightener. So in *City of Gold* (1979), the voice begins in shrill exasperation: "You're a nasty rude little boy! . . . " and ends in calmer menace: "so off you go at once to

your auntie and tell her you're sorry, before Elisha's bears come and get you!"

Told like that the story may remain nasty and trivial, but it regains its purpose. It has rediscovered its voice. When I told my publisher I had an idea, what I meant was that I had found a voice—or rather, voices.

Most of the Old Testament stories had begun in the oral tradition. There they had had their very varied purposes—explanation of a taboo, precedent for a legal case, reinforcement of a ritual, all the way up from the little matter of teaching children to mind their manners to the great purpose of binding a people together in the unified worship of the One God. By recreating these voices I would (this is crucial) be true to the material, in a way that neither the high style nor the low style can any longer be.

Of course I did not think of what I was doing in such hifalutin' terms. Like any writer, I simply thought "This is an interesting idea—I hope I can make it work." And of course, I could not really recreate the voices. Even suppose I had magically been able to listen in to a ballad singer of the tribe of Dan (if they *had* ballad singers) telling the story of Delilah, and then had translated it into English, it would not have worked. The references, the cultural assumptions, the modes of story telling, are too remote. All I could do was *pretend* to recreate the voices. Moreover, for the sake of variety, and to give an impression of the immense stretch of time during which the stories of the Bible came to their final shape, I transposed some of the stories away from their original contexts and purposes. It seems to me both plausible and proper that a father should tell his children the story of the first Passover while they are hiding from the persecution of Antiochus some twelve hundred years later; this story is central to the tradition, and has served the same purposes for another two thousand years. But it is far from plausible that a Babylonian drill sergeant should tell the story of David and Goliath as a preliminary to training his squad in the use of the shield against the sling. It made a change and amused me.

So what I did was not what it might at first sight appear to be—a return from the outworn sophistications of literary storytelling to the pure simplicities of the oral tradition. (The oral tradition is in any case far from simple and has sophistications of its own.) *City of Gold* is if anything more literary than the traditions I rejected. These are not voices, they are imitations of voices. They have their own literary ancestry—the Browning, for instance, of "My Last Duchess" or of "An Epistle," which is itself incidentally a Bible story, about Lazarus; and the Kipling of *Puck of Pook's Hill* and *Rewards and Fairies*. But that is not to say that they are hollow, sham, or false to the material. (I am assuming for the sake of the argument that I did the job well and embodied my idea satisfactorily. Whether that is in fact the case is not for me to say.) It is in such permutations, developments, sloughings of old skins, that literature stays alive and finds fresh voices to speak into the ears of new generations.

REFERENCES

Dickinson, Peter. *City of Gold*. London: Gollancz, 1979.

THE CRITICAL VOICE

9

Smoky, Animal Romance, and the Cowboy Narrator

JAMES E. HIGGINS

The animal story is an ancient genre kept existent by writers of great merit like Kenneth Grahame and E. B. White, who created modern masterpieces of animal fancy in which talking animals represent both man and their own species. Animals speak in classics like Kipling's *Jungle Books* and Felix Salten's *Bambi*, though in all other respects within these tales they remain creatures of nature, bound only by the laws of the jungle and the forest.

The realistic animal story, in which animals are given no power of speech, evolved and took root in the expansive wilderness and frontier of North America. Ernest Thompson Seton's *Wild Animals I Have Known* was published in 1898, and five years later came *Call of the Wild* (1903) by Jack London. It is to this last category of animal tales to which *Smoky, the Cow Horse* (1926), by Will James, belongs.

Although "realistic" animal tales do possess very distinct characteristics and aesthetic elements by which they must be judged, they are by no means unrelated to animal stories of a more fanciful nature, past or present. They are all connected beneath the surface, and all are a part of a rich and important tradition that speaks to man concerning his place in the nature of all things.

The fanciful tales are stories of "supposal." Suppose the animals could speak, what would they have to say? The realistic tales on the other hand, in seeming contradiction to the label put on them, are based on the premise that the animals do "speak," and despite the fact that most civilized men have found it difficult, for a variety of reasons, to hear what they have to say, there are others who have indeed learned to understand animal language and to heed the messages they communicate. The term "realistic" has been used here only to distinguish these stories from those of a fanciful nature, not to place them in the literary school of realism. They can be more fittingly characterized as animal romances, for they are marked by the kind of writing that, in the definition of Frank Norris, goes " . . . straight through the clothes and tissues and wrappings of flesh down into the red, living heart of things" (Norris, 797).

Smoky, a keystone work in the brief history of realistic animal stories, has been given very little critical attention beyond its enthusiastic reception in 1926. In the case of children, it is virtually unknown and certainly read by only a small number. It, like many other great books with a timeless theme, should still have a place in the marketplace, for it is the prototype of the nature romance, set in the rugged terrain of the American West.

The first paragraph of *Smoky* leaves no doubt in the reader's mind that this will be a romance.

It seemed like Mother Nature was sure agreeable that day . . . stems of new green grass was trying to make their way up thru the last year's faded growth, and reaching for the sun's warm rays. Taking in all that could be seen, felt, and inhaled, there was no day, time, nor place that could beat that spring morning on the sunny side of the low prairie butte where Smoky the colt was foaled. (3)

It ends just as fittingly in the romantic tradition, having come full circle, after years of pain and separation, when the green grass was growing an inch a day. As the cowboy Clint goes out to get a bucket of water, " . . . the morning sun throwed a shadow on the door; and as he stuck his head out a nicker was heard" (263).

In his preface to *Smoky*, Will James makes it clear from the outset that it is a story for animal lovers. He makes no excuses for the reciprocal affection that will pass between man and horse, and he does not shy away from the realization that he may be accused of sentimentalization. The cowboy Clint is a composite of the many men James encountered during his life on the range. He witnessed and experienced for himself the strong bond that can develop between man and animal, especially when their work together demands long hours in all kinds of weather and over rough terrain. His drawings that accompany the prose are in the tradition of those artists of the West he greatly admired: Russell, Remington, Dixon, and Wyeth. His illustrations have an air of the romantic about them, but no one would accuse them of being inaccurate or unrealistic. His writing has that same quality.

James writes of Smoky in the preface:

He's not a fiction horse that's wrote about in a dream and made to do things that's against the nature of a horse to do. Smoky is just a horse, but all horse; and that I think is enough said.

As for Clint, . . . I'm here to say that I can produce many a cowboy what can show feelings for a horse the same as Clint done. (vi)

The above sample of James' prose gives just a hint of the style that brought protests from several reviewers when *Smoky* was first published. And, of course, even stronger objections were raised when it won the Newbery Award in 1927. One would guess that even today, in some quarters, there still remains disapproval for this kind of writing being put into the hands of youngsters. Maxwell Perkins, James' editor at Scribner's, on the other hand, recognized immediately that the verisimilitude of the work was greatly dependent upon the cowboy vernacular and that the misspellings and even the ungrammatical structures were aesthetically appropriate.

James *tells* the story. The cowboy speaks directly to the reader. It is unlikely that he could have successfully told the story in any other way. Mark Twain speaks for James and other storytellers like himself, who found themselves in the same fix: "With the pen in one's hand narrative is a difficult art: narrative should flow as flows the brook down through the hills and leafy woodlands" (xiv).

Will James is a cowboy first and foremost. His writing exudes the subtle essence and flavor of the desert, mountains, and sagebrush. It is the spirit of what has become known as the Old West. It seems he took the advice given him by C. M. Russell in a letter dated May 12, 1920, and applied it not only to his drawing, but to his writing as well. "I know you have felt a horse under you. Nobody can tell you how to draw a horse . . . the real artistick may never know you but nature loving regular men will and thair is more of the last kind in this old world . . . " (Amaral, 35).

Though he was not a naturalist, James the cowboy, like any farmer or shepherd or woodsman who spends his working life in the outdoors, and who is also blessed with talent for telling a story, brings a fresh quality to his descriptions of the natural environment. As an example:

The first of winter had come and hit the mountains of the southern country. Big, dark clouds had drifted in, drenched the ranges down to bedrock with a cold rain, and hung on for days. Then the rain had gradually changed to a wet snow, kept a falling steady, and without a break, till it seemed like the country itself was shivering under the spell.

Finally, and after many long days, the dark clouds begin to get lighter and lighter and started lifting and drifting on. Then one evening, the sun got a chance to peek thru and smile at the country again. It went down a smiling that way. And after it disappeared over the blue ridge, a new moon took its place for a spell, and like as to promise that the sun would smile again the next day.

And it did; it came up bright and real fitting to that Arizona country. The air was clear as spring water in a granite pool, and as still. The whole world seemed dozing and just contented to take on all the warmth and life the sun was giving. A mountain lion was stretched out on a boulder, warm and comfortable, where the day before he'd been in his den all curled up and shivering. Then a few deer come out of their shelter, hair on end and still wet thru, but as they reached the sunny side of the mountain it wasn't long when it dried again, and layed smooth.

Further down the mountain and more on the foothills, a little chipmunk stuck his head out of his winter quarters and blinked at the sun. He blinked at it for quite a spell like not believing, and pretty soon came out to make sure. He stood up, rolled in the warm dirt, and in more ways than one made up for the long days he'd holed away. Other chipmunks came out, and then he went visiting. More seeds was gathered as he went from bush to bush and even tho he already had a might big supply already stored away, he worked on as tho he was afraid of running short long before spring come. (189–90)

The *voice* of the narrator, who is obviously also a cowboy, is always present; and though the vernacular, misspellings, and breaches of correct grammar can at first be a bit troublesome to the reader, it only takes a page or two before the printed obstacles fade away and the reader is rewarded by the sound of the telling, as the tale is immensely enriched.

James does not follow the tenets of written language; he adheres to the more informal conventions of the oral storyteller. The tone is conversational. From time to time the narrator mentions himself, as when he is describing Smoky's early encounters with wild animals: "Smoky . . . had scrambles with 'em, but that came later in his life, and it's a good thing it was later, for I most likely wouldn't be telling about Smoky now" (24).

In this kind of telling the indefinite "you," when it appears, gives way to direct address as it does in the live storytelling situation when the "you" is accompanied by eye contact. James may use it instinctively, without giving much thought to the matter, but the editor surely was aware of it and let it stand because of its effectiveness. It may have been edited out in some places, because it is used sparingly: "[I]f you could of felt his warm hide and seen how thick the hair had growed on it, and how long, you'd never wondered why it was that the cold raw winds never fazed him" (31).

Sometimes James goes further and moves unobtrusively into the use of third-person observations other than the narrator himself, such as when he describes the movement of a group of drifting range horses: "—A feller watching 'em would of figgered that something or other had started 'em on the move . . ." (37). Still at other times he will be careful to keep human observations distinct from the animal's awareness. For instance, in describing Smoky's third year, when he was "a picture to make any cowboy miss a few heart beats," James is quick to add, "to the bunch, all of them qualities and good points of Smoky's was lost and not at all noticed" (42–43).

Smoky flows with the naturalness and spontaneity of a yarn being spun in the bunkhouse. Nevertheless, James takes great care not to ascribe human reasoning to his animals. Smoky is an animal that grows, learns, and matures, but always within the limits of the species.

The moment Smoky comes into the world his senses begin making connections with one another and recording impressions in the brain.

[S]omething moved right in front of his nose about a foot; it'd been there quite a good spell but he'd never realized it before, besides his vision was a little dim yet . . .

Being it was right close he took a sniff at it. That sniff recorded itself into his brain and as much as told him that all was well. It was one of his mammy's legs. (4)

The narrator often serves as the translator of the horse's actions, as in the above description, where the words "as much as told him" are inserted. The horse is not given human speech, but he does communicate, and here again the author translates the meaning. James uses the word "nicker" for the sound of horse talk, making it clear that each one sends its own message.

[A]t the first move the colt made she run her nose along his short neck and nickered . . . and his first little answering nicker was heard. (4)
     His mammy nickered encouragement . . . (4)
     . . . his mammy nickered "that's a good boy." (7)

At other times, of course, messages are sent by actions. As a colt Smoky is big of size and temper, making it difficult for some of his elders "to eddicate him and *show* that they could" (43). And when he acts up at one point, "Smoky felt like he hadn't even been noticed, . . . the actions of the stud had said plainer than words 'fool kid' " (45). Throughout the book James subtly reminds the reader that the horse is not behaving beyond his own capacities:

He looked at the far away hills of his range and he seemed like to think on the subject . . . (53)
     If Smoky could only of knowed . . . (67)

Smoky matures from colt to gelding while time in the story is measured in the same way that time on the range is recorded, by the passing of the seasons. When he is no longer considered a "child horse," his "mammy" is now referred to as his "mother," and slowly she is distanced into his past. Without making direct comparisons, James nevertheless depicts the "adolescent" horse as having some of the same traits as his human counterpart.

It all kept getting to be less of a puzzle for him till finally there come a time when Smoky got so he thought he knowed it all. He figgered he had the world by the tail and with a downhill push. Like all the other colts of his age he was just where conceit had the best of him, he got strong headed and full of mischief, and then's when the older horses figgered him to be a regular pest and began knocking on him. (41)

When Clint finally rounds up Smoky and begins to train him as a cow horse, James describes first hand the learning capability of the horse:

He was all for catching on and not a nerve in him was idle as Clint would take him of evenings and ride him out for a spell, and chase, cut out, or rope at the critter. Them goings on had his mind occupied and the fact that he'd figger and think on the subject between times was proved by the way he'd go at things in a decided and knowing how way, when the day before the same thing had left him puzzled and wondering. (107)

Instinct is the prime "thinking" power of Smoky, and time and time again this innate gift saves him from approaching trouble. For instance, when he is only a foal, curious but "innocently" unafraid of anything in the environment, he wanders off following a coyote. When they are well away from the herd the coyote suddenly turns and leaps at his throat. "The generations of mustang blood that'd fought the lobo and the cougar and which was the same blood that flowed in Smoky's veins is all that saved the colt. That inherited instinct made him do the right thing at the right time . . . " (11–12).

Later, when he has matured and learned to better use his senses, it is the same mustang inheritance that helps him endure fear and pain. When Clint first ropes him, "Smoky figgered the end of the world had come as he felt the human touch him, and if it'd been in his blood to faint away, he'd done it easy . . . " (29).

The rest of the narrative revolves around the relationship between man and horse. It is indeed a "love story." For the cowboy it is love at first sight: "[A]s he stood there, his eyes taking in every move the mouse colored gelding was making, there was a smile showed under the stetson. That smile was just for the glad way he felt as he sized him up . . . He was glad to know that he'd be the first to touch that pony's hide . . . "(68).

For the horse, of course, the initial meeting is another matter. He is roped and lies helpless on the ground. "In a dazed way he seen the cowboy bend over him; a knee touched his neck and the muscles along there quivered the same as if a snake's fangs had been feeling for a holt. A hand touched his ear and another his forehead; there was no pain but if there had been the little horse would of never felt it" (69).

So the "bronco busting" begins. With patience and understanding of the breed and special affection for this particular gelding, Clint begins the slow taming of the wild horse. Smoky gradually begins to respond to the singular smell and look of this two-legged creature and to trust his movements. The author does not trace the animal's growing trust through Smoky's "thoughts," but rather through his actions and by other subtle changes in the narrative itself. For instance, just as earlier Smoky was distanced from his mother, as this relationship grows closer references to the man evolve from "crethure" to "human" to "cowboy" to finally his proper name, "Clint."

A similarity between *Smoky* and *The Call of the Wild* is the absence of references to sexual feelings or responses. Measured against nature books of today, of course, this would have to be viewed as a shortcoming. One can surmise that it was probably the publisher who deleted such passages, or requested James beforehand not to include them, for it would seem unlikely that he would have had any qualms about including them. There are a few references in the opening chapter to nursing, and before Smoky has his first encounter with the cold and snow of winter, his mammy has already " . . . give him to understand that he was weaned. There was no arguing with her, and Smoky knowed better than try . . . " (32).

The following spring Smoky experiences his first roundup, and like the other new members of the herd he is cut out and branded, but there is no mention of the gelding procedure: he is suddenly referred to as "that mouse colored gelding" (47). The terms "stud" "mare," and "gelding" are used throughout the book, but for the uninformed reader their meanings are left for a run to the dictionary or to another source for explanation. Obviously in the 1920s any sexual reference in an animal story was still a taboo, especially in a book that might be read by or shared with children. It turns out that the publishers' concerns abut the strongly negative reception the public might give to any such inclusion were well founded. Over twenty years later Mary O'Hara's very popular best seller, *My Friend Flicka* (1947), came under heavy attack by censors and some reviewers for the graphic gelding description she included, even though it was for the expressed purpose of showing that the procedure was not as painless for the animal as many people believed.

It is interesting to note here that whereas editors of fifty years ago or more were on constant watch lest there be some offense taken because of a scene of a sexual nature, little vigilance was given to racial stereotyping, especially of a negative type. The narrator of *Smoky* has sympathy for the animal, but a 1926 prejudice against "outsiders." Except for Clint no other humans really step clearly into focus as characters in *Smoky*, but the two men who are singled out from among the many who are responsible for his bad fortune and ill treatment are both racial "outsiders." The cowboy who first rustles Smoky, and moves him off his home range, is described as "a halfbreed of Mexican and other blood that's darker . . . a halfbreed from the *bad* side, not caring, and with no pride" (180).

At the climax of the story Clint doesn't recognize the old mouse colored horse that he rescues. The horse is pulling a vegetable wagon and is being beaten by its owner. The vegetable man is not physically described, but when the sheriff arrives on the scene he says to Clint: "Say, cowboy . . . don't scatter that hombre's remains too much, you know we got to keep record of that kind the same as if it was a white man, and I don't want to be looking all over the streets to find out who he *was*" (257). This bit of dialogue would be edited out of a manuscript today.

Any yarn that springs from the bunkhouse would have the melodramatic elements of the Old West so apparent in cowboy ballads and tales. Any cowboy narrator will have sympathy for the animal and antipathy for those outside the cowboy range, both attitudes bordering on melodrama. For the cowboy narrator, it is the "breed" that initiates Smoky and us into the world of pain, and, in the context of the melodrama, we approve as Smoky turns on the "breed" and stomps him to death. The cowboy narrator too brings the reader to awareness of the degree of decline from the plains horse into a cart horse, as Smoky ends up in the traces of a vegetable wagon.

[T]hem straps even seemed to wrap around his heart at times and keep it from beating.

[T]he old pony even got so he couldn't hate no more; abuse or kindness had both got to be the same, and one brought out no more result or show of interest than the other . . . He didn't mind anything, any more. (250–51)

The child reader, outraged by the degradation, is then set up for the book's joyful reunion.

Will James is the cowboy narrator, though his origins are not those that he fictionalized in *Lone Cowboy* (1930). He was not born in a covered wagon; he did not live on the Montana prairies; his parents did not die when he was a small child (Viguers, 557). Instead he was born of French parents in St. Nazaire de Acton and as Joseph-Ernest-Nephtali Dufault he grew up in the province of Quebec. In his study of James' life and work, *Will James: The Last Cowboy Legend* (1980), Anthony Amaral states, "When he was fifteen he solemnly announced to his mother and father that he was going to the Canadian West . . . In 1907, with ten dollars from his father and the prayers of his mother Ernest went West " (101–03). In the Canadian West he began to live the life of a cowboy and rapidly improved on the smattering of English he learned as a child. In 1910 he crossed the border and drifted down to the range country of southwestern United States.

It is a story more remarkable in its own way than the ones James invented. He probably thought that knowledge of his origins would detract from his image as an authentic cowboy and the veracity of his stories. The truth is that the deep yearnings of his boyhood to go West, become a cowboy, and ride the great outdoors astride his own horse constructed an indelible reality of their own *within* the boy-man. This is what marks *Smoky* with a truth of its own also—the truth of romantic fiction.

Without explicitly setting out to do so, authors of books such as *Smoky* sensitize the reader, especially the young reader, to the realization that each creature of nature has a measure of power peculiar to itself and its kind. Like the animal tales of old, without argumentation or evangelization, they raise the fundamental issue concerning the human's place in the nature of things.

REFERENCES

Amaral, Anthony. *Will James: The Last Cowboy Legend.* Reno: University of Nevada Press, 1980.

Clemens, Samuel. *The Complete Short Stories of Mark Twain.* Edited by Charles Neider. Garden City, N.Y.: Hanover House, 1957.

———. *Lone Cowboy: My Life Story.* Lincoln: University of Nebraska Press (rpt. 1985).

James, Will. *Smoky the Cow Horse.* New York: Scribner's, 1926, 1929.

Norris, Frank. "A Plea for Romantic Fiction." In *The Norton Anthology of American Literature*, Vol. 2. Edited by Ronald Gottesman et al, 797. New York: Norton, 1979.

Viguers, Ruth Hill. "Experiences to Share." In *A Critical History of Children's Literature*, edited by Cornelia Meigs, 557. New York: Macmillan, 1953.

10

Children's Novels and Welsh Mythology: Multiple Voices in Susan Cooper and Alan Garner

EMRYS EVANS

Most children learn early to appreciate stories, both for what they tell and how they are told. The guardians of the world's mythologies—from Homer to the tale-tellers of the Australian Outback—are the trustees of story. Later writers who draw on the materials of myth or legend to enrich their own poems, novels, or plays have at their disposal all the techniques of modern narrative with which to repay their debt of fidelity while giving new life to their sources.

Children's experience of narrative and narrators grows with age. The first narrator sits in the room with them: probably they sit on his or her lap. The voice is the voice of a mother or grandfather, nurse or teacher, though that voice may also take on the voices of characters in a story. The first tales are the tales of early childhood—memorized rhymes, folk tales, family stories, religious tales, and parables. Next, stories are read aloud from books, so that the children's interest in the new medium develops, and they learn to read for themselves. The narrator now speaks to them from the page, and the techniques available to teller or reader increase in sophistication.

Growth can be reflected in a child's experience of any particular tradition of myth or legend. Welsh myth is no exception. Its custodians are relatively late, the medieval manuscripts of the Mabinogion holding pride of place among them. A first glance at the monstrous catalog of half-remembered names from Pan-Celtic mythology that is stored in "Kulhwch and Olwen," for example, may not suggest much sophistication of narrative skill. Yet Kulhwch's question on his arrival at Arthur's court—"Is there a gatekeeper?"—or Yspaddaden's consistent refrain in the imposition on Kulhwch of the thirty-nine tasks—"Though you get that, there are things you will not get"—are the tropes of a skillful tale-teller, holding the audience's attention.

In "Math Son of Mathonwy," the fourth branch of the original Mabinogion, we find the tale of Blodeuwedd, on which Alan Garner bases *The Owl Service* (1967). Susan Cooper's use of Arthurian material in the sequence *The Dark Is Rising* (1973) ranges beyond the Mabinogion, but Cafall, the curiously equine name of Arthur's dog, appears among the hunters of the boar, Twrch Trwyth, in "Kulhwch and Olwen" itself.

By looking at two recent children's novels, which are set in Wales and which draw on Arthurian material, I mean to examine the way the stories are told, using Seymour Chatman's analysis of the roles of implied author, narrator, narratee, and implied reader. I also want to argue that novels of this kind, apart from their ability to give pleasure to their readers, to introduce them to a particular mythology, and to illustrate its continuing power even in the twentieth century, invite and demand increasing sophistication in their readers, to the point at which they come close to parity with adult novelists like those Seymour Chatman uses as his exemplars—writers like James Joyce, Ernest Hemingway, and Virginia Woolf.

Susan Cooper's sequence of five novels, *The Dark Is Rising* (the title is used both for the series as a whole and for the second novel in it), varies a good deal in style. The first volume, *Over Sea, Under Stone*, was first published in 1965; the last, *Silver on the Tree*, in 1977. Adult critics and children who have read the books with pleasure have pointed out how the author's voice develops over this period of writing. *Over Sea, Under Stone* has been said by J. Gough to be "like a superior metaphysical version of Enid Blyton's holiday thriller for children, *Five on Treasure Island*"; and there is a tendency to return to a similar style and form in *Greenwitch* (1973), the third volume, which is set, like the first, in Cornwall. By general consent, *The Dark Is Rising*, the second volume, is the most powerful and successful of the five. The appearance of Will Stanton, the "Old One," gives a focus to the material drawn from history, myth, and legend that is absent in its neighboring volumes; and his encounters with Merriman, the Merlin figure, have an immediacy and an equality of standing that is lacking when the other children encounter him as their odd magic uncle. The final episode of the Wild Hunt, drawing on the legend of Herne the Hunter in Windsor Park, can court comparison with other literary appearances of the same figure, as in Shakespeare's *The Merry Wives of Windsor* or Harrison Ainsworth's *Windsor Castle*.

The final volume of the sequence, *Silver on the Tree*, brings together all the major characters, children and adults, of the previous volumes, but unfortunately it suffers from an attempt to include too much legendary or magical content, and so lacks the structural tautness of *The Dark Is Rising* or *The Grey King* (1975), the fourth volume, which is my main concern here.

The Grey King, like *Silver on the Tree*, is set in Wales. The little town of Tywyn, where the story begins, with its church and the ancient stone of

Cadfan and the Dysynni Valley, where most of the book's main incidents occur, are real enough. The "liberties" which Susan Cooper acknowledges have been taken with the geography of the area are minute, and anyone who knows Bird Rock and the lake at Tal y Llyn will find extra delight in the story. Although *The Dark Is Rising* has its great set pieces and is very firmly rooted in the viewpoint of Will Stanton, *The Grey King* shows Susan Cooper's narrative style at its most varied and accomplished.

In *The Grey King*, Susan Cooper uses at least four narrative voices. There is the voice of the implied author, propelling the narrative and addressing itself clearly and directly to the implied (child probably, adult possibly) reader. There is the slightly different voice of a close observer of this particular scenery, this particular part of Wales at this time of year. Possibly we are closer to the real author here, if we may take it that Susan Cooper herself knows Tywyn and the Dysynni well and loves them, because here we are being addressed by someone who knows the birds, the plants, the houses, and the weather and who wants us to share her enjoyment of them:

The little road was narrow here, like a tunnel, with its high grass banks and looming hedges like green walls on either side. Whenever they passed the gap where a hedge opened to a field through a gate, he could see the green-brown bulk of hillsides rearing up at the grey sky. And ahead, as bends in the road showed open sky briefly through the trees, a higher fold of grey hills loomed in the distance, disappearing into ragged cloud. Will felt that he was in a part of Britain like none he had ever known before: a secret, enclosed place, with powers hidden in its shrouded centuries at which he could not begin to guess. He shivered. (11–12)

Third, we have the voices of the characters. Cooper, unlike Garner, does not experiment with dialogue presentation, and occasionally her characters deliver rather obvious lessons to each other, as when Bran teaches Will about spelling and pronunciation in Welsh (39–43). But generally the voices of the two boys are unaffected and colloquial, and the Welsh-English voices of John Rowlands, Caradog Prichard, Owen Davies, and others are reasonably authentic and add an appropriate richness to the narrative. Finally, there is a "high" language, drawn from the area of what Cooper calls the High Magic, which informs the whole series. It is concentrated in the three English stanzas and two Welsh lines presented on the fly leaf before the contents page, but the meeting of the three Lords within Bird Rock also draws on this speech, as does the language of the Grey King himself (134–38). And it is one of Will Stanton's acquired skills as an Old One (how he acquires them we are shown in *The Dark Is Rising*) that he, too, is able to command this high language on appropriate occasions.

In the straightforward narrative passages, the point of view is nearly always that of Will. Before this first meeting with Bran, we find Will walking up the hillside, searching for Cadfan's Way (22–31). The narrative is economical, moved on by phrases like "Stuffing the map into his pocket, he went on, higher . . . " and "He turned to go on up the slope." With this is interspersed the second voice, for Will hears the skylark and observes the coloring and movement of Cafall, Bran's dog, with the eyes of someone who has watched sheepdogs on a Welsh farm. Such passages can be found throughout the novel. But this second voice is strongest in certain descriptive passages. Aunt Jen's kitchen (17), with its dresser and its willow pattern china; John Rowlands' face, with its "well-shaped, modelled mouth of the Celt" (19); or the cottage on the hillside "stone-walled, slate-roofed, sturdy-looking, but with the glass broken in its two small windows" (51) are examples of this concern for attention to the details of the scene.

The voices of the characters constantly diversify the texture of the narrative. The first words actually spoken are in Welsh: "Beth sy'n bod?" ("What's the matter?") (9). Will's cousin Rhys and his English but Welsh-sounding Aunt Jen establish the Welsh presence early. Some slight unease in the presence of an alien culture appears even in the second chapter when Will, looking at his uncle, is "not sure whether or not he was laughing at them" (20). Bran, at first encounter with Will, does not want to give too much away, and we see hints of the mutual suspicion between Englishman and Welshman that is so much stronger and more hurtful between Gwyn and Roger in *The Owl Service*. Much of the sting of this conflict is removed here by Will's universal status as an Old One; indeed, some readers might want to argue that this also removes some reality from the story. However, when John Rowlands tells his own story of "the girl from the mountains" (121–27), it is a strong and genuine Welsh voice we hear, somewhat tragic but without self-pity, in a skillful and convincing shift of the narrative stance as a whole.

The high language may enter the text not only as gobbets of special virtue, as in quotation from the preliminary verses or the speech of the Grey King, but it can also permeate the whole texture of the narrative at special moments. This seems to occur especially at the end, when the Sleepers arise from the slopes of Cader Idris and vanish into the shadows of the pass at Tal y Llyn.

They were horsemen, riding. They came out of the mountain, out of the lowest slopes of Cader Idris that reached up from the lake into the fortresses of the Grey King. They were silvery-grey, glinting figures riding horses of the same strange half-colour, and they rode over the lake without touching the water, without making any sound. The music of the harp lapped them round, and as they drew near, Will saw that they were smiling . . . Each one had a sword hanging at his side. Two were hooded. One wore a circlet about his head, a gleaming circlet of nobility, though not the crown of a king . . . The music rippled bell-like round the valley from the harp in Will's hands . . . (200)

Such language is spellbinding and has to be shattered like a spell: Here this is done by the crude uncomprehending tones of Caradog Prichard, who returns us from the land of the High Magic to the quarrels of the valley and the bitterness of human rivalries.

What, then, does *The Grey King* demand of its reader? If we accept as a base line for the reading of children aged, say, eight to thirteen, a Famous Five story by Enid Blyton, we find that they need only be able to pick up from the page the chatty, collusive style of a narrator who carries the story forward episodically from incident to incident and the predictable dialogue of the children and their allies and victims.

To these basic abilities, Susan Cooper adds the opportunity to enjoy at least three further skills. A good reader of *The Grey King* will appreciate the voice of the implied author when it asks him or her, looking generally through the eyes of Will Stanton, to take pleasure in Aunt Jen's kitchen, the moorland birds, and the changing lights on the flanks of Cader Idris. The Welsh voices of the men, the sneering tones (rather more conventional, perhaps) of Caradog Prichard, and the undertones, varying from serious attempts to understand each other and what is going on around them to the light banter of pre-adolescents at play, in the voices of Will and Bran: all these are there to be picked up. And finally there is the high language of the verse, of the Old Ones, and of the high points in the narrative.

It is difficult to imagine any readers, young or old, finding *The Grey King* a thoroughly enjoyable book unless they are sensitive to these variations in its author's presentation. Certainly there do seem to be people, children and adults alike, who do not care for anything like "high" language: they do not understand other readers' admiration of Tolkien and generally prefer "reality" to anything smacking of fantasy. This particular kind of perception or blindness (whichever it is) deserves a study to itself, and I suppose such readers would not be likely to rank Susan Cooper highly, though there is much in her writing that might appeal to them, too. However, The Dark Is Rising sequence in general, and *The Grey King* in particular, seems to me a considerable, if not an unqualified, success in the field occupied by writers like J. R. R. Tolkien, C. S. Lewis, Lloyd Alexander, Ursula Le Guin, and Alan Garner, and the variations in narrative presentation that I have tried to outline are part of the reason for this success.

All the evidence, internal and external, suggests that Alan Garner is a more self-conscious author than Susan Cooper, more uniquely committed to his writing, and more dedicated to development and necessary change in the way he writes. Although I have tried to show ways in which some of the later volumes of Cooper's sequence do become more sophisticated in their narrative presentation than the earlier ones, I have also had to admit some degree of regression, and earlier styles remain present even when increased use of dialogue and changes of viewpoint begin to be important. In Garner's case, however, a reader who picked up *Red Shift* (1973) or *The*

Stone Book (1976) and then *The Weirdstone of Brisingamen* (1977) or *The Moon of Gomrath* (1963), not knowing they came from the same hand, might well be surprised to learn that this was the case. An article in the London Sunday *Observer* on January 25, 1970, reports that even then "Garner can hardly look at his early stories," and his dissatisfaction with them has been reported elsewhere since then, as in Neil Philip's 1981 study of Garner's work, *A Fine Anger.*

The Owl Service, our main concern here because of its Welsh setting and its strong debt to the Mabinogion, undoubtedly stands on its own feet as a novel of very high quality (whether exclusively a children's novel or not). It is also, with *Elidor* (1967), part of a transition from the more clearly child-oriented world of the early books toward the less easily classifiable terrain of *Red Shift* and the "Stone Book" series. It is perhaps evidence of its narrative sophistication that, in looking at it to try to discover the voices used by its implied author and its narrators, and to identify the qualities of its implied reader, observations by Seymour Chatman in *Story and Discourse* (1978) become more directly relevant than they were to the Susan Cooper books.

Describing the features of the voice of the implied author, Chatman writes: "It instructs us silently, through the design of the whole, with all the voices, all the means it has chosen to let us learn" (148). After rereading the first four chapters of *The Owl Service*, I noted how it is difficult to grasp an overall narrator's voice. Most of the story is presented as dialogue between the characters, in direct speech. Perhaps the implied author is there in the organization? (Whom do we hear next? Who hears whom? Where are we? What time of day is it? What happens? Who knows how much? What are the relationships, e.g., between Nancy and Huw, Clive and Margaret, Roger and Alison, Roger and Gwyn, Gwyn and Alison?) These questions continue to concern us throughout the novel, and certainly Garner changes the slant from which we view scene, characters, and events of the story from chapter to chapter and even within chapters. For the majority of the novel, the viewpoint is Gwyn's, but there are scenes and stretches of dialogue when Gwyn is not present, and the viewpoint changes, for example at the beginning of chapter thirteen, where the opening dialogue is between Clive and Alison. The stepfather's difficulty in approaching his new responsibilities are obvious, as is the teenager's mixture of desire to respond and unwillingness to be articulate.

Then Alison leaves Clive and walks by the river, where she meets Gwyn (as much by chance as *The Owl Service* ever allows) near the hen hut. There follows a longer dialogue between Alison and Gwyn, in which the viewpoint seems to shift subtly between the two characters, and the reader's concern and sympathy is enlisted equally for either. When at the end of the chapter Roger interrupts, Gwyn changes his tone and leaves. The very last remark, made by Roger, more or less assumes Gwyn is out of hearing and leaves us contemplating him with his "chip on the shoulder a mile high" as he retreats.

"Stories that are uniquely dialoguic or rely heavily on it require the implied reader to do more inferring than other kinds, or if not more, at least a special kind," writes Chatman (175). One does not need to search hard for such dialoguic instances in *The Owl Service*. At the end of chapter twenty, Roger's intrusion on the dialogue between Gwyn and Alison, with its implication (quickly taken by Gwyn, as it must be by the reader) that Alison has told Roger about Gwyn's self-conscious deprecation of his Welsh accent, leads to a mutual confrontation between the three twentieth-century adolescents that is as powerful and as frightening as the Blodeuwedd-Lleu-Gronw triangle of the legend. This is a good deal for any reader to infer, but infer it he or she must.

Conversations between Gwyn and Alison become increasingly opaque as they get to know each other better and as we get to know them and share their experiences, thoughts, and conversations. The exchange " 'Did you scrape the painting off?' said Alison. 'Did you scrape the pattern?' said Gwyn" (196) is enough to confirm to them and to us that other forces are at work. At the same time, of course, it is plausible adolescent dialogue, moving toward the intimate "private" language of lovers. As such, it demands a good deal of its readers—again hardly less, I think, than Hemingway.

Chatman draws some interesting distinctions in his analysis of discourse between "soliloquy," "records of thought," and "stream of consciousness." I do not think Garner uses stream of consciousness in *The Owl Service*. Throughout the novel, we are too strongly rooted in a particular character's point of view for the freedom of that technique to be appropriate. Yet the very end of the story, which has always presented problems to readers and commentators (Who wins in the end? Is it Roger or Gwyn, Lleu or Gronw, who is finally able to offer help to Alison/Blodeuwedd?), has moments between and after the dialogue when the reader looks directly at the scene, sharing the dream-nightmare of all the characters: "The walls were shedding their texture and taking another in the pouncing feathers" (156), or the very last sentence, when the owls seem at last to turn to flowers, the flowers from which the flower maiden was created, and the petals fall fragrantly around them all.

Soliloquy, however, does occasionally occur: Gwyn, at the beginning of chapter eleven, waiting in the dark for Alison to leave her bedroom, says aloud to himself "Not bad. Not bad at all" (62), and in the same passage we have what Chatman calls "record of thought"—not spoken by the character, but given in the words he or she might have used if it had been spoken. This style is interspersed with third person narrative, as in these three paragraphs from the beginning of the chapter and the parody of Clive's voice in the last few words is a nice extra touch:

She'll not go through the kitchen, because Mam bolts it. She'll not go out the front, because it's two doors to unlock. So it'll be the cloak-room. Right, girlie. Don't hurry.

Gwyn stood on the high terracing of garden above the back of the house, over-
looking the cloak-room. He stood against a tree by the hedge, where the road came
nearest the house, passing a few yards away at roof level as it curled round the Bryn.
He had been standing there for two hours, and had not moved.

You're going to come out of that door, and the only way to nab you is to watch,
and keep watching, and nobody would have the patience to stand here and do that,
would they? Such a bore, old stick. (61)

Earlier, when Gwyn first begins to realize the connection between what is
happening in the valley and the story of Blodeuwedd (chapter 8), and the
sight and scent of meadowsweet that pervades the whole story (and which
I find strongly evocative of family August holidays in another corner of the
same country) strikes his senses, he exclaims cryptically, "By, there's axiomatic." On the next page, the legend is quoted from Gwyn and Thomas
Jones' Everyman Library translation of the Mabinogion (68, 74), the book
that Gwyn has borrowed from his English master and that has hurled itself
at him very literally a moment before.

The Owl Service would, I am sure, lend itself to a much more detailed
analysis of its variations of discourse than I can give here. The narrative uses
many voices, and the reader's power of effectively moving among them is
considerably challenged. But here I can only briefly return to Seymour
Chatman's description of the role of the implied author. We have just considered some out of "all the voices": "the design of the whole" is equally
important. What the words of the text offer us is a partial account of what
we as readers can infer to have occurred and of the different experiences of
all the characters. When we hear Clive talking with Roger, Gwyn with Alison,
or overhear the local women talking in the village, we are always invited to
be aware that there is more going on around us than the author can, or will,
tell us. There is a very powerful invitation to us as readers to respond to
this text in the ways described by Wolfgang Iser in *The Act of Reading* (1978)
or by Louise Rosenblatt in either of her two major volumes. Garner's is a
challenging, in some ways difficult, even almost an "obscure" text (in the
sense used by Winifred Nowottny in *The Language Poets Use* [1962]).

In sophistication of narrative presentation, then—or "discourse," as Chatman calls it—we see considerable differences between the work of Cooper
and Garner, and particularly between the two novels in question. In subtlety
and complexity of psychological and moral content they differ, too; and the
demands made on the reader by "story," using Chatman's terms again, run
parallel with those of "discourse." These demands made on readers by increasingly subtle narrative discourse in the novels they read—as in this case
from, say, Blyton through Cooper to Garner—form a parallel strand in this
development.

It is not necessary to regard children's literature as mainly a stepping stone
toward literature written for adults in order to appreciate the use of a wider

technical palette by its writers. *Red Shift* and *The Owl Service* give as much intellectual stimulus and pleasure to adult readers as they do to children. But the role of the author in stimulating readers' abilities to use inference, to extend their own imaginative capabilities by appreciating irony, ambivalence, and an increasingly wide range of moral and psychological relationships and choices is considerably bound up with the complexities of the narrative discourse used.

REFERENCES

Barthes, Roland. *S/Z*. Translated by Richard Miller. New York: Hill and Wang; London: Collins (Fontana), 1975.

Chatman, Seymour. *Story and Discourse: Narrative Structure in Fiction and Film.* Ithaca and London: Cornell University Press, 1978.

Cooper, Susan. *The Dark Is Rising*. New York: Macmillan, 1973.

———. *Greenwitch*. New York: Macmillan, 1973.

———. *The Grey King*. New York: Macmillan, 1975.

———. *Over Sea, Under Stone*. New York: Harcourt Brace, 1966.

———. *Silver on the Tree*. New York: Macmillan, 1977.

Corcoran, B. and Emrys Evans, eds. *Readers, Texts, Teachers*. Montclair, N.J.: Boynton/Cook and Milton Keynes; United Kingdom: The Open University Press, 1987.

Garner, Alan. *Elidor*. New York: Walck, 1967.

———. *The Moon of Gomrath*. London: Collins, 1963.

———. *The Owl Service*. London: Collins, 1967.

———. *Red Shift*. London: Collins, 1973.

———. *The Stone Book*. London: Collins, 1976.

———. *The Weirdstone of Brisingamen*. London: Collins, 1977.

Gough, J. "A Critical View of Susan Cooper's Fantasy Quintet, *The Dark Is Rising*." *English in Education* 19:2 (1985): 55–56.

Harding, D. W. "The Role of the Onlooker." *Scrutiny* 6 (1937): 246–58.

Iser, Wolfgang. *The Act of Reading*. Baltimore: Johns Hopkins University Press; London: Routledge and Kegan Paul, 1978.

Jones, Gwyn and Thomas Jones, trans. *The Mabinogion*. London and New York: Dent, 1949.

Nowottny, Winifred. *The Language Poets Use*. London: Athlone, 1962.

Philip, Neil. *A Fine Anger: A Critical Introduction to the Work of Alan Garner.* London: Collins, 1981.

Rosenblatt, Louise. *Literature as Exploration*. 3rd ed. New York: MLA: London: Routledge and Kegan Paul, 1976.

———. *The Reader, the Text, the Poem: The Transactional Theory of Literary Work.* Carbondale: Southern Illinois University Press, 1978.

11

Singing the Blood Song: The Narrator's Choices in Retelling Norse Myth

ALICE MILLS

In retelling Norse myth for children, narrators face problems encountered by every twentieth-century reteller of myth. The audience when a myth was originally told or sung knew a great deal that a modern audience cannot be assumed to know. The Norse audience would have been familiar with many tales about Asgard and the land of the giants, Thor and Odin, the ancient beginning and the approaching end of the world. Not only would they have known the chief characters and places and the general outline of the stories (while expecting to be pleased and surprised by the bard's imaginative rendering each time), they would also have understood the cultural assumptions underlying the myths in a way that a modern audience does not. What, for instance, is the most approved way for a hero to die? What are the appropriate funeral rites? If a stranger enters a hall, how should the lord respond? How should a human being behave in the presence of a god?

The narrator of a myth to twentieth-century children or adults cannot assume that any teaching about these stories has occurred. All the places, names, personalities and events have to be introduced, without daunting the reader or weighing the story down with instruction. Whether to provide a guide to pronouncing names, a map, an introductory synopsis or background information, whether to jump into storytelling and hope that the narrative will carry the reader through—such choices suggest a tension between trusting the story and anchoring it, between safety and excitement, the known and the unknown. The author must establish a narrator while considering such questions of framework.

Ensuring that the child reader knows from the start who the gods and heroes are, or whether the gods will finally destroy the giants at the end of the world provides a very rough equivalence to the myth's original audience and allows for powerful tragic effects. Kevin Crossley-Holland took up such a narrative role when he retold all the Norse stories dealing with gods in *The Norse Myths* (1980); in 1985 a selection from this book was published for children as *Axe-Age, Wolf-Age*. Also in 1985 Michael Harrison published *The Doom of the Gods*, a copiously illustrated work telling many of the same stories for children. In all three books the narrator's challenge is to make the old myths fully available, meaningful, and alive to modern readers.

Harrison and Crossley-Holland both choose to ground the reader at the start of the story. Both begin their retellings (after a short foreword in *Axe-Age, Wolf-Age* and a much lengthier introduction in *The Norse Myths*) with brief accounts of the geography of Norse myth. Both alert their readers at once to the doom of the gods, a theme stressed in Harrison's *The Doom of the Gods* from its title onward.

The introductory paragraphs of the two texts differ most significantly in the narrator's stance with regard to the time sequence of the stories. The story proper, for Harrison, is all set in the past tense, so that the last days of Ragnarok and the coming of a new world have already occurred in the storyteller's past. The only excursions into the present are a direct address to the reader on the last page and on the first page, the description of Asgard, Middle Earth, and the land of Hel as existing timelessly, forever present until the doom of the gods arrives and—with a jolt into past tense—destroyed Asgard and Middle Earth:

Three worlds encircle the Ash Tree's mighty trunk, one above the other. The highest is Asgard, the land of the gods where Odin rules. From Asgard the Quaking Bridge, Bifrost, links the gods with Middle Earth where men like us live, and where dwarves have their mines and tunnels . . . It was spoilt and destroyed by rivalry between gods and giants. The forces of dark and cold from Utgard overwhelmed the sunshine and joy of Asgard and swept Middle Earth away with it.(1)

The first chapter of both *The Norse Myths* and *Axe-Age, Wolf-Age* briefly chronicles the creation of the world and looks ahead to its ending:

Burning ice, biting flame: that is how life began. In the south is a realm called Muspell. That region flickers with dancing flames. It seethes and it shines. No one can endure it except those born into it. Black Surt is there: he sits on the furthest reach of that land, brandishing a flaming sword; he is already waiting for the end when he will rise and savage the gods and whelm the whole world with fire. (*Axe-Age, Wolf-Age*, 15)

Like Harrison, then, Crossley-Holland chooses an eternal present for the places and people of his introductory paragraphs. For the bulk of his narrative after the creation chapter all is told in past tense, but he turns to future tense for the story of Ragnarok. According to the narrator of *Axe-Age, Wolf-Age* and *The Norse Myths*, the doom of the gods is yet to come. Crossley-

Holland thus adopts the Norse perspective as he narrates the stories, setting the reader within a myth sequence yet to be completed, while Harrison treats the sequence as a long-ago and finished story to be recounted throughout in the past tense. One choice is truer to the surviving texts of Norse myth, the other to the realities of a twentieth-century reader.

Nevertheless, Crossley-Holland is conscious of the needs of his twentieth-century audience. A lengthy introduction is provided for *The Norse Myths* dealing with the Norse world and its cosmology and pantheon and offering a scholarly account of the writer's sources. Specific interpretation of the stories is left to notes at the back of the book cross-referenced to each myth and ranges among the etymological, lineage-validating, agricultural, seasonal, sociological and archetypal (following Eliade in particular). Placing these interpretations at the back of the book with page references following each myth allows the reader a choice of consulting the note in full awareness that it will offer an interpretation or to ignore it.

There is another problem for the narrator of Norse myths: what to do with the strange names, so hard to pronounce, remember, or connect with all the characters and places in the stories. A reader confronted in the first few pages with the names of a dozen gods, their weapons and steeds and dwelling places, their enemies and battlegrounds, may easily give up at that point. In his introduction to *The Norse Myths* Crossley-Holland sets out his solution:

The myths teem with unfamiliar and, at first sight, alarming names. You cannot do away with them: to deprive the gods and other characters of their original names would be to deprive them of part of their power. I decided to use the Old Norse originals . . . but have also worked their translations into the fabric of the story wherever I could. Where a name is of little consequence . . . I have occasionally made an exception to this rule, sometimes using the original for its sound value, sometimes using only the translation. (xli)

Axe-Age, Wolf-Age does not follow the rule set out here but usually simplifies, especially in omitting many of the names of places. As a result, it presents very few of the unfamiliar, alarming names that Crossley-Holland is so well aware may be obstacles to the reader. The children's version not only eliminates many difficult names, but at least twice it offers necessary help for the reader, to make sense of an episode, where the decision in *The Norse Myths* to retain the Norse names without translation obliges the reader to resort to the notes if the passage is to be understood. A minor example is the description in "The Building of Asgard's Wall" where the giant labors through the winter, "Hraesvelg beat his wings and, outside Asgard, the cold wind whirled" (12). *The Norse Myths* simply names the creature, leaving explanation to the note, while the corresponding passage in *Axe-Age, Wolf-Age* speaks of "the corpse-eating Hraesvelg."

Such a choice, explaining the reference or relying on the evocative power of the name, is hardly consequential, but in *The Norse Myths* "The Lay of Harbard," called "Thor and the Ferryman" in *Axe-Age, Wolf-Age*, the point of the story is lost when Crossley-Holland withholds explanation. In this tale Thor comes to a deep channel of water on his travels and asks the ferryman to carry him across. From the other side of the water the ferryman refuses; instead he responds with a series of insulting challenges, which Thor tries to match. For once Thor is defeated. The point of the tale is that the ferryman who refuses to carry Thor across and who insults him so cuttingly is Odin in disguise. There is no hint of the ferryman's true identity in *The Norse Myths* except in the notes: "Harbard or 'Grey-beard' is, of course, Odin in disguise" (217). In *Axe-Age, Wolf-Age* Crossley-Holland adds a detail near the start of the story: "The ferryman slowly got to his feet and pulled his wide-brimmed hat well down over his one eye" (114). Enough of a hint is offered here for the reader to make sense of the story.

In general, the policy in *Axe-Age, Wolf-Age* of simplifying and explaining renders the stories easier to read and understand while still retaining some of the Norse joy in naming. The manifold titles of the gods are reduced to a few recurrent phrases that take on the force of kennings when the stories are read as a whole. This does not work quite so well in *The Norse Myths* with its more faithful rendering of the Norse phrases, some of which are baffling except to the scholar. Other names, where they play no significant part in the story, are generally omitted in the children's version. In "Loki's Children and the Binding of Fenrir," *The Norse Myths* names the large chain that eventually binds Fenrir as Gelgja and the huge boulder it is looped through as Gjoll, while the river of slaver streaming from the wolf's jaws "ran from the middle of the island into the lake of Amsvartnir and was called Von, the river of Expectation." (36) In the corresponding story in *Axe-Age, Wolf-Age*,

The gods fixed a large chain to the end of the silken ribbon. They passed the end of this chain through the hole in a huge boulder, looped it back, and secured it to itself. . . Slaver streamed from his jaws. It ran from the middle of the island into the lake and was called the River of Expectation. (48)

What has been lost is the exotic resonance of the Norse words: what is assured is ease and confidence in reading, especially important when the narrator considers a child audience and the possibility of parents or teachers reading aloud from the book.

Harrison solves the problem by omitting all but essential names. In the case of this episode, *The Doom of the Gods* omits the entire sequence, ending when Fenrir has been bound by the magic cord only. The final mention of the wolf in this version is of his "howling to the darkening sky. And there he stayed, until the last days" (17). This retelling lacks the cosmic intensity of the wolf's travail in the Norse original, which Crossley-Holland has conveyed in both of his versions of the story. *The Doom of the Gods*, however, has another resource in Tudor Humphries' illustrations. Below the inadequate text is a picture of the wolf's head, slaver jetting from its open jaws, rising from behind a rock and above a turbulent flow of foamy water. The illustration, suggesting that the wolf is as large as mountains or a river in flood, restores the story to something of the cosmic scale that the text has lost.

The narrator of the Norse myths must also decide on the handling of their sexuality: rape, menstrual blood, genitalia. Odin boasts of how he "sank [his] shafts into heroes and virgins." Loki jokes about tying a thong behind his testicles. And in "Thor and Geirrod," Thor and Loki encounter traps intended to destroy them with menstrual blood.

After a while the two gods came to the Vimur—a wide torrent of water and menstrual blood. . . .
    Thor paused to regain his breath and looked upstream into a rocky ravine. And there he saw the cause of their hardship: Geirrod's daughter, Gjalp, was standing astride the torrent and blood was streaming from her, increasing the depth of the river. "Aha!" shouted Thor. He stooped, ducked and gouged a rock from the river bed. "A river must be dammed at its source," he called, and with huge strength he hurled the hunk of rock at Gjalp. He aimed well. Gjalp was maimed. (129–30)

This episode, which suggests (as Crossley-Holland's note proposes) the dread and power of women's secret magic, is reduced in *Axe-Age, Wolf-Age's* version "Thor Visits Geirrod" to no more than a story of the gods melting a torrent of water. There is no mention here of the giant's daughter deepening the flood with her bleeding or of Thor maiming her.

In general, *The Doom of the Gods* simplifies and shortens its stories in comparison with Crossley-Holland's retellings, but in this instance Harrison is closer to the Norse myth than *Axe-Age, Wolf-Age*. He makes no mention of menstrual blood, but tells how

Thor looked up and saw, at the end of the ravine, Geirrod's massive daughter damming the narrow exit. He bent down through the icy water and felt for a stone. He hurled it and it struck her full in the forehead so that she fell back and was drowned in the rush of the water. (49–50)

The accompanying illustration shows the jagged stone just about to hit the giantess' distorted face.

One other significant choice the narrator must make is that of structure, of the ordering of the tales. *The Doom of the Gods* is narrated as a single long story in episodic form, each episode only making full sense when taken in context. The choice of stories is dictated by this narrative strategy. All the tales involve Loki, and all but "Utgard" describe his ever-increasing malevolence that finally brings ruin on the gods and the world. Harrison's is a tragic sequence and invites the reader to pass judgment on Loki. Crossley-Holland's *Axe-Age, Wolf-Age* and *The Norse Myths* present a group of stories connected by recurrent characters and a general chronological development toward Ragnarok, but the tales are separate and usually complete in themselves. *The Norse Myths* is presented as a full collection, and Crossley-Holland justifies his selection from the ancient texts by an explicit definition of myth as "sacred history set in a mythical time, involving supernatural beings who create man and whose actions provide paradigms for men" (xxxix). Although this is open to challenge as an adequate definition of myth, as a working principle it does ensure a boundary and an inner coherence to the tales. Nevertheless, the reader of either of Crossley-Holland's texts has to work harder than Harrison's reader to make connections. The reward, though, is a wider range of stories, tragic and comic, than Harrison offers.

Underlying the choices being made by the narrator is the narrator's understanding of myth itself. Questions of framework, tense, naming and explanation, sequence, and illustration all depend on the narrator's confidence in the intense power of myth to sustain itself for a new and unfamiliar audience. Both Crossley-Holland and Harrison offer narratives where the myths are presented without apology or copious explanation. Crossley-Holland claims, in the foreword to *Axe-Age, Wolf-Age*, that "the myths are not imprisoned in their own time and place; they tell us of their makers but they also tell us a lot about ourselves—our own deep longings and fears" (12).

It is a mark of each narrator's success that the myths are so readily available; the way is open for each reader either to enjoy the story as an adventure or to look deeper, to seek out the mirror for our longings and fears, the mythic image of ourselves. In the end the highest praise for a modern reteller, and the aim of each narrative strategy, is not to get in the way of that power.

REFERENCES

Crossley-Holland, Kevin. *Axe-Age, Wolf-Age*. London: André Deutsch, 1985.
———. *The Norse Myths*. New York: Pantheon, 1980.
Harrison, Michael. *The Doom of the Gods*. Oxford: Oxford University Press, 1985.

PART III
Fantasy

Introduction

CHARLOTTE F. OTTEN

Critical writing on narrative theory is having difficulty establishing firm distinctions between fiction and nonfiction. Forms usually viewed as non-fictional—biography and autobiography, for example—now appear to have a fictive narrator, and all such writing seems to have fictive characteristics.

Distinctions between fantasy and realism are also being blurred; and, as the nature of narrative is examined, the traditional view that fantasy occurs in a secondary world and realism in a primary world, although useful, has undergone scrupulous reexamination.

The blurring persists in this section called *Fantasy*. Here the term is used to describe narratives as different as a novel about talking rabbits, a series of novels with the realistic title "chronicles," novels usually regarded as science fiction, adventure stories, and eighteenth-century satire. Attempting to identify the voice of the narrator in these particular cases may not help to clarify the difference between fiction and nonfiction, or between fantasy and realism, but it may raise important questions about such matters as whose voice is heard in a novel in which most of the characters are nonhuman and not natively equipped with speech?, whose voice is heard in a hero chronicle whose roots are in Celtic mythology? is whose voice; heard in futuristic scenes but also in places that resemble Waukegan, Illinois?; whose voice is heard projected into an ideal companion?; and whose voice is heard in a sophisticated satire written for adults but adopted by children?

Richard Adams' voice was originally the voice of a father telling a story about rabbits to two little girls. As the story unfolded and turned from oral to written form, Adams drew, perhaps unconsciously at first, on the narrative voices he had heard in his childhood. The narrator's voice in his rabbit saga, *Watership Down*, begins with the voice of Greek drama: Fiver's vision of blood is infused with Cassandra's "terrible vision of the whole palace running with blood and her own terrible danger, her death, and the disaster of the whole house of Atreus" in the *Agamemnon* of Aeschylus.

As a schoolboy Adams participated in the performance of Greek drama; his narrator remembers that the chorus not only talked to the audience and commented on the action but also gave the drama its intuitive, visionary, prophetic, metaphysical dimension. The voice of the chorus is unobtrusive in *Watership Down*, but it is no less a metaphysical presence in the voice of the narrator there than in Greek drama.

There are other voices from his childhood experiences that are integrated in the narrator's voice: the Bible, especially the narrative parts, the Gospels, and the Acts; and the Book of Common Prayer. Both influences helped the narrator to deal with the whole human situation on earth (though in the experiences of fantasy rabbits) and gave the narrator a sense of the moral ascendancy so vital to leadership.

His experiences in World War II gave Adams Kehaar's (the seagull's) voice; the wide reading of adulthood gave him epigraphs from voices as different as those of St. Augustine, Dostoevsky, and Mozart. The voices of childhood and adulthood, however, did not interrupt the narrator's voice but deepened it with resonances found in the voices of universal storytellers. They told their stories to an audience, as did Adams to his two little girls.

The narrator of Lloyd Alexander's Prydain Chronicles has his roots in medieval romance. Like the narrator of Sir Thomas Malory's Arthurian legends and of Marie de France's lais, he reports fantastic happenings with no surprise, no dismay, no amazement, no despair. Enchanted swords, dread castles, prophecies, supernatural interventions, metamorphoses, unnatural births into a fearsome immortality—all are woven into the fabric of romance.

Focusing upon the acts of Taran, Alexander's narrator tells of the coming of age of Taran Wanderer. The central conflict in the Prydain Chronicles is Taran's intense desire to know who he is: both in terms of his parentage and in terms of heroic qualities. Throughout the chronicles Taran struggles with a self-imposed axiom: to be a hero one must be nobly born. The process of the novels is Taran's progression away from that axiom; and although the narrator makes no comment upon, nor shows any emotion toward, this growing self-knowledge, he leads to this revelation for over twelve hundred pages. Like the narrators of medieval romance, the narrator of the Prydain Chronicles has structured the inevitable resolution into the telling.

Since this resolution is a matter of high seriousness, as Alexander claims, the narrator does not participate in the laughter found in the comic episodes. At the end of *The High King*, for example, Taran hesitates and is almost paralyzed by the awesome duty of going out to meet his subjects. Eilonwy, the future queen, reassures him and then suggests, "Right now, there's only one question: are you going in or out of this doorway?" This is a comic moment for the reader and for Taran but not for the narrator, who steps in and resumes the high seriousness of the tale: "In the waiting throng beyond the cottage, Taran glimpsed Hevydd, Llassar, the folk of the Commots, Gast and Goryon side by side near the farmer Aeddan, King Smoit towering over them, his beard as bright as flame" (303)—a listing of witnesses to a moment of high seriousness, for the reader and the narrator.

The reader of the Prydain Chronicles, like the reader of medieval romance, comes to the narrative with certain expectations. The reader expects Taran to be nobly born, expects Taran not to be merely an assistant pigkeeper, suspects Taran to have been a prince all along. But Alexander's narrator departs from the traditions of medieval romance. A twentieth-century narrator, he subverts the text by overthrowing the reader's expectations. He has led both Taran and the reader to see that nobility comes by virtue of spiritual qualities, not by birth. By being unintrusive and nonmanipulative, the narrator can join Taran and the reader in revelation and recognition of the central truth in the chronicles: "A grower of turnips or a shaper of clay, a Commot farmer or a king—every man is a hero if he strives more for others than for himself alone" (*The High King*, 292).

At the opening of Bradbury's *Dandelion Wine*, Doug Spaulding takes out a yellow nickel tablet and a yellow Ticonderoga pencil and begins to record all the things he does and all the things he learns in the summer of 1928. "You do things and don't watch," he tells his brother. "Then all of a sudden you look and see what you're doing and it's the first time, really." Since publishing his first story in 1939, Ray Bradbury, like Doug Spaulding, has been looking at and recording the things he has done and the things he has learned in such a way that they are as new and vital as they might have been the first time.

Part of this vitality comes from the voice of the narrator of Bradbury's fiction, a voice that uses memory and imagination to project material from the past into the present and into the future. This combination of memory and imagination enables the narrator to comment upon the present and the future from the perspective of the past. In *Farenheit 451* Bradbury pictures a dehumanizing and dehumanized society that has cut itself off from the arts. In *The Martian Chronicles* he shows a world at war with itself and with all order and beauty. In *Something Wicked This Way Comes*, he suggests that the devils who create misery in others live in our own souls and are exorcised only by a celebration of love and life. And in *Dandelion Wine* he recreates the mystery, awe, and wonder a child may feel upon encountering something that, to an adult, may be completely and absolutely ordinary.

Bradbury sets the last two novels—*Something Wicked This Way Comes* and *Dandelion Wine*—in Green Town, Illinois. It is Bradbury's hometown of Waukegan, Illinois, and although the narrator preserves the old town as it is, he also gives it a mythical quality. Many of the details of Green Town are taken from Bradbury's own memory, as are many of the events and characters of these novels. The public library, the ravine, his grandparents' house, John Huff, the maraudings of the Lonely One—all are in the memory of the author. And all are shaped by the voice of the narrator, who maintains the contours of the old Waukegan, even as they take on qualities of fantasy.

In his discussion of the voice of the ideal companion in adventure stories, Nicholas Tucker goes to the world of developmental psychology to identify children's need for a mature voice. Young protagonists—immature, naive, inexperienced—find strength and identity in the voices of older companions. The stories Tucker examines range from the "more fantastic" to the "less fantastic"; they may use the voice of a father in a collaborative fantasy with his young son as in *Winnie-the-Pooh*, or the voices of gangs to speak for the individually weak as in the more realistic Arthur Ransome boating stories. As long as the growing child needs voices that represent authority, wisdom, courage, stability, omnipotence, these companion voices will be a source of comfort, stability, even growth. When children grow out of this need and enter the sexually aware stage of development, however, they break with the fantasy world of ideal companions, leave these kinds of adventure stories, and enter the realistic world to listen "for a responding echo in someone of the opposite sex." In the abandoning of these voices the narrator, the protagonist, and the reader-growing-older participate.

Lionel Basney reviews the history of the publication of *Gulliver's Travels*, including its bowdlerized, truncated, and rewritten versions. Since *Gulliver's Travels* early on was adopted by children (or adapted by adults for children) and is today read by children in a number of editions—Penguin, Golden Illustrated, even one inherited from their parents' childhood—Basney maintains that the key to the adoptions by children is not in the alteration of the form of *Gulliver's Travels* but in children's perceptions of the narrator, Gulliver. Although the Gulliver created by Swift for his satire is often the subject of Swift's "severest laughter" and the target of Swift's irony, the narrator Gulliver in the child-reader's perceptions is a true fantasy narrator of incredible adventures, who reports back to children like "a friendly camera." The adventures that focus on the painful (as well as on the exciting, even terrifying) aspects of physical disorientation and that reveal the discomforts (as well as the advantages) of size are precisely those with which children associate in their own lives. Their narrator Gulliver, no matter how exotic his experiences, tells them through his fantasy narrative what they already knew about themselves. This affinity is the reason why children have adopted *Gulliver's Travels* and helps to explain its continuing power.

THE AUTHORIAL VOICE

12

To the Order of Two Little Girls: The Oral and Written Versions of *Watership Down*

RICHARD ADAMS[1]

The golden rule for parenthood is to keep the child's company—not necessarily to be always teaching the child or instructing the child, but just to keep the child's company. Children should realize unconsciously that there's no one's company that a parent seeks or wants more than theirs and that the parent enjoys spending time in their company. I think this is of great importance in building up confidence and trust between parents and children.

One very pleasant way in which an adult can spend time in a child's company is by telling stories. In our family, whenever there was anything tedious that had to be done, like waiting around, or a car journey or anything like that, it was my practice to tell stories. Sometimes I would improvise the stories off the top of my head, or sometimes they would be the great stories of the world, like "Jack the Giant-Killer," or sometimes I would tell them part of the *Odyssey*, like the encounter with Polyphemus in the cave. Anything that would hold their attention and broaden their minds and imaginations. When the children were still quite small, we began going to Stratford on Avon every summer, sometimes twice, to see the Shakespeare plays. It's quite easy to interest young children in Shakespeare. They used to love it; there was no compulsion about it.

I think it was one day in the 1960s when we were driving up to Stratford in the afternoon—we always went to evening performances to help the children think they were more grown up; they would have dinner in a hotel and go to the evening performance and they'd have the next day off from school—and while we were driving they asked for a good long story to while away the car journey, one that they'd never heard before. I began improvising the story of the rabbits off the top of my head. I had to think of something at once. This is why *Watership Down* (1972) begins with Fiver's vision of blood. The first thing that came into my head is the terrible scene in the *Agamemnon* of Aeschylus when Cassandra is left outside the palace; Agamemnon has gone in, ostensibly to have a bath and actually to be murdered by Clytemnestra. Cassandra left alone with the chorus suddenly has this terrible vision of the whole palace running with blood and her own terrible danger, her death, and the disaster of the whole house of Atreus; she tries in vain to get this across to the chorus. Cassandra has been cursed by Phoebus Apollo. (She swore an oath to Phoebus Apollo; it was a lie, and she was cursed.) The curse was that she should always prophesy the truth and always be disbelieved. These are, in fact, the lines that are quoted in Greek in the beginning of *Watership Down*. This was the first thing that came into my head, and I thought that I could transfer it to a bunch of rabbits. I went on telling it as we went along, about how they left the warren and the journey across country. In fact, many of the incidents in *Watership Down* can be traced to episodes and happenings in other books and stories.

The story lengthened as it went on. It became quite a long journey story, and it wasn't finished by the time we got to Stratford. It was continued on morning trips to school. (I drove the children to school every morning. This used to take about fifteen to twenty minutes.) About a fortnight later the story was finished. The children said, "That's too good to waste, Daddy, you ought to write it down." I resisted this for some time. I said, "Well it takes a long, long time to write a book. You would have forgotten all about it long before it was finished. Anyway, it's very arduous writing a book. I have a job to do; I'm working in the Civil Service all day, and I don't know when I'd write the book." But they were very, very persistent; they kept on about this for a month or two. Then one night I was reading a book to them at bedtime that wasn't very good. Finally I threw the book across the room and said, "I can write better than this myself." So nine-year-old Juliet in a very acid voice said, "I wish you would, Daddy, instead of keep on talking about it."

Thus stimulated, I went and got some legal paper and set about writing in the evenings. I would come home and have the evening meal and have a look at the news on television, and then I'd settle down and write for a couple of hours before going to bed. I never thought twice about it. It wasn't particularly arduous. There never was a book written less self-consciously, I think, or with less trouble. I was just writing for my little girls. I had no ambition for the book, except to get a modest hardback edition published. I would be able to put a copy into their hands and say, "There is the story you asked me to write."

The written story was, of course, very different from the oral story, although the narrator's voice did not change. Also, all the principal features remained—that is to say Fiver's vision of blood, the leaving of the Sandleford Warren, the journey across country, the arrival on the downs, the realization that there were no females and that they had to get females somehow or other, the journey to the strange warren, the final attack, and Hazel's desperate venture when he went to the farm to loose the dog—all those were part of the original story. Nevertheless, other things were added as I moved from the oral to the written text, and these enriched the narrative. I read a book about rabbits—R. M. Lockley's *The Private Life of the Rabbit* (1964), to add a certain amount of authenticity—all this stuff about reabsorbing embryos and chewing pellets and so on that came in later as a result of my study of rabbits. General Woundwort was also an addition.

There are also rather self-conscious lengthy descriptions of the natural world. I put into the book a great deal of my own passionate love of the Berkshire countryside where I was born and grew up. And sometimes this was quite deliberate, like the sunset on Watership Down that opens part two of the book, or the rabbits coming to the River Test, or the swallows gathering for their autumn migration. This is self-indulgent in a way; it was expressing my own love of nature round here where I've always lived. I think my favorite passage is the description of approaching autumn in the last chapter of the book.

It was a fine, clear evening in mid-October . . . Although leaves remained on the beeches and the sunshine was warm, there was a sense of growing emptiness over the wide space of the down. The flowers were sparser. Here and there a yellow tormentil showed in the grass, a late harebell or a few shreds of purple bloom on a brown, crisping tuft of self-heal. But most of the plants still to be seen were in seed . . . The songs of the insects were fewer and intermittent. Great stretches of the long grass, once the teeming jungle of summer, were almost deserted, with only a hurrying beetle or a torpid spider left out of all the myriads of August. The gnats still danced in the bright air, but the swifts that had swooped for them were gone and instead of their screaming cries in the sky, the twittering of a robin sounded from the top of a spindle tree . . . The sky, too, was void, with a thin clarity like that of water. In July the still blue, thick as cream, had seemed close above the green trees, but now the blue was high and rare, the sun slipped sooner to the west and, once there, foretold a touch of frost, sinking slow and big and drowsy, crimson as the rose hips that covered the briar. As the wind freshened from the south, the red and yellow beech leaves rasped together with a brittle sound, harsher than the fluid rustle of earlier days. It was a time of quiet departures, of the sifting away of all that was not staunch against winter. (464–65)

This isn't the kind of thing you do when you're telling a story, but a written story is quite different. I call this one of the set piece fireworks.

In writing the book I deliberately wanted to make big demands on the child reader. I take the view that the books an adult reads aloud to children ought to be something just a little bit more demanding, not much more demanding, but a little bit more demanding than what children read for themselves. An adult ought to be stretching children a bit and helping children to reach out.

In writing *Watership Down* I set out to write a book that a parent like myself might enjoy reading to children like my own. *Watership Down* was intended to be a real novel, readable with enjoyment by someone age nine or ten; I have even had fan mail from six-year-olds. I think this is because it is a real novel and has the two essential characteristics of the novel, which have been the two essential characteristics of the novel since the eighteenth century. First, the story grows naturally out of the characters of the protagonists. Second, and even more important, the novel deals with some fundamentals of the human situation here on earth.

Watership Down is a real novel because it has both of these qualities. It's about a small tenacious band of comrades discovering how to settle down and live together. At the beginning of the book Hazel is not accepted as a leader; he can't keep Bigwig in order. He gradually gains ascendancy, moral ascendancy. The big payoff point of the book is the bit when Bigwig says to Woundwort, "My Chief Rabbit has told me to defend this run, and until he says otherwise, I shall stay here." The Efrafans think that the chief rabbit must be a bigger rabbit than Bigwig. It's impossible for them to grasp that Bigwig might respect Hazel as his chief rabbit, even though Hazel is not physically stronger. That to me is the point of the book. *Watership Down* is about leadership, a fundamental of human existence. Leadership is gained by people who can acquire moral ascendancy by example and ability. During the first half of the book the good leader gradually establishes his moral ascendancy, and then during the second half of the book, the bad leader, the bully, comes up against him. The good leader wins out against the bad leader by his readiness to sacrifice everything if necessary. In writing my book I had very much in mind these two ideas: One, that it wouldn't talk down to the child reader. (That's why I say there's no such thing as a children's book.) Two, that it would be a real novel.

Of course, all of this is filtered through the storyteller, who has himself been influenced by many other tales. Greek drama influenced the telling of the story in more than one way. It gave me the narrator's voice. I heard the voice of the Greek chorus when I went to Bradfield school. In one respect Bradfield is entirely unique: in the late nineteenth century the then headmaster, a rather enterprising man called Dr. Gray, had the idea that he and his senior pupils should convert a disused chalk pit that belonged to the school into a Greek amphitheater. And this they did; they actually dug it with their own hands, then had the stone for the tiered seats imported. For a hundred years now Bradfield has had a Greek amphitheater, a miniature of the great ones in Epidaurus and places like that. It's three parts of a circle with what is known as the orchestra, the central space at the bottom, and then the skene, which is the equivalent of our modern stage. There they performed the Greek tragedies—Aeschylus' *Agamemnon*, Sophocles' *Oed-*

ipus and *Antigone*, Euripides' *Oresteia* trilogy, all in the original Greek. This has become a tradition at Bradfield; the Greek play is performed every third year.

Greek drama, half a religious liturgical service beginning with an invocation to Apollo or to Dionysos, is conducted on a tripartite basis: You have the protagonists who are up in the skene, which is, as it were, behind the proscenium arch. Then you have the chorus in the orchestra, the central space. The chorus would be continually sprinkling incense throughout the action on the altar to Dionysos. When I was at Bradfield, the way they did this they had the altar in the center of the orchestra and inside it was a cylinder, and a little way down there was a biscuit tin lid, and under the biscuit tin lid there was a Primus stove, which was kept going throughout the action; you couldn't hear it. So when the chorus put the incense onto the altar, it automatically went up in smoke. And then you have the audience, which participates in the action as it is mediated by the chorus.

In writing *Watership Down* I had very much the concept in my mind that I was the chorus, talking to the reader and commenting upon the action. The job of the chorus, that never leaves the stage from the beginning of the play to the end, is to mediate the action, to tell the audience what it should be thinking, to pray to the gods, to ask them perhaps to intervene or put their blessing on the protagonist or in some way to help. The leader of the chorus will have dialogues with the protagonist, with the principal characters, and tell them what the audience is thinking. You're never free, if you're seeing a Greek drama, from the intervention of the chorus, commenting on the action, talking to the protagonists, telling the audience how it ought to be feeling, speaking on behalf of the audience, or even praying. And I in writing, and in any creative work I do, constantly have this in mind.

The chorus in Greek drama invoked the gods in recognition of the metaphysical dimensions of human life; I felt that *Watership Down* would be richer if the rabbits had some kind of metaphysical dimension to their lives. Of course this would have to be kept very simple. For example, the rabbits have respect for what seems a creator or at least some type of providential, protecting care. At moments of exhilaration or rescue, they say, "Oh, Frith," with an awareness of something beyond themselves. There are prayers of gratitude to Frith: "Oh Frith on the hills," cried Dandelion, when they arrive at Watership Down for the first time, "he must have made it for us." Frith is the sun, and they acknowledge the sun as the source of all life. They also show sympathy for the intuitive, the visionary, and the prophetic. It is Fiver's original vision of blood and his continuing prophecies that cause much of the action of the story. And at the end, when young Threar predicts the coming of a man on a horse, Hazel says, "Fiver's blood? As long as we've got some of that I dare say we'll be all right."

Of course, there is also the presence of death—the chorus in Greek tragedy is honest about death, as is the narrator of *Watership Down*. Death enters as that faint silver light, in sharp contrast to that opening quotation from Aeschylus, the *Agamemnon*, "the house reeks of death" and the narrator's comment, "the primroses were over." El-ahrairah's ears shone with a faint silver light because Frith gave him a new pair of ears when he got back from the Black Rabbit. He says, "I have something for you, some new whiskers and some new ears." Then he says, "I put a little starlight into them, but you needn't worry; it's not nearly enough to give away a clever thief like you. It's only very faint." And so one of the attributes of El-ahrairah, as a result of this adventure, is that his ears shone with a faint silver light. This was how Hazel recognized him when he turned up. In this way, the narrator makes death a friendly person who ushers Hazel into a new life, "where the first primroses were beginning to bloom" (475).

The end of the book came about quite naturally in my relationship with my own daughters. They said, "What happened to Hazel in the end?" and I said, "Well, I've never told you a lie in my life. We've all got to die sometime, but I tell you what we'll do. We'll give him what Pallas Athene promised Odysseus; she promised him the gentlest death that may be, she says in the *Odyssey*. And that's what we'll give him." So he was meant to have as easy and perfect a death as possible to please my little girls.

As I told and wrote the story, I never forgot my listeners and readers. At least two characters entered the story because of my daughters. I came home one evening from work and found young Rosamond in tears over her violin practice. I said, "What's the matter?" and she said, "That horrid Rowsby Woof, I can't play it." Rowsby Woof was a celebrated teacher of violin who wrote a lot of exercises and pieces for children. She was struggling with a piece by Rowsby Woof. I said, "I'll fix it for you; I'll put him in the story." And there, the immediate world of the children entered the world of the story in the shape of Rowsby Woof.

Because the children were commenting all the time on the writing of the book and making suggestions as we went along, Bluebell comes into the story when he does. When I got as far as Holly turning up on Watership Down, Juliet said, "But Daddy, you've forgotten about Bluebell." I said, "I can't remember Bluebell." She said, "Yes, Daddy, he was the comic rabbit who was always making jokes. You can't have forgotten, we've got to have him." And this is why Bluebell turns up halfway through the story with Captain Holly because I was ordered to put him in. The oral form of the story entered the written form because the children remembered what I had forgotten.

In a way, my daughters were also the arbiters of the choice of quotations at the beginning of each chapter. I asked Juliet about those epigraphs. "Look," I said, "do you want them in or not?" And she said, "I like them, Daddy, because when you read the quotation, you can't imagine how it's going to fit in with what's going to happen. And then as you read on, you see how it does, and I like that. I think that's fun." I tried to get in all my favorite authors; but I couldn't get in a bit of Proust and I couldn't get in a bit of Tolstoy. I did manage to get in a bit of Dostoevsky and a bit of Jane Austen, and even a bit of *Cosi fan Tutte*. I placed their distinct voices in the context of *Watership Down*.

The voices of the Bible and the Book of Common Prayer, important parts of my education both at home and at Bradfield, also came to be part of the narrative voice. I've always been grateful to my father and Bradfield for grounding me in the narrative parts of the Old Testament, the Gospels, and the Acts. This has remained with me all of my life, and I think it resonates in the narrator's voice. It appears consciously in the epigraph from Psalm 59, where the psalmist's enemies "grin like a dog." And Charlotte F. Otten has suggested that it appears unconsciously in phrases like "in the fullness of time."

The seagull comes out of my experience in World War II. Kehaar's character, even his voice, is based on a Norwegian Resistance man whom I knew in the war, a splendid chap, Johansen. For some reason I don't quite understand, Johansen had been in World War I. Norway was not involved, but he had been anyway. We met on a troop ship, and one night Johansen got very drunk, and finally the purser of the ship semiforcibly conducted Johansen downstairs to his cabin. And I cherish the memory of Johansen being led away shouting, "You say you in the last war? I was there too! I never see you!" Johansen was very Kehaar-like.

Of course, the storyteller, the narrator, is not merely a product of home and reading and education and personal experience. Storytelling is a timeless and universal occupation. People have been doing it since time immemorial. And it is a wonderful thing to have people hanging on your every word. When I was a boy at school, I used to tell stories in the dormitory before lights out, and it was terrific. They'd say, "Go on, Adams, what happened then?" Then the master comes round and says: "Time for lights out." "Oh sir, just another three minutes, sir, while Adams finishes the story. What happened then, Adams, what happened to him?" You feel the power in your fingertips as you build up the tension.

I didn't imagine that anybody else would go for this particular private story told to my own two little girls, told for their pleasure as we drove to Stratford, and written at their insistence. Yet naturally it's intensely gratifying that this rather private and personal idea of mine, which started as nothing but that, has sold itself all over the world. But like Lewis Carroll's *Alice*, which was improvised by Charles Dodgson in a boat on the Isis on a summer afternoon, *Watership Down* was entirely spontaneous and unselfconscious, and written to the order of two little girls.

NOTE

1. Based on an interview with Charlotte F. Otten, June 17, 1987, in Whitchurch, Hants, U.K.

REFERENCES

Adams, Richard. *Watership Down*. London: Rex Collings, 1972.
Lockley, R. M. *The Private Life of the Rabbit*. London: André Deutsch, 1964.

13

A Manner of Speaking

LLOYD ALEXANDER

When, years ago, I tried learning to play the piano—with dazzling lack of success—I never understood why composers wrote in anything but C major. To me, it was a fine key, without annoying sharps or flats. If one wanted a gloomier atmosphere, C minor struck me as perfectly adequate. A piece of music with three sharps, four flats, or worse, threw me into fumbling confusion. Composers, I believed, chose outlandish keys through spite and malice, for the sadistic bedevilment of young students. Only when I first tried to write—with equally dazzling lack of success—did I gradually realize the importance of tonality, not as an arbitrary or whimsical choice, but as the very fabric of the work itself, musical or literary.

Crucial though it is, tonality is a mysterious concept. Ineffable, perhaps, yet unmistakable. We know it when we hear it. I use the word "hear" deliberately, for we hear literature as clearly as we hear music. The narrative voice, unique and personal, is an audible fingerprint.

Some quick and random samples:

Hast thou given the horse strength? hast thou clothed his neck with thunder? . . . He swalloweth the ground with fierceness and rage. . . . He saith among the trumpets Ha, Ha; and he smelleth the battle afar off, the thunder of the captains, and the shouting.

It is a truth universally acknowledged that a single man in possession of a good fortune must be in want of a wife. However little known the feelings or views of such a man may be on his first entering a neighborhood, this truth is so well fixed in the minds of the surrounding families that he is considered the rightful property of some one or other of their daughters.

Call me Ishmael. Some years ago—never mind how long precisely—having little or
no money in my purse and nothing particular to interest me on shore, I thought I
would sail about a little and see the watery part of the world. It is a way I have of
driving off the spleen, and regulating the circulation.

Even if we did not know that passage from the King James Bible (*Job* 39:
19, 24–25), the opening lines from Jane Austen's *Pride and Prejudice*, and
from Herman Melville's *Moby Dick*, we would instantly perceive the difference in voices. They ring in our ears, maybe in our bone marrow. A
matter of acculturation? Long familiarity? A question of style? There is, I
think, more to it than that.

What precisely that may consist of, I suspect I shall never find out, let
alone analyze and articulate. Still, ignorance of a subject has never been
much hindrance to statesmen, economists, or philosophers, and certainly
not to authors. The best way to learn something is to write a book about it.

My own concern is with fantasy for young people and, in these pages,
how the voice of the narrator functions in that genre. As Gary D. Schmidt
wrote to me, "The narrator affects the telling of the tale, the tone, and the
reader's response."

Undeniably so. The intriguing questions, though, are: How? Why? What
is the nature of the narrative voice itself?

First, it might be useful to put the subject very briefly in a larger context.
What we may discover about the narrative voice in fantasy has some bearing
on literature in general, for the young and otherwise, and on all the arts.

I have always believed in the underlying unity of the arts. If there is
basically one life process, there is by the same token one art process. It
simply takes different forms and uses different media. I would even say that
the arts, at some deep level, strive to imitate one another, to break the
limitations of their individual forms.

Each art has its own blessing. And its own curse. Painting, for example,
has available every color of the rainbow, but its canvas is doomed to stay
forever mute. Drama can make a world of its stage but not enlarge its little
wooden stage into a world. Music has sound without language. Poetry has
the music of language without the language of music.

To make up for those built-in handicaps, painting hopes to make its colors
sing, its portraits speak. Dance tries to be sculpture in motion. Poetry wants
to become music; and music, poetry.

The novel would appear to suffer the most restrictions. True enough, the
novel can turn a page into a stage, conjure up lovers, clowns, warriors on
horseback, change day into night, winter into summer, and circle the globe
in a single sentence. Its curse is to be locked into the alphabet. Spinning
tales from black squiggles presents a task more daunting than spinning straw
into gold.

Novelists, of necessity, are a resourceful lot. They turned the curse into a blessing. If a picture can be worth a thousand words, the right word can be worth a thousand pictures. The mechanisms of language allow the storyteller to work wonders by merely shifting adjectives. "No spell or incantation in Faerie is more potent," says J. R. R. Tolkien in *Tree and Leaf* (1965). "We may put a deadly green upon a man's face and produce a horror; we may make the rare and terrible blue moon to shine; or we may cause woods to spring with silver leaves and rams to wear fleeces of gold . . ." (22).

The novel, using only words, can journey anywhere in the world, or out of it, in past, present, or future. It can depict what is ordinarily possible. It can also depict what is extraordinarily impossible. When it does this latter, we call it fantasy, which is merely a convenient term. At heart, all forms of literature are fantasies—works of art, not works of nature. As I've said often and elsewhere, realism is a dream pretending to be true; fantasy is truth pretending to be a dream.

The novel has a few other tricks up its sleeve. A child of the printing press, it was not only imprisoned by the alphabet, it was also confined to the page as mute as the painter's canvas. To escape from silence, the novel adapted the strengths of its ancestors: poets, bards, ancient storytellers. That is to say, it tried to give the illusion of being an oral medium. It spoke to the reader as if it were a storyteller speaking to the listener, an oral-aural relationship.

Despite changes and developments in the novelistic form, the closer the novel stays to its oral ancestors the greater its vitality as a verbal structure. Poets have always known this. Even when poetry itself was captured by the printed page, the poets insisted that their medium continued to be the human voice. Most poets still prefer to have their poetry read aloud.

This applies, in large measure, to the novel. Authors, I believe, in the course of their work should ask themselves: Does it read well aloud? How does the page *sound*? Deprived of rhyme, meter, and poetic form, the novel nevertheless has its own cadences, rhythms, and sonorities.

These may not have any bearing on whether the novel is any good—as a novel. Some of our most important novels are awkwardly written, others read aloud marvelously well. My point is simply that we can usually tell— or hear for ourselves—whether or not a particular writer has a tin ear.

How does the novel convey the impression of having its own voice? How does it give the illusion of a living presence within the silent page? The ancient storytellers were there in the flesh, sitting in bazaars, around fireplaces, in kitchen corners. What they spoke might have been less important than how they spoke it: vocal timbre, gesture, personality; just as a great actor can make us laugh or cry by reading the telephone book.

The novel, as physical object, as a book, does not have this presence. Live authors don't accompany each copy of their books—a blessing for the writer and maybe the reader, too. Yet, the author is there on every page.

At one stage, authors unashamedly intruded themselves, addressing the reader directly. To give one example out of hundreds, in *Tom Jones* Fielding constantly pops up with such comments as "Reader, I think it proper before we proceed any farther together . . . " and "My reader may please to remember. . . . "

Except in first person narratives, authors seldom these days allow themselves this direct relationship with the reader. Sometimes I think we may be the poorer for it. Even so, lacking the author as commentator, stage manager, or companion, the novel achieves the same result through style, tone, and especially through narrative voice.

These are elusive terms, overlapping and merging with each other. For my purpose here, I'll try to keep them separate and offer my own very loose definitions—or suggestions. If nothing else, they may provide starting points for disagreement.

For the sake of argument, then, I would suggest that style in its most rudimentary form is merely the process of stringing words together. By that process, style automatically results. It can be good or bad, elegant or awful. "One loaf rye brd. 3 qts. milk" constitutes style—grocery list style. That little booklet telling us how to put together our new lawn mower has a style, inscrutable and enigmatic though it may be. Style, in the sense that I am using the term, does not necessarily have a voice. Except in the case of official regulations, where the voice is bureaucratic drone.

Tone, I suggest, is something else again. It involves such things as level of discourse, diction, the techniques of rhetoric, the trope that uses a word or phrase in an unexpected way. Tone may convey a certain flavor. It does not always have a voice. Or, put it that we can have tone and style without voice, but not voice without style and tone.

Tone can be an enticing but fatal trap, a Lorelei that wrecks too many authors who should know better. Tone can lead us easily into the purple passage, a kind of literary posturing, flaunting our vocabulary, mistaking bombast for persuasion. Perhaps it is an attempt to prove we are literary, as we try to prove we are genteel by saying "Would you desire a beverage?" instead of "Do you want a drink?" or "She returned to her domicile" instead of "She went home."

Tone, by itself, can build the literary equivalents of baroque palaces, gothic cathedrals, stately mansions—all empty, if there is no substance behind the spender. It becomes, as Pooh-Bah says, "Merely corroborative detail, intended to give artistic verisimilitude to an otherwise bald and unconvincing narrative."

Encompassing style and tone, voice is the most important and the most difficult to describe. Definitions tend to fall into the same category as "I don't know anything about art but I know what I like." Or, as someone (a Supreme Court justice?) said, "I can't define pornography but I know it when I see it."

Since each of us is unique, each of us has a unique voice. The voiceprint is as unmistakable as the fingerprint. In literature, however, this is not always the case. In so many novels, usually mediocre or worse, the voice of one is barely different from the voice of another, much like the anonymous background chatter at a cocktail party.

Authentic narrative voices are unmistakable. To use Henry Fielding again as an example, reading him we have the impression not only that we hear him but, as well, that we know him personally: wise, witty, gracefully and wickedly satirical, making outrageously humorous comments on the world at large. We would like to invite him to dinner.

Other voices may be exciting, reassuring, inspiring, or intense. Still others may be graduates of the Ancient Mariner Academy of Charm and Personality. They hold us with a skinny hand and glittering eye, and practically grab us by the throat.

As a reading experience, it may not be especially joyful. Like Coleridge's Wedding Guest, we may go "like one that hath been stunned, / And is of sense forlorn." But, if we are sadder we are also wiser. We cannot belittle the power and magnetism of the voice. Although the Wedding Guest beat his breast as the Mariner went on—and on and on—nevertheless he "stood still, / And listens like a three years' child: / The Mariner hath his will."

Whether we happen to like or dislike certain narrative voices, whether we would want them as friends or heave a sigh of relief when they stop talking, they produce an effect on us. If literature does not do that, it does nothing.

Here it might be interesting to ask, Does the fantasy genre have its own particular style, tone, and voice? Given fantasy writers' individual differences and personalities, is there anything they have in common? In the broadest terms, there is a shared voice among writers of tough detective stories and British-style country house mysteries, for example. Is this true of fantasy?

The answer has to be Yes. No. Maybe.

Or, so as not to beg the question completely, it might be more accurate to say that it depends on the kind of fantasy.

For instance, there is a type that I would call, for lack of a better term, "Jock Strap Fantasy." It has all the subtlety of a junior high school locker room. The heroes (and heroines, too) are incredible hulks with mighty thews and a wardrobe of sandals, loincloths, and studded armbands. The characters express themselves with such comments as "Aaargh!" The narrative voice is closer to the comic strip balloon than to literature.

As for high fantasy, creating what Tolkien calls a "secondary world," the narrative voice ranges from E. R. Eddison's graceful archaism to the evocative simplicity of Kenneth Morris. Even so, since the subtext of high fantasy deals with intellectual, spiritual, and philosophical matters, the narrative voice should be able to accommodate them. To quote Marshall B. Tymn, Kenneth J. Zahorski, and Robert H. Boyer:

The elevated stature of the characters, the Everyman quality of the heroes, and the evocative archetypes blend nicely with the supernatural or magical causality and the secondary world of high fantasy. But the final ingredient, and perhaps the greatest challenge to the writer, is a style that can support these elements and clothe them in appropriate language. The dialogue must befit the stature of the speakers; descriptive passages must be in an elevated style that necessarily works through imagery and comparison to create the imaginary worlds. (9)

While this does not preclude humor, irony, or satire, perhaps what the various narrative voices of high fantasy have in common is a seriousness of purpose. Or, call it elegance, in the mathematical sense. Or economy, which is to say, using precisely what is needed to produce a given effect, neither more nor less.

Despite all the foregoing, the narrative voice still refuses to be pinned down. It embodies, in language, writers' attitudes, viewpoints, visions of the worlds they create, and of the real world in which we all live. To try to understand how the narrative voice works, the best thing is to let it speak for itself.

Regarding my own work, Gary D. Schmidt observes that the narrator seems to be striking a balance between comic, mundane events, and marvelous events. "When Dallben is introduced in *The Book of Three*," says Schmidt, "the narrator, in a completely unruffled tone, tells us the rather spectacular news that Dallben is three hundred and seventy-nine years old."

Exactly so. The narrative voice that emerged in the Prydain Chronicles was, by and large, very simple and straightforward in dealing with a world in which attaining an age of nearly four centuries was not especially unusual, a plain statement of fact.

But I have to confess right away that the narrative voice in the Prydain Chronicles and, indeed, in any of my books, did not come about through a prior conscious intellectual decision separate from all other aspects of the creative process. My comments here are made only in the light of hindsight.

For me, as no doubt for every author, the early stage of the creative process is a messy and incoherent piece of business, an appalling stew where bits and pieces float around with no apparent relationship or meaning: a face partially glimpsed, an enigmatic setting or stretch of scenery, snatches of dialogue. The narrative voice—at that stage more like a mumble than a voice—is one ingredient. Part of the creative process lies in trying to rationalize the irrational; to externalize, to put into language what one poet has called "a taste in the head."

The narrative voice, to me, grows naturally and organically along with all the other elements. It must certainly be suitable to the nature of the story. At the same time it must also be, above all, intensely personal. In my own unobjective opinion, the voice of each story is, in its own way, different. But there is no question who wrote it. "The voice is Jacob's voice, but the hands are the hands of Esau." So, at least, I hope.

While maintaining the underlying personality, the narrative voice should also be susceptible to change within the story, depending on the requirements and mood of a given situation. Writers are not distinguished by excessive modesty when it comes to seizing an opportunity to discuss their work, so I'll try to demonstrate through some examples of my own.

The Book of Three (1964), for instance, begins: "Taran wanted to make a sword; but Coll, charged with the practical side of his education, decided on horseshoes. And so it has been horseshoes all morning long." (9)

And the closing passages:

> "You're to stay!" Taran cried. "I've asked Dallben!"
> Eilonwy tossed her head. "I suppose," she said, "it never occurred to you to ask *me*."
> "Yes—but I mean . . . " he stammered, "I didn't think. . . . "
> "You usually don't," Eilonwy sighed. "No matter. Coll is straightening up a place for me."
> "Already?" cried Taran. "How did *he* know? How did *you* know?"
> "Humph!" said Eilonwy.
> "Hwoinch!" said Hen Wen. (224)

Then, the opening of *The High King* (1968), the final book of the Chronicles, reads: "Under a chill, gray sky, two riders jogged across the turf. Taran, the taller horseman, set his face against the wind and leaned forward in the saddle, his eyes on the distant hills." (9) And the closing lines read: "Yet, long afterward, when all had passed into distant memory, there were many who wondered whether King Taran, Queen Eilonwy, and their companions had indeed walked the earth, or whether they had been no more than dreams in a tale set down to beguile children. And, in time, only the bards knew the truth of it." (304)

The Prydain Chronicles would be categorized as high fantasy. It might be interesting now to compare and contrast a passage from *The Black Cauldron* (1965) with one from the second volume of the Westmark Trilogy, *The Kestrel* (1982). (While the Westmark books may not meet a strict definition of fantasy, they deal with a country that never existed and events that never happened; and my private perception is that the Westmark Trilogy is a sort of fantasy.)

Here are two passages involving the death of a character:

In *The Black Cauldron*, Adaon, son of the chief bard and himself a charismatic figure, has been mortally wounded and insists on giving Taran a magical brooch:

> "Take it," Adaon repeated. "This is not my command to you, but the wish of one friend to another." He pressed the brooch into Taran's unwilling hand.
> Eilonwy had come with water to steep the herbs. Taran took it from her and knelt again beside Adaon.
> Adaon's eyes had closed. His face was calm; his hand lay outstretched and open on the ground.
> And thus he died. (100–101)

In *The Kestrel*, Theo and his band of partisans have found their comrade Stock, also a poet but one quite different from Adaon, killed during a Regian ambush:

Theo jumped down from his mare. What looked like a side of beef had been propped against a tree trunk. The eyes were open, staring at him. The mouth seemed full of red mud. It took him several moments to realize it was Stock. . . .

Theo grew aware of the Monkey cursing endlessly and monotonously. He paid no attention. Something should be done about Stock's body; this seemed a matter of great importance. (132)

In both instances, the narrative voice is steady, objective, factual. Yet, at least to my own ear, it is essentially the same voice, in one case speaking of a certain epic heroism, in the other, of the brutalization of war, where there is no heroism at all.

While the narrative voice in the Prydain Chronicles and the Westmark Trilogy also accommodates humor, the stories are "serious." I put the word in quotation marks because a work need not be constantly grim in order to be serious. There is a difference between "serious" and "solemn."

The adventures of Miss Vesper Holly, the sixteen-year-old Philadelphian with marmalade-colored hair, the digestive talents of a goat, and the mind of a chess master have, I hope, a measure of serious substance. They are far from solemn. They came about as an attempt to heal my own spirits after the anguished dilemmas raised in the Westmark Trilogy. In an entirely different vein, they were intended as entertainment for the author as much as anyone, with a gloriously fearless heroine, fiendish villains, outrageous melodrama in the grand tradition of the Victorian thriller and penny-dreadful.

With Vesper and her devoted guardian, Professor Brinton Garrett ("dear old Brinnie," as Vesper fondly calls him), the narrative voice is literally the voice of the narrator. The stories are told in the first person by Brinnie himself, a proper Philadelphian, stouthearted and well meaning, not always quick to grasp the dreadful dangers of a situation but unfailingly polite and reasonable.

The technical problems here are interesting. Dear old Brinnie, as narrator, must always speak in character but, at the same time, keep the action moving with Vesper as the focus of attention. He must also be unwittingly funny and affectionate and, at the same time, convey an underlying attitude and viewpoint.

Describing one of the characters in *The Illyrian Adventure* (1986), for example, Brinnie comments: "He was tall, broad-shouldered, and alarmingly muscular. His eyes, deep-set, burned with what could have been some intense, inner fire or simply a bad disposition. A clean shirt would not have harmed him." (36)

In *The El Dorado Adventure* (1987), defending his beloved Vesper, Brin-

nie fires a rifle at the abominable Dr. Helvitius and is so upset by it that
he feels obliged to stop in the middle of a desperate situation to explain:

I cannot forgive myself for what I did. It has long been one of my strictest principles
not to interfere with the life of any individual, let alone attempt to shorten it. If an
exception were to be made, Dr. Helvitius would surely qualify. It might be argued
that, having neither scruples nor conscience, he had no claim upon the conscience
of someone else—least of all his intended victims. But that is a question to be resolved
by a judgment higher than mine. In the event, my responsibility toward Vesper
outweighed every other consideration. I can state in all honesty: I meant only to
wound him. I cannot forgive myself—for missing the villain completely. (119)

Unmistakably Brinnie, and probably his author too. Looking back over
these pages, I find my original suspicions confirmed. I have still been unable
precisely to pin down and dissect the nature of the narrative voice. As in
music, we might, through technical analysis, be able to explain *how* a passage
works but not essentially *why* it works.

The important thing is: It works. Whatever the peculiar combination of
style, tone, and voice may be, we hear and respond to it. Sometimes it stays
with us to become part of the complex counterpoint of our personality.
Sometimes it changes our lives.

Narrative voice, perhaps, may come down simply to a matter of one human
being speaking to another, telling us what we are and what we could be;
where we have been, where we are, and where we may be going.

REFERENCES

Alexander, Lloyd. *The Black Cauldron*. New York: Dell, 1965.
———. *The Book of Three*. New York: Dell, 1964.
———. *The El Dorado Adventure*. New York: E. P. Dutton, 1987.
———. *The High King*. New York: Dell, 1968.
———. *The Illyrian Adventure*. New York: E. P. Dutton, 1986.
———. *The Kestrel*. New York: E. P. Dutton, 1982.
Tolkien, J. R. R. *Tree and Leaf*. Boston: Houghton Mifflin, 1965.
Tymn, Marshall B., Kenneth J. Zahorski, and Robert H. Boyer. *Fantasy Literature*.
    New York: Bowker, 1979.

14

Memories Shape the Voice

RAY BRADBURY

When I began to write *Dandelion Wine* (1975), first I rummaged through my mind for words that could describe my personal nightmares, fears of night, and time from my childhood. Then I took a long look at the green apple trees and the old house I was born in, and the house next door where my grandparents lived, and all the lawns of the summers I grew up in, and I began to try words for all that. I shaped stories from these.

What you have in *Dandelion Wine* then is a gathering of dandelions from all those years, all the summers of my childhood in one book. The wine metaphor that appears again and again in these pages is wonderfully apt. I was gathering images all my life, storing them away, and forgetting them. Somehow I had to send myself back, with words as catalysts, to open the memories out and see what they had to offer.

So from the age of twenty-four to thirty-six hardly a day passed when I didn't stroll myself across a recollection of my grandparents' northern Illinois grass, hoping to come across some old half-burnt firecracker, a rusted toy, or a fragment of a letter written to myself in some young year, hoping to contact the older person I became to remind him of his past, his life, his people, his joys, and his drenching sorrows.

It became a game that I took to with immense gusto: to see how much I could remember about dandelions themselves, or picking wild grapes with my father and brother, rediscovering the mosquito-breeding-ground rain barrel by the side bay window, or searching out the smell of the "goldfuzzed" bees that hung around our back porch grape arbor. Bees do have a smell, you know, and if they don't they should, for their feet are dusted with spices from a million flowers.

And then I wanted to call back what the ravine was like, especially on those nights when walking home late across town, after seeing Lon Chaney's delicious fright, *The Phantom of the Opera*, my brother Skip would run ahead and hide under the ravine-creek bridge like the Lonely One and leap out and grab me, shrieking, so I ran, fell, and ran again, gibbering all the way home. It was great stuff.

Along the way I came upon and collided, through word association, with old and true friendships. I borrowed my friend John Huff from my childhood in Arizona and shipped him east to Green Town so that I could say goodbye to him properly.

Along the way, I sat down to breakfasts, lunches, and dinners with the long dead and much loved. For I was a boy who did indeed love his parents and grandparents and his brother, even when that brother "ditched" him.

Along the way, I found myself in the basement working the winepress for my father, or on the front porch Independence night helping my Uncle Bion load and fire his homemade brass cannon.

Thus I fell into surprise. No one told me to surprise myself, I might add. I came on the old and best ways of writing through ignorance and experiment and was startled when truths leaped out of bushes like quail before gunshot. I blundered into creativity as blindly as any child learning to walk and see. I learned to let my senses and my past tell me all that was somehow true.

So, I turned myself into a boy running to bring a dipper of clear rainwater out of that barrel by the side of the house. And, of course, the more water you dip, the more flows in. The flow has never ceased. Once I learned to keep going back again to those times, I had plenty of memories and sense impressions to play with, not work with, no, play with. *Dandelion Wine* is nothing if it is not the boy-hid-in-the-man playing in the fields of the Lord on the green grass of other Augusts in the midst of starting to grow up, grow old, and sense darkness waiting under the trees to seed the blood.

Waukegan, visited by me often since, is neither homelier nor more beautiful than any other small midwestern town. Much of it is green. The trees do touch in the middle of streets. The street in front of my old home is still paved with red bricks. In what way then was the town special? Why, I was born there. It was my life. I had to write of it as I saw fit.

I was amused and somewhat astonished at a critic a few years back who wrote an article analyzing *Dandelion Wine* and the more realistic works of Sinclair Lewis, wondering how I could have been born and raised in Waukegan, which I renamed Green Town for my novel, and not have noticed how ugly the harbor was and how depressing the coal docks and rail yards south of town were.

But, of course, I had noticed them and, genetic enchanter that I was, was fascinated by their beauty. Trains and boxcars and the smell of coal and fire are not ugly to children. Ugliness is a concept that we happen on later and become self-conscious about. Counting boxcars is a prime activity of boys.

Their elders fret and fume and jeer at the train that holds them up, but boys happily count and cry the names of the cars as they pass from far places.

And again, that supposedly ugly rail yard was where carnivals and circuses arrived with elephants who washed the brick pavements with mighty steaming acid waters at five in the dark morning.

As for the coal from the docks, I went down in my basement every autumn to await the arrival of the truck and its metal chute, which clanged down and released a ton of beauteous meteors that fell out of far space into my cellar and threatened to bury me beneath dark treasures.

What the teller of *Dandelion Wine* tells comes out of the accumulated richness of my childhood. Children are cups, constantly and quietly being filled. The trick for the adult writer is knowing how to tip the cup over and let the stuff run out. And so what went into *Dandelion Wine* was not the sum of things I've read or imagined or dreamed, but the sum of things I am, or at least was, shaped to its own truth.

The fact is simple enough. Through a lifetime, by ingesting food and water, we build cells, we grow, we become larger and more substantial. That which was not, is. The process is undetectable. It can be viewed only at intervals along the way. We know it is happening, but we don't know quite how or why.

Similarly, in a lifetime, we stuff ourselves with sounds, sights, smells, tastes, and textures of people, animals, landscapes, events, large and small. We stuff ourselves with these impressions and experiences and our reaction to them. Into our subconscious goes not only factual data but reactive data, our movement toward or away from the sensed events. This is the storehouse, the file, to which we must return every waking hour to check reality against memory, and in sleep to check memory against memory, which means ghost against ghost, in order to exorcise them, if necessary.

Here is the stuff of originality, the totality of experience reckoned with, filed, and forgotten. For no writer sees the same events in the same order in his life. One man sees death younger than another, one man knows love more quickly than another. Two men, as we know, seeing the same accident, file it with different cross-references, in another part of their own alien alphabet. There are not 100 elements, but two billion elements in the world. All would assay differently in the spectroscopes and scales.

As we can learn from every man or woman or child around us when, touched and moved, they tell of something they loved or hated this day, yesterday, or some other day long past. At a given moment, the fuse, after sputtering wetly, flares, and the fireworks begin. But they only begin after the writer has reached into the storehouse of his whole childhood and allowed these memories to determine a narrative voice.

I have had this happen not once but a thousand times in my life. My father and I were really not great friends, until very late. His language, his thought, from day to day, were not remarkable, but whenever I said, "Dad, tell me about Tombstone when you were seventeen," or "the wheat fields, Minnesota, when you were twenty," Dad would begin to speak about running away from home when he was sixteen, heading west in the early part of this century, before the last boundaries were fixed—when there were no highways, only horse paths, and train tracks, and the gold rush was on in Nevada.

Not in the first minute, or the second, or the third minute, no, did the thing happen to Dad's voice, did the right cadence come, or the right words. But after he had talked five or six minutes and got his pipe going, quite suddenly the old passion was back, the old days, the old tunes, the weather, the look of the sun, the sound of the voices, the boxcars traveling late at night, the jails, the tracks narrowing to golden dust behind, as the West opened up before—all, all of it, and the cadence there, the moment, the many moments of truth.

Oh, it's limping crude hard work for many, with language in their way. But I have heard farmers tell about their very first wheat crop on their first farm after moving from another state, and if it wasn't Robert Frost talking, it was his cousin, five times removed. I have heard locomotive engineers talk about America in the tones of Tom Wolfe who rode our country with his style as they ride it in their steel. I have heard mothers tell of the long night with their first born when they were afraid that they and the baby might die. And I have heard my grandmother speak of her first ball when she was seventeen. Their souls grew warm as memories shaped their voices; they were all, at least for the moment, storytellers.

If it seems I've come the long way around, perhaps I have. But I wanted to show what we all have in us, that it has always been there, and so few of us bother to notice. When people ask me where I get my ideas, I laugh. How strange—we're so busy looking out, to find ways and means, we forget to look in and back. All that is most original lies waiting for our summons. For nothing is ever lost: the continual running after loves, the checking of these loves against one's present and future needs, the moving on from simple textures to more complex ones, from naive ones to more informed ones, from nonintellectual to intellectual ones. If you have moved over vast territories and dared to love silly things, you will have learned even from the most primitive items collected and put aside in your life. From an ever-roaming curiosity in all the arts, from bad radio to good theatre, from nursery rhyme to symphony, from jungle compound to Kafka's *Castle*, there is basic excellence to be winnowed out, truths found, kept, savored, and used on some later day. To be a child is to do all these things, to be a writer is to recall all these things.

The experience of the child. The labor of the writer. These are the twin sides of the coin which when spun is neither experience nor labor, but the moment of revelation. The coin, by optical illusion, becomes a round, bright, whirling globe of life. It is the moment when the porch swing creaks gently and a voice speaks. All hold their breath. The voice rises and falls. Dad tells of other years. A ghost rises off his lips. The memory stirs, rubs its eyes, ventures in the ferns below the porch, where the summer boys, strewn on the lawn, listen. Story is there. It sounds big in the summer night. And it is, as it always was down the ages, when there was a storyteller with something to tell, and listeners, quiet and wise.

So I have always tried to write and to tell my own story, the stories of man trying to throw the very phosphorescence of his insides long on the wall. Give it a label if you wish, call it science fiction or fantasy or the mystery or the western. But, at heart, all good stories are the one kind of story, the story written by an individual from individual truth.

Green Town did exist, then?

Yes, and again, yes.

Was there a real boy named John Huff?

There was. And that was truly his name.

He truly could pathfind more trails than any Choctaw or Cherokee since time began, or leap from the sky like a chimpanzee from a vine, or live underwater two minutes and slide fifty yards downstream from where you last saw him. He did hit the baseballs you pitched him into the apple trees, knocking down harvests. He did remember all the words to the cowboy songs and the names of all the wildflowers and when the moon would rise and set and when the tides came in and out. He was, in fact, the only god living in the whole of Waukegan, Illinois, during the twentieth century that I knew of. But he didn't go away from me, I went away from him. But, happy ending, he is still alive, forty-two years later, and remembers our love.

Was there a Lonely One?

There was, and that was his name. And he moved around at night in my home town when I was six years old and he frightened everyone and was never captured.

Was Grandma a woman with a broom or a dustpan or a washrag or a mixing spoon always in her hand?

She was. You saw her cutting piecrust in the morning, humming to it, or you saw her setting out the baked pies at noon or taking them in, cool, at dusk. She rang porcelain cups like a Swiss bell ringer, to their place. She glided through the halls as steadily as a vacuum machine, seeking, finding, and setting to rights. She made mirrors of every window, to catch the sun. She strolled but twice through any garden, trowel in hand, and the flowers raised their quivering fires upon the warm air in her wake. She slept quietly and turned no more than three times in a night, as relaxed as a white glove to which, at dawn, a brisk hand will return. Waking, she touched people like pictures, to set their frames straight. And when she came to the end of her life, she slipped into the long dream.

Fire balloons.

You rarely see them these days, though in some countries, I hear, they are still made and filled with warm breath from a small straw fire hung beneath. But in the Illinois of 1925, we still had them, and one of the last memories I have of my grandfather is the last hour of a Fourth of July night sixty some odd years ago when Grandpa and I walked out on the lawn and lit a small fire and filled the pear-shaped red-white-and-blue-striped paper balloon with hot air, and held the flickering bright-angel presence in our hands a final moment in front of a porch lined with uncles and aunts and cousins and mothers and fathers, and then, very softly, let the thing that was life and light and mystery go out of our fingers up on the summer air and away over the beginning-to-sleep houses, among the stars, as fragile, as wondrous, as vulnerable, as lovely as life itself.

I see my grandfather there looking up at that strange drifting light, thinking his own still thoughts. I see myself, eyes filled with tears because it was all over, the night was done. I knew there would never be another night like this.

No one said anything. We all just looked up at the sky and breathed out and in and we all thought the same things, but nobody said. Someone finally had to say, though, didn't they? And that one is me.

The wine still waits in the cellars below.

My beloved family still sits on the porch in the dark.

The fire balloon still drifts and burns in the night sky of an as yet unburied summer.

Why and how?

Because I say it is so.

Is the ravine real and deep and dark at night? It was, it is. I took my daughters there a few years back, fearful that the ravine might have gone shallow with time. I am relieved and happy to report that the ravine is deeper, darker, and more mysterious than ever. I would not, even now, go home through there after seeing *The Phantom of the Opera*.

Most importantly, did the big house itself, with Grandpa and Grandma and the boarders and uncles and aunts in it exist? I have already answered that.

So there you have it. Waukegan was Green Town, with all the happiness that that means, with all the sadness that these names imply. The people there were gods and midgets and knew themselves mortal and so the midgets walked tall so as not to embarrass the gods, and the gods crouched so as to make the small ones feel at home.

Here is my celebration, then, of death as well as life, dark as well as light, old as well as young, smart and dumb combined, sheer joy as well as complete terror written by a boy who once hung upside down in trees, dressed in his bat costume with candy fangs in his mouth, who finally fell out of the trees when he was twelve and went and found a toy-dial typewriter and wrote his first "novel."

A final memory.

REFERENCES

Bradbury, Ray. *Dandelion Wine*. New York: Knopf, 1975.

THE CRITICAL VOICE

15

Finding the Right Voice: The Search for the Ideal Companion in Adventure Stories

NICHOLAS TUCKER

Some of the most attractive characters in children's fiction have always been those loyal companions who accompany the young hero or heroine on their main adventures and indeed often make such adventures possible in the first place. Such supportive characters do not occur only in stories for children; one has simply to think of the various brave companions in adventure stories from Beowulf to Tolkien and beyond. But in the children's adventure story, devoted supporters often play a particularly important role. More than the rest of us, child readers must know that even in the flattering excesses of private fantasy neither they nor their young fictional representatives can usually hope to take on the adult world single-handed and win in the approved adventure hero style without straining credulity in quite extreme ways. Some extra help from elsewhere must therefore be generally forthcoming, but quite from whom can be something of a problem. Assistance from other child characters might do, yet all too often this also cannot totally escape the young reader's awareness of the limitations of what children can normally hope to achieve in an adult world, imaginary or otherwise. But if child readers and their fictional young heroes look for older, wiser companions in their adventures, there may soon be problems with that very dependence on adult authority, which children increasingly wish to escape from in their own private fantasy world. Differing ways of solving this problem as readers grow older reveal interesting developmental shifts both in what children look for in fiction and in how writers progressively cater to such changes.

For the very young reader, happy in a dependence upon parents, this is not too serious an issue. Accordingly their favorite characters in fiction may be perfectly content to take their main guidance from older figures. Whatever their occasional timid initiatives, for example, Pooh and Piglet never dream of questioning the superior understanding of Christopher Robin, nor does Christopher Robin doubt the authorial voice of this father who is shaping Christopher Robin's "remembering voice" into the collaborative story voice of son and father. If by any chance a bold young hero ever does try going against the wishes of his olders and betters, then, like Beatrix Potter's Peter Rabbit, he soon comes to see the error of his ways, with writer and audience at one over the general inadvisability at this age of ever seriously questioning what mother says, although Peter's "testing voice" continues to operate in the illustrations. As for fictional young friends, they too are seen not as valued counterweights to a parent's natural authority when it comes to suggesting independent action, but more as potentially mischievous influences, with Benjamin Bunny involving himself as well as his cousin Peter in dangerous escapades before they are both finally rescued by old Mr. Bunny and given a whipping.

But examples of ready obedience to parents do not on the whole last very long in twentieth-century children's adventure literature, something that reflects the greater emphasis that has been placed on the necessity for children to start finding their own way in life as soon as possible. By contrast, the nineteenth century, with its lingering belief that children should principally follow in their parents' footsteps, could still get away with family adventure stories where father himself is the key figure giving out orders while confidently expecting general submission; thus the idealized parents in *The Swiss Family Robinson* or *Masterman Ready*. There is also an echo of this type of model and its easy acceptance in Laura Ingalls Wilder's series about her pioneering childhood toward the end of the nineteenth century. Here again father is both friend and authority figure, heavily involved in the perpetual adventure of his family's struggle to survive in a hostile environment. The young Laura in her turn identifies with both her parents; their battle for survival is her own, and their authoritative voices are heard clearly in the third person voice of Laura, a voice chosen to detach hers from the psychological needs and limitations of a first person narrator.

Yet although first appearing in the 1930s, these stories describe a pattern that was already fast disappearing during the childhood Laura Ingalls Wilder was recalling fifty or so years ago. For the newer, smaller family, more often set in suburbia than in the remote countryside, and for children who now receive their most important education and later job prospects outside the home, adventure stories have more frequently come to represent psychological release from parents rather than the necessity for continual dependence on them. Given the fearsome nature of such a step, even in the imagination, it is not surprising that the first stories to embody such bold ideas of independence were those most clearly belonging to the world of fantasy than to anything more alarmingly like real life. Thus the safely distanced "Once upon a time" voice of traditional fairy stories, where child heroes set out from home with nothing and finally end up with economic independence and sexual maturity in the form of marriage to a princess, plus untold riches from wherever else.

On hand to help fairy story heroes in their quest are paradoxically those very parental figures children are trying to break away from in their imagination but here made tolerable through impenetrable disguise. In this way fairy godmothers or talking animals like Puss-in-Boots embody a child's fantasies of his or her parents' omnipotence in the way of casting magic spells and foreseeing the future ("This will end in tears").

Modern children wishing to find the same type of message in settings closer to their own experience can look among others to the works of E. Nesbit that also involve magical older characters such as her Psammead or Phoenix, still casting spells or granting wishes but now set within the more recognizable scenery of Edwardian England. While the children involved do not leave home and parents for long in their quests for adventure, they are certainly absent a good deal on their various time travels. Nor are their parents particularly interested in what their children were doing, too absorbed in their own affairs ever to thwart such splendid opportunities for independent action. These children escape into a world where their own voices take on the voice of parental authority and stability.

Another example of the modern fairy story and a different type of ideal companion can be found in P. L. Travers' story *Mary Poppins* (1934), still popular today and continuing to reach new audiences in the shape of Walt Disney's popular film made in 1964. On the face of it, Mary Poppins herself would seem the last choice for an ideal companion, since as a nanny of the old school she "Never wasted time being nice." One of her characteristics is a permanent sniff (the sniff speaks as loud as a voice), and she can be as rude to other adults as she can be abrupt and crushing to her young charges Jane and Michael Banks. The other servants with whom she works detest her "airs and graces" and the way she is "always keeping herself to herself." So why should the young Banks children love her so, not to mention over fifty years' worth of young readers of this and subsequent Mary Poppins adventures?

The answer lies in Mary Poppins' capacity to introduce magic into the otherwise humdrum lives both of Jane and Michael and those of her readers. Flying up to the ceiling on one page, talking to animals in the manner of another twentieth-century magician, Dr. Dolittle, on the next, her voice transcends physical limitations and gives her young charges and her young readers unlimited power. Although herself authoritarian, this power does not always link up with the authority of parents, policemen, or those other members of the adult establishment with whom Mary Poppins is on somewhat distant terms. The children certainly obey her; it would be foolish otherwise given her supply of magic treats. But bending the knee to Mary Poppins does not mean obedience to those other grown-ups excluded from her secret existence; rather, it guarantees entrance into a world where the children alone have access to powers denied everyone else.

It therefore does not really matter that Mary Poppins constantly scolds Jane and Michael for bad table manners, too much curiosity, or other small infringements of adult lore. Constriction in day-to-day behavior co-exists here with an exciting freedom elsewhere, and there are other ways in addition to sharing this secret fantasy world in which Mary Poppins is more childlike than her hectoring manner initially suggests. Although she has a boyfriend, the pavement artist Match-man, their infrequent courtship follows very childish lines, with raspberry-jam-cakes and trips on a merry-go-round providing the climaxes of their one outing. In looks, Mary Poppins resembles a Dutch doll, "with large feet and hands, and small, rather peering eyes." Yet she is still vain, enjoying her reflection in shop windows, particularly when she happens to be wearing new shoes or "nice new gloves with fur tops." In this way, she combines the most exciting fantasy aspects of adult omnipotence (her capacity for magic) with a delightful immaturity that constantly brings her down to child level whenever she threatens to become too superior or unapproachable. Although she leaves Jane and Michael by the end of her first story, her final "Au revoir" means exactly what it says: four more books of adventures to come. She is not an ideal companion for all ages, since older readers will find her magical adventures harder to swallow, but for children who still find fairy stories acceptable, Mary Poppins continues to speak with a voice that confers omnipotence upon the powerless.

Eventually children will want stories closer to reality, so once again the choice of hero-companion becomes important. Having now passed through the more extreme dependency needs on parents or parent-substitutes, young readers will sometimes look for younger, less generally managerial adult characters in their stories to help child heroes with the continuing uphill task of making an impression on the adult world, albeit only in the imagination. But as the boy hero in L. P. Hartley's far from childish novel *The Go-Between* (1953) has to discover, children must always to an extent risk ultimate betrayal by such companions, not to an enemy but rather to a young adult's almost inevitable final gravitation toward someone else closer in age and of the opposite sex. However gallant their companions in battle or escape, however close the identification, however necessary the projection into the voice of someone older and more glamorous, young readers always face being left behind at the point at which their more mature companions finally have the opportunity to progress to the area of sexual maturity—the only field where being young automatically rules out anything like an equivalent triumph.

This is something all child readers must get used to, and elements of anger or envy at being deserted in this way can always be balanced by pleasant anticipation of the time when they too will be able and willing to make such choices. Nor would they wish for glamorous hero-companions to renounce all interest in marriage and parenthood; this would then make them less desirable in other ways. Yet the occasional unwillingness of young readers to measure up against such fully mature companions and so find themselves still somewhat wanting does lead at times to the desire for different types of supporting characters.

Fiction involving more aged hero-companions, for example, can also be popular, with such characters well past economic or sexual ambitions and so better able to devote a flattering proportion of their time, attention, and approval to the young heroes or heroines in their stories. Wizards like Gandalf in *The Hobbit* (1937) or Merlin in T. H. White's *The Sword in the Stone*, grandmothers as in Roald Dahl's *The Witches* (1983), or even old sea captains as in Edward Ardizzone's *Little Tim* (1937) series—all combine the virtues of experience with fewer of the disadvantages of still belonging to the normal adult authoritarian establishment. Indeed, the old in children's fiction are often themselves somewhat disapproved of by the parents and parent-representatives concerned. If such elderly characters also follow off-beat professions such as the Punch and Judy man in John Masefield's *The Box of Delights* (1935) or tramps, as in various *William* (1922) stories by Richmal Crompton, then their alienation from ordinary types of parental authority may be even more satisfyingly complete. Here the voice of age distances the child from conventional authority and provides maturity of a peculiarly exciting kind.

Yet elderly hero-companions also have their disadvantages. While their advanced age and occasional infirmity mean they often leave a gratifying proportion of the dangerous work for their young heroes or heroines to do, their age can be something of a liability when the going gets really tough. Once hero-companions risk becoming something of an encumbrance, socially or otherwise, they quickly begin to lose this appeal—one reason why canny writers see to it that aged wizards or magicians often pay only comparatively short visits to whichever young hero or heroine they are out to befriend.

Middle aged hero-companions, though, are hard to find, possibly because they are too alike in age to the parents that children are now increasingly trying to free themselves from, at least in the imagination. Even so, a few rogue parents or parent-substitutes still manage to make it into adventure stories as hero-companions, but only when such characters are themselves delinquent or in general set against the rest of society, as in Roald Dahl's story about a son and his poacher father, *Danny, the Champion of the World* (1975). Elsewhere, a few children's writers have experimented with the idea of very small adults as hero-companions, as in Mary Norton's *Borrowers* (1952) series or Lynne Reid Banks' novel, *The Indian in the Cupboard* (1952). Once again, such heroes can combine something of the general competence of adults when it comes to taking part in an adventure with a very satisfying dependence upon the practical help of the child hero in what is this time an outsized world for adults rather than for children. By contrast, Roald Dahl in *B. F. G.* (1982) creates a giant hero-companion, who although immeasurably stronger than the child heroine, still needs her help in more mundane ways. In Dahl's "The Boy Who Talked with Animals," the boy who rescues the giant turtle shouts at forty or fifty adults on the beach; his voice leaves the adults speechless. The voice of the boy-hero invokes shame in the adults and tranquilizes the giant turtle. The young boy's voice resonates in the turtle who is "full of the wisdom of great age." The cruel voices, the fearful voices, are those of the "immature" adults.

Another choice of child hero-companion settles instead upon child gangs as sources of strength in early fiction. Children who might well feel impotent on their own can imagine themselves or their fictional representatives as far more capable once surrounded by the collective resources of a well-organized gang. The fact that such gangs tend to be unreliable, ever-shifting affairs in real life, only makes their idealization in fiction more attractive to the solitary child reader, who may well have never belonged to any gang at all and who would be only too happy to identify with a hero or heroine suddenly blessed with a number of atypically loyal friends of his or her own age. In Enid Blyton's Secret Seven (1949) and Famous Five (1942) series, such gangs regularly hunt down crooks, just as they do rather more convincingly in Erich Kastner's classic story in this genre, *Emil and the Detectives* (1931). In J. M. Barrie's *Peter Pan* (1906) the lost boys plus Peter and Wendy prove more than a match for Captain Hook and his pirates, just as the children in C. S. Lewis' Narnia series always manage to help their leader Aslan achieve his noble ends. More realistically, the weather-beaten young gangs in Arthur Ransome's boating stories also enjoy final collective success, despite coming up against numerous obstacles on the way. The gangs speak for the individually weak.

When the stress on relationships as opposed to adventure occurs in a child's life, the eventual end of a child's need for children's books heralds the end of childhood itself. For the obvious next step after this is to turn to those stories that take the search for the ideal hero or heroine companion into the ranks of the opposite sex of the same age and with the same aims of courtship in mind. The new world of sexual adventure in fiction involves different types of voices catering to more mature needs than those found in younger children still looking for fantasy companions with whom they can outwit crooks, find buried treasure, and finally prove to parents and the rest of the outside world that at least in the imagination they are so much more competent than anyone before ever appeared to believe. The voices of sexually aware young people, however, are distinct voices, no longer searching for a companion. The need for a mate demands that a child assume his or her own voice. It is this voice that listens for a responding echo in someone of the opposite sex.

REFERENCES

Ardizzone, Edward. *Little Tim.* Oxford: Oxford University Press, 1937.
Banks, Lynn Reid. *The Indian in the Cupboard.* London: Dent, 1952.

Barrie, J. M. *Peter Pan*. London: Hodder and Stoughton, 1906.

Blyton, Enid. *Famous Five*. London: Hodder and Stoughton, 1942.

————. *Secret Seven*. Leicester: Brockhampton, 1949.

Crompton, Richmal. *William*. London: Newnes, 1922.

Dahl, Roald. *B. F. G.* London: Cape, 1982.

————. *Danny, the Champion of the World*. London: Cape, 1975.

————. *The Witches*. London: Cape, 1983.

————. *The Wonderful Story of Henry Sugar and Six More*. New York: Knopf, 1977.

Hartley, L. P. *The Go-Between*. London: Hamish Hamilton, 1953.

Kastner, Erich. *Emil and the Detectives*. London: Cape, 1931.

Lewis, C. S. *The Lion, the Witch, and the Wardrobe*. London: Geofrey Bles, 1950.

Masefield, John. *The Box of Delights*. London: Heinemann, 1935.

Norton, Mary. *The Borrowers*. London: Dent, 1952.

Tolkien, J. R. R. *The Hobbit*. London: Allen and Unwin, 1937.

Travers, P. L. *Mary Poppins*. London: Collins, 1934.

16

Gulliver and the Children

LIONEL BASNEY

It seems only natural to us that the eighteenth century should have taken *Gulliver's Travels* for a children's story: It is a children's story for us still, the fabric of cartoon, films, and popular myth. But there is an issue of critical importance in this apparently inevitable popularity because it is evident that Swift did not mean the book as a children's book. The text's primary use— taking as much of it into account as we can, giving full value to its anger and ambivalence—is to be read as a scathing and complex indictment of human pretension, including the pretense that we know all of Swift's intentions. It was a book, Swift said, to vex the world, not divert it; a book that would be hard to read and hard to take; "a direct, plain and bitter satire," wrote Swift's relative and biographer, Deane Swift, "against . . . innumerable follies and corruptions" (Williams, 139); a fitting successor to the *Tale of a Tub*.

But this use of the text is primary only in a rather restricted and academic sense. In the democracy of actual reception and reading, *Gulliver's Travels* has become one of the most compelling of fantasies. We enter it as children and retain its imaginative structure, for countless uses, as we grow up. Its being a children's book to us at first does not inhibit its imaginative impact; it is *as* a children's book, as a ludic world, that it makes its lasting impact on our minds. Many changes, of course, have been made in Swift's text to shape and expedite its children's use; the greatest change, in this story told by its hero, is the alteration of the narrator's voice itself. But we cannot explain (or explain away) what has happened to Swift's text by the mechanical simplification and bowdlerization of the style. Something in the story invited, or even compelled, the rewriting. Something in Swift's design got away from the restrictions of even his supreme stylistic control.

EARLY VERSIONS

Gulliver's original publication, in London in October 1726, was received with a burst of popularity. Like most explosions, however, this one is not altogether clear. The book was instantly serialized—because, said the *Penny London Post* of November 25, the *Travels* "have so considerable a Share in almost any Conversation." Three days later *Parker's Penny Post* claimed that "for their Variety of Wit and . . . Diversion, [the *Travels* had] become the general Entertainment of Town and Country . . . " (Teerink, 203–04). The common implication is breadth of appeal, which seems to be confirmed by Gay's writing to Swift that the book was "universally read, from the Cabinet-council to the Nursery" (Williams, 62). But how, or for what, was it read in these extremes of audience? Setting aside the Scriblerians' involvement in Swift's coy pre-publication maneuvering, and Gay's knowledge that Swift had not meant the book to entertain, Gay's evidence is not very helpful. Half a century later James Beattie would say that "Gulliver has something in him to hit every taste" (Williams, 196), without offering any useful analysis of how Swift's farrago was divided up and savored.

We can initiate this analysis by noting that the Gulliver mythology had from the start four fairly distinct uses: it was used for satiric ends other than Swift's; it was extended into new voyages; it was simplified for children specifically; and it was co-opted for a general "Lilliputian" style of children's literature whose function and rhetoric countermanded both Swift's intentions and the children's uses *Gulliver's Travels* came to attract.

The book's incendiary political satire was obvious from the beginning— already in 1726 someone thought it capable of "throwing ourselves, and all *Europe* into a flame" (Williams, 68). Swift must have been delighted. Samuel Brunt attacked the South Sea Bubble (the eighteenth-century equivalent of the 1929 Stock Market crash) in his Gulliverian *Voyage to Cacklogallinia* (1727), and Samuel Johnson disguised his illegal reports of parliamentary debates in Cave's *Gentleman's Magazine* by calling them "Debates in the Senate of Lilliput." Such things were not for children. On the other hand, the book's childlike side was part of its power as a satiric fiction. The point of calling Robert Walpole "Walelop" is partly to reduce him to the league of little men. The works in the second category, new voyages, were likewise not specifically for children. But children who read or heard the original travels might have read volume three, parts one and two (1727), which took them back to Brobdingnag and on to Sporunda and Sevarambia. *Memoirs of the Court of Lilliput* (1727) are more clearly adult fare; among its appearance *à clef* of English luminaries there is an attack on Pope, which earned its possible author, Eliza Haywood, a place in the 1728 *Dunciad* (Welcher, 3:ix).

Despite the confused state of scholarship in the third category, it is clear that abridgements soon appeared that were meant for the nursery alone.

How soon it is probably impossible to tell. The first abridgement (1727) listed by Teerink (207) was not clearly intended for children. But later ones, such as *The Adventures of Captain Gulliver* (published by Francis Newbery in 1772), began the long tradition of detaching Lilliput and Brobdingnag from the rest of the story and publishing them as a unit (Bator, 555). John Sadler's small octavo (published by Darlington in 1773) announces both kingdoms on its title page but offers only a twenty-eight-page abridgement of Lilliput (Teerink, 212). Much earlier, however, chapbooks clearly meant for children were published and republished, with simplified prose and woodcuts. Gottlieb (161) suggests 1750 as a speculative date for a chapbook printed in Aldermary Church Yard, London, a twenty-four-page version of Lilliput; but he points out, significantly, that its woodcuts are badly worn, suggesting many earlier printings (cf. Teerink, 210).

It may have been this provenance that stimulated Jonathan Smedley's angry reaction to *Gulliver's Travels* as a children's story. He guesses that Swift owes something to *Tom Thumb*, a popular chapbook subject (Williams, 91). The difficulty is that the entertainment is bought with waste of time, since *Gulliver's Travels* has no useable moral—or if is has, "when it is found out, [the moral] does not teach Religion and Virtue, but the very Reverse of them" (Williams, 91). Smedley's expectation of a moral and his perception of Swift's actual subversiveness are not unorthodox for his time. *Gulliver's Travels* may have invaded the nursery in his chapbooks and octavos, but the official taste in children's stories was against him.

We need to keep this in mind when approaching the most celebrated popularizer of *Gulliver*, John Newbery. Fielding put the adjective "Lilliputian," meaning tiny, on the London stage in 1727. This obvious enough neologism led, however, in one further Lilliputian step, to a reversal of Swift's imaginative design. For Lilliputian came almost instantly to be a synonym for "child" (Pickering, 61), so that in "Lilliputian" writing from the 1750s on, the pygmies are the children themselves, and Gulliver (instead of being, as the original design suggests, the figure with whom readers including children would identify) becomes the adult, the mentor, the power over the throne.

Newbery's *Lilliputian Magazine* was advertised in the *General Evening Post* in March 1751 as ready to be issued in monthly numbers; " ' my Design is,' " Newbery wrote, " 'by way of *History* and *Fable*, to sow in [children's] Minds the Seeds of polite Literature and to teach them the great Grammer [*sic*] of the universe: I mean the Knowledge of Men and Things' " (qu Barry, 63). Though it was apparently published only once in book form (1752), the magazine introduced a half-century of Lilliputian moral fictions, courtesy books, stories published by Newbery's competitors (such as *The Lilliputian Masquerade*, published by T. Carnan in 1787), and "Lilliputian" versions of famous novels (*Tom Jones*) and periodicals (*The Juvenile Tatler*, 1783) (Barry 230, 235–36).

Newbery's scheme extended the influence of the Gulliver-world, and therefore indirectly of Swift's book, until it blanketed eighteenth-century thinking about children's literature. But it has never been adequately considered that this scheme delivered a children's imaginative world over to adult purposes. Newbery took away from his young readers the amorphous play world *Gulliver's Travels* offered them, and replaced it with a simply educative world in which the child is reduced to a Lilliputian and the adult, correspondingly, exalted into a Brobdingnagian. To say that Gulliver was adopted by children is to put the process too simply. Most of the time the story was adopted *for* children *by* adults; and Newbery's success stemmed, I think, as much from his securing the Gulliver-world for adult-controlled educational purposes as from his popularizing it for children's pleasure.

It is evident that Gulliver's attractiveness for children depends, as John Traugott has shown, on the amorphousness, the malleability, of the Lilliputian world. The child can "be" a little person confronting a big one; from this perspective she can "see" the ludic quality of adult preoccupations such as war and politics. Or she can "be" Gulliver playing with dolls which, more wonderfully than any actual doll, move, speak, initiate contact, build a world for the child-explorer to enter (Traugott, 129–40). In Swift's text this playfulness is obscured by the corrosive ironies of his satire. If making a children's version means clearing the text of its ironic complexity and thus of Swift's designs on his adult reader, it meant, in Newbery's redaction, flattening out the ludic dimension of the Gulliver-world as well. Later redactions flattened less; but even they, bowdlerizing and selecting as well as rewriting, made Swift's text into something else. Which raises, once again, the central conundrum of whether Swift's text was ever, or could ever be, a children's story in its original design.

AN ADULT WORK

Since at least the 1770s, children's versions of the story have been made out of the first two voyages alone. Johnson's acute if unkind remark—that once Swift had thought of little men and big men, there wasn't much more to it—focuses the attractiveness of the truncated story very well: the two voyages give sharp, easily grasped images of a universal somatic experience, the sense of one's own size in a world of rough averages. Among the Lilliputians, Gulliver is huge; among the Brobdingnagians, he is tiny. But these contrasts are superseded by the almost cosmic distance between Lilliputian and Brobdingnagian (144 times the height and a thousand times the bulk)—and this, by the imaginative effect of a world where both could exist. This effect belongs to that vague territory the critics of Swift's time called the "sublime"; the range of size is almost unimaginable, and a little (pleasantly) spooky.

Of course the Lilliputians are not sublime. They are so absurd, as well as so small, that they are rather nonhuman, toylike—"animalcules in human shape," wrote Lord Orrery (1752), "ridiculously engaged in affairs of importance" (Williams, 122). (The King of Brobdingnag takes Gulliver for a toy [142].) The Brobdingnagians are giants out of fairy tales; the Lilliputians are the dolls and small animal pets we keep around our children and toward which (to some extent like Gulliver) children feel tenderness and precocious parental affection—just, that is, what Glumdalclitch feels for Gulliver (133–34).

It is easy to see why book three, the voyage to Laputa and other places, did not become a children's favorite. It has no controlling, convincing pictorial center but is a passel of assorted satire ending in the horrifying Struldbruggs, the damned and decaying immortals. The book contains isolated comic images—the flying island, the flappers, the men burdened like peddlers with all the things they used for words—but one has to know a good deal about seventeenth-century science and linguistic philosophy to make sense out of them. More importantly, Gulliver has no clearly visualizable place in all of this. He simply wanders from place to place and sees what is there to see.

Perhaps it is with book four, however, that we run seriously aground. Talking animals with good lessons to teach were a staple of children's literature late in Swift's century. It is hard, however, to imagine him liking a moral tale like *The Life and Perambulation of a Mouse* (1783). The Yahoos and the Houyhnhms are at best parodies of Aesopian animals. They are fantasy, not fable. The Yahoos are disgusting, the rational horses are just that, lofty and rational. But the crucial difficulty, again, is Gulliver. Here, in the hardest test of his sense of reality, he moves steadily toward absurdity and then into a kind of schizophrenia, without Swift's sympathy and indeed at the point of Swift's severest laughter.

This is not to say that a consistent, detailed fictional character for Gulliver was one of Swift's projects or that it is necessary even for the appeal of books one and two. It would be more accurate to say that Swift has made Gulliver a narrative mouthpiece, endowed with a body and a jumble of ordinary opinions. In books one and two, Gulliver's transparency and malleability are just what make him an accessible narrator. He goes, sees, wonders, and reports; he is curious, credulous, and energetic; he is a friendly camera. He picks up languages with a child's ease and attaches himself to the nearest available authority figure. If we pay little or no attention to the irony he sometimes uses, or to the irony Swift is always using on him, he is the perfect children's narrator. And irony is just what a young reader will not see.

Reading *Gulliver's Travels* as a children's book depends directly on reading Gulliver, the narrator, in a specific way. The issue of the narrator leads us to the plain conflict between this way of using the story and the larger, probably more Swiftian way. Gulliver is a literalist child in an allegorical world. So much is standard narrative practice: the allegory educates us by educating the narrator, our representative. But in *Gulliver's Travels*—including now all of Swift's irony—the allegory comprises an outright attack on the character and beliefs of any reader who manages to comprehend it. To read Swift's allegory rightly is to come within range of his guns. Sometimes Gulliver cooperates in the attack, in a limited way; more often he is a target too; but always he is an instrument for the larger satiric purpose.

The book has two uses, then, both centering on Gulliver, the narrative voice. The thinness as a character that keeps him from getting in the way of the wonders of books one and two also makes him endlessly malleable to Swift's satire. If Swift needs Gulliver to be shocked at the behavior of an emperor who refuses to have him killed for no reason, but who orders him to be blinded instead (also for no reason), Gulliver admits that he is naive in the ways of princes; but since Swift has to get him out of Lilliput quickly, he endows Gulliver in the same paragraph with enough book learning about the *history* of princes to make him take to his heels (Penguin, 109). Swift will never let Gulliver be; and even at the blandest moments we are at a loss to interpret Swift/Gulliver's tone:

I thought this account of the Struldbruggs might be some entertainment to the reader, because it seems to be a little out of the common way, at least, I do not remember to have met the like in any book of travels that hath come to my hands: and if I am deceived, my excuse must be, that it is necessary for travellers, who describe the same country, very often to agree on the same particulars, without deserving the censure of having borrowed or transcribed from those who wrote before them. (Penguin, 260)

The irony of this is so bland that at first we think it is unimportant. But then why include it? If it is purposive, it must be a gesture of contempt—Swift does not bother to be subtle, apparently because he thinks us too dense to bother with, except that *this* judgment of us must be made clear.

This is the style that impresses us with what Claude Rawson calls Swift's "fundamental unfriendliness" (11). The most profound effect of Swift's ironies, sent through and around Gulliver, is to cut the ground from under our feet, to keep us from feeling sure, for longer than a moment, that we know what is going on. Swift is mounting a gradually more stark and venomous attack on pride, on our implicit belief that we are rational creatures. Hence the constant sabotage of certainty. The attack is venomous because of Swift's angry conviction that nothing he reveals about human beings is new, that the ideals he invokes are obvious. Man's pride is clearly excessive, lawyers are plainly cheats, war is obviously horrible; anyone who thought about it would say so; but before we can think about it, our complacent sense of rational control must be destroyed. We must be convinced, by repeated experience, that we cannot answer for ourselves.

In this way we come to see that *Gulliver's Travels*, on Swift's largest plan, is not a children's book at all. To read it as one is to take Gulliver's part, to see as he sees. But to read it in full recognition of Swift's ironies means to abandon Gulliver's perspective and accept another that does not so much transcend his as it definitively and even bitterly rejects it. Gulliver's childlike receptiveness, the innocence of his responses, leads him in the end to a kind of insanity; but the only alternative to being a child in this way is Swift's contorted irony. Swift does not accept childlikeness, nurture it, expand on it; he manipulates it and finally explodes it. There is not much comfort in his drastic adulthood; but it is what he values.

A CHILD'S BOOK

This accounting for the text makes it seem impossible that *Gulliver's Travels* could ever become a children's book. But beneath, or beside, Swift's bitter flouting of readerly conventions there remains the clear, meticulous imagined world of little men and big men. The age of wholesale rewriting of Swift's text began with the insight that it was this world, and not the ironies and indecencies, which made *Gulliver* a classic: "the interest," Francis Jeffrey wrote in 1816, "does not arise from the satire but from the plausible description of physical wonders . . . " (Williams, 320). Richard Payne Knight and Walter Scott made the same observation, and Scott added: "In fact, the work rests upon an axiom, in itself certain, that there is no such thing in nature as an absolute standard of size, and that all our ideas upon the subject are relative, and founded upon comparison" (Williams, 310; cf. 272). The games of wonder and empathy Traugott lays out, that is, depend not on Swift's original narrative voicing, but on images; and the children's version that neuters the voice, or makes it friendly, and lets the images through will be most successful for this range of uses.

The critical problem raised by this fact of reading is profound and far more complicated than this discussion can pursue. Briefly stated, it is this: how does the image-world of a literary work escape the properties of the text and impress itself (directly?) on our imaginations? All we can do here is to note the ways in which Swift's text has been modified to make this imaginative reception easier. At least three modifications have been repeatedly made: the text has been truncated, bowdlerized, and simply rewritten. All of these involve the narrative voice. Truncation traditionally drops the last two voyages, in which Gulliver's voice becomes increasingly shrill and disordered. Bowdlerization cleans out Gulliver's unconscious indecencies and also the physical literalism that Swift saw (in part) as comic but that people of later times saw as obscene. The rewriting, finally, changes the narrative voice by subtracting its ironies, making it blander, more transparent, and a better conveyor of images.

Little more needs to be said about truncation of the story. Sometimes it has gone along with expurgation: *Stories from Seven Old Favorites*, volume five of The Children's Hour series (1907), chooses incidents from the first two voyages that contain no questionable material but leaves Swift's text as he wrote it.

Perrin maintains that none of the eighteenth-century *Gullivers* was expurgated (225)—he is not considering, I suspect, the shrunken chapbook editions—and this suggests that if the original text was (as Gay claimed) read "in the Nursery," the time's general freedom from squeamishness was extended in some degree to children. Walter Scott's text (2d ed., 1824) was still complete. Half of the nineteenth-century texts from then on (according to Perrin's tally) were expurgated in line with the era's discomfort with anything that gave too vivid a sense of the human body as body (225–28). The nineteenth century cut the notorious passage in which the Lilliputian soldiers, marching beneath Gulliver's legs, glance upwards (with "laughter and admiration," says Gulliver) through his torn breeches (Penguin, 78). It excised the descriptions of Brobdingnagian bosoms (Penguin, 130, 158). The twentieth century has stuck by some of these excisions, as in the popular and often reprinted Dent edition (at least into the 1950s). In addition we have sometimes removed the account of the Brobdingnagian execution (Penguin, 158–59); we have, as Perrin observes, more reason than our forefathers had to be uncomfortable with cruelty (228).

Four versions of the beginning of Lilliput, chapter two, will illustrate the imaginative effect of bowdlerization in tandem with rewriting: Swift first; then an 1894 Macmillan edition, anonymously edited; then the Aldermary chapbook (c. 1750), and a Golden Illustrated Classic (adapted by Sarel Eimerl, 1962). Swift writes:

When I found myself on my feet, I looked about me, and must confess I never beheld a more entertaining prospect. The country round appeared like a continued garden, and the inclosed fields, which were generally forty foot square, resembled so many beds of flowers. These fields were intermingled with woods of half a stang, and the tallest trees, as I could judge, appeared to be seven foot high. I viewed the town on my left hand, which looked like the painted scene of a city in a theatre. (64)

The next paragraph is devoted to Gulliver's excremental needs. All three children's versions simply omit it, and with it Swift's typical undercutting of his narrator: "I would not have dwelt so long upon a circumstance, that perhaps at first sight may appear not very momentous, if I had not thought it necessary to justify my character in point of cleanliness to the world . . . " (64). Then:

When this adventure was at an end, I came back out of my house, having occasion for fresh air. The Emperor was already descended from the tower, and advancing on horseback towards me, which had like to have cost him dear; for the beast, though very well trained, yet wholly unused to such a sight, which appeared as if a mountain moved before him, reared up on his hinder feet: but that prince, who is an excellent horseman, kept his seat, till his attendant ran in, and held the bridle, while his Majesty had time to dismount (64).

The 1894 Macmillan edition retains Swift's original language, except to drop the offensive paragraph, and the first sentence of the third paragraph, with its "occasion for fresh air." With the scatology goes Swift's irony at Gulliver's expense and what Swift no doubt would have regarded as admissible (if rough) comedy; what is retained is the good-natured, childlike, unstrenuous observer who is delighted with small trees and small town and is ready to assimilate all the wonders of the small land—to be taken in, that is, according to Swift; to see and wonder, in the children's version.

The 1750 Aldermary chapbook, in line with its extreme brevity, discards everything but Gulliver's observation of the town and the emperor's near accident; its language is also simplified.

When I found myself on my feet, I looked about me, and saw trees about seven feet high, and a town upon my left hand like the painted scenes at a play house.
The Emperor advanced to me on horseback, when the beast unused to such a sight, reared upon his hinder feet; but the prince being a good horseman, kept his seat, while some of his attendance ran in and held [the horse] . . . (Gottlieb, 163).

This adaptation discards Gulliver's statement of reaction ("I never beheld a more entertaining prospect"), and with it almost all sense of Gulliver as a character distinguishable from the event he is narrating. The Lilliputian measurement ("stang") is discarded, and "scene of a city in a theatre" is simplified and generalized to "scenes at a play house." These revisions are clearly meant to increase the ease of comprehension, but they sacrifice much of the vividness with which Gulliver describes his surroundings and the vidid image (seen through the horse's eyes) of the moving mountain.

The Golden Classic adaptation is a compromise between the chapbook and the 1894 expurgated reprint.

When I found myself on my feet, I looked about me. I must confess I never saw a more delightful view. The country around looked like one huge garden, and the fields, which were about forty feet square, resembled flower beds. These fields were intermingled with woods, and the tallest trees appeared to be about seven feet high. The town was on my left hand. It looked like the painted scene of a city on a theatre stage.
The Emperor had already descended from the tower and was advancing on horseback toward me, which almost cost him his life. For although the beast was well trained, it was wholly unused to such a sight, which must have looked like a mountain moving in front of him. It reared up on its hind feet, but the Prince was an excellent horseman and kept his seat until his attendants ran in and held the bridle so that he could dismount. (18)

This text restores a certain amount of the original language; it omits the Lilliputian word and substitutes modern for eighteenth-century usage ("one huge garden" for "a continued garden," "cost him his life" for "cost him dear"). It restores Gulliver's innocuous response to the scenery and makes more clearly subjective (that is, more clearly Gulliver's) the image of the moving mountain: While the original says that Gulliver "appeared" like a mountain, the Classic says that he "must have looked" like a mountain. The effect is not, perhaps, to bring us much closer to Gulliver. It may betray our loss of perceptual innocence: Swift was more willing to believe that what he or his narrator saw actually was there.

Gulliver's Travels is a good example for the study of the narrator in children's writing, simply because so much depends on Gulliver. Swift bends the text back on his hero because Swift's true theme is not adventure but the failure of adventure, not the variety of the world but the sameness of human folly. Even the original, controlled Gulliver, however, sometimes betrays a moment of genuinely childlike insight; he is sometimes just the narrator of intelligible wonders. To pick up the theme Scott articulated, Gulliver's sheer physical disorientation yields experiences we recognize, "I slept about two hours, and dreamed I was at home with my wife and children, which aggravated my sorrows when I awaked and found myself alone in a vast room, between two and three hundred foot wide, and above two hundred high, lying in a bed twenty yards wide" (Penguin, 131). The absurdity this moment contains stems from its exaggeration. But aloneness in an enormous room is a familiar childhood experience. Swift means, by the work as a whole, to force his readers to confront "what everybody knows" and no one will admit about man's true stature in the scheme of things. But children do not know "what everybody knows." One thing they do not know is how big they are (in all senses). To them the disorientation of common notions is not a form of salutary moral shock. To them it is the sort of attraction and terror that constitutes the essence of fantasy.

REFERENCES

Barry, Florence V. *A Century of Children's Books.* 1922. Reprint. Detroit: Singing Tree, 1968.

Bator, Robert. "Jonathan Swift." In *Writers for Children: Critical Studies of Major Authors Since the Seventeenth Century,* edited by Jane M. Bingham, 555–59. New York: Scribner's, 1988.

Gottlieb, Gerald. *Early Children's Books and Their Illustration.* New York and Boston: Pierpont Morgan Library in association with David H. Godine, 1975.

Perrin, Noel. *Dr. Bowdler's Legacy: A History of Expurgated Books in England and America.* New York: Atheneum, 1969.

Pickering, Samuel, Jr. *John Locke and Children's Books in Eighteenth-Century England.* Knoxville: University of Tennessee Press, 1981.

Rawson, C. J. *Gulliver and the Gentle Reader*. London and Boston: Routledge and Kegan Paul, 1973.

Stories from Seven Old Favorites. The Children's Hour, vol. 5. Boston: Houghton Mifflin, 1907, 1929.

Swift, Jonathan. *Gulliver's Travels*. Adapted by Sarel Eimerl. A Golden Illustrated Classic. New York: Golden Press, 1962.

———. *Gulliver's Travels*. Edited by Peter Dixon and John Chalker. Harmondsworth and Baltimore: Penguin, 1967.

———. *Travels into Several Remote Nations of the World, by Lemuel Gulliver*, with preface by Henry Craik. 1894. Reprint. Ann Arbor, Mich.: University Microfilms, 1967.

Teerink, H. *A Bibliography of the Writings of Jonathan Swift*. 2d ed. Edited by Arthur H. Scouten. Philadelphia: University of Pennsylvania Press, 1963.

Traugott, John. "The Yahoo in the Doll's House: *Gulliver's Travels* the Children's Classic." *Yearbook of English Studies* 14 (1984): 127–50.

Welcher, Jeanne K., and George E. Bush, Jr., eds. *Gulliveriana* 6: 1–3. Gainesville, Fla. and Delmar, N.Y.: Scholars' Facsimiles and Reprints, 1970–1972.

Williams, Kathleen, ed. *Swift: The Critical Heritage*. New York: Barnes and Noble, 1970.

PART IV
Realism

Introduction

CHARLOTTE F. OTTEN

Realistic fiction for children shares at times with adult postmodern fiction an awareness of, perhaps even a preoccupation with, the technical aspects and theories of narration. By interrupting the narrator's voice with an examination of the structure of voice, the author may show that the apparent interruption is no interruption at all but only another way of establishing the credibility or unreliability of the narrator and the credulity or sophistication of the reader.

In this section, three authors examine the voice of the narrator in books as different as those in which an old woman narrator metamorphoses into a young woman narrator, in which the narrator is the whole of West Africa, in which the narrator reflects the culture of Appalachia. The critics' approaches, too, are as different as those of the authors, with one applying the narrative theories of Henry James to four children's books, and the other using her own experiences as editor and author to detect the distinct voice of the narrator for the middle-age child.

Jill Paton Walsh, acknowledging the slipperiness and metaphoric quality of the term "narrative voice," argues that a term so rich in suggestion cannot be considered apart from adult fiction: The narrator's voice is not what separates children's fiction from adult fiction. In either case, voice has "two elements, a voluntary and an involuntary one," and, insists Walsh, the voice of the narrator is not the voice of the author. In order to understand how voice works, Walsh uses the term "mask," a term that conceals the actual author and that enables the narrator to speak with a number of voices.

In her analysis of *Unleaving*, Walsh describes her narrative voice—her voluntary mask—as metafictive, as one of the few instances in her books in which voice examines voice as part of the voice. This is obviously a sophisticated use to which writers of postmodern adult fiction have also turned. Although the young readers of *Unleaving* have expressed interest in the narrator's voice, Walsh doubts that her adoption of the metafictive mask is central to their experience of the book.

When speaking about the involuntary narrative voice, Walsh recognizes that behind the mask is an identifiable human being—the author—who cannot obliterate her own identity. The author, by using a mask, has tapped into deeper, stronger voices that allow the author "to speak with a better, wiser, finer voice" than her own.

For Ann Grifalconi, voice is rooted in culture. Going to central West Africa for her series of books on this culture, she heard there "the word and the texture and the beat—the infectious rhythm of life itself." As she traveled through villages, she discovered new images and fresh ways of relating universal truths.

For *The Village of Round and Square Houses*, she chose a narrator who could combine realism and myth. The young woman, Osa, who brought Grifalconi to the village, became the character-narrator of her story. In her own voice Osa transmits the mythic voice of truth, which is her grandmother's voice. This unique blending of voices of the present and of the past is the voice of the African culture in which the two voices are indistinguishable.

For *Darkness and the Butterfly*, where the subject is the child's fear of the dark, Grifalconi chose an adult African narrator to address this fear, not through condescension or moral instruction, but through the image of a butterfly, who "found the way to carry her own light through the darkness."

In her third book, *Osa's Pride*, Grifalconi returned to Osa as first person narrator, who, by "telling on herself," and through the use of parable, achieves self-knowledge.

Grifalconi stresses that behind her African stories is the author herself, who transmits these stories through her own authentic voice; and in the author herself is the realistic narrator, who, working in the tradition of the African storyteller, mediates the "wonder and validity of the West African experience."

About a year before she began to write her story about Appalachia, Lois Lowry heard the voice of a girl, later to be called Rabble Starkey. Lowry wrote down the two sentences that this girl spoke to her, and those two sentences gave her the elements that were the key to the voice: "summer, neighborhood, war, and Gunther."

Lowry makes a point about distinguishing between her own voice as author and the voice of the realistic fictional character she has created. The strange thing, however, about hearing and creating a narrative voice is the circularity of the process. Lowry observes that the voice of Rabble Starkey has the cadences and diction of Lowry's life and experiences in Appalachia, South Carolina, the Blue Ridge Mountains, but that as the voice of Rabble Starkey emerged at the typewriter—clear and distinct—it became suddenly also Lowry's voice. Not wishing to sound magical or mystical, Lowry simply expresses the wonder of the transformation. At the heart of her narrative, then, is the mystery of voice identity.

In his critical theories on narration, Henry James developed the concept of a central consciousness or intelligence as narrator. Not a first person voice, nor an omniscient third person narrator, the central consciousness works through the experiences of a single character but is controlled by an "unintrusive third person narrator." The advantages of the central consciousness as narrator in realistic fiction for children, Lois Kuznets suggests, are those that James describes for adult realistic fiction: the reader has a stable point of identification from which to measure the central character and the action, and the author has greater freedom in the use of language.

In her detailed consideration of four books—*The Yearling, Sounder, Julie of the Wolves*, and *A Sound of Chariots*—Kuznets identifies the central consciousness in each and shows the effects on the young reader of the choice of narrative voice. The central consciousness can be "the lonely son," as in *The Yearling*; "the boy, alone," as in *Sounder*; "the girl alone," as in *Julie of the Wolves*; "the girl artist," as in *A Sound of Chariots*; but in all four instances, Kuznets shows that children guided by the central consciousness acquire "an appreciative understanding of the complexity not only of language but of the human experience that fictional voices both represent and shape."

Tracing the uses of the narrator's voice through the last half of the nineteenth century into the early twentieth century, Jean Karl notes that authors of realistic fiction for children usually took the omniscient position, which enabled them to be observer, commentator, instructor. Karl shows that today's authors have more choices but also greater challenges. No matter which voice the narrator assumes, it must not be perceived as an "assumption"; rather, the author must become a child—a middle-age child—in outlook, perception, and knowledge. Karl describes three ways in which authors can become the voice of the child: by honestly recalling their own childhood, listening to and observing children around them, and exploring the past in order to grasp the lives of earlier children. Authors who can slough off the accretions of adulthood will not betray the child but will guide the child in the voice of a child.

THE AUTHORIAL VOICE

17

On Wearing Masks

JILL PATON WALSH

"Voice" of course, in expressions such as "narrative voice" is a metaphor. And it is a very slippery one, used as shorthand to name a varying bundle of techniques, effects, stylistic tones and strategies. We shall have a hard time being precise and precisely understood discussing such a topic.

Let's start by confronting two potential culture gaps. First is the supposed difference between children's books and adult books. I am not one of those who would deny that there are any differences, but the differences are not necessarily differences of technique. Although there may be areas of literary discussion in which it is necessary to hive off children's books and consider them separately, there are other areas in which such hiving off produces rubbish. Once, for example, I unwisely embarked on a discussion with a young woman who was eagerly interested in historical writing, especially with the complex "dating" of work to the time in which it was written, which shows through the careful dating contrived by the author, to the time the work is about. It was an interesting discussion, with an intelligent interlocutor. But I was soon baffled. She had not read Tolstoy, or Stendhal, or any novel by Walter Scott, or Marguerite Yourcenar's *Memoirs of Hadrian* or Gore Vidal's *Julian*, or *Vanity Fair*, or *The Red Badge of Courage*. However good *Johnny Tremain*, *My Brother Sam Is Dead*, and *The Slave Dancer* may be, they are not enough to sustain a discussion of the nature of historical fiction *without reference* to any adult work. They were certainly not written by people who had not read any adult historical fiction. My discussion was not with a person who was interested in historical fiction, even if she thought she was.

To discuss time horizons in historical writing, but only in examples culled from the children's list, is perverse and unproductive because there are no important distinctions between children's books and general books in this area of discussion, and many illuminating insights for which Tolstoy or Stephen Crane would be excellent illustrations. Narrative voice is another topic that can hardly be considered exclusively in respect of works written for children. Perhaps in this case there are some differences between the narrative voices in children's books and in adult books. But how shall we discern them without considering the techniques in both kinds?

My second culture gap is the one that increasingly yawns between writers and critics. Only a short time ago it was possible to graduate from a university cognizant with the state of literary criticism, and by subscribing to one or two literary journals, reading the occasional seminal book, and generally keeping an eye on things, to remain broadly familiar with the state of criticism for most of one's life. Now criticism is so arcane, so technical, and so full of rapidly changing mutually homicidal schools and "isms," that it is a full-time job to keep up with it. Nobody who has taken time out to write fiction could expect to have a grip on the state of criticism, and the works that one has missed are written in an impenetrable thicket of technical terms, which makes attempts to catch up without taking a second degree doomed to failure. The literary culture of writers and the literary culture of critics are going separate ways, with cultural consequences that are as yet unclear, although certain to be profound.

The analysis of a literary question offered by a writer, then, is a workshop sort of thing, and not the same kind of artifact as analysis offered by a critic.

From a writer's viewpoint what is commonly called "voice" has two elements, a voluntary and an involuntary one. A narrative voice might mean the strategy deliberately adopted by the writer, fully self-aware, for telling a story, and it might mean that indefinable quality that makes it possible to recognize small fragments of a writer's work, and that distinguishes it, even in dialogue, where it mimics the voices of characters, from the work of other writers. Just as with one's real voice, one can control what one says, and many aspects of utterance—how loud, how fast, whether angry, loving, authoritative—yet one cannot control what one sounds like, or easily sound like someone else, and voices once known are intensely recognizable and identifiable, even if they are those of actors speaking in dialects or accents different from those in use the last time one heard them.

It is obviously easiest to start by discussing the consciously controllable aspects of narrative voice. First one must realize that none of the voices audible in the book is that of the author. When we open a book and start to read, it is natural to think that it must be the author whose words we read, the author who is telling us the story. This natural assumption, which is wholly untrue, is a booby-trap for writers as much as for readers, and is underpinned by the phrase "self-expression" so often applied to literary art.

But it is not as themselves that authors enter their books, and those who wish to express themselves require the services of a lover or a psychiatrist; the services of a reader have to be earned. The rhetorical devices available to a modern fiction writer are, however, many and complex, so that I must elaborate this point a little.

Let us start by thinking of a book—Thackeray's *Vanity Fair*—in which the author introduces himself to us on the first page, as a puppeteer, and keeps jumping up and down apostrophizing the reader and making comments on the "puppets" as the story progresses. Is the puppeteer Thackeray himself? Is it his voice that tells us in the opening paragraphs of "Before the Curtain" that, " . . . the famous little Becky Puppet has been pronounced to be uncommonly flexible in the joints . . . " (5), and if so, whose is the voice that opens chapter one: "While the present century was in its teens, and on one sunshiny morning in June, there drove up to the great iron gate of Miss Pinkerton's academy for young ladies, on Chiswick Mall, a large family coach. . . . " (11)?

Is this second voice, which tells us the vast majority of the story, also Thackeray's? When the puppeteer pops up and makes a comment, "In a word, everybody went to wait upon this great man—everybody who was asked—as you, the reader (do not say nay), or I the writer hereof would go if we had an invitation" (458), is Thackeray interrupting himself?

I think it is rather obvious that the puppeteer, though presented to us as the author, is simply another character in the book. Detached, cynical, Olympian, and often making comments to guide the reader's reaction and produce a particular "shrinking" effect, constantly nudging us into remembering how insignificant human lives are, he is part of the apparatus for telling the story. Perhaps in some ways he does resemble the real-life Thackeray. But there is no need for him to do so. Even if one of the characters in the book is actually called the author, the author is not on oath to be sincere, or to speak in his own voice. If the real Thackeray was not a cynic at all, but a sentimental old duffer (and we might feel free to think he was when we read his portrayal of Amelia!), it is very obvious that he presents himself within the book as just what the book requires him to be. Within the book "the author" is a persona, not a person.

It is only one step less obvious that the other voice, the anonymous disembodied one that tells the bulk of the tale, is also a character in the book, however nebulous, and not the author. The narrative voice is not the voice of the author in private life; it is a professional "stance." And much the clearest way to think about this is to think in terms of masks. "The mask of the narrator" is worn while the utterance that forms the words on the page is not being spoken through the mask of any of the characters, though we must not forget that characters too are narrators. The author's self must be set aside, or be concealed by the masks. It is a *story* that is being expressed through the speaking masks, not a *self*.

I think many otherwise very promising books have been wrecked by the intrusion of the author—the real one whom you can invite to dinner, or ask to talk at your school—because the anonymous nature of the narrative voice had not been understood; it is simply that if you are wearing a mask your face is covered and unseen. To understand this is to grasp a fundamental truth about literary technique.

Of course, people often think that whereas writing for adults may require a sophisticated understanding of technique, writing for children needs only a simple kit of tools. They think this because they are focusing on the children, not on the task of writing fiction. And children are usually thought of as needing simple books. I do not know where children acquired the reputation of being simple, but it was not, I imagine, an idea that arose in the mind of anybody who knows a lot of children, or works with them and their books. But even if they were simple, it would not necessarily follow that simple literary technique would be all that you needed to please them. A proper understanding of narrative voice is in fact very complicated, but it is also simple in the sense that there is no narrative we would call a story that does not involve this voice, so that thinking about it is lesson one.

Before I expound for you some author's-eye views of narrative voice, however, I would like to make another point. A good deal of discussion of literary works contrives to consider author and reader, while forgetting about the subject. Now books tend to be about something, and all literary devices stand or fall by their usefulness in getting the reader to think and feel about that something. Because the subjects of fiction tend to be rather grand and shapeless—"the human predicament," "time and change," "love," "growth," and so on—the subject and the setting can become confused and the subject overlooked. This produces a rather unpractical and eerie feel to abstract discussions, as though one were taking a course on how to be a museum guide, without ever learning, or asking, what is in the museum around which one will conduct people!

It is important to understand the central position of the subject in the author's mind while the book is being written, and, if the strategies are working well, in the reader's mind while the book is being read because once you see that we are involved in a triangle, you see why mask dropping is so disastrous. Quite simply, if the real author pops out from behind the mask and starts showing his or her own feelings, then the reader's attention is distracted from the subject.

Two different temptations make authors want to drop the mask for a few sentences, or pages, and get into the act themselves.

One is a little touch of megalomania—the author is deeply interested in his or her feelings or opinions and chiefly motivated by a desire for self-expression. If it's getting rather difficult to manuever the story into voicing the great ME, then perhaps, the author thinks, "If I get on stage myself, and just say a few words. . . ."

The other, and it particularly afflicts writers for children, is a lack of trust in the audience, a terrible anxiety that they won't understand art. If you show them something cruel happening, you are afraid that they will think you are in favour of cruelty. Just in case you are misunderstood, you had better just get a word in here, speaking in your own voice... But the problem is that masks are magic, and if you drop them you break the spell. The problem is that the aim of fiction is to arouse emotion and understanding in readers, and you do that by showing them the subject. Once you make yourself into the subject of the book you are guaranteed to bore everybody!

Writing is actually a rather self-abnegating activity, in which you subordinate yourself to the job in hand. If an ugly, cruel mask is the best one for this story, then you must wear it and not be vaingloriously concerned in case someone thinks you are cruel in your real, your personal opinions. I will try to illustrate what I mean with an example. In *A Chance Child* (1978) I wrote about cruelty to children in the Industrial Revolution. I found myself reading, while researching for this book, personal testimonies from little children of the early nineteenth century which were harrowing and heart-breaking in the extreme. In fact I found the research reading so upsetting I could only do it for quite short periods at a time, and then I had to rest from the emotional battering I was getting. I don't mind telling you, in a critical article, that this was how I felt, but for the purpose of fiction how I felt is quite useless. Can I move you to tears by telling you that I, JPW, safe and comfortable upward of 140 years later, am bitterly opposed to the practice of sending five-year-old girls down coal mines for twelve hours a day with tallow candles? So what? Who doesn't disapprove of that? Who cares what I approve of? The disapproval must be kept well out of sight, behind the mask, and I must simply tell you about the subject—what it was like then, how people lived. The subject will move you to sorrow and anger, as it has done me. That's what the narrative mask is for—to get the author out of the way and allow the reader unpestered, unobstructed, to experience the subject.

But once one has learned that one's book is not going to be a platform for one's personal feelings and opinions, that one must go masked, there is then a choice of masks. And there are many to choose from. There are a number of different first person masks, for example. Any of the characters in a story can serve as the mask for the narrative voice. An older or wiser version of one of the characters is a much used mask—both interesting and easy, that one, but hard to make sympathetic to very young readers. Then there is the mask marked "author," which Thackeray was wearing in the passages from *Vanity Fair* referred to above. There are a number of invisible masks, allowing the storytelling to follow along, closely observing the characters, but not among them so as to be observed by them, and playing no part in the action. And then there are masks of gods—who know and see everything, unlimited by time and space. The advantages and disadvantages of these sorts of masks—usually called "points of view"—are very well known and are the subject of innumerable "how to write" books, and in the higher reaches of literature, the subject of a good deal of high-powered critical analysis. I do not have anything very new to say about deliberate authorial strategies, though such deliberate strategies are never exercised with more effect than in choosing the mask of the narrator.

Very occasionally in my working life I have used the masks to play a deliberate game with the reader. There seems to me to be a fundamental difference between choosing and wearing the narrative masks for storytelling—what I would call a "fictional" use—and playing about with the very fact that masks must be worn—what I would call metafictional use. Metafiction is very much a dominant form in modern adult fiction; it is difficult to write it for children, who being newly started as readers are apt to miss the sort of cultural and cross-cultural reference on which metafiction often depends. I rather tend to deplore messing about with the mask instead of just picking it up and speaking through it, but in *Unleaving* (1976) I did try a trick with the masks. Safely out of sight myself, behind one of the god's-eye-view covers, I tried to induce young readers to identify with a character—Madge—so strongly when she was young that they would be tricked into finding themselves inside the skin of an old woman later in the book. That the old character and the young character are the same person is knowledge withheld until late in the story. I wondered how many readers would guess, and how far they would read before guessing. This book is much more widely liked than I had expected it to be and has brought me some of the best readers' letters I have ever had, but the readers' reactions are disconcerting just the same. Some readers guessed too soon, and others didn't guess at all what I was up to, and I have yet to hear from a reader who finds the trick central to his or her experience of the book. Truly, what is going on in a work of fiction is much larger than what the author thinks is going on.

I have played a trick with narrative voice in a much simpler book than *Unleaving*, and one for younger readers—*The Green Book* (1981). In this the fact that the story you are reading is being told—written into a green notebook, by one of the characters—is not revealed until the end. And here I have clear testimony that the strategy doesn't work very well. The book has been abridged several times for inclusion in anthologies and English textbooks, and unfailingly the adult abridgers remove the little touches, the comment on the child's courage, the childish turns of phrase, that might clue you to guessing who the narrator is.

There's very little doubt, really, that games with the narrative voice are always chancy and simple mask wearing best, but not, if I am to believe my letter file, because children don't understand metafiction. Some of the sharpest comments I have ever had have come from young readers, and some of the most obtuse from the grown-up.

I would like to return now to the more shadowy meaning of "voice" and consider the meaning that "narrative voice" has when we recognize a passage as being by a certain author, or feel that the whole effect of a work is recognizably that of a personality we know from other books. In one sense an author's narrative voice is not designed or chosen, and cannot be altered, any more than a speaking voice can, or a fingerprint, or a time in which to be born or die. You might think, after what I have been saying about masks, that the mask would entirely eliminate this personal aura, and it is true that mask wearing has some wonderful effects. The masks, which put the author in touch with things that the flesh-and-blood waking author did not know he or she knew, gives, sometimes, extra stature, extra understanding, in a way that astonishes everyone.

The process of writing, when you stand yourself out of the way, sometimes allows the mask to speak with a better, wiser, finer voice than your own. But, alas! There are limits. For one thing, not everybody can wear every mask. Some are just too heavy, too difficult, too light, too small, somehow outside one's range. Even masked, even a brilliant elderly male actor would have trouble playing a delicious bimbo; the most wonderful high school actress ever, however masked, would have trouble with King Lear.

And however professionally you have laid aside your personal, conscious feelings and opinions, the things you don't know you think, the feelings you wish you did not feel, somehow get into the utterance through the mask. These uncontrollable things are part of the impression you give as a mask wearer; they are nearly impossible to pin down, and yet they hallmark every paragraph you write. This penumbra is what we love, like, hate, in the writers that we read, as it is in people that we know. If you dislike someone it is often for things they cannot help; if you don't like a writer's work it may be just the same thing, but you may not be able to help it either!

And here we have reached a matter which is at the heart of writing for children. Some adults don't like children much. Many more think they like children but cannot bring themselves to take them very seriously. The only mask they think appropriate for telling stories to children is a cheap and vulgar one. Children like fooling and will watch a clown for an hour or two. The pretend friend, the one who wears a simple or vulgar mask because he or she assumes you would be baffled by a finer one, on the other hand, is not much liked. And most tiresome of all is the person who is only pretending to be a storyteller, who dodges around the mask all the time, telling you what to do and think, spoiling the show.

One final point. The masks we have available to choose from are almost all very ancient and were first made in societies that did not divide the audience into young and old, educated and ignorant. They do not adapt very well to talking down to people. They sit most comfortably and work best when they are used to enable the author to claim—just for a while, just while the story is being told—equality with the audience. There are masks for enacting superiority to an audience—the masks of preachers and teachers and visionaries. But the narrative masks are all apt to fall off if you look down with them, leaving you barefaced. You must find an audience you can look level at, or leave the masks on the wall.

REFERENCES

Thackeray, William M. *Vanity Fair*. 1st pub. 1847; London: Methuen, 1963.
Walsh, Jill Paton. *A Chance Child*. New York: Farrar, Straus, Giroux, 1978.
———. *The Green Book*. New York: Farrar, Straus, Giroux, 1981.
———. *Unleaving*. New York: Farrar, Straus, Giroux, 1976.

18

The Search for the Authentic Voice for the Telling of a West African Experience

ANN GRIFALCONI

The attempt to condense an experience, develop a tale or tales, and capture the right voice to tell the tales—all these are woven out of the experience and upon the loom the mind's eye creates.

One goes to a place because in one's heart and mind, one is there already. But one must concentrate on this—it seems—for a long, long time, until the other side is a real, firm, solid place to be.

For me, this other place, the place I wanted to be—from at least the age of sixteen—was Africa. Twenty-five years later I went there. But by that time, I had made it real for me—a place to stand.

When I got there, it also became a place to feel, a people to listen to, a way of life that became a part of my own experience. And so it was that form became filled with substance; outlines filled with color; imagination became suffused with sounds and voices and odors, intermingled with the equatorial heat of day and the mountain coolness of night.

And the journey of years of "going to" became a turning point, becoming years of savoring what had been verified, what had been made new, and those infinitesimal thousand wonders of people and place, of nature and resistance, and love and perseverance that would one day integrate themselves into my own understanding of life.

But in truth, upon reflection, I believe I was not looking for just a place or variety, but for something in common—the "voice" that I had known and recognized all my life, the universal human voice. For the African voice is a richly human voice, a family voice speaking, creating possibilities and change, creation itself.

In Africa, they say "Word is Seed." It is believed that the husband whispers into the shell of his wife's ear and so the word-child becomes the human-child, that one says "courage" and becomes courageous, that one says "water" and the rains come. So the power of the spoken word imbues the imagination—an uttered seed flowers in the ear of the world.

And "Africa!", once uttered, became real for me.

I discovered that the oral tradition in Africa is a tradition of creative power and strength. Stories are born for a purpose and as instruction to the imagination of the young, becoming real in their actions and relationships. Every African is an actor in the family and tribal dramas and also a teller of those tales. Respondents hear, call back, move in a chorus of response and answer, a rhythm of voice and gesture. There is humor and laughter and a fine and dramatic sense of timing, based on clear-eyed observations of human foibles and from a life lived in communion with field and fowl, and creatures of all kinds.

And here the conveyance of ideas is not limited to voiced words: in drums as well as speech, texture is important. The rough, mixed chorus of male and female voices is equivalent to the leaf-muted drum, the single trumpeted voice and the drummed chorus answering, even over great distances.

In Africa, there are the famous and traveled storytellers too, the Griots, who also carry the entire history of the tribe in their heads. Those of this captivating trade usually develop impressive and formal beginnings and endings to their tales and use all the nuances of tone, rhythm, caricature, and gesture that an experienced African village audience expects and enjoys.

How do storytellers go about attracting and capturing their audiences? Through the ear first of all, through the voice, using the word and the texture and the beat—the infectious rhythms of life itself—telling a story first created in the heart's eye and then made real in the imagination of the listener.

An African narrator may have a different set of possibilities than other narrators, yet shares the universal human need to convey a special view of the ways of the world and of human relationships.

So much of this texture and way of telling was already resting in my own inner ear when I decided to write about this experience. I had been there, had heard so much African speech and so many spoken tales, and had picked up something impossible to find simply by reading: the significant emphasis, the attitude toward life, and the reverence for the spirits of all forms of life about us.

These emphases suggested that my chosen narrator must be open to wonder, the awe in all of us for the powers of love or nature or magic. It is this special quality that makes a good storyteller—one who knows, but does not know everything, one who reveals as it is being revealed. The narrator's voice rings with the truth and immediacy of discovery: the diver bringing back a pearl from the sea; the old woman revealing the accumulated wisdom of a people through a lifetime of loving, stern experience; the adult remembering the joys and discoveries of childhood and how to be; the child revealing the pain and anguish of growing up to that later revealed understanding, yet finding solace in those small moments of impressive comprehension that we call awareness. It is the author's task to listen honestly and with the purest of intentions to that voice, to that set of unique moments of convictions that is perhaps imaginary, yet very real, the narrator tells us. In this way, the narrator may offer others authentic moments of discovery.

How does an author decide to listen to one and not to another's voice, preferring one voice over another, one view over another? By choosing that voice which seems to know.

We as viewers/listeners really only want to carry away with us one clear view, a way to understand the whole from a true part representative of that whole, enough for one small moment. So we seek the narrator who can give the reader the gist, the live chunk of experience, with words the reader can understand (and a few magic new ones to think on), and powerful images so that the reader can "see."

In my *Village of Round and Square Houses* (1986), first of a series of tales about a unique African village where I had actually stayed, I chose the girl who brought us there as the narrator, Osa. As a character/narrator, Osa could tell, in the first person, what it was like to grow up in a village where the women lived in round houses and the men lived in square ones.

From this immediate experience, it was natural then to turn to her grandmother to find out "How did all this come about?" Known as the best storyteller in the whole village, she would be the one who knew best how to tell of such far-off times of legend, as a skillful weaver of mysterious effects is needed here! So while the girl remembers, it is Gran'ma Tika's voice that tells the founding myth, but both use the rhythmic, African storyteller manner.

Darkness and the Butterfly (1987), another book set in the same African village, deals with young Osa's fear of the dark. I chose an adult narrator to speak soothingly and rhythmically, as if telling us this was a fear any child could conquer, as the unfolding of the story shows. Thus, from the outset, by the narrator being an omniscient observer, the child's fears were placed in the context of the larger African culture, which recognized magic, dreams, and transformation in handling its fears, in a way admitted to even by the "wisest" adult, and Osa is allowed to reach her own solution within the universal context of a protected, evolving childhood.

Now if the child Osa had told the story, she would have been buried in her fears and might have buried the fearful child reader with her! Yet the adult narrator faithfully follows the child's own experiences in a process that ventures slowly and carefully, both wider and deeper, into self-recognition and change.

To establish this universal storyteller context in *Darkness and the Butterfly*, the narrator, in order to get the attention and cooperation of the listener/reader, begins in a conspiratorial, intimate manner (probably in a half-whisper): "Have you ever been afraid of the dark?" Then the narrator commences the story itself in a more typically formal storyteller's manner: louder, slower, with "big" rhythms:

> Not too long ago, nor far away,
> Where spirits live in the trees and rocks,
> And in the animals that roam at night,
> There was a bright and pretty girl named Osa
> Who was *so* afraid of the dark. . . .

After Osa has adventured, been lost, been rescued, and shared the reason for her fears with the Wise Woman ("that she is too small—the smallest of the small"), the Wise Woman points out that the butterfly is still small, but flies on. Then Osa finally falls asleep. "Osa dreamed that the yellow butterfly flew by, / shining brightly—as if it carried its own light inside."

Osa tries to follow it, doubts herself, and loses its guiding light. The dream allows her to fail and then to find her own strength, transforming her understanding upon awakening, as Osa finds that she is willing to go home alone through the darkening night and that she need not be afraid anymore.

The narrator/storyteller resumes the more formal voice in rounding off the end of the story:

> And that is how it came about
> That Osa—the smallest of the small—
> Found the way to carry her own light thru the darkness
> For all the days and nights of her life to come!

In a third book, *Osa's Pride* (1989), set in the same African village, I returned to the first person girl narrator, Osa, as she tells us how she learned that such things as foolish pride can be recognized, even in oneself. Again looking back on herself from an adult point of view, we see that she is "telling on herself"—it must not be that bad! This time, the focus is on the way the adults in her family handle her pride, in a manner typically indirect and African: by parable (Gran'ma telling and showing a story about someone else) and allusion (Uncle Domo relating an adage)—bringing Osa to her own ultimate conclusions, which she states in her own language: " 'I may not be any *better* than anyone else . . . / But I'm no *worse*, either!' "

But behind the scenes, of course, is the author, the true and authentic narrative voice actually transmitting the tales. And onstage, by the author's choice, is the narrator, working here in the African storyteller's tradition—through the use of musicality and parable, of symbol and fable—to demonstrate the wonder and validity of the West African experience, an experience that is real and imagined and remembered.

REFERENCES

Grifalconi, Ann. *Darkness and the Butterfly*. Boston: Little, Brown, 1987.
———. *Osa's Pride*. Boston: Little, Brown, 1989.
———. *Village of Round and Square Houses*. Boston: Little, Brown, 1986.

19

Rabble Starkey: A Voice from a Surprising Place

LOIS LOWRY

I was a child in the 1940s—the great comic book years. While in retrospect I would love to be able to say that I disdained such things and concentrated instead on the classics, the truth is that I spent countless months of my childhood obsessed by comics, squandering my allowance, hoarding, sorting, stacking, storing, trading, and poring over the flimsy issues of Captain Marvel, Little Lulu, and the rest.

And I loved the back covers. Those were the pages, you'll recall, that promised you grand things for a small price. The Charles Atlas ads promised muscles and power over bullies. The decoder rings and invisible ink promised detecting skills the equal of Dick Tracy's.

I liked the ads that talked about voice. THROW YOUR VOICE AND AMAZE YOUR FRIENDS. The promise of amazing my friends was not really the seductive element to me. It was simply the idea of *controlling* my own voice, placing it somewhere else, speaking out of a milk bottle, perhaps, or from the pleated valance at the top of the draperies, rather the way the voice of God might come, from on high.

Wisely, I never sent money off to the box number that promised to make me a ventriloquist. I don't know why. Probably I never had the required amount of cash—I think they were talking three figures. Perhaps I suspected, even then, that disappointment would be the outcome.

Maybe it was simply enough to speculate, to speculate on the power of hearing my own voice speak from a place beyond my usual reach. Me—and recognizable—but from a new and surprising place.

And so, eventually, I became a writer.

"We had us a big war in our neighborhood that summer, and the only one on my side was Gunther. And shoot, Gunther was worthless as sin, he was only five and he had pinworms, to boot."

The voice of the narrator whose name would prove to be Rabble Starkey appeared unbidden, in the form of those two sentences, about a year before I began to write the book. I wrote the sentences down, of course. They intrigued me. I could picture Gunther; whoever he was, he was clearly scrawny and sickly, probably a misfit, even at five.

I had no idea who the narrator was, or where she (it was quite clear to me that it was a "she") came from. And I was puzzled by the "war" that was part of the image. I couldn't figure out what battle this less-than-articulate narrator was waging.

But I knew she would come back, and so I wrote the sentences down, and waited.

The waiting is always the hard part. I think most writers of fiction must go through it—that period when an image: audible, as mine was, or visual (John Fowles describes the months before he wrote *The French Lieutenant's Woman*: "A woman stands at the end of a deserted quay and looks out to sea. That was all. This image rose in my mind one morning when I was in bed half asleep. . . . I began to fall in love with her.") begins to surface in the consciousness.

It floats to the top again and again. It changes, expands, and reveals itself. But it is a slow process.

When, at last, I sat down with the opening sentences, the narrator's voice seemed more focused, and indeed it focused on four words: summer, neighborhood, war, and Gunther. From those elements, and from the speaker herself, I would begin to make a story.

By the time the story was complete, those original sentences were gone. Many things were changed: on a trivial level, Gunther's pinworms were elevated into a slightly more socially acceptable ringworm; and higher up the literary scale, the reference to "war," which I had envisioned as a childhood scuffle, had expanded to include all the emotional battles through which one achieves maturity.

As for Rabble—who, incidentally, told me her name as I was typing her story (I'm sorry. But that's how it happened, and other writers will tell you the same thing)—hers was the voice through whom I spoke, and it certainly is not the voice I use when I am speaking to my mailman, or my children, or to the American Booksellers' Association. Nor is it a voice I hear on the streets of Boston or New Hampshire, the two places where I now live.

But the voice of any writer comes through the voices that pervade that writer's past: the voices of parents and grandparents and siblings and friends and teachers and nursemaids, and the voices of the bullies who lived in the next block, and the trashy children you weren't supposed to play with because they might have lice.

Many of those tangential voices from my own past are those of long-forgotten people. I wouldn't be able, now, to tell you the names of every classmate in the small southern Pennsylvania town where I went through elementary school, or every friend in the northern tip of the Blue Ridge Mountains where I spent childhood summers. Nor could I tell you many names of people from the part of South Carolina where I lived for a year when I was twenty-two.

But their cadences and diction have stayed with me, as part of my perception and experience. They became the cadence and diction of Rabble Starkey's voice, and each day, when I sat down at the typewriter, they became part of my voice, as well.

Why did that voice, that diction, that tone, emerge for that particular book? Why not the wry and outspoken voice of Anastasia Krupnik, or the more lyrical, innocent, and introspective voice of Elizabeth of *Autumn Street* (1980)? I can only guess. My guess is that Anastasia and Elizabeth's lives are too much like my own: secure, almost predictable; conventional, comfortable, and safe. Their voices—my voice, writing through and about them—contain that certainty; and even when plot demands in those books inflict tension, the sureness remains.

But *Rabble Starkey* (1987) was to be different. This was a book about life of a different sort—the life of families, once again, to be sure, but families of an unconventional sort, whose lives were to be less predictable, less secure. These were people of a different world from the world of my own childhood. Here was a world where pickups are the vehicle of choice, wedding pictures might be a strip from a dime store booth, and the beauty queen of yesterday might well today be waitressing in a restaurant where the orders are shouted to the kitchen through a hole in the wall. I needed a unique tone and sense of place. I needed a setting where uncomplicated values were treasured and where sophisticated trappings were alien. When I put fourteen-year-old Sweet Hosanna Starkey on a Greyhound bus with her unnamed baby, and let her travel home, I needed a home that would welcome her back. I needed a place where people would speak in a slow and unschooled way, so that their welcome would be believable.

I began to see, in my mind, the place where my brother lives today. He is a doctor in the foothills of the Appalachian Mountains. His patients have more often been mauled by bears than shot in a subway. They are people of slow speech and strong sentiment, simple lives and sturdy virtues.

I began to hear their voices, and among their voices was Rabble Starkey's. So I let Rabble herself tell me about her early years in rural West Virginia. She did it in her own voice. It is difficult to describe that phenomenon without sounding uncomfortably New Age and Shirley MacLainian. But it is, take my word for it, something that simply happens. When—after the necessary waiting—I sat down that first day, and typed, "We had us a big war in our neighborhood that summer, and the only one on my side was

Gunther," I *became* Rabble Starkey, and she became me. Or, to be more precise, we had always been the same person and the same voice, but for the first time we discovered and acknowledged that.

It was the old THROW YOUR VOICE AND AMAZE YOUR FRIENDS trick, after all. It was me—it was me all the time—but it was coming from a new and surprising place.

But let me put things into a lighter perspective, too, by telling you of a conversation I once had with a New York cab driver, an aspiring author himself, who had asked about the process of writing. I talked—at too great length, I suspect—about memories and imagination and dreams, and about how all of those things come together with a kind of magic that creates the writer's voice.

I could see that he was shifting in his seat, increasingly glum.

Finally, when I paused for breath, he sighed and said, "Leon Uris was in this cab once and he didn't say nothing about all that magic shit. He told me to use index cards."

REFERENCES

Fowles, John. "Notes on an Unfinished Novel." In *Afterwords*, edited by Thomas McCormack, 161–62. New York: Harper and Row, 1969.

Lowry, Lois. *Autumn Street*. Boston: Houghton, 1980.

———. *Rabble Starkey*. Boston: Houghton, 1987.

THE CRITICAL VOICE

20

Henry James and the Storyteller: The Development of a Central Consciousness in Realistic Fiction for Children

LOIS R. KUZNETS

The critical theories of Henry James have been, for the most part, applied only to adult fiction. Indeed, as Felicity Hughes demonstrates, James took some pains to disassociate his realism from the "family novel," disparaging both the child and the female reader in the process. He can be seen as partly responsible for the low critical esteem into which children's literature fell after the early twentieth century. Moreover, James' ideas about narrative stance and his followers' disdain for the intrusive, often didactic narrator— the typical voice of early realistic children's literature—made children's fiction seem especially unpalatable aesthetically (Booth, chaps. 1, 2). Nevertheless, James' criticism and practice—particularly his concept of a central consciousness or intelligence—provided one promising direction for aesthetically satisfying and subtle development of point of view in realistic literature for children and young adults in the twentieth century.

As a critic of his own writing, James was concerned with working out an aesthetic for the novel that would account for his own practice with regard to point of view, a practice that he developed over time and that found its fullest—and to James most satisfying—embodiment in Lambert Strether of *The Ambassadors* (1903)—the creation of a central intelligence or consciousness, which is not, however, expressed in the first person. The narrative of the central consciousness through which all of the scenes and action are filtered is distinguished from omniscient narration by the stringency of its limitation to the experience and perception of a single character, controlled from without by an unintrusive third-person narrator who engineers a plot and a supporting cast that will eventually bring that character, and the reader along with him or her, to some recognition of what is "really" going on (Blackmur, xvii–iii).

In his prefaces to the New York edition of his novels (1907–09), James explored the nature of this consciousness. He saw it as both perceptive and blundering, working its way and developing through the course of the novel, and striving toward a kind of moral enlightenment based on experience (James, 63). On the way to Strether, he used both the consciousness of a young woman, Isabel Archer, in *The Portrait of a Lady* (1881), and of a female child—Maisie— of *What Maisie Knew* (1897). In the prefaces of these novels, he examines the problem of making the perceptions and the concerns of the young female and of the child as "interesting" as he conceived Strether's intrinsically to be. To his credit, James succeeded in expressing the consciousness of both young females without conveying any of the disdain that he, in earlier essays, evinces for the child and/or female reader of the family novel.

James is most satisfied by an achieved enlightenment that is finally ironic. In the case of Maisie, irony lies in the fact that this enlightenment is against conventional morality; in the case of Isabel Archer, it is prematurely crippling and, in the case of Lambert Strether, too late in arriving. This particular kind of irony does not lend itself well to children's novels, although it can often be found in young adult fiction. Nevertheless, the fact that James conceives of this central consciousness as both inherently competent and developmentally vital makes it an excellent vehicle for the *Bildungsroman* or novel of individual development, a form with an important place in realistic children's and young adult literature.

In fact, however, the development of a central consciousness was not the point of view of choice of many realistic novels for children and young adults in the twentieth century. Until the mid-twentieth century, children's writers often opted for an unobtrusive omniscient narrator, creating the illusion of an unmediated story, or, on occasion, still chose the intrusive storyteller, no longer explicitly didactic, but now rather chummy or expository.

During the mid-twentieth century, moreover, the most apparent voice of choice became that of the protagonist in the first person, which, by eliminating the mediation entirely, directly confronts the reader and tells its own story. First person child narration had been used with comic effect by Charles Dickens in his *A Holiday Romance* (1868) and with ironic effect by Mark Twain in *Huckleberry Finn* (1884). But, in the late nineteenth and early twentieth centuries, with the exception of E. Nesbit in her Bastable stories (*The Story of the Treasure Seekers* [1899], *The Wouldbegoods* [1901], and *The New Treasure Seekers* [1904]), few writers had experimented extensively with the use of the first person child narrator in realistic fiction for young readers.

Then, with the advent of J. D. Salinger's *Catcher in the Rye* (1951), a wave of first-person stories for young adults began to appear. This form of narration seemed particularly attractive for the problem-oriented domestic story in which the adolescent protagonist saw himself or herself in opposition to surrounding adults, when adults became—in total contrast to the early domestic realism—"part of the problem" rather than "part of the solution." As time went on, this point of view became associated with "New Realism" and books for pre-adolescent readers as well. For instance, this voice suits the purposes of popular writer Judy Blume. Through such a narrative stance, she seems able to bring about quick, relatively unquestioning identification of young readers with her protagonists.

This skill is not to be scorned as a means of circumventing an intrusive omniscient narrator and focusing on the young protagonist. Still, the first-person form of narration has limitations that James himself noted in regard to realistic fiction. This voice, according to James, leads to a certain "loose-ness" in composition (which he finds in Proust for instance) and, somewhat paradoxically, may be used to prevent "real contact" with the consciousness of the central character, who can be an unreliable witness even of his or her psychological events (James, 320–21). DeLuca, surveying adolescent liter-ature, has also commented upon the narrowness of vision that the first-person point of view seems to create. This narrowness seems particularly evident in first-person fiction for young adults and children when the author seems unable to incorporate in the text any measures of the narrator's re-liability. The child reader is then never forced to question identification with this character.

For those who, as I do, consider unquestioning identification with the protagonist to be not only naive but a type of reading to be gradually shed as one matures, first-person point of view as it appears in children's and young adult literature can seem severely limited. This limitation can, of course, sometimes be overcome by very skillful writers who manage to incorporate measures of the narrator's reliability in the text. For example, one of the charms of Nesbit's Bastable stories is the manner in which Oswald is forced to convey the ways he himself is obtuse and self-serving in the very process of pretending to be alert and modest. His exaggerated sense of his own importance and superiority to girls and poets is checked by the events and the eloquence of others that he duly records. Similarly, in *Where the Lilies Bloom* (1969), the Cleavers skillfully circumvent their very attractive and generally perceptive first-person narrator, Mary Call, in scenes like the one where she suddenly discovers that Devola, the "simple" older sister whom Mary Call patronizes, has learned to drive. This scene requires a reassessment on the part of the reader, who hitherto may have assumed that Mary Call's view of reality constituted *the* reality of the book; it prepares those readers for an ending that is not the one most desired by Mary Call.

Other first-person narrators, like Karana in Scott O'Dell's *The Island of the Blue Dolphins* (1960), help the young reader to overcome a distance from a protagonist of another race and time. The use of a central conscious-ness might not at the same time have enabled O'Dell to leave to the epi-logue—where it would not overshadow the affirmation of the novel—the ironic, historically accurate ending to Karana's struggle to create a community on an island abandoned by humans.

In Nesbit's or in the Cleavers' work—where subtle reversals of identification may occur—even adult readers are frequently fooled by these reversals. Such reversals contribute to the complexity of the books: they assume an experienced young reader, but they provide no supportive material to help the young reader to determine the reliability of the narrator. Books, however, that employ a central consciousness provide a different kind of support for the young reader, establishing a point of identification but giving more opportunity for measuring that central character's perceptions within the total world created by the book.

Another reason for an author to use the central consciousness is aesthetic. As James says in his discussion of *What Maisie Knew*, "Small children have many more perceptions than they have terms to translate them; their vision is much richer, their apprehension even constantly stronger, than their prompt, their at all producible, vocabulary" (145). In practice and in contrast to the first-person point of view, the use of a central consciousness seems frequently to give freedom to the author to expand the boundaries of language aesthetically. An author may use syntactically complex and imagistic prose that might seem realistically inappropriate to a child or even adolescent narrator, and, hence, produce a stylistically dense work.

Although first-person narration has been the most striking development in realistic fiction for young people, books employing some version of the Jamesian central consciousness have appeared throughout this century. An interesting early example is Nesbit's exploration of the consciousness of only one of the three children she depicts in *The Railway Children* (1906). There Nesbit employs a mixed point of view, alternating between a chummy intrusive narrator and insight into the consciousness of a responsible older daughter, Roberta, called Bobbie, whose superior sensitivity and perception (with the help of some narrative coincidence) make her not only her mother's principal support but the virtual rescuer of her falsely imprisoned father. Bobbie's narratively undeveloped consciousness, which Nesbit combines with the more obvious intrusive narrator in this early twentieth-century realistic text, adds a special dimension to an otherwise rather formulaic family story of survival through hard and jolly good times.

Partly because Bobbie's perceptions frequently seem to run directly counter to those of her younger brother Peter, whose consciousness is not explored, Nesbit seems to be confirming James' dictum about his own choice of central consciousness in *What Maisie Knew*: "I at once recognized, that my light vessel of consciousness . . . couldn't be with verisimilitude a rude little boy; since, beyond the fact that little boys are never so 'present,' the sensibility of the female young is indubitably, for early youth, the greater, and my plan would call, on the part of my protagonist, for 'no end' of sensibility" (James, 143–44).

Such sexual stereotyping, rather similar to Lewis Carroll's implication that little boys turn easily into pigs, is *not* confirmed by the four following examples of the use of a central consciousness, the first two of which focus on young boys who are very much "present" and far from "rude": Marjorie Kinnan Rawlings' *The Yearling* (1938), William Armstrong's *Sounder* (1969), Jean George's *Julie of the Wolves* (1972) and Mollie Hunter's *A Sound of Chariots* (1972). I will consider each book briefly from two angles: what version of a central consciousness appears in the work and what effects on the reader this choice of narrator might create.

THE LONELY SON AS CENTRAL CONSCIOUSNESS

In contrast to *The Railway Children*, Rawlings' *The Yearling* makes full use of a central consciousness in a text thoroughly purged of the intrusive narrator. Signal is given almost immediately of the particular narrative voice. The first three sentences impersonally establish the rural setting; then we move right into this consciousness and never leave it: "The boy Jody watched it [the sky], speculating." The close relationship between the setting and consciousness maintains itself throughout the story of an adolescent boy, living on an isolated farm in backwoods Florida, who must find fulfillment of his needs for companionship largely through nature and animals, and who must bend to the hard laws that such a landscape imposes on its dirt poor inhabitants. As she states in the introduction to the 1941 edition, Rawlings set out to write a *Bildungsroman*, "to tell of a year in the life of a sensitive boy who should be a man, through sorrow and knowledge, at the end of it" (x).

Jody's consciousness permits empathy with a parent. His closest connection is with his alert, nature-loving father, Penny Baxter, rather than his mother, whose own consciousness seems to have been maimed by the harsh life and the early deaths of several other children. In this fully developed use of the central consciousness, we can see Jody's consciousness as first formed by Penny and then perpetuating the close relationship between them. Penny's nurturing of Jody is then passed on by Jody to Flag, the yearling deer whom Jody brings up and then must destroy.

This consciousness becomes a vehicle not only for the transmission of Penny's nurturing ways and of love for this harsh countryside, but for the expression of Rawlings' own love for the Florida scrub. Through it, long descriptions of nature are made palatable to the young reader by Jody's connection with them—his imbuing them with his own emotional set— although they are not expressed in the English of the dialect that Jody and his family speak, which has both charm and limitations.

One example will have to suffice to show a consciousness that makes connections at a deep level unlikely to be expressed in a first-person narration for reasons of age and understanding. Here Jody must run for help to the

Forrester clan, with whom his family has recently quarreled. Penny has just been bitten by a rattlesnake and has shot a doe in order to use its liver to draw out the poison. The doe's fawn (Flag) has appeared, sniffing her carcass. Jody sets off, running:

> He came to the tall trees of the island. They startled him, because they meant that he was now so close . . . he halted a moment under the shadowy live oaks, planning. It was twilight. He was sure it was not time for darkness. The rain clouds were not clouds, but an infusion of the sky and had now filled it entirely. The only light was a strand of green across the west, the color of the doe's flesh with the venom on it. (149)

Such vivid associative imagery as found in the last line of this passage pervades the book, enmeshing the reader in this consciousness.

The use of this central consciousness permits a sense of identification with Jody throughout his love and loss of the yearling, but also allows for a vision that picks up what might not register consciously with an adolescent with his or her own needs and hostilities, such as the overheard interchange between his father and mother:

> She said: "Seems like bein' hard is the only way I kin stand it [sorrow and loss]."
> He [Penny] left his breakfast and went to her and stroked her hair.
> "I know. Jest be a leetle mit easy on t'other feller." (212)

Strangely enough, Rawlings herself set out to depict in Ma Baxter "a picture of all nagging wives and mothers" and found herself more understanding as she continued with the story (x). This understanding might not have been achieved had all been depicted not only through Jody's eyes, but in his own limited first-person version of their relationship. Hostility rather than understanding seems especially likely because it is Ma who, because of Penny's illness and Jody's refusal, is left to fire the first shot at Flag, the yearling, who has been devastating their crops; Ma, a poor shot, so maims the creature that Jody is forced to put him out of his misery.

Jody's subsequent anger and rejection are given full vent in his running away. The use of a central consciousness, however, permits Rawlings to create in *The Yearling* a vivid world wider than that of the protagonist's conscious recognition. She does this without loss of immediacy and identification with the lonely boy forced by circumstances beyond his control to kill the thing he loves and then forgive his parents for the roles harsh necessity has forced upon them.

THE BOY, ALONE, AS CENTRAL CONSCIOUSNESS

William Armstrong's *Sounder* provides another fine example of the use of a central consciousness within a *Bildungsroman*, although here clearly a

mixed use, combined as it is with the distant voice of an omniscient unintrusive narrator. The effect of this combined point of view has been the focus
for controversy over the nature of the book as representative of Black life.
The world here, both as perceived omnisciently and through the eyes of the
unnamed boy, has met with much resistance from Black critics and others
who, with some justification, find this world lacking in the familial, communal, and emotional supports that they perceive to be characteristic of the
Black community (and part of the southern White community as well) (Huse).

The first chapter begins with a distant omniscient point of view exercising
godlike privileges not only of viewing the Black sharecropping family as a
whole as they are balanced on the edge of tragedy, but of surveying a lonely
landscape in which the "white man who owned the vast endless fields had
scattered the cabins of his Negro sharecroppers far apart, like flyspecks on
a whitewashed ceiling" (2). The same voice describes the opposite, socially
integrating effect of Sounder's booming voice: "Each bark bounced from
slope to slope in foothills like a rubber ball. . . . It filled up the night and
made music as though the branches of all the trees were being pulled across
silver strings" (5). Toward the end of the chapter one begins to enter the
boy's consciousness as he crawls into bed, taking comfort in the freshness
of his pillow and the warmth of his little brother's body.

The boy's consciousness, like that of Bobbie in *The Railway Children*, is
thereafter highlighted in the midst of a family, parents and siblings, to whom
we do not have similar access. In *Sounder*, however, even more than in *The
Yearling*, we see a child whose family cannot form a protective barrier against
the harsh demands of a world in which adults as well as children have
relatively little power. Our access to the intensity of experience of the boy
becomes almost overwhelming—isolated as his consciousness is in a world
painfully silenced and largely helpless or hostile. Armstrong insists on making
this experience all the more vivid by tuning the boy's receptivity to the
highest pitch, so that every sight and smell, the slightest sound, carries a
heavy load of associations that reinforce our sense of the violence that has
been done to his family and the mutilation that surrounds him, symbolized
at first by the maiming of the dog.

The *leitmotiv* of mutilation is particularly important to the novel (Kuznets).
The central consciousness sustains this theme, which is eventually articulated
by the Black male teacher who becomes the point of identification for that
consciousness, taking the place of the father (chap. 7). Particularly inspiring
is the way in which the boy's consciousness is *not* maimed in spite of his
bearing witness to the mutilation of father and beloved dog, his being
forced—in order to read—to fish out of a trash bin a torn volume of supportive
prose, his suffering physical injuries at the hands of a prison guard.

The bestiality of the forces of law and order—contrasted with the humanity
of such beasts as Sounder—might well have been met by physical hostility
on the part of the boy. One longs for it; however, Armstrong's book is a

testament to the philosophy not only of Montaigne—who claims that "malicious and inhuman animosity and fierceness are usually accompanied by weakness" (90)—but to the passive resistance of Gandhi and Martin Luther King. Nevertheless, through access to the boy's consciousness the reader is permitted some relief. We can visualize with him, for instance, the red neck of the prison warden as that of a bull in the slaughterhouse after this warden has mutilated the Christmas cake that stands for the family's love and sacrifice. The boy's daydreams of reactive violence provide a necessary outlet for both boy and reader alike, until both can rest easy at the home of the teacher. This resting place can be reached only at the end of the "lonesome road" that is the subject of the mother's song.

Armstrong's attempt to write the story of an individual Black man who influenced his own childhood (if we are to believe the introduction to *Sounder*) led him to intensify the identification through the use of a central consciousness that must struggle to bear the practically unbearable; in it one can find no excuse for the violence that seeks to destroy a family whose existence is already marginal. *Les Misérables* is here seen through the eyes of a child. In this case, the use of a central consciousness supports the reliability of the protagonist, who starts out bewildered by events and ends wise.

Escaping, through the use of a central consciousness, a "realistic" reproduction of the language that the young boy and his family would have spoken in a first-person account, Armstrong employs also a prose that he attempted, in its omniscient voice, to make close to the voices of the Old Testament. However controversial this presentation, its devastating power cannot be denied.

THE GIRL, ALONE, AS CENTRAL CONSCIOUSNESS

Through the consciousness of Julie-Miyax, the Inuit protagonist of *Julie of the Wolves*, we suddenly find ourselves looking at the arctic sun, which, like the natural landscape in *The Yearling*, is imbued with the perceptions of the protagonist: "It was a yellow disc in a lime-green sky, the colors of six o'clock in the evening and the time when the wolves awoke" (5). We are also led quickly to watch the wolves as she does—as her father taught her. Thus we see them not as enemies and embodiments of evil, as would be natural to *us*—bred as we have been until recently on horror stories of wolves—but as possible allies, a ready-made family, in the battle against the arctic winter.

The identification with this child of another race and experience begins at once, at the most thrilling moment, for the story is not told in the order that it might well have been in a first-person narrative, that is, from the beginning. Rather, it begins *in medias res*. This structure allows George to build desired connections with the bleak natural setting and the wolves, to establish sympathies that cannot be broken. She does not permit the reader, for instance, to hope with Julie for a pink bedroom in San Francisco offered by her American pen pal as the solution to present problems. By the time the reader learns about that room, an arctic year has already passed in a far more exciting setting, which Miyax has mastered through the help of the wolves and memories of her father's practice and teaching.

The glory of part one, where Julie has changed into Miyax, permeates the flashback in part two, where the reader learns how Julie has left behind the unsatisfactory solutions that she and her society sought after her mother's death and her father's later disappearance. By part three, the reader is ready for Miyax's decision to remain in the traditional way of life, but perhaps not prepared for the irony in store for all in the impossibility of that decision. This irony is embodied in Miyax's last song to the wolf father who sustained her through the winter and who was shot from an airplane possibly flown by Julie's real father, Kapugen. (Now called "Charlie," this father, whom she eventually finds, has married a White woman and succumbed to the pleasures of American domestic plenty.) Her song reads:

> Amaroq, Amaroq, you are my adopted father.
> My feet dance because of you.
> My eyes see because of you.
> My mind thinks because of you. And it thinks, on
>   this thundering night,
> That the hour of the wolf and the Eskimo is over. (170)

So flexible is the use of the central consciousness that it permits here the opposite understanding to emerge from the one at the end of *The Yearling*. Rawlings permits no alternatives to loss because she sees the necessity for Jody's bowing his head to a natural law in which the family's survival is dependent on the death of his animal friend. Jody's return, "sadder but wiser," is imbued with little irony because Rawlings has made it seem simply another stage of his development and an expansion of consciousness. In contrast, George, a staunch conservationist, predicates her novel on the idea that natural law has been distorted by technological intervention and genocide—physical in the case of the wolves and cultural in the case of the Inuits. When Miyax returns to her father, she returns because no other place exists for her. We know, however, that this return to a father corrupted by "civilization" directly contradicts all that she has learned—it reverses the development of an Inuit identity that permeates this *Bildungsroman*. The shutting down of Julie-Miyax's consciousness is one of the many changes implied in her sad song. George's use of the central consciousness comes close to the usual Jamesian twist into irony in the harsh ending to the development of Miyax's consciousness.

THE GIRL ARTIST AS CENTRAL CONSCIOUSNESS

In *A Portrait of the Artist as a Young Man* (1916), James Joyce uses a combination of stream of consciousness with an omniscient narrator to bring alive the *Künstlerroman*—the novel of the artist's development. I am certainly not the first to point to Mollie Hunter's *A Sound of Chariots* (1972)—which uses a more noticeably controlled central consciousness—as an excellent example of what one can do with that species of realistic novel in the realm of children's literature (Molson, DeLuca). In this book, the reader is drawn into the consciousness of talented and passionate young Bridie, whose father has just died. She is forced, henceforth, to create a life for herself of which he would be proud, in an atmosphere unconducive to the full expression of the androgynous self that he had from birth encouraged in this—his favorite—daughter.

The funereal scene into which Bridie walks on the second page is first described in an omniscient voice, but from the moment someone present says, "Here's Bridie," we are plunged into her alert consciousness: "A chill of uneasiness ran over her and the picture presented by the two women focused suddenly in her vision with unnatural clarity of detail" (4). This alert consciousness is the one with which we remain throughout the rest of the book as Hunter, like George, manipulates the structure to begin *in medias res* and to include a flashback, which establishes Bridie's special relationship with her forceful, radical, war wounded father. When Hunter then brings us back to the moment when Bridie learns of his death, we know Bridie must face not only the material alterations of their lives, which have never been financially secure, but her loss of her special "place in the sun" of his esteem and her sense of identification with his consciousness.

In *A Sound of Chariots*, Hunter is working with a protagonist far more articulate than protagonists in the other books discussed above. Yet Hunter still does not choose the first-person voice, which would require giving up the central consciousness and the ways in which that point of view tests the protagonist's perceptions and expands upon them. By choosing this route, she is able also to stand back from the openly acknowledged autobiographical nature of the narrative and move beyond probable limitations of her early perceptions of her own life.

This fictionalizing of Hunter's *own* past development is accomplished without distorting its authenticity. Hunter recreates that past, emphasizing the ways in which language expressing experience plays a magnified part in development that it does not in the other novels considered. In addition, Hunter provides a complex overreaching imagistic structure in which dreams and reality continually overlap. This structure transcends Bridie's conscious recognition.

Particularly potent in this imagistic network is blood, which serves as a marker of experiences that betray "the closed circle of life and death in which she was caught" (170). This blood imagery is initially connected with night-mares of dismembered bodies that resemble the war wounded veterans in their state-provided housing, nightmares that develop power and scope after Bridie finds a medical book in which her mother had hopelessly searched for the answer to the father's illness. Blood then plays a part in other initially terrifying experiences that mark Bridie's determination to live life fully, unlike the grief-ridden adults that she sees around her. Yet these experiences, which remind her of her own mortality and spur her creativity, eventually bring about an empathy that she at first does not have with both the maimed veterans and her own frighteningly mournful mother. That empathy, a link with her father, is depicted here as an important development beyond the linguistic imagination and intellectual power that she has developed along the way.

The heightened consciousness that has become almost a cliché for the young artist ever since Joyce's paradigm of the *Künstlerroman* is here bound up in a web of connections and obligations of precisely the kind that Joyce attempts to have his hero slough off. But, in creating her own past consciousness through a Jamesian central consciousness that cannot cut itself off, Hunter seems to be emphasizing these very connections. One, therefore, might read the ending in which Bridie, constricted by corsets, is sent off to help her grandparents keep shop, as ironic in some of the ways *Julie of the Wolves* might be.

However, not only did Hunter herself succeed despite these encumbrances, but her portrait of the artist as a young woman seems to confirm the kind of development in community, rather than through separation, that feminist theorists like Carol Gilligan postulate as women's moral and ethical strength. Hunter depicts Bridie's father, modeled on her own, as consciously abjuring for himself that very separation for which the usual models of male strength have prepared him, enhancing our sense of androgynous possibilities signaled by his delighted words on the birth of still another daughter, Bridie: "You can have the other bairns, Agnes. This one's *mine!*"

Much remains to be said about ways in which these particular books are similar and yet different from each other. This study has emphasized their common debt to a modern, fully realistic yet aesthetic tradition. Looking back on his *The Portrait of a Lady*, James himself was forced to admit that "the Isabel Archers, and even much smaller female fry, insist upon mattering" (James, 49). In children's literature also, this basically humanistic tradition has provided a wide range of female and male protagonists worthy of exploration and demonstrated to several generations of young readers that such children do indeed matter. In addition, this tradition has supportively guided the child reader to an appreciative understanding of the complexity not only of language but of the human experience that fictional voices both represent and shape.

REFERENCES

Armstrong, William H. *Sounder*. New York: Harper and Row, 1969.

Blackmur, Richard P. "Introduction." In *The Art of the Novel, Critical Prefaces*. New York: Scribner's, 1934.

Booth, Wayne. *The Rhetoric of Fiction*. Chicago: University of Chicago Press, 1961.

Cleaver, Vera, and Bill Cleaver. *Where the Lilies Bloom*. Philadelphia: J. B. Lippincott, 1969.

DeLuca, Geraldine. "Unself-Conscious Voices: Larger Contexts for Adolescents." *The Lion and the Unicorn* 2 (Fall 1978): 89–108.

George, Jean Craighead. *Julie of the Wolves*. New York: Harper and Row, 1972.

Gilligan, Carol. *In a Different Voice, Psychological Theory and Women's Development*. Cambridge: Harvard University Press, 1982.

Hughes, Felicity. "Children's Literature: Theory and Practice." *ELH* 45 (1978): 542–61.

Hunter, Mollie. *A Sound of Chariots*. New York: Harper and Row, 1972.

Huse, Nancy. "*Sounder* and Its Readers: Learning to Observe." *Children's Literature Association Quarterly* 12 (Summer, 1987): 66–69.

James, Henry. *The Art of the Novel. Critical Prefaces*. New York: Scribner's, 1934.

Kuznets, Lois. "Sweet and Sour Land: A Critical Comparison of the 'Sounder' Novels." *Illinois English Bulletin* 65 (Spring, 1978): 23–29.

Molson, Francis. "The Portrait of the Young Writer in Children's Fiction." *The Lion and the Unicorn* 1 (Fall 1977): 77–90.

Nesbit, E. *The Bastable Children*. 1901–03, rpt. New York: Junior Literary Guild, 1929.

———. *The Railway Children*. 1906, rpt. New York: Penguin, 1960.

O'Dell, Scott. *The Island of the Blue Dolphins*. Boston: Houghton Mifflin, 1960.

Rawlings, Marjorie Kinnan. *The Yearling*. New York: Scribners, 1938.

21

The Process of Finding the Voice in Realistic Fiction for the Middle-Age Child

How do you become a child again? This is the problem that confronts almost every adult writer of fiction for the middle-age child. For today, in most instances, a writer of books for middle-age children is not the apparent narrator of the book, as once might have been the case. Instead, today's author is writing not about children but through one child, or perhaps even several children. The author does not stand outside the book, but within it, and the voice in which she writes must be the voice of one or more of her child characters; she must, in essence, become one or more of her characters as she describes the events in which they are all involved. In a book in first person, this would seem obvious, but today, even in third person, the narrative must take on the traits of one or more viewpoint characters. Yet, the whole of the novel must be shaped by the adult who writes from behind the voice she is creating. In other words, the author holds the reins, but the characters control both speech and movement.

An author today does not say "let us watch as Little Trudy makes her way to school. We know she is unhappy because we saw that she did not know how to do her math homework, but will her friend Octavia be able to help her?" Instead the author says, "Trudy moved slowly down her front steps. That awful math. She'd never understand it. She wondered if she could possibly manage to miss the school bus. It would make things so much easier if she could get out of going to school at all. But then she'd miss seeing Octavia, and they had so much to talk about. She wondered if Octie knew how to do the math. Sometimes she understood surprising things. Trudy's step quickened. If Octavia could help her. . . ."

In the first example above, a poor example of this style it must be admitted, the author is obviously outside the character and simply telling us what is happening and reminding us of things we have seen before. In the second example, the author is viewing the situation through Trudy's eyes and we are given her feelings about something we may already know but that bears repetition because something else is about to happen.

What is true today in the matter of the voice of the narrator in books for middle-age children, has not always been true. Louisa May Alcott did not make much attempt to enter her characters, though she was not as blatantly outside her characters as the narrator in my stiff example above. She viewed her characters from an omniscient position, able to see into children and adults alike. She not only told us what everyone was thinking, when it seemed important to her narrative, but also commented on the actions and reflections of her characters, and was never above moralizing about what she saw.

Children of that time seemed to expect that sort of book. Many of the books published in the last half of the nineteenth century and into the early years of this century followed the same pattern, most of them not nearly so enjoyable today—and perhaps not then—as the Louisa May Alcott works because she did have a very real sense of what children were like and how their lives and thinking developed, even though she tended to idealize certain traits.

It was not long, however, before writers began to enter more completely into the scenes they portrayed. Perhaps it was the influence of the dime novel and the endless series books that developed around the turn of the century that made writers of more serious works realize that stories written not from outside and above the main characters, but from inside could more easily create a setting into which a young reader could step.

The idea grew until by the late 1940s and early 1950s it was strongly believed that a book of fiction for a middle-age child could have only one viewpoint character. But it must never be told in first person. First person was too difficult for children. Yet the book must be presented and the entire scope of the book be limited to those things that the viewpoint character did, heard, or thought.

This was an extremely limiting factor for authors. Imagine, for example, Mark Twain's *The Prince and the Pauper* told with only one viewpoint character! But that was the standard of the 1940s, 1950s and even much of the 1960s. And it had its advantages. It tended to help the author create a character that was interesting and involved in events that would draw child readers. Furthermore, there is always a tendency when writing for children to point out the pitfalls of childhood—the wrong attitudes, the wrong choice of friends, the wrong activities—but when an author is writing through a single character this is much more difficult to accomplish. The viewpoint character cannot criticize his own approach to life, nor is the character likely to find problems in similar traits among his friends. The character may come to regret certain thoughts or actions, but only for reasons that are reasonable for that character and therefore acceptable to readers. Consequently moralizing diminished a great deal.

Writing through one child also had the advantage of helping authors structure a work in ways that focused attention on the main character and the plot and kept out extraneous material. It brought the reader into the book and into the action in a very direct way that helped the reader identify with the main character. Children like to identify with characters in books that appeal to them. The characters become friends whose adventures become the adventures of the reader. In this way, readers take on new identities, explore new ideas and circumstances, and enlarge their own experiences. For middle-age children, then, a book that takes them into the mind and activities of one child and lets them explore there an adventure and a way of life that may not be too different from their own but is different enough to be novel is a book that gives them exactly what they are looking for in a book.

In addition, writing through one child made the author think about voice, language, the understandings of children. If you are writing through a ten-year-old—or more commonly for this level book, a twelve-year-old—you must speak as a child speaks, think as a child thinks, view the world as a child does. The author, in effect, becomes that child.

At the same time, by general consensus, it was and still is assumed that an author need not take on the total structure of language as it is used by the average child. To do so could too easily result in a book that was dull and repetitive. It is enough in most books to incorporate the rhythms of children's speech and some of their phraseology. Authors can, on the whole, use decent grammar, though some modifications must be made, especially in conversation.

The strictures that developed over the years and came to flower in the forties, fifties and sixties were useful, both in attracting children to books, and in helping authors find a level where both they and their readers could feel comfortable. But today, there is a realization that children can grasp more than was once thought, so there can be more than one viewpoint character, and books can be told in the first person, as well.

Yet some of the strictures of writing for middle-age children remain, and rightly so. The characters must be portrayed as they see themselves, not as adults see them. Characters must speak and act on their own, not as adults would have them behave. Writers must not moralize or criticize the characters they are writing about, except as the situations that develop in the novel do this for them. And those things that happen in the book must test real to the child reader, just as the characters themselves must.

All of this means that though the writer sees from an adult point of view where the child's thoughts and actions will take him, this must never be betrayed before the inevitable happens. It is a difficult role that the author plays, one that not every adult can assume. It is always hard not to point out what we know better than someone else. But more to the point is the fact that the joys and triumphs of childhood, the disasters and woes of the young must assume in a book the proportions they have for the child, who does not have as wide a life of experience to measure them by as the adult. Not all adults can slough off, even for the time of writing, the knowledge they have acquired through the years. To do so seems demeaning to some, a waste of wisdom to others. And yet, there are many things children can only learn as adults did, by experience, and books, well done, can give them that experience, if they are real and if they do not preach but are simply lived in the way that life most often goes, or at least in the case of the novel in question must inevitably go.

So how does an author do it? How does an author become a child? This varies from author to author. Just as no two people are alike, so no two authors are alike in how they invade the body of a child, or in some cases of several children, characters they have created in their minds that yet take on a life of their own and become as alive and real as a flesh and blood child.

For some, it is finding the child within. All of us have memories of childhood. We remember some of what happened to us—the best and the worst, usually. And we remember how we felt on certain occasions. But more important than these memories are the memories we do not consciously remember. Psychologists tell us that everything that has ever happened to us is imprinted in our brain. It would be terribly confusing if we had to consciously remember every single thing we had ever experienced. We couldn't concentrate on today for our thoughts of the past. So, fortunately, most of the events we have experienced in our lives are hidden from us and come back only when events, sights, sounds, smells or feelings recall specific incidents or places or people. But for some individuals, the memories and feelings of childhood seem very close to the surface. Though they have matured into adults physically, mentally and spiritually, they know still how it felt to be a child. They are open to childhood, especially their own. They may not even like children. (Some authors of children's books do not really feel comfortable with children—maybe because they understand all too well the discomforts of childhood and they do not want to be reminded too directly of what may be painful to them.) Yet the child in them can rise to the surface and speak in ways that children of another generation can appreciate.

It is important that authors remember that childhood is not the great golden glory sentimental authors for adults often make it seem to be. In a recent episode, the cartoon character Calvin, after a very trying experience, says (in a very unchildlike way—but true nevertheless) "People who get nostalgic about childhood were obviously never children." It is important that authors know the pain and the deprivations and the mental misery that invade all childhoods, as well as the moments of unalloyed delight, the wonderful surprises and the splendid feelings of achievement that childhood can give. And it is especially necessary that authors for children know that there is nothing cute, coy, or simpering about children, unless adults have made them that way.

Authors who write out of their own memories of childhood, out of their own deep feelings for the struggles of childhood, even when they do not always recall why they know about these things, do not fall into the traps of creating children as adults would like them to be, think that they are, or hope that they will be. They know what children already know, though some adults are not aware of it: life is both good and bad and you have to live it day by day, doing the best you can with what you have.

When such authors write today, they may, because they are allowed to do so in the textures of today's accepted patterns for books, write as often in the first person as in the third. Sometimes they are accused of always writing about themselves, whether it is first person or third that they choose as their vehicle, and whether it is one viewpoint character that they use or several. But this is not true. They are writing out of themselves, out of their forgotten memories, buried feelings, and still festering hurts or all-encompassing joys, but the characters they create are not themselves; they are characters that take on some of the aspects of the writer, but not his whole personality. These characters are as likely as the characters of any other kind of writer to assume a life of their own, become creatures the author did not know existed, and live their lives in ways the author had not imagined they could.

The voice with which these characters speak is their own voice, created in part by the author to express the kind of person the author sees his character as being, and in part by the characters he or she develops. The voice and character become one as the nature of that character becomes apparent. If the character is brave and active, the language of the story is strong and forthright. If the character is shy and uncertain, the language is tentative and hesitant. If the character is tough, the language is tough. If the character is overeducated, so is the voice of the book. The book is the character, and the character makes the book. And all come from the author's sense of her own childhood, but grow into people who are not the author.

But not everyone creates out of memory, remembered or forgotten. Some authors create their characters, their voices, their plots out of children around them—their own children, children they have taught, or children they have known in some other way. Some authors find themselves spending a good deal of time at the local mall, listening to the children who come there. For older children, the mall is like the drug store or the school store of the past, a place to meet and talk. And authors are there, too, listening, to find characters and voices for the books they want to create. Busses, subways, libraries, any place that children appear, authors use to learn what their characters are like, how they speak, and what concerns them. The problem for this second kind of author is developing a realistic voice and maintaining it throughout, consciously doing so because she is not drawing on an inner voice. Again there may be one viewpoint character or several, the story may be told in first person or third. But whichever, characters must speak with their own voice and out of a sense of who and what they are. Their thoughts, actions and conversation must be consistent, though these may grow and change as the story proceeds. For the author who is getting the voice from outside herself—listening to young people, choosing one, perhaps, to be the model for the viewpoint character, studying the character, coming to know the character as a person—recognizing what her protagonist would do and would not do are all important. Yet so is letting the character live and move as a real person, apart from the model that has been chosen.

There is a third kind of approach for authors. (Actually, there are probably as many kinds of approaches as there are authors, and some authors use more than one approach, but speaking in general terms, these are the three major ones.) This is the approach of the writer of historical fiction, stories of children in other lands, tales of adventures in areas the author is unlikely to have experienced. These authors are also writing realistic fiction. But sometimes they were not even born when their characters lived, so they can't write out of themselves. Or perhaps, their characters lived in a place the author visited only as an adult, or maybe has never visited. Maybe the place no longer exists to be visited. Maybe the place is too dangerous for a casual visitor. It is only by dint of careful attention to as much reference work as can be found about the time, place, and people there that a true story can be told.

Once the research is done, the author faces a further problem: how much of the thinking, speech patterns, real conditions of another time or place can be conveyed in a book for children and be understood by the reader for which it is intended? Like authors of realistic works set in our own time and place, the author lets the material sink into her mind and rise again as a story, with the flavor of the time and place, with the essence of what those people were and did, with a true perspective—as far as can be gained—on what life was like then and what people might have done and said, but cast into a form that uses all of this in ways that hide the research and lets the characters—the viewpoint character or characters especially—speak for themselves in language that is comfortable for them and comfortable for the author and not too difficult for the intended reader. Not easy. Especially when the author has read a great deal of adult material and yet must keep that viewpoint the viewpoint of a child. Yet some authors do succeed, and when they do, it enables young readers to explore the past, or to explore another country in ways that make them feel at home there and give them a grasp of a life far beyond their own.

Today's author then has advantages over authors of the past in finding a voice, or voices, for her middle-age children's novel. But the essence of what she must do remains the same as it has always been: she must create a believable milieu of words in which characters, background, and plot can function in ways that attract and speak convincingly to children of today, and maybe even tomorrow.

PART V
Poetry

Introduction

CHARLOTTE F. OTTEN

If poetry is the most complex of verbal forms, if poetry can be considered another mode of apprehension, then it follows that voice in poetry will seem to be more complex and less apprehensible than voice in prose. In this section three contemporary poets attempt to unravel the complexity of voice in their own poetry and to show the reader ways to apprehend voice in their poems; one critic focuses on the voice of the child-narrator of *A Child's Garden of Verses*, the other on the child-participant in the orality of the poems of Dennis Lee, Ted Hughes, and Nikki Giovanni.

Myra Cohn Livingston's poems are a study in a wide variety of poetic forms. As Livingston travels back into her poems searching for a theory of voice, she discovers that in her earliest poems, *Whispers and Other Poems*, as well as in her latest, *Space Songs*, it is the voice of the narrator that creates the meaning of the poems. Recognizing that poets have always had available to them narrative, lyrical, and dramatic voices, she discerns three components in voice: the conversational, the mask, and the apostrophe. These three components can be found in various combinations in her poems. When she is using mask, she is creating an authentic childlike voice, a voice that is sometimes a persona, sometimes an inanimate object. When she is using apostrophe, she is creating a voice that is neither the persona nor the inanimate object but the one that she maintains "communes with the in-animate, that asks questions and reveals again something of the inner monologue within each of us." When a poet has a poem in her head asking to be written, the most conscious decision to be made is this—which voice does the poem call for. The voice of the poet, she concludes, reaches into the form of the poem: rhythm, rhyme, figures of speech, subject matter, all bend to voice.

This theory of voice, which Livingston discovered when she was teaching children to write poetry, is rooted in the express desire of the poet to make "the reader a part of the poem"—whether the poem is about seasons or space, the sea or the earth, or about herself, or Josh or Jennie or Anna, or about potato chips, or about trucks, cats, or construction vehicles in Dallas. Mask and apostrophe, both of which seem to put distance between poet and reader, in the poetry of Livingston become the voice-bridge from the poet's consciousness to the reader's.

Nancy Willard's *A Visit to William Blake's Inn* began with her search for a narrator, as did the searches of Alice and Martin Provenson, the illustrators. Alice Provenson suggests that "it was clear in *The Voyage of the Ludgate Hill* who was speaking, but it took us a while to discern in *A Visit to William Blake's Inn*. (It was interesting to puzzle it out from the text without consulting Nancy.) The Tiger, the King of the Cats, the Marmalade Man, Blake, the Sunflowers speak in the first person, but then so does the Traveler. Who is *he*?" (Personal letter to Charlotte F. Otten, October 31, 1987).

For Nancy Willard, the search ended when she discovered that William Blake had already chosen her to be his narrator, rather than the reverse. Thus chosen, she invoked William Blake's "spirit" to inspire and lead her, not on a mystical path, but on the road of poetic inspiration traveled by a long line of English poets who had invoked the spirits of earlier poets. With Nancy Willard selected by Blake, and William Blake's spirit invoked by Nancy Willard, the complex narrative structure of *A Visit to William Blake's Inn* was ready to be built.

What Nancy Willard erected was a narrative structure with both a superstructure and a substructure. The "spirit" of William Blake operates in Nancy Willard as creator of the poem and its superstructure. The poet William Blake, quoting his own poetry, creates the substructure of the poem. The reader, invited by Nancy Willard to become a fellow traveler and a visitor to the inn, joins William Blake and Nancy Willard as both observer and participant. Once having traveled with them, the initiated reader and the poet Nancy Willard see that "our lives have the shape of [William Blake's] story."

Nancy Willard's poem *The Voyage of the Ludgate Hill* has as its direct source a volume of Robert Louis Stevenson's letters. Working within the historical constraints of these personal documents, Nancy Willard wrote a poem that she thought Stevenson would have sung. The narrator of the poem is the historical character Robert Louis Stevenson; the characters accompanying him are the imagined characters of Nancy Willard. By giving Stevenson a voice in her poem, Nancy Willard deepens the epistolary voice with a poetic one. Although the poetic voice rescues Stevenson from mere historicity, he remains, nevertheless, an authentic historical figure in the poem. This narrative technique makes Stevenson a poet in his own story and the creator of his own imaginative, though not imaginary, voyage.

Some of Eve Merriam's earliest memories are of sounds—the sounds of the world around her, the sounds of words, the sounds of names. She recalls how intrigued she was when she discovered that "Pennsylvania" meant "William Penn's Woods"; how she listened to the sound of the voice of Franklin D. Roosevelt during his Fireside Chats; how she sang the alliterative songs of children's games. When she began to write poetry, she began in sound. The titles of many of her collections of poetry indicate her continuing fascination with sound: *There Is No Rhyme for Silver, It Doesn't Always Have to Rhyme, Catch a Little Rhyme, Finding a Poem,* and *Out Loud.*

Sound is an important element in poetry; to say that the poet works with sound is simply to name one aspect of the poet's craft. In its essence poetry involves the use of sound to produce certain effects on both the text and the reader. In Eve Merriam's poetry, however, sound is more than an essential element: it is also the voice of the narrator. Through sound the narrator establishes her identity. Like the Pied Piper, the narrator's sounds entice children into the poem, where they are not merely followers and listeners but creators and contributors.

Sound becomes the creative interplay of the poem; together poet and child explore the range and resonance of sound. The voice of the narrator is not the solitary voice of the poet but the creative joint voice of poet and child. When Eve Merriam brings her poems to a child audience, she makes it clear that she depends upon the child-listener to play the poetry sound game with her. She cannot play it alone: In " 'I,' says the Poem," Merriam has her poetry declare "I cannot speak until you come. / Reader, come, come with me."

For Eve Merriam, the text of a poem is not sacrosanct. Open-ended, it is subject to the oral/aural contributions of the child audience. Clearly, the poet loves the sounds of words for their own sake—what she calls "word-mongering"—but the narrator's love of sounds is a call to the child-reader to develop, or at least to become aware of, the beauty, merriment, playfulness of the world, particularly as it is evidenced in sounds and in their duplication in written and spoken language.

The problem with adults writing poetry for children is often, as Joanne Lewis points out, a problem of voice. Some adult poets adopt a child's voice so selfconscious as to sound condescending, even pretentious. For Robert Louis Stevenson it was not a matter of adopting a voice for his *A Child's Garden of Verses* but of reentering his own childhood and recapturing the voice deep in his consciousness. Lewis examines the rhetorical strategies outlined in the critical writing of Brower, Wright, and X. J. Kennedy and provides a context for hearing the authentic narrative and lyrical voices of Stevenson in *A Child's Garden of Verses.* As fictive narrator of his own childhood, Stevenson reexperiencd his (and the universal child's) emotions and, hence, was able to create a poetic voice free of condescension and pretension.

Applying the critical theories of Bakhtin, Barthes, Hartman, and Ong to the poetry of Dennis Lee and Ted Hughes, Roderick McGillis locates the voice of poetry in orality. Orality and voice, however, are more than oral/aural. McGillis stresses the importance of *hearing* poetry with a voice: "It is through such a voice that we come closest to understanding the literature we read." Voice is what the poet uses to write the poem; it is also what the hearer/reader uses to hear/read the poem. When the hearers of poetry are children who actively participate in the orality of poems, the poems become the voice of the creator/hearer. The narrator's voice in children's poetry, then, is a dual voice: it is the voice of poet and hearer.

THE AUTHORIAL VOICE

22

Some Thoughts on Voice in Poetry

MYRA COHN LIVINGSTON

One of the discoveries I made at a shockingly late stage in my writing career was that of the importance of voice, its variety and possibility for turning what otherwise might be dull narration into a more meaningful piece of work.

This moment of epiphany (or was it, rather, a series of moments?) happened not, as might be supposed, while I was writing but in an elementary school classroom. There as poet-in-residence I experienced continual frustration with second graders whose verse, unlike their personalities, was banal and lifeless. "The flower is red," one began, or "The tree is near the window," or "The rain is coming down." How, I wondered, could I encourage children to use their observations and thoughts more effectively? Continually reading to them the best in poetry, knowing that they possessed in common with poets a fresh way of looking at the world, a penchant for simile and metaphor, a keen imagination and the ability to pretend, to endow the inanimate with life (sensibilities usually lost in later years), I sought to find a way to guide their honest responses beyond fact, beyond narration, into the realm of poetry.

Teaching children to write poetry is impossible. What one can do is to stress the importance of observation, encourage journal entries, offer good models in literature, and respect the imagination of each child. It is not difficult to teach basic forms: the couplet, tercet, quatrain, haiku, cinquain, and free verse; to introduce rhythm patterns, syllabic pattern, and the elements of sound. The difficulty lies in meshing all of this together in order that the voice of childhood be translated onto paper. Was it possible, I puzzled, to find a clue in the better use of the child's voice?

There are, as I see it, three voices available to the poet: the narrative, the lyric, and the dramatic. The narrative voice is that which tells a story, recalls an event, a rather matter-of-fact, impartial third-person voice that offers some sort of information. It can be as short and simple as a nursery rhyme or as complicated and rich as an epic. Narrative poetry is often interlaced with some aspects of the lyric and dramatic voices. It can be rooted in reality or in fancy, but it is in my mind largely the voice that bids readers to listen.

The lyrical voice, certainly the most fashionable in current adult poetry, is that in which poets speak of experiences and/or images in relationship to themselves. The traditional technical aspects of lyrical poetry (a musical rhythm, usually end-rhymed, to be sung originally to a lyre) have for the most part vanished, dismissed by many adult contemporary poets as part of an out-worn order. Yet with few exceptions lyrical poetry remains intact in the world of children's poetry, a reminder of Dr. Isaac Watts' injunction that children remember best what is said in rhyme and its accompanying metrical patterns.

The lyrical voice may remain self-contained, intent on relating the ex-perience or thoughts of the poet, but it may also speak directly to the reader. Most lyrical poetry seems concerned with personal response and feeling. Asking children to turn observations into the lyrical voice, the outcome is predictable. "I see the tree near the window" or "I found a red flower" or "I watch the rain coming down." Hardly an improvement!

The discovery of the three components of the dramatic voice, the con-versational, the mask and the apostrophe, voices whose potential had never occurred to me before, unleashed not only for my students, but for me, a new way of looking. I had been reading some poems written in these voices all my life, yet had never really stopped to examine their possibilities.

The mask is a childlike voice. It is a voice that pretends to be something it is not and is used, in a sense, by every writer who becomes another character in a story or novel. In this voice the writer creeps into another's skin, adopting a different persona. To me it is the mask, pretending to be the inanimate, which is unique to poetry. It is Walter de la Mare's "Snow-flake," and Lillian Moore's "Message from a Caterpillar." By the use of this voice students may not only indulge their natural penchant for pretending, but stretch their imaginations. Indeed I found this voice to prod them into expressing a variety of hidden feelings about themselves. Their beginnings now changed. "Come, look at my red petals," or "I scratch at the window," or "Hear what a noise I can make!" A fifth grade boy, whom I shall always remember, spoke about himself as a lonely root. "Everyone looks at the beautiful flower," he wrote, "but nobody sees me, for I am the lonely root." And, unfortunately, he was.

Another component of the dramatic voice, the apostrophe, is a voice uncannily true to childhood. It is the voice that communes with the inanimate, that asks questions and reveals again something of the inner monologue within each of us. Apostrophe is, for the children, both an opportunity and a challenge to examine more deeply the particulars of what they observe, to ask questions that reflect their personal concerns about the nature of the world. "The smog has speckled your leaves, tree," or "Why do they pick you to take inside?" or "Do stop, rain, so I can get out of this stuffy room."

It may well be that my analysis of voice is idiosyncratic, but from a pragmatic viewpoint the quality of the children's work, based on attention to voice, did improve immeasurably. What occurs to me, looking back, is that once I had bumbled through the stages of defining the voice, choosing poetry that reflected the different voices and planning lessons accordingly, I began to think about my own writing in new ways. I tried out voices that, heretofore, I had used only intuitively. I asked questions as to how I could engage my readers more effectively. Before this time it had never even crossed my mind to define, let alone investigate, such matters.

LYRICAL VOICE

Whispers and Other Poems (1958), written when I was eighteen, is a book of verse using both the lyrical and narrative voices. This choice had to be wholly intuitive. It would be natural for me, drawing upon my own childhood experiences, to present myself as the center of the world, to relate all images to this self.

> I like to peek
>   inside a book
>   where all the picture people look.
> ("Picture People," *Whispers and Other Poems*)

Narrative poems are almost as frequent, yet always endemic to my small world:

> The mourning dove has built a nest
> Up where the latticework is best...
> ("The Mourning Dove," *Whispers and Other Poems*)

or

> The merry-go-round
>   whirls round and round
>   in a giant circle on the ground...
> ("The Merry-Go-Round," *Whispers and Other Poems*)

The use of the lyric voice predominates in the next book, *Wide Awake and Other Poems* (1969), but there is a marked difference in its use. In *Whispers and Other Poems* the voice was my own, a child responding to my first ten years of life in Omaha. In *Wide Awake* the lyric voice has been transferred to our first son, Josh, whose world of buses, trucks, cars, construction vehicles in Dallas became my world. I was using the lyric voice as though we were one person.

> Cab over engine,
> Goose-neck trailer,
> Half-cab diesel
> And moving van
>   I watch you rumble
>   The Northwest Highway;
>   I wave at the corner
>   When I can . . .
>
>   ("Josh's Song," *Wide Awake and Other Poems*)

It would be proper, I suppose, to call this voice a mask, yet I do not consider it such because I note a verse in the book where I am not myself nor Josh, but my niece Anna. In this instance, I have noted the difference by using her name within the poem:

> Out of my window
> A long brown string
> Of winter leaves are whispering
> And dancing in the happy day
> And calling—Anna, come and play—
>
>   ("For Anna," *Wide Awake and Other Poems*)

Strangely enough, the same peculiarity shows itself in the next book, *The Moon and a Star*, with two poems for Anna and for my twin nephews, whose names also appear within the body of the verses. What hindsight seems to be telling me here is that in these early books of poetry as well as in books of rhythmic prose such as *I'm Hiding*, *See What I Found* and *I'm Not Me*, I used the lyric voice not only for myself but for our second son, Jonas, as though we were one person. My use of the voice as mask, for anyone outside the immediate family, necessitated that I present real names as a part of the poem, as though to establish a distinction. As I view it now, I must conclude that in watching my children through early childhood, I was reliving my own childhood, its experiences and feelings. Watching my niece, nephews or other children, I felt a compulsion to note this separation by the use of a name. Theirs were *not* my feelings, yet they needed my childlike lyrical voice. It was at that time the only voice with which I was most comfortable.

A Crazy Flight and Other Poems (1969), as I look at it now, is a strange book for it marks the end of looking backward to my own childhood recalled again through my children's actions, thoughts and dreams. There are a number of poems for our daughter, Jennie, whose worlds of fantasy recalled my own:

> I know the language of the ocean,
> A language we speak together often,
> A secret language we share.
>
> ("Someday," *A Crazy Flight and Other Poems*)

The poems which deal with dreams and with flight are the last vestige of my childhood, all written in the lyrical voice, as though her make-believe world held some echo of my own. In this book, however, there is an entirely new influence, that of children I was encountering in the classroom, most evident in poems like "Being Fat," "Skinny Jim" or "Why?": I don't know why I'm so crazy. / It just happens some days . . . ("Why?" *A Crazy Flight and Other Poems*).

My own children were now fourteen, eleven and six, and I had begun to teach many classes, particularly at the second to sixth grade levels. The transfer of lyric to mask becomes strikingly evident in the next four books, *The Malibu, The Way Things Are and Other Poems* (1974) *4-Way Stop*, and *O Sliver of Liver* (1979). Seldom is the lyrical voice used, either that of my children or of myself as a child, but of students, of conversations overheard, of response to feelings as evidenced by these young people. Watching them at lunch hour I wrote "Street Song":

> O, I have been walking
> with a bag of potato chips,
> me and potato chips
> munching along . . .
>
> (*The Way Things Are and Other Poems*)

Observing a child unable to make contact with others, I empathized:

> We could be friends
> Like friends are supposed to be.
> You, picking up the telephone
> Calling me
> > to come over and play
> > or take a walk . . .
> > ("We Could Be Friends," *The Way Things Are and Other Poems*)

The Way Things Are, influenced particularly by fifth graders, contains a preponderance of lyrical-mask poems. The true lyrical voice is suddenly reserved, I discovered, for those poems that have only to do with myself, with my reaction to images seen without children, as though perhaps in growing older I have shed the memories of my own childhood. But it is also true that at this same time in the mid-seventies I was practicing my ideas about voice, caught up in experimentation. Apostrophe occurs four times in *The Way Things Are,* more often than in the total of six earlier books, and eight times in *4-Way Stop* with fifteen instances of its use in *O Sliver of Liver.* It is also in *O Sliver of Liver* that the mask becomes, for a time, a true mask. I am no longer my children nor other children, but a chambered nautilus, a bed, a ghost.

From 1946, when I wrote *Whispers,* until the seventies I must conclude that my use of voice was wholly intuitive. For about five years I practiced using a variety of voices. Some of these succeed, a great number seem to me now somewhat strained. It was not until I began *No Way of Knowing: Dallas Poems* (1980) that I began to think in terms of sustaining a single voice—in this case, a lyrical mask. The people I was portraying had to speak in their own language, a Black vernacular peculiar to Dallas, which could only be heard through direct transmittal. I became Arthur:

> When Kennedy
> Come to our town
> He come with dreams
> Got shot right down.
> ("Arthur Thinks on Kennedy," *No Way of Knowing: Dallas Poems*)

I became Minnie's admirer:

> Lace sure favor Minnie.
> Makes her look so bright.
> She been luring me along
> Since we first dance tonight.
>
> No question she the spider.
> No question I the fly.
> No way I gonna miss that web
> When Minnie spin on by—
> ("Minnie," *No Way of Knowing: Dallas Poems*)

At this point I also believe that the exercises I had asked my students to undertake, changing a lyrical poem to a narrative poem or a dramatic poem, became part of my own approach. Voices whose possibilities had never concerned me were now a challenge. It was also about this time that I began to consider how the reader might respond to the various voices. I am aware that *Monkey Puzzle and Other Poems* (1984) with its strong use of the dramatic mask in nineteen poems, the apostrophe in two, the lyrical in two and the narrative in seven poems was probably the last book in which I did not trouble with thoughts of more fully engaging the reader. I had no choice in

A Lollygag of Limericks or *Higgledy Piggledy* as these were books based upon place names and double dactyls, which both required a narrative voice. *Worlds I Know and Other Poems* had to be written in a lyrical voice for it was my first book, *Whispers*, rewritten from the point of view of one who no longer ignored the devils of childhood. *There Was a Place and Other Poems* because of its subject matter—the problems and worries of children caught in difficult family situations—demanded the immediacy of the lyrical voice, the identification such a voice offers to troubled young people.

The five picture books which I did with Leonard Everett Fisher, however, presented a challenge both as to voice and form. I was by now, in the early eighties, greatly troubled by the atrophy of imagination in the young as well as an overconcern, particularly in children's writing, with the attention to the autonomous self. My work on *The Child as Poet: Myth or Reality?* convinced me that the symbolism of nature was a positive antidote to the overly precious dream, wish, and lie syndrome that had run rampant for a number of years. How could I appeal to readers through subject matter that is a source of universal wonder in a voice to which they might listen? In writing earlier books I had not needed to choose one voice or form because of the variety of subjects. In these five books there had to be some unifying form and voice, for all of the poems were connected and concerned with nature.

DRAMATIC VOICE

Strangely enough, it is only now that I began to comprehend, after poking about in past work, that the choice of voice is very largely determined by subject. Those poems which fall into the arena of experience, of personal life, demand the lyrical voice. Their images need not, but can be factual or scientific, but must always convey a particular way of viewing the world, peculiar to one person, one writer.

The dramatic voice enables a writer, and most particularly a poet, to try on different skins, to pretend or imagine in the same way, I suppose, that novelists and dramatists use dialogue or plot. There is also in the dramatic voice an opportunity to engage in an inner monologue which, at its best, will allow the reader to not only enter another's mind but serve as a springboard to further reflection for that reader. It will also honor the imagination as a vital force in life.

The narrative voice, as that which bids a reader to listen, may be embellished by forays into both the lyrical and dramatic modes, but in the poet's hands it may be the playground for a variety of figures of speech that, under control, enrich the commonplace world and invite the reader to see beyond scientific fact. The narrative voice may be serious or humorous, as may all other voices, but is always a voice that, however far it may choose to stray from fact, honors the realities of life. The most imaginative narrative such as the Alice books, the finest examples of nonsense, such as the Lear story poems, always acknowledge reality.

To have written *A Circle of Seasons* (1982) as a lyrical poem would have been possible had I wished to speak of my own reactions to the four seasons. The fact is that I had done that so often that I recognized in early and aborted beginnings that the poem would have been only a repetition of things already said. Nor did I feel that using the voice of apostrophe or mask would work. Apostrophe would have been but another panegyric to nature. I could hardly imagine myself as a season and so mask was dismissed. Therefore to honor the reality of the seasons I chose the narrative and to indulge imagination I chose personification. A four line stanza in sprung rhythm with an *aaba* pattern seemed to fulfill the need for variety in rhythm as well as satisfy the musical appeal of end rhyme.

> Winter etches windowpanes, fingerpaints in white,
> Sculptures strange soft shapes of snow that glisten in the night,
> Filigrees the snowflake, spins icicles of glass,
> Paints the ground in hoarfrost, its needles sharp with light.

To draw in the reader I added for each verse an apostrophe in language simple enough for the youngest child:

> O bush
> And pine,
> You, too, shall brightly shine.

The voice chosen for *Sky Songs* (1984) can best be explained by the book's working title, *Sky Secrets*, which in its first drafts seemed to be a narrative poem. To talk about the sky would require certain facts about the sun, moon, clouds. Yet I did not wish to make this a book of information. Another early draft reminds me that "Secrets / live in the sky / that can never be told" became "Secrets / live in you that / can never be told" which seemed when written (although never used) to allow room for the metaphoric stance of the moon as earth's night mother, the midday sun as a white eye and the morning sky as an astrodome. Further, as the work got underway, I realized that I had gone back to my own childhood belief in the sky as a heaven in which, like *Green Pastures*, God must live. The book became, therefore, not only an apostrophe to the sky and to what could be seen in it, but the unseen presence of God (a fact incidentally that no reviewer has commented upon).

> You have
> held the hot sun
> so long that it has bleached
> you white. This morning you carried
> it up

to chase
the dark shadows
away, but now you have
pushed it so high that it sits there
gloating,

staring
with one white eye
on the sweltering earth,
laughing at the wildfire it sets
ablaze.

("Noon," *Sky Songs*)

Throughout *Sky Songs* metaphoric observation, inner monologue, fact, questions, and often syncretic answers are offered in the hope that child readers might ask their own questions, create their own similes and answers for cloud shapes, the changing phases of the moon, the effects of rain, snow, smog, and the color of a sunset. Each poem is at triple cinquain, a form I had experimented with in *O Sliver of Liver*.

Sea Songs might have taken any voice, yet it is doubtful that I could have described the many moods of the sea, its rhythmic force and its various levels of life as a lyrical poem. I have never visited the depths of the oceans. Nor would a mask work, for I could not pretend to be vast amounts of water. Again, to bring in factual material I resolved to use a narrative voice that could not only recount the sea's mystery but the lives of fishermen, summer bathers, and the ocean's underground inhabitants. To intensify the movement of water, I returned to sprung rhythm and a five-line stanza, unrhymed and disordered as the waters themselves.

Crashing on dark shores, drowning, pounding
breaker swallows breaker. Tide follows
tide. Lost in her midnight witchery
moon watches, cresting tall waves, pushing
through mist and blackness the cold waters.

To tie this opening stanza in with other stanzas that describe the shift from night to day, from mystery to reality, I decided on an unrhymed apostrophe to both moon and sun, which moved from the opening lines

Moon, you have worked long
Now rest . . .

to

Sun, you climb higher
and higher.

and closes with

> Moon, speak once more
> the dreams...

In this way I hoped that with the simplest of words children might be inclined to focus on both sun and moon as subjects for their own songs.

In *Earth Songs* I was attempting in some way to relate the child's concept of the vastness of earth's deserts, mountains, forests, with its relatively small position in the universe. Shakespeare's line from *Anthony and Cleopatra*, "The little o, the earth" had haunted me since college days. Indeed the seeds of this book occur in *O Sliver of Liver* with a cinquain:

> little
> o, the earth, bathed
> in ocean, how bravely
> you tumble through the black nothing
> of space

> ("little o," *O Sliver of Liver*)

To further this idea I conceived of a conversation, the dramatic voice, between a child and earth and had originally intended to carry this through each stanza. The form I created, however, relied so strongly on sound and became so figuratively heavy that a simple apostrophe, as in *A Circle of Seasons* or *Sea Songs*, would have been crushed under the weight of these stanzas. For better balance, therefore, I conceived of an opening conversation:

> Little O, small earth, spinning in space
> face covered with dizzy clouds, racing,
> chasing sunlight through the Milky Way,
> say your secrets, small earth, little O,
> Know where you lead, I follow. I go.

> (*Earth Songs*)

Earth then answers in the following stanzas, with an eventual return to the opening conversation but with an ironic twist that allows the child to see the world as large while the earth, which has been describing itself, finally views itself as small. The voice is largely that of the mask. The form is one I invented; here the last word in the first line rhymes with the first word in the second line, a pattern that continues until the penultimate line where the last word must rhyme with both the first and last words in the final line.

It was a pattern I wished to repeat in *Space Songs*, but the subject matter with its many place names did not respond to the newly created form. The element of sound was not important here, nor as I began to work could I conceive of the mask of myself as a sun, moon, or satellite. Further I wished to include not only stars and planets but something of the nature of discovery and dreams of space. I dabbled with the lyrical voice,

> I will imagine
> in my hand
> ten thousand shining grains of sand

[holograph]

But this led me nowhere in terms of the rest of the work. I did not wish to use sprung rhythm, nor even a triple cinquain. Indeed this would have been impossible in view of the proper names. The form had to be simpler and preferably compatible with my desire to replicate the shape of sun, moon, comet, and satellite. So not only did I read about space for a year and a half, I struggled with form, deciding at last on a rhyming sestet, *abcabc*. The need to mix fact with flights of imagination dictated the use of the narrative voice, as in "Comets":

> Long distance travelers
> from the cold
> of space,
> ice-clad,
> dirty,
>
> tugged by a passing star,
>
> journey to see the sun
> whose searing burn
> swells them with gas
> as on they race
>
> streaming their blowing, sunlit hair.
> These are comets.
> They come.
> They go.
> They will return.

(Space Songs)

Here the rhyming pattern can be seen as space/race, star/hair, and burn/return. The use of perfect rhyme and occasional disorder in off rhyme lent themselves, I believe, to the subject, which mixed fact and imagination, known and unknown.

With another book in my head, indeed with all the notes written over several years of observation and with a new approach to the potential of voice, I am at the moment still searching for the right form, the best voice in which to put this new long poem. I am reminded of John Ciardi's insistence that we do not ask "What does a poem mean?" but rather "How does a poem mean?" It is a matter, I believe, of balancing subject, form, and voice, as well as attention to finding a way to make the reader a part of the poem.

Sometimes the narrative voice is what is needed to recount fact yet introduce fiction, imagination, and fantasy. Sometimes it is a matter of encouraging the child-reader to adopt an inner monologue or to urge that reader to make the imaginative leap of addressing the inanimate as in the dramatic voice. Sometimes it is an invitation to the reader to adopt a mask, to feel as one with the inanimate; such a poem is "Monterey Cypress: Pt. Lobos":

```
at whim of winds
        my limbs are bent
    to grotesque shape
      by element
        of ocean spray
          and salty wind
    and who may see
        my bleached bole pinned
          into the sand
            shall
          wonder
            why
            I
              twist
              alive
              while
              others
              die
```

(*Monkey Puzzle and Other Poems*)

There is no easy answer to the matter of voice. A poet is able to use several voices that would be difficult in any other form of writing. When and how and why to use them, in combination with the narrative or lyric voice, or simply by themselves, remains another matter for speculation and struggle and must be dealt with as each poem enters one's head and asks to be written.

REFERENCES

Livingston, Myra Cohn. *A Circle of Seasons*. New York: Holiday House, 1982.
———. *A Crazy Flight and Other Poems*. New York: Harcourt, Brace and World, 1969.
———. *Earth Songs*. New York: Holiday House, 1986.
———. *Monkey Puzzle and Other Poems*. New York: Atheneum, 1984.
———. *No Way of Knowing: Dallas Poems*. New York: Atheneum, 1980.
———. *O Sliver of Liver*. New York: Atheneum, 1979.
———. *Sea Songs*. New York: Holiday House, 1986.
———. *Sky Songs*. New York: Holiday House, 1984.

————. *Space Songs.* New York: Holiday House, 1988.

————. *The Way Things Are and Other Poems.* New York: Atheneum, 1974.

————. *Whispers and Other Poems.* New York: Harcourt, Brace and Company, 1958.

————. *Wide Awake and Other Poems.* New York: Harcourt, Brace and World, 1969.

23

Tellers and Travelers: The Voices of *A Visit to William Blake's Inn* and *The Voyage of the Ludgate Hill*

NANCY WILLARD

One of my favorite scenes in the whole kingdom of fairy tales is the uproar that greets Ole Shut-Eye, the magic gnome who pays nightly visits to a little boy in Andersen's story of the same name:

As soon as Hjalmar was in bed, Ole Shut-Eye touched all the articles in the room . . . , and they immediately began to talk together, and each one spoke of itself, with the exception of the spittoon, which stood silent, and was vexed that they should be so vain as to speak only of themselves, and think only of themselves, without any regard for him who stood so modestly in the corner for everyone's use. (Jacobi, 603)

Isn't Ole Shut-Eye a little like a writer to whom an idea has just arrived, carrying on its back a dozen characters clamoring to tell *their* side of the story?

Writers know that there are as many different stories in the simplest tale as there are characters to tell them. A little girl is sent by mother to take a basket of goodies to her sick grandmother. On the way she meets a wolf. Dreadful events follow. It's Red Riding Hood's story, of course. She is the one making the journey. But suppose you let the wolf tell his version. Or the mother, filled with guilt at having sent her child into the woods alone. Or the grandmother, devoured and reborn in a sort of Cesarian rebirth, with the woodsman acting as rough midwife. Without the distance an omniscient storyteller gives it, "Little Red Riding Hood" would be as heartrending and astonishing as our own dreams.

Fortunately writers do not always have to choose their narrators. Sometimes their narrators choose them. Such was my experience writing the two books I've done with Alice and Martin Provensen, *A Visit to William Blake's Inn* (1981) and *The Voyage of the Ludgate Hill* (1987). The books have this in common: the main characters in both are real people, William Blake and Robert Louis Stevenson. Dreaming your way into history has its problems. To narrate a story from the point of view of Blake—who but the spirit of William Blake could do it?

The narrator who relates the doings at William Blake's Inn is an outsider. Like Red Riding Hood, he is the one making the journey. He has the broad curiosity of a traveler; he reads the King of Cat's postcards, he overhears Blake conversing with the Wise Cow, and when he recounts what he's seen and heard of the Tiger or the sunflowers, he has enough sense to leave himself out of it and let these creatures speak for themselves, using the phrases and stanza forms Blake himself gave them in "The Tyger" and "The Sunflower." Most important, the narrator is not one of the permanent residents. Like all mortals on this planet, his stay has a beginning and an end. So his point of view is close to mine and, I hope, to my reader's. Our lives have the shape of his story.

The narrator in *The Voyage of the Ludgate Hill* is also a traveler—Stevenson himself. The poem was inspired by a voyage that Stevenson actually made from London to New York, which he describes in a letter as follows.

O, it was lovely on our stable-ship, chock full of stallions. She rolled heartily, rolled some of the fittings out of our stateroom, and I think a more dangerous cruise (except that it was summer) it would be hard to imagine. But we enjoyed it to the masthead, all but Fanny; and even she perhaps a little. When we got in, we had run out of beer, stout, cocoa, soda-water, water, fresh meat, and (almost) of biscuit. But it was a thousandfold pleasanter than a great big Birmingham liner like a new hotel; and we liked the officers, and made friends with the quartermasters, and I (at least) made a friend of a baboon (for we carried a cargo of apes), whose embraces have pretty near cost me a coat. (Colvin, 6–7)

Several years earlier, Alice and Martin Provensen sent me their small green volume of Stevenson's letters and asked me if I would write a text for them to illustrate based on his account of the voyage of the Ludgate Hill. Delighted to be doing another book with them, I read two biographies of Stevenson and set out to write it.

Every story takes its writer on a journey that moves from "Once upon a time" to "happily"—or unhappily—"ever after." The journey from Stevenson's letter to finished poem was not easy. I'd thought of the Ludgate Hill as a latter day Noah's ark and filled it with exotic animals not mentioned in Stevenson's letter. I had forgotten the Provensens' high regard for historical accuracy. They were polite but distressed. The final version of the poem invents the human characters—I didn't have a passenger list—but not the animals. The Provensens were right. Horses and apes it would have to be, if I wanted to let Stevenson tell the story for himself.

Or rather sing it for himself. *The Voyage of the Ludgate Hill* is a sea chanty. I hope Stevenson would find that appropriate. And I hope Martin, who died only a few weeks before the publication of our book, would feel that the three of us had worked so that Stevenson could tell his own story.

REFERENCES

Colvin, Sir Sidney, ed. *The Letters of Robert Louis Stevenson.* Vol. 3. New York: Scribner's, 1925.

Jacobi, Frederick, Jr., ed. "Ole Shut-Eye." In *Tales of Grimm and Andersen.* New York: Modern Library, 1962.

Willard, Nancy. *A Visit to William Blake's Inn.* New York: Harcourt Brace, 1981.

———. *The Voyage of the Ludgate Hill.* New York: Harcourt Brace, 1987.

24

Out Loud: Centering the Narrator in Sound

EVE MERRIAM

For me the major function of poetry is to give pleasure. Doublemeant pleasure—the exactitude of the language and the musicality of the phrasing.

When I hear a poem I feel it through my whole body, especially in my throat, in the pit of my stomach, and in my extremities: toes twitter, fingers start feathering. It's like a shot of adrenalin or a whiff of pure oxygen. The techniques used in the poem may vary: rhyme or non-rhyme, assonance, alliteration, plosives, gutturals, sibilants, repetitions, refrains: more more, my plea is more.

And when I hear—or recite—a poem I prefer to stand rather than sit because a dance is involved. It may be a stately waltz or a hopping limerick; langorous or lively, the rhythms are there to embrace.

Please notice that I say *when I hear* and not *when I read.* Poetry is above all a verbal pleasure. In 548 B.C. Simonedes of Ceos remarked that poetry is vocal painting as painting is silent poetry. Recently a child said to me, "When you read it out loud, it understands itself better."

Agreed, agreed to both statements. I love (yes, love, not paltry like) the sounds of syllables, especially onomatopoeic delights, words that sound like what they mean. It pleases me enormously, like some kind of mathematical elegance, that one has to open one's mouth wide to say the words "Out Loud." You can't purse up your lips and be a tight miser; you have to be prodigal, spendthrift. The sound is WOW! OUT LOUD.

The very word "sound" is particularly felicitous, a centering for me. I enjoy the layers, the wrappings to be unpeeled in that monosyllable—sound as something auditory, and also laudatory, since the word also means something that is *solid, ripe, in a state of health, to be depended upon.* Depended a-pun.

Meanings and minings. Merry-go-sounds, mischief. I think it is not accidental that my favorite character in mythology has always remained my childhood favorite: Loki, the Norse god of crafty behavior. Loki. Lucky. Look, key!

The double richness of language is what I try to explore: words and the music therein, sense and the nonsense therein, the spacious expanse of vowels, the cacophony of consonants.

> It doesn't always have to rhyme,
> but there's the repeat of a beat, somewhere
> an inner chime that makes you want
> to tap your feet or swerve in a curve;
> a lilt, a leap, a lightning-split:
> thunderstruck the consonants jut,
> while the vowels open wide as waves in the noonblue sea.
>
> ("Inside a Poem," *A Sky Full of Poems*)

My aim is to convey to myself, the first hearer, and then to others, a sense of the sport and playfulness of language. It's a game. A surprise. An unexpected and yet everyday celebration. There's a physical element in the poem when it's read aloud, akin to skipping rope or throwing a ball. That's the idea I had in mind with the very first poem I wrote for young people, back in 1960:

> A rhyme is a jumprope, let's begin.
> Take a turn and jump right in.
> What can we do with a rhyme for *today?*
> Perhaps we'll go sailing in the *bay.*
> We could feel the silver dots of *spray* . . .
>
> How long do you think this rhyme will *stay?*
> Until the sky turns dark and *gray?*
> (If you were a horse you could answer *Neigh* . . .)
>
> ("A Rhyme Is a Jumprope," *Jamboree Rhymes for All Times*)

I find it great fun to fool around with onomatopoeic sounds. The rrrrrroar of ocean waves upon the sh-sh-shore. In the country, the dry click of crickets, the creak of a wicker rocker. The whispering susurrus of leaves on a quaking aspen.

Sounds of creatures. The velvet soft as fur purr of a kitten that changes into a yowling howl of a MeOW! The word "serpent," how satisfying! Starting out with its slithery slippery S so sinuously, magically draping its pliant self into the letter shape.

Sounds of objects. The tick tick tick pop of an electric toaster. Slip slap of the windshield wiper. Swish swash of the washing machine. Drip drop drip of the leaky faucet.

I try to avoid invented sound effects. The words I use (with the exception perhaps of *Mean Song* where I deliberately made up swear words to replace the standard trite ones), the words I enjoy and employ are all to be found in the dictionary. Sometimes an uncommon word can set off a verse for me. A gazebo. A kibitzer. A gallimaufry.

My hope is that each hearer may respond with her or his idiosyncratic voice. And with alacrity. Passive is for television staring; poetry demands an active ally, the human voice and the human body in motion. I want poems to snap at the hearer, to tickle a child into unlocking folded hands. I want poems to make you fidget and get up on your feet, punch out the rhymes or rhythms, laugh, yelp, stamp, stomp, shake your head, wriggle, bounce, jounce.

When I first started writing for young people, I felt particularly conscious of speaking—and therefore wanting to write in—the American language rather than English. Some of the poems that I recalled from my childhood were puzzlingly anglicized: counterpane, it turned out, was not some sort of window but a bedspread. A macintosh was not a ruddy sweet-scented apple but a raincoat. So I set out to write in an American idiom. I use a mishmash of words and do not necessarily scorn slang or cartoon vocables.

> Slam, slam, slam goes the steel wrecking ball;
> Bam, bam, bam, against a stone wall . . .
>
> Crash goes a chimney, pow goes a hall,
> Zowie goes a doorway, Zam goes a wall . . .
> ("Bam, Bam, Bam," *Jamboree Rhymes for All Times*)

Some of the influences on my work date back to my childhood pleasures. The daily newspaper in Philadelphia, where I grew up, carried a column on the editorial page that often featured light verse by Tom Daly. I can still recite "Ebenezer had a girl, / Ebenezer's girl was Flo; / Talk of tides of love, great Caesar! / You should see them Eb and Flo." I also appreciated the folk wisdom of "I eat my peas with honey, / I have done so all my life. / They do taste kind of funny, / But it keeps them on the knife." The notion of such bad table manners appealed greatly to an outwardly well-behaved little girl. I was also fortunate in that the illustrious D'Oyly Carte Light Opera Company brought Gilbert and Sullivan's repertoire to our city every year, so the tongue-twisting narrative lyrics of the brilliant W. S. G. were familiar to me. I never was forced to memorize poems, but I did, for the joy of it, for the pleasure of being able to dance my secret dance with rollicking rhymes and rhythms whenever I wanted.

It may be possible to sort out three strands in my work. (Three, by the way, is my favorite number, and I have written "A Throw of Threes" in my most recent collection, *Fresh Paint* (1986):

Three Questions for an Angel:
Do you take it off when you go to sleep?
Do they fold back so you can put on a jacket?
Do you have dreams?

and

Three Cures for Melancholy:
a barrel organ
a conversation with a mynah bird
a sprinkle of cinnamon inside your socks

The first, and perhaps main strand, is my delight in word play, in the mellifluous and ridiculous aspects of language, in oddities and quirks. I am happy when I am clowning around with language, brandishing slapstick nonsense, falling down over polysyllables, balancing on the thin wire of riddles. I like horseshoe curves and unexpected turns.

By the Shores of Pago Pago
Mama's cooking pots of couscous,
Papa's in the pawpaw patch,
Bebe feeds the motmot bird,
and I the aye-aye in its cage. . . .
Kiki hopes her juju beads
will help to ward off tsetse flies,
Lulu's looking very chichi
in a tutu trimmed with froufrou:

does all this mean our family's cuckoo?
("By the Shores of Pago Pago," *Rainbow Writing*)

The second strand stems, I think, from my having been almost continuously in my life a city cave dweller. I am aware of pollution, of noise, of urban crises, and, of course, of the shadow that hovers everywhere, the threat of the destruction of our planet by humankind's inhumanity to nature. I write poems about such matters, because a subject such as nuclear war matters to children as much as to adults. It is a peculiar kind of ostracism to deny the real world to children.

The third strand that shows up in my work over and again is not a denial of the second, but an extension of it, into an affirmation of the quotidian, the daily caresses and comforts in the world, a being alive with all five senses. I am not an interstellar buff; I am a traveler in the "Here and Now." My credo can be summed up, I think, in the two quatrains of "Beyond Sci-Fi":

Birds in the sea,
fish skyed above:
dream of the marvels
in worlds that may be.

Wake to the wonders
this world shows to me:
birds in the air,
fish in the sea.

(Fresh Paint)

REFERENCES

Merriam, Eve. *Fresh Paint*. New York: Macmillan, 1986.
————. *Jamboree Rhymes for All Times*. New York: Dell, 1984.
————. *A Sky Full of Poems*. New York: Dell, 1986.
————. *Rainbow Writing*. New York: Macmillan, 1976.

THE CRITICAL VOICE

25

How Far from Babylon? The Voices of Stevenson's Garden

JOANNE LEWIS

In the envoy "To Minnie" near the end of Robert Louis Stevenson's *A Child's Garden of Verses*, the poet speaks directly to his cousin as an adult, recalling their days at Colinton Manse. He contrasts the innocence of their childhood games with the complicated exotica of the separate adult worlds they have subsequently entered. He hears "phantom voices" of remembered children calling out a question from the nursery rhyme, " '*How far is it to Babylon?*' " The speaker answers his phantom children with a sigh of nostalgia: "Far, far enough from here—" (*Collected Poems*, 409). In this dramatic situation lie most of the problems faced by the poet writing for children. Since the adult has long ago gone on to the Babylon of adulthood, between the adult poet and the child audience stands the gulf of experience, bridged more or less successfully by memory and talent. Robert Louis Stevenson, in some ways a victim of his own clarity, bridged that gulf in *A Child's Garden of Verses*, skirting the mires of sentimentality and sociopolitical limitations, by developing the voice of a child narrating his own childhood in deceptively simple rhymed verse.

HISTORY OF THE GARDEN

A few years ago, in a remarkable tough-minded discussion of poetry for children, Sheila Egoff described Robert Louis Stevenson as an inventor of the "domestic lyric," an outgrowth of the romantic movement's celebration of childhood as separate from and better than adulthood, a kind of poetry capitalizing on the self-absorption of children in their own everyday interests. The description is only partly accurate. Egoff, like many another commentator on *A Child's Garden of Verses*, lays the reputation for smugness in poetry for children, the perpetuation of an unquestioned white, middle-class society, at the feet not of Stevenson, but of his imitators (226). Because the context of her discussion calls for an examination of new directions in children's literature, she compares Stevenson's followers unfavorably with poets for children who have followed, instead, Ferlinghetti, Ginsberg, and Leroi Jones, who she claims created "a new mandate to explore themes of their own time" (226–27), and whose themes are "anxiety, alienation, racial and social injustice, war, technological overload, and the dangers of urban life" (228).

Fortunately, most of Stevenson's critics and biographers have recognized the honesty and clarity of *A Child's Garden of Verses* even when they may have underrated their value to literature as a whole. James Pope Hennessey describes *A Child's Garden of Verses* as "that fetching record of the workings of the child-mind" (53). John A. Stewart notes that though *A Child's Garden of Verses* "does not escape the sophistication which is the inevitable fruit of knowledge and experience," the "little book mirrors, or reproduces, the joys, the griefs, the ongoings of childhood with a fidelity and happiness of effect probably unequalled in our poetic literature" (1:344). David Daiches provides probably the most complete and balanced assessment of *A Child's Garden of Verses*, calling it "first-rate children's poetry—that is, poetry which uses the devices of the poet naively, not sentimentally or corruptly" (184).

Certainly, the modern world differs radically from the apparently comfortable Victorian world into which Robert Louis Stevenson brought *A Child's Garden of Verses* in 1885. The jaded sensibilities of twentieth-century children, one hears, demand sterner stuff. Children need, they say, more realism, by which is apparently meant writings dealing with social injustice, ecological awareness, nuclear disarmament. While one must admit that surface differences between Stevenson's world and that of the modern English-speaking child are enormous, the childhood concerns that Stevenson rendered best do not appreciably change. Children still fear the dark, still feel weak and small and dependent, still rejoice in the creation of private worlds in which they are strong and in command, still are tugged by simultaneous attraction to the adult world and belief in the superiority of their own more manageable one.

Stevenson is better than his imitators. He continues to speak not only to nostalgic adults but to contemporary children despite his unfashionable, "incorrect" sociopolitical views because he located a voice that could retrieve genuine childhood emotions. Finding the right voice, the sure tone in bridging the gap between the adult's world and the child's in writing poetry for children is far more difficult than it seems. From time to time Stevenson trips on the same wire that tangles weaker poets for children. Most of the time, though, he succeeds because he disciplines himself to plain diction, simple verse forms, confines himself to images from a child's reality, not to a grown-up's projection of it, and creates a world separate from but intimately connected to the adult world into which this imagined child audience must grow.

Another common way modern poets for children have bridged the gulf between adult and child has been to adopt a tone of somewhat raucous humor. Poets like Jack Prelutsky and Shel Silverstein have produced a number of volumes of popular verse for children. The voice they have developed is the voice of the iconoclastic clown. Both poets pretend to hold the adult world at bay with a bold rebelliousness, counterattacking naughtiness, or ebullient irrationality. Poets like Valerie Worth, on the other hand, reduce or ignore the difference between the adult world and child world, and thus the problem of voice, by narrowing the scope to lyrical renderings of closely observed natural phenomena. One of Stevenson's enduring strengths is that while he stays closely within the limits of a child's consciousness, he neither denies the adult world nor loses touch with the child's actual dependency on adults. The adult world hovers all around the fragile cocoon of security constructed by nanny, memory, remembered imaginative play. His child speakers often oppose adult sensibility, make adults at times the enemy, but his children also accept as facts of life the fears and dependencies intrinsic to human childhood. Even as Stevenson vividly remembers and recovers the real joys and pains of childhood, he keeps his audience aware that this world of innocence and security is doomed to fade.

Stimulated by reading Kate Greenaway's *Birthday Books for Children*, Stevenson wrote most of *A Child's Garden of Verses* during bouts of illness at Hyeres in 1883 and 1884. He chose to write verse while he was ill, thinking it would be less demanding than prose. His exacting standards instead made the project occupy his full attention. He wrote to his friend W. E. Henley (October 1883): "I can do whistles [his name for *Child's Garden of Verses*] by giving my whole mind to it: to produce even such limping verse demanding the whole forces of my untuneful soul" (*Letters*, 2:165). In fits of self-deprecation, he seemed unable or unwilling to evaluate what he was accomplishing: "You see how this d——d poeshie flows from me in sickness: Are they good or bad? Wha kens?" (*Letters*, 2:220). He defended them to literary colleagues by belittling them: "These are rhymes, jingles; I don't go for eternity and the three unities" (*Letters*, 2:165). On the other hand, in the same letter he reveals his search for precision in the verbal creation of a child's voice: " 'Twinkled' is just the error; to the child the stars appear to be there; any word that suggests illusion is a horror."

In the dedication to the frankly autobiographical verses Stevenson thanked his nanny, Allison Cunningham, "who did so much to make that childhood happy" (*Letters*, 2:120). Because he writes simply of simple things—swinging, digging in the sand at the seashore, being tucked in bed—some critics feel that these poems are dominated by what David Daiches called a "goody-goody" note (182), but to read the whole volume is to be aware that Stevenson was quite conscious of the shadow side of childhood, though he approaches it obliquely in these poems. To William Archer he explained why he did not directly deal with childhood pain:

My childhood was in reality a very painful experience, full of fever, nightmare, insomnia, painful days and interminable nights; and I can speak with less authority of gardens than of that other "land of counterpane." The sufferings of life may be handled by the very greatest in their hours of insight; it is of its pleasures that our common poems should be formed; these are the experiences we should seek to recall or provoke; and I say with Thoreau, "What right have I to complain, who have not ceased to wonder?" and, to add a rider of my own, who have no remedy to offer." (*Letters*, 2:280)

When *A Child's Garden of Verses* was finally printed, Stevenson wrote with a perhaps disingenuous humility to Edmund Gosse that "They look ghastly in the cold light of print," but, he added, "there is something nice in the little ragged regiment for all; the blackguards seem to me to smile, to have a kind of childish treble note that sounds in my ears freshly; in song if you will, but a child's voice" (*Letters*, 2:271). That voice is the precise quality that has made Stevenson's verses outlast the world of British class-consciousness and imperialism into which they were born. It is indeed a child's voice that Stevenson captured in the best of *A Child's Garden of Verses*.

DEFINITIONS

When we speak of a narrative voice in literature we normally think of story: epic, novel, perhaps ballad—forms of fiction, whether poetry or prose. But if every tale must have a teller, so every song must have a singer. The lyric poem as well as the predominantly narrative or dramatic poem has a narrative voice. Once we spoke of character, point of view or persona. Nowadays we tend to speak of rhetorical strategies and the narrative situation, concepts more often applied to forms of prose than forms of poetry. Nevertheless, a poem, like every other form of communication, is a rhetorical situation, and every rhetorical situation demands a speaker as well as an audience. A sense of the voice of a single person speaking, even if the composition may originally have been collective, arises out of the words printed on the page (in the more common case) or words stored in the memory to be recited (in the case of traditional literature). Because most poetry reaches young children through the ear rather than through the eye, one further distinction may be necessary: the "voice" we speak of here is the voice of the poetry as maker, not that of reader or reciter. We must not confuse the "voice' of the poem with the "voice" that is composed of air vibrations falling on a listening ear. Reciter or reader may indeed add new elements to the text, as may the listener(s), but the "voice" of the text is that voice controlled by a human mind choosing the words for a fictive speaker whose characteristics determine diction, images, rhythms.

Beyond the normal questions asked of the rhetorical situation, "What is the relation of the poet to the reader?" lies the further question of the relation of poet to this narrator, and beyond that, the relation of that narrator to implied audience. This network of relationships directs the matter of tone. Analysis of tone depends on "minute language signs." Tone is set by the complex set of relations among such signs, becoming the tonal pattern projected by the poet-speaker (Brower, 101–2, 108). As George T. Wright points out in his analysis of the varying relations among poet, persona, and audience, no matter how direct the expression of the poet's own thoughts and feelings seem to be, as, for instance, in the lyric, "art is formal, and there must always be a distance, minimized or emphasized, between the maker of the poem and the persons in the poem" (110). I would add the distance between persons and reader, maker and reader, and yet another factor, attitude. X. J. Kennedy clarifies: "tone, strictly speaking, is not an attitude by whatever in the poem makes an attitude clear" (16). Tone is whatever conveys an attitude toward the audience, and thus includes all the options available to the poet, the choices with which he must come to terms.

This point becomes particularly relevant in a discussion of poetry directed to a child audience. If the poem, for instance, has a child speaker, that speaker presumably has a closer relationship to a child reader/listener than to the adult poet. One of the reasons that finding a proper voice in poetry for children is such a fragile and difficult operation is that the relationship between persona and implied poet (neither of which is the living poet himself/herself) shifts continuously, within the poem, and from reading to reading. At any point, the adult poet can lose control of his chosen limits. "In fact," observed Wright, "the poet in the poem, the intelligence with which the poet identifies himself and with which the reader is invited to identify himself, may exist anywhere, and at more than one point, along a sort of sliding scale between the person and the whole poem . . . " (117). In the case of the poet of childhood, the rhetorical situation may be further complicated by awareness of a double audience. Tone, expressed primarily through diction and imagery, is the sum of these shifting attitudes. Choice of persona controls diction as well as the range of imagery available, and thus controls voice.

The trap in writing or selecting poetry for children lies in the belief that an adult must adopt a different "voice" when speaking to children. How shall I speak? As a child? As a teacher? As a fanciful being of some sort? The voice of the narrator in poetry for children will vary as much as it does in poetry for adults. It can play, growl, laugh, shriek and weep, as well as sing. It can indulge in irony. It can direct itself to the double audience of child and adult. What it must not dare to do is become self-conscious. The poet writing for children often speaks through some version of his own phantom child. The poet's choice of a narative voice—a persona speaking in a particular manner, in a particular situation, using a particular tone, selecting a particular diction, choosing particular images—will be crucial in creating a world that can be shared with an audience inexperienced in life but supersensitive to condescension and pretension. Stevenson found that narrative voice.

STEVENSON'S VOICES

The voices Stevenson employed in reconstructing his childhood typify the range of voices employed in most signed poetry for children: teacher, observer, adult playmate, nostalgic adult, and the child himself. Though he used them all in A Child's Garden of Verses, he is least successful as the didact, most successful as he moves across the continuum to the consciousness of the child himself. Early collections of poetry for children commonly employed the voice of the teacher proffering moral or pragmatic homilies. Mark Daniel's recent anthology of verse, A Child's Treasury of Poems (1986), beautifully illustrated with nineteenth-century paintings though it is, demonstrates the heavy hand of the didact in children's poetry. (Daniel includes selections from A Child's Garden of Verses, often the more didactic verses.) Such models were undoubtedly as much a part of the matrix of Stevenson's tradition as Kate Greenaway's books. Some readers and critics in fact remember Stevenson best for the complacency of such verses as "A Happy Thought" ("the world is so full of a number of things / I'm sure we should always be happy as kings," Collected Poems, 375), "A Thought" (362), or "Whole Duty of Children" (363). The first three lines of "Whole Duty" admonish the child to tell the truth and have good table manners; the fourth line qualifies realistically: "At least as far as he is able." Why should his adult speaker suddenly step back from his tone of prim propriety? In the role of teacher or preacher, Stevenson can never maintain the consistently serious tone necessary to the moral instructor. He plays this role seldom, and when he does, the voice is often colored by an ironic subtext.

The speaker's voice, for instance, in "Good and Bad Children" takes its top note from the role of instructing adult, but its undervoice is that of playful caretaker. None of the proffered advice is meant to be taken literally: children know that their bones are not "very brittle," nor do children generally want to grow "great and stately" into "kings and sages." Though the teacher-speaker firmly recommends sedateness and a simple diet, disapproves unkindness and greed, the punishment offered in the last stanza to "Cruel children, crying babies" is clearly mock serious; they will grow up "Hated, as their age increases, / By their nephews and their nieces" (377–78). The child may recognize the threat as an unpleasant fate, but can also recognize the distance between the silliness of the message and the tone in which it has been delivered. Stevenson masters the almost impossible: he allows children to share his gentle irony, trusting them to hear his speaker's undervoice.

If one were in any doubt about Stevenson's delight in subverting didacticism, one has only to read through *Moral Emblems*, which he wrote for his stepson Lloyd Osbourne to print on his toy printing press in 1881–82. The publication history of this project of literary play between Stevenson and the child for whom he wrote *Treasure Island* is well documented in Janet Adam Smith's notes to the *Collected Poems* (560). It offers an excellent example of Stevenson's complicated awareness of his own childhood, his responsibilities as an adult, and his relationship to a real child. In one entry Stevenson's woodcut shows two men, one punching the other who is then hurled into the sea below. The speaker moralizes on the aggressor thus:

> Poor soul, his unreflecting act
> His future joys will much contract;
> And he will spoil his evening toddy
> By dwelling on that mangled body. (420)

The verse warns against aggression in the blackly humorous vein of a "Little Willie" jingle. Smith suggests the *Moral Emblems* were stimulated by Stevenson's reading of Isaac Watts' *Songs Divine and Moral for the Use of Children* (560). She offers as evidence the existence of a copy among Stevenson's childhood books. Perhaps Watts' clarity and simplicity did serve as a model of how to write for children, but the adult speaker in Stevenson's "didactic" verse nearly always has his tongue in his undidactic cheek.

Modern poets for children, consciously eschewing the direct role of moral instructor, frequently employ a variation on the didact: an adult, impersonal observer of natural phenomena. One of the best modern practitioners of this voice is Valerie Worth whose "small poems" are lyrical meditations on animate or inanimate objects. A friendly adult observer describes common objects in a series of brilliant analogies and strong musical effects. The "voice" in Worth is dispassionate, dry, calm, yet approachable. Perhaps because of his penchant for gentle irony, Stevenson does not find this voice a particularly congenial one. The adult speaker in his "Looking-Glass River" (382–83), for example, guides his companions to experience the mirror of the still, smoothly flowing river in which "we" will see our faces reflected. "Patience children," he cautions, thus establishing his imagined audience, as he urges his listeners to watch the circular ripples fade. In "From a Railway Carriage" (384) the speaker disappears into the camera eye, recording the rapidly passing scene from the train for a disembodied listener. A child listener is implied by the strong rhythm of representational dactyls, but is not otherwise present in the poem. In "Fairy Bread" (383) a supernatural being specifically entices the "dusty-footed children" up to his or her "retiring room" with food and stories. The title claims "Fairy," but the "voice" of the poem sounds more like companionable nanny than like the mystical folk who inhabit the poetry of Margery Allingham or Walter de la Mare. In all three poems Stevenson's voice shifts its locus, pitches itself somewhat uncertainly.

While Stevenson can and does indulge in playful irony, he cannot be said to be writing within, or anywhere near, the nonsense tradition of Carroll and Lear, whose ironies are massive and structural. Nonsense poems written for children usually spring from the role of adult as child playmate, in collusion with the child against a somewhat hostile, or at least irrational, adult world of rules. When this is the expression of a genuine and necessary psychological position on the part of the writer, as it is in the cases of Edward Lear and Lewis Carroll, the results can be brilliant. When the role is adopted arbitrarily out of a mistaken sense of how to play with a child, the result is heavy-handed self-consciousness. The adult poet peeks over the edge of the manuscript or watches closely out of the corner of the eye to see if the child is being properly seduced by the adult's humor. Stevenson avoids the genre of nonsense altogether and uses infrequently the role of adult playmate.

He prefers the direct to the oblique. When he creates an imaginary world, it is the play world of a real and lonely child. The solitary child is the speaker Stevenson chooses most often and most successfully in A Child's Garden of Verses. Sometimes the child's voice is tainted or at least colored by sophisticated perceptions. Most often the child's voice speaks cleanly of child experience, evoking universal recognitions in both child and adult. In the first group are those poems that seem surrounded by the knowledge that the child speaker must grow into adult responsibility. The child either resists this "truth" or faces and embraces it, welcoming the exotica that adulthood seems to bring. In the second group, the child speaker recreates a lived experience, then reacts to it with curiosity, joy or fear. This latter, larger group contains most of Stevenson's best known poems. (The end section, "Envoys," addresses specific adults, always in an adult voice; they are tributes or explanations, but are not really part of the main body of poems.)

Let me illustrate the notion that the child voice is sometimes "tainted" with an adult perception. In "The Gardener" (404) a child speaks to a workman. The speaker separates himself from the adult world of work and responsibility as he describes the gardener who "does not love to talk," and who insists that the playing child keep to the garden paths. The child's mind controls concrete, unsubtle images in the first two stanzas: the flowers are "red, green, and blue," the gardener works silently, refusing to play. At the third stanza, an adult ventriloquist enters the child voice: "Silly gardener, summer goes," winter comes, life ends. "O how much wiser you [the gardener] would be" to play, the child declares. Children can indeed be impatient with adults who refuse to pay attention to them, but it is the adult, not the child who is conscious of the brevity of life, who fears time's swift passage. "Looking Forward" (368) also mixes the voices of child and adult, but with more success. The childish "I" imagines himself grown "to man's estate," an adult phrase, but locates the evidence of adult potency purely in images drawn from a childish consciousness; he'll "tell the other girls and boys / Not to meddle with my toys" (368).

"Keepsake Mill" (376) maintains a double consciousness throughout its six stanzas. Two boys, one of them the speaker, crawl under branches to the forbidden site of the weir. In the fourth stanza, this speaker, hearing the mill wheel turning "today" suddenly attains an adult's temporal sense: this mill wheel will still be turning "Long after all of the boys are away." The child, with unnatural prescience, predicts a future in which he and his friend, "old and all gaily apparelled," will "meet and remember the past." Still, Stevenson retains the sense of a child speaking by envisioning these old men keeping into old age the beans and marbles over which they quarrel in the present. Stevenson rarely succumbs to sheer nostalgia, but one rejoices that *A Child's Garden of Verses* contains few of these mixed or "tainted" blossoms.

Like Kipling, Stevenson has been charged in recent years with the sins of his class, nationality, and period. The western industrial nations are (quite rightly) examining their consciences, saying their mea culpas for the smugness of white supremacy, the assumptions of imperialism. One hears cited as evidence against Stevenson such poems as "Foreign Children" (378) and "Travel" (366). "Little Turk or Japanee, / O! don't you wish that you were me" may sound to the politically sensitized like purest chauvinism. Such a reading overlooks Stevenson's irony. A curious counterpoint prevails here between the exotic images the speaker associates with "Foreign Children" and seems to be rejecting in favor of the complacent security of his own ways: being fed on "proper meat," living safely at home. The child speaker does have a natural childhood conservatism, but he simultaneously entertains an even stronger natural childhood attraction to the novel, the colorful, the strange. Though he seems to say, "You poor little foreign children," he reveals his attraction in enumerating the very details which are supposed to make them benighted: "the scarlet trees," ostrich eggs, giant turtles, lions. He doesn't have to admit his fascination. The images confess for him. The point was not lost on me as a child. Are today's children duller and more humorless? I think not.

Stevenson's child personae frequently develop understanding of their own world by contrast with images of the unknown and exotic. Such images Stevenson naturally drew from his remembered childhood world, which was the flourishing world of British colonialism. In "The Sun's Travel" (379), the speaker contrasts his own play in Scottish daylight while "Each little Indian sleepy-head" is being put to bed. The catalog of exotic places in "Travel" (366–67)—Crusoe's island, the Great Wall of China, Egypt and the Nile— may sound to overattuned political ears like rampant expansionism, but images of apes, "cocoa-nuts," camel caravans legitimately fill the head of the speaker as a child of his culture. What does this child speaker imagine himself finding on his travels? Stevenson's speaker makes the strange familiar as he imagines finding not exotic jewels and heaps of treasure, but the "toys / Of the old Egyptian boys." Repeatedly, Stevenson's child persona extends imaginative sympathy toward "Other little children." In "Where Go the Boats?" (369) he wonders about domestic "other children" living further downstream in England.

The bulk of Stevenson's children's verses employ a child speaker free of such mixed perception, free from this "adulteration" by a sophisticated awareness beyond the capacity of the fictive persona. Confined to child perceptions, this voice expresses the childhood universals of vulnerability, loneliness, fear of the dark, and, on the other hand, restless curiosity about his immediate world, the pleasures of shared dramatic play, an unmitigated joy in being. Most of Stevenson's best work in *A Child's Garden of Verses* employs this unstrained child voice.

Vulnerability and fear mingle in the voices that speak in Stevenson's going to bed poems. "Bed in Summer" (362) captures a normal and ubiquitous resentment at being excluded from communal activity in being put to bed. (The outrage must burn even more fiercely in long northern Scottish twilights than in the Southern California in which I grew up.) The "you" to whom the child speaker pleads his case in stanza three ("does it not seem hard to you . . . to have to go to bed by day?") is all of us, cast as adults forced to remember the frustrations of childhood. Expression of resentment escalates to more fully articulated resistance and fear in "North-West Passage" (387–88). In part one, the voice sounds a false bravado: "Must we to bed indeed? Well then, / Let us arise and go like men." Part two, "Shadow March," makes the "jet-black night" almost palpable as it "stares," "crawls," hides from the child's light, but "moves with the moving flame" held in a trembling hand as the child feels "the breath of the Bogie in my hair." The necessity for courage and the bliss of reassurance are everywhere in poems such as "My Bed Is a Boat" (380). Comforting allegories invented by kind adults tame night fears in "The Land of Nod" (371), "Young Night Thought" (363), and "The Land of Counterpane" (370). (Contemporary children may need a gloss on counterpane. As a child I preferred the mystery of an unknown "counterpane" to definitions.)

Curiosity and exhilaration override night fears in such poems as "Escape at Bedtime" (374). The child speaker has slipped away from the bedtime-bound adults to marvel at the "crowds of stars" in the night sky. The adults catch him at last "with cries" and pack him off to bed, but the stars keep on "going round in [his] head." The child speaker cherishes this talisman against fear, a charm that seems to have come directly from the universe. The night sky for modern urban children may be so filled with smog and neon that the stars have dimmed or disappeared, but the capacity to invent protections to ward off the evil eye of the night remains.

Producers of children's television know that children still puzzle over natural phenomena: stars reflected in a body of water, windstorms, snail trails. One of Stevenson's most anthologized, most quoted poems, "My

Shadow" (371–72), employs a child speaker to express a child's delighted bafflement with the phenomenon of one's own shadow. The poem not only records the puzzle of a shadow's apparent defiance of the rules of growth and behavior, but the child voice sounds a triumph in scolding the "errant" shadow as a lazy coward. What an opportunity to feel superior to something in this world over which he has so little control. In the less well-known four-line poem, "Auntie's Skirts" (370), the speaker simply records the passage of a Victorian woman through the house by the sound of her skirt on the floor and its bulk as it "trails behind her." As in Herrick's "Whenas in silks my Julia goes," the verse creates a speaker attentive to the minutest detail of his physical world.

The sheer and solemn joy of dramatic invention at play with playmates or alone is Stevenson's real métier. In this category he has never been matched. We know that "Pirate Story" (364) reconstructs an actual scene of play; he wrote to his cousin Henrietta Milne identifying her as one of the children in that poem, and specifying the scene of "A Good Boy" (373) as the "B[ridge] of A[llen] when we had a great play with the little Glasgow girl" (*Letters*, 185). The child speaker in both poems employs first person singular to include other children; the time is the present. In the first, three children imagine that a basket becomes a pirate ship. In "A Good Play" (368) two children construct another ship "of the back-bedroom chairs" full of pillows. In "Marching Song" (374) six children play at being grenadiers, at least until they've had "enough of fame and pillage." In each case though the speaker says "we," his details describe the drama of the activity, not social interchange.

A number of poems record scenes of solitary dramatic play. In "Block City" (393) the child addresses an implied child ("What are you able to build with your blocks?"), but the text of the poem describes only the speaker's activity. One of Stevenson's favorites (not one of his best poems, however) was "The Little Land" (396–97), in which a child shuts his eyes and imagines the real world from a diminutive point of view "Where the clover tops are trees," "And the ants go marching by / Carrying parcels with their feet." Imaginative projection into a disproportionate world is part of an honorable literary tradition (Queen Mab, Gulliver, Tom Thumb, Thumbelina) as well as a psychological solace. Typically, the Stevenson child solemnly manipulates the details of a well-known physical world, usually to make loneliness, illness, or boredom more bearable. His play in a sickbed he detailed in "The Land of Counterpane." In "The Hayloft" (385) heaps of sweet-smelling hay become "Mount Clear, Mount Rusty-Nail, Mount Eagle, and Mount High," inhabited by mice.

Stevenson's solitary child does not always need to heighten landscapes with exaggerated fancy. Before Stevenson, few had caught a child's sheer pleasure in everyday activity. His child narrators report a variety of ordinary experiences in ordinary language, but with an accuracy of observation that raises the effect to wonder. At the seashore the tide moves in on holes the child has dug with his spade ("At the Seaside," 362), the personified wind moves elements of the landscape about like a bully or a large animal ("The Wind," 376), the upward arc of a swing gives the speaker a chance to "look down on" various aspects of the landscape, expressing happy momentary dominance of the world in which one is normally small and impotent ("The Swing," 382).

The voice in this group of poems is always a child's, but Stevenson varies his implied audience. The child in "At the Seaside" seems to be meditating in tranquility on a phenomenon he has observed. The audience is allowed to overhear his thought. In "The Wind" he addresses an unseen force directly; he challenges, accuses: "I saw you do all these things. Who are you? Where are you?" In "The Swing" the speaker yearns to share his exaltation with someone else, perhaps another child, perhaps a friendly adult, implied by his opening question: "How do you like to go up in a swing . . . ?" The remaining ten lines of the poem report the speaker's reaction; childlike, he has forgotten his audience.

Memory by memory, small experience by small experience, Stevenson dredged the recesses of his childhood and fitted them out with scene and character. In spite of limitations of place and time, in spite of occasional falterings, Stevenson moved with confidence through the world of childhood memory. His garden is not heavily scented with sensory images; the range of his musical effects is narrow. What he did do he did brilliantly indeed. What he did do was to think himself so thoroughly back into his young consciousness that he seems to have been able to reach across temporal barriers. His fluid capacity to shift his full consciousness and attention into the mind of a remembered child, and his extraordinary discipline in fitting words and images to suit the limits of that mind invest A Child's Garden of Verses with a living voice, a genuine "childish treble note" to which we still respond.

REFERENCES

Brower, Reuben. "The Speaking Voice: Dramatic Design." In Perspectives on Poetry. Edited by James L. Calderwood and Harold E. Toliver, 98–108. New York: Oxford University Press, 1968.

Daiches, David. Robert Louis Stevenson. Norfolk, Conn.: New Directions, 1947.

Daniel, Mark, ed. A Child's Treasury of Poems. New York: Dial Books for Young Readers, 1986.

Egoff, Sheila. Thursday's Child: Trends and Patterns in Contemporary Children's Literature. Chicago: American Library Association, 1981.

Hennessey, James Pope. Robert Louis Stevenson. London: Jonathan Cape, 1974.

Kennedy, X. J. An Introduction to Poetry. Boston: Little, Brown, 1960.

Prelutsky, Jack. The New Kid on the Block. New York: Greenwillow Books, 1984.

Silverstein, Shel. A Light in the Attic. New York: Harper and Row, 1981.

Stevenson, Robert Louis. *Collected Poems*. Edited by Janet Adam Smith. London: Rupert Hart Davis, 1950.

————. *The Letters of Robert Louis Stevenson*. 2 vols. Edited by Sidney Colvin. New York: Greenwood Press, 1969. Reprint of *The Valima Letters, Being Correspondence Addressed to Sidney Colvin by Robert Louis Stevenson*, 1894.

Stewart, John A. *RLS: A Critical Biography*. 2 vols. Boston: Little, Brown, 1924.

Worth, Valerie. *More Small Poems*. New York: Farrar, Straus and Giroux, 1976.

————. *Small Poems*. New York: Farrar, Straus and Giroux, 1972.

————. *Small Poems Again*. New York: Farrar, Straus and Giroux, 1986.

————. *Still More Small Poems*. New York: Farrar, Straus and Giroux, 1976.

Wright, George T. "The Faces of the Poet." In *Perspectives on Poetry*, edited by James L. Calderwood and Harold E. Toliver, 109–18. New York: Oxford University Press, 1968.

26

Reactivating the Ear: Orality and Children's Poetry

RODERICK MCGILLIS

Young children live as close to a primary oral culture as anyone can. They learn to understand language through the ear, not the eye: they learn to retain what knowledge they need mnemonically. How many children, of my generation at least, remember when North America was discovered by Europeans by recalling that "In 1492 Columbus sailed the ocean blue"? The numbers of days in a month we remember by recalling the rhyme, "Thirty days hath September, April, June and November." Going to bed was often accompanied in my family with the adage, "Early to bed and early to rise / Makes a man healthy, wealthy and wise." Such oral formulary works its way into the singing games and school yard lore of all children, as the Opies, the Knapps, and others have shown. Not only is this lore a means of retaining knowledge, but it is also, in its many manifestations including jeers, jokes, tricks, riddles, and games, a means of creating community, of drawing children together in a shared experience and culture.

Inside the school, however, children learn to read, to see language spread across the pages of their textbooks, flattened and supine. To accumulate knowledge, children turn to the printed book. Retrieval of this knowledge becomes a silent search through pages of books or through the data base of the computer. Powerful loss and powerful victory.

Traces of the speaking voice grow faint as literature commits itself more and more to the visual temptations of print. Print seduces the voice into abandonment; voice flattens onto the page, spreads as the printer's ink wills, and loses its timbre. Yet the seduction of language to the horizontal printing bed cannot silence it entirely. Speech refuses to lie silent. Neither is it stimulated by a terminal that echoes but does not itself speak. Speech recumbent waits only the willingness to be heard. Once heard, it becomes speech resonant of many voices.

We are inescapably tied to language as print. We are a literate society and all the illusions of pre-literacy, of oral community, cannot disguise the loss of immediacy that the voice had in oral societies. There the mother tongue was at its liveliest. Speaking of the voice of passion, Herder laments that what he calls the "language of nature" is deprived of life once it is written down; script turns it into "an arbitrarily penciled symbol" (90). This language of true feeling, he goes on to say, "was meant to sound, not to depict" (91). Unity, clarity, and immediacy are all aspects of hearing. The language we hear keeps us in tune with others, with the past, with our origins. The visual language of print separates.

Much literature for young children, however, attempts to recreate the immediacy of oral speech. The best illustration of this in process is the practice of Robert Munsch, who writes his stories (most of them anyway) only after he has told them orally for three years. Then "Munsch the writer simply [writes] what Munsch the storyteller [dictates]" (24). Poetry is even more insistent upon its oral origin. Nancy Larrick has commented upon the connection between poetry and orality: "Poetry, beyond any other literary form, solicits participation from the listener or reader. Indeed, some people insist that a poem is not complete until there is a partner adding his own experiences and feelings to those of the poet" (3). She uses the example of folk song that encourages "every child to get into the act, by singing, by clapping and by improvising with new words." She also notes that Pete Seeger asks children to invent stanzas to his songs (50). The Canadian poet, Dennis Lee, does the same. In his postlude to *Alligator Pie* (1974), Lee writes,

One thing I discovered is that the words should never be sacred. A rhyme is meant to be used, and that means changing it again and again. For children's verse passes around in weird and wonderful versions, and the changes always make sense—to the tongue and the ear, if not necessarily to the mind. If your child inadvertently rewrites some of these poems, please take his version more seriously than mine. (63)

Lee goes on to offer brief suggestions for improvising his poems "Alligator Pie" and "Willoughby Wallaby Woo." At first reading, we see that Lee thinks of his poems as occasions for oral performance. The "weird and wonderful versions" that children come up with please the tongue and ear. Lee notes that the poems ought "to be brought to life almost as tiny plays," performances. Their communal and participatory nature comes to Lee as a surprise: "I had never realized how soon a child can take part in 'doing poems.' " All this suggests orality. When Lee speaks of "reading" nursery rhymes to his children, he means reading out loud, and, I suspect, more pertinently, reciting while he pulls faces and bounces young rear ends on his knees. However, the confusion of "reading" and "speaking," as my use of the word "speaks" in the last sentence indicates, is deep in our thinking. Note that Lee mentions the child "rewriting" some of his poems. Normally, however, we think of the written text as sacrosanct; once written words become reified. When we read these reified words, we do so silently, and more often than not quickly and without a sense of their origin in sound. If we reflect a moment, we recall that the word was first spoken and to hear it is the prelude to seeing it; in fact, to hear is to see and to see in this sense is to understand. Writing that can be heard offers us "language lined with flesh," as Roland Barthes puts it.

"Writing aloud" is Barthes' term for writing that is as "delicately granular and vibrant as an animal's muzzle" (67). Such writing we feel along the blood. But "writing aloud" is paradoxical in the way the more familiar term "oral literature" is. For writing and literature are, in themselves, necessarily silent, marks on a page that may have typographical and chirographical life, but that can have no oral-aural life until they are voiced, that is until the collusion of voices within and without the text sound. "Voice" is necessarily heard, and in hearing we participate. In short, when we experience writing orally, we are closer to participating in the literary experience than when we simply see marks on a page. And to participate in the literary experience is, Barthes would remind us, to take pleasure in the text. Such pleasure is playful, delightfully polymorphous. Pleasure derives from performance, but the performance of literature voices a text; it is not primary the way ancient oral performances were. Yet literature in the postmodern culture aspires to the condition of what Walter Ong calls primary orality; it aspires to sing and dance.

Perhaps poetry for the very young has always expressed the postmodern condition since it has never ceased to sing and dance. It is connected to ancient oral-based culture in which, as Nancy Larrick says, the passion for poetry and music "is one of the distinguishing features" (3). Oral poetry and story were participatory, and those who came to hear the minstrels or storytellers "were soon singing or changing repeated lines and sometimes adding new stanzas on the old pattern" (3). In this culture, the teller or singer performs.

Performance is the condition of literature for children, and the residue of this condition sounds in all literature. In pre-literate societies language could not "be seen and not heard"; it had to sound. To communicate was to speak or at least to voice. The same is true for children up to seven years of age. For them, as for those in pre-literate societies, "relationships between human beings are governed exclusively by acoustics (supplemented by visual perception of bodily behavior)" (Havelock, 65). Adults may read literature, but the child can only hear it. We educate the ear before the eye. When we begin to read we transfer the act of communication from the ear to the eye, and what was before acoustically passed on becomes "materially preserved visible artifacts that are capable of rearrangement" (Havelock, 103). The eye, however, comes to dominate, and, as it does, the communal sharing of literature and the singing and dancing of language shift to the silent edicts of the eye. Geoffrey Hartman notes that reading, "especially in print culture, is often used to blind the ear." That is why, Hartman goes on to say, "poetry makes its curious alliance with critical reading, in order to reactivate the ear. Both are auscultations that have the capacity of putting us on the alert toward the silence in us" (142). When the freedom of the voice diminishes, play becomes work.

Under the authoritarian eye, communal play becomes structured work. To "see that this is done" is to act alone, while to "hear what someone did" is to commune. To see is to separate; to hear is to take in. Poetry is for the ear, and consequently, as June Jordan argues, it "overcomes the subject to object relationship" (in Larrick, 58). Poetry, Jordan continues, "presents an opportunity to control the meaning of separation or to obliterate separation" (58). For the very young child, the reading of poetry is a performance, that is, as Richard Bauman defines performance, "a mode of communication, a way of speaking, the essence of which resides in the assumption of responsibility to an audience for a display of communicative skill, highlighting the way in which communication is carried out, above and beyond its referential content" (3). In terms of literature, this suggests oral interpretation that, as Thomas Sloan points out, takes literary meaning to be "not so much discursive as dramatic." Sloan argues:

Meaning should be grasped not merely in terms of denotation and connotation but also in terms of speaker, situation, and action. Meaning is, in short, what "happens" in literature. The "happening" is typically a speaker responding to or within a situation. . . . At any rate, meaning emerges through words, movement, gesture, the character of the speaker, and the nature of his situation. It cannot be expressed as a statement, as a theme, or even a paraphrase. It can be partially expressed by critical talk about the literature. But it can be more than partially expressed by the oral interpreter who, with the language of the literature itself, *performs* the "happening." (7)

Children's poetry never loses its performative aspect.

This is not to say that an understanding of poetry demands that the reader perform it in front of an audience. Rather, we must, if we are to participate in the call and response that all utterance invites us to participate in, realize that the text we read is a speech act performed by a speech subject. Understanding of the speech act is "inherently responsive" and sooner or later, as Bakhtin says, "what is heard and actively understood will find its response in the subsequent speech or behavior of the listener" (*Speech Genres*, 68, 69). When Bakhtin speaks of "what is heard," he speaks of both spoken and written language. To be truly responsive, we must hear what we read. What we hear is a voice that reverberates with other voices since no voice is singular; it can only be a "relative voice." It is through such a voice that we come closest to understanding the literature we read.

Poetry for young children draws attention to its voice, to its oral base, as Dennis Lee's poetry exemplifies. He tells us that he thinks he "learned most from the nursery rhymes" (63). A poem like "Willoughby Wallaby Woo" bears this out. The first lines of the four couplets echo many nursery rhymes, rhymes such as "Handy dandy, riddlety ro, / Which will you have, high or low" or "Diddlety, diddlety, dumpty." But the poem is openly participatory the way the nursery rhyme "There was a monkey" is; the speaker may add verses at will and encourage the listener to do the same: "Willoughby, wallaby, wince. / I want to sing like Prince." In short, we hear in this short poem the echo of many singing and action rhymes that date back hundreds of years. Although the "I" of the poem feels kind of glum, he or she is as unindividualised as the speaker of "Cock a doodle doo! / My dame has lost her shoe. / My master's lost his fiddling stick, / And knows not what to do." In both Lee's and the traditional rhyme, there is a sense of closure, in Lee's by the repeated line, "I don't know what to do," and in the traditional rhyme by the happy recovery of the lost shoe and the fiddling stick. Yet both the sense of closure and the rather flat feeling (in Lee's verse) are overcome by the sound of the verses, their jauntiness, their playful manipulation of language. The "woo" is not a woe, but a wooing; the verse woos the speaker to invent further verses, to take part in creating the rhyme, to utilize his own fiddling stick or trip her own soft shoe. The verse is truly participatory in its wooing. To participate is to engage in verbal play, to create a language that sings and dances, and to break free of the limitations of meaning. The meaning of "Willoughby Wallaby Woo" is right here, in its creation of community through the invitation to play with the text. The authority of the author transfers to the reader and the text is no longer fixed and sacred.

The voice of an oral culture sounds in "Willoughby Wallaby Woo," a voice that is and is not Dennis Lee's. Of course, Lee's voice is here, but it echoes and reverberates with the voices of the whole tradition of the nursery rhyme. The voice is necessarily connected with flow and desire more than with meaning, if by "meaning" we understand a "theme" or "point" to the verse. Unavoidably, something is lost: a centering and stabilizing presence. Yet something conservative is here too: the desire to return to an oral language.

This desire is clearly evident in the nursery language and musical cadences of poems for the very young, poems such as Lee's "Alligator Pie" and "Singa Song." More complex poems for somewhat older children also express this desire. Take, for example, Ted Hughes' *Moon-Whales and Other Moon Poems* (1976). The poems in this volume are playful fantasies of moon creatures, but the most powerful fantasy of all is the fantasy of a pure language, an unmediated communication between author and reader. The poet is not so much an authority reflecting on meaningful aspects of life, as he is an orchestrator calling for the reader to sing words and to feel deeply. In *Poetry in the Making* (1967), Hughes describes poems as "a sort of animal" with their "own life" that is "separate from any person, even from their author." He emphasizes that poems are written things, however, when he remarks that "nothing can be added to them or taken away without maiming and perhaps even killing them" (15). The reader must not tamper with the text.

Hughes writes poems that sing and dance, that beg to be heard. Alliteration, recurring rhyme, and quickening rhythm trip off the tongue. In "Moon-Hops" Hughes plays with sound to invite the reader to participate in the performance of the poem. Hughes' longer, more "writerly" poems also express what Ong might call oral residue. "Moon-Wind" is about silence; the poem's center is in language that repeats and resounds and holds fast to an utter stillness that utters aloud. The poet speaks of disruption, rupture, and darkness dropping again. Yet the voice speaks not only of loss and dislocation; it also invokes imaginative participation. The poem performs an about-face on our notions of both moon and wind, and in so doing draws us into collusion with it. When we perform the poem, speak it, we are the speaker addressing a disoriented "you."

Walter Ong reminds us that "written texts all have to be related somehow, directly or indirectly, to the world of sound, the natural habitat of language, to yield their meanings. 'Reading' a text means converting it to sound, aloud or in the imagination, syllable-by-syllable in slow reading or sketchily in the rapid reading common to high-technology cultures. Writing can never dispense with orality" (1982, 8). The short "Word Poem" by Nikki Giovanni appears to demand silent reading by inhibiting our ability to read it fairly out loud. Absence of punctuation forces us to look at the poem and take it in silently to establish its sense. As the subtitle indicates ("perhaps worth considering"), we are to reflect on this poem and consider the ways of reading it; its meaning alters as we note the orthographic trick with the word "become." How are we to vocalize this poem? The slash tells us to read the word "become" as two words, yet the slash also tells us that this is one word separated, one word we may read as one word. This gives us potentially two ways of hearing the poem. The two readings are, however, one. The poem is distinctly oral in its incantatory voice. Its repetitions, the rise and fall of its cadence hark back to the oral chant, the rhythmic call to action and participation of an oral community. The voice here is the voice of the oral poet who knows her audience, knows its dreams and feelings. But in the sense that the poet shares her audience's dreams and feelings, she participates in the singing spirit that has passed down through generations. The voice of the poet is intimate, confident in the deep sympathy of the audience; the poet touches the audience's spirit and in turn reveals personal inner depths.

Levity does not necessarily preclude intimacy. Arnold Lobel's *The Book of Pigericks* speaks from the long tradition of the limerick, and in its personal voice it harks back to Edward Lear. Lobel hitches on to the tradition of laughter that equalizes, that undermines authority; he speaks as one of the pigs and delights in writing of a rude pig from Duluth who is uncouth, a poor pig on the street whose garbage stew is a treat, and a strange pig who after dark alarms folk in the park. Many of these limericks concern the body and food. Messy and abundant eating, awareness of the body, these do not embarrass but rather bring us together. As Bakhtin says of Rabelaisian laughter: "Laughter created no dogmas and could not become authoritarian, it did not convey fear but a feeling of strength. It was linked with the procreating act, with birth, renewal, fertility, abundance" (1984, 95). What better form than the limerick to hook into the tradition of laughter since the whole point to the limerick is abundance: one good limerick deserves another and the reader feels the urge to create more. Everyone participates; everyone laughs together.

Despite the closed form of the limerick, it is never complete. The creator of limericks is never concerned with completion. To be full of rhyme is to be flush forever. Also of little concern is theme or what the work is all about. More important are the entertaining possibilities of language, the music of words. Despite the socializing urge of print culture, the power of oral language to "rhapsodize" continues to sound from the page.

REFERENCES

Bakhtin, Mikhail. *Rabelais and His World*. Translated by Helene Iswolsky. Bloomington: Indiana University Press, 1984.

———. *Speech Genres & Other Late Essays*. Translated by Vern W. McGee. Austin: University of Texas Press, 1986.

Barthes, Roland. *The Pleasure of the Text*. Translated by Richard Miller. New York: Hill and Wang, 1975.

Bauman, Richard. *Story, Performance, and Event*. Cambridge: Cambridge University Press, 1986.

Giovanni, Nikki. *ego-tripping and other poems for young people*. New York: Lawrence Hill, 1973.

Hartman, Geoffrey H. *Saving the Text: Literature/Derrida/Philosophy*. Baltimore: Johns Hopkins University Press, 1981.

Havelock, Eric A. *The Muse Learns to Write*. New Haven: Yale University Press, 1986.

Herder, Johann Gottfried. "Essay on the Origin of Language." In *On the Origin of Language: Two Essays*. Translated by Alexander Gode. Chicago: University of Chicago Press, 1986 (1966).

Hughes, Ted. *Poetry in the Making*. London: Faber, 1967.

———. *Moon-Whales and Other Moon Poems*. New York: Viking, 1976.

Knapp, Mary and Herbert Knapp. *One Potato, Two Potato*. New York: Norton, 1976.

Larrick, Nancy, ed. *Somebody Turned on a Tap in These Kids*. New York: Delacorte, 1971.

Lee, Dennis. *Alligator Pie*. Toronto: Macmillan, 1974.

Lobel, Arnold. *The Book of Pigericks*. New York: Harper and Row, 1983.

Munsch, Robert. "Whatever You Make of It," *Canadian Children's Literature*, 43 (1986): 22–25.

Ong, Walter J. *Orality and Literacy: The Technologizing of the Word*. London: Methuen, 1982.

Opie, Iona and Peter. *The Lore and Language of Schoolchildren*. London: Oxford University Press, 1959.

Sloan, Thomas O., ed. *The Oral Study of Literature*. New York: Random House, 1966.

PART VI

Historical Fiction

Introduction

GARY D. SCHMIDT

In *Friedrich* and *I Was There*, Hans Peter Richter uses a first person narrator to experience and describe the growth of the Nazi machine in Germany of the 1930s. His narrator is, in many ways, himself, for the books are written as a testament to his times and as a warning to the present. Everything the narrator sees, Richter saw. However, the books are classified as historical fiction in that the characters are fictionalized, the events manipulated into a linear narrative progression, and the chaos of real characters and situations ordered into a story that has unity, purpose, and a consistent ominous tone.

In presenting real events under the guise of fiction, Richter is struggling with the tensions of the genre of historical fiction. The writer within this genre works on the interface of history and imagined story, playing the dual narrative role of the historian and the storyteller. Though bound by historical fact, the writer is free to create characters, manipulate perspectives, suggest unifying connections between plot situations, and recreate events that are unrecorded or only sketchily recorded.

In historical fiction, narrators place real events into a fictive mode to sharpen their sense of reality and drama for the child reader. Esther Forbes recreates the meetings of the revolutionary committee of Boston during the 1770s in *Johnny Tremain*. Elizabeth George Speare tells of the preaching of Jesus in first-century Galilee in *The Bronze Bow*. Rosemary Sutcliff envisions a ritual of manhood among the Picts during the Roman occupation of Britain in *The Eagle of the Ninth*. James and Christopher Collier picture the political infighting during the Revolutionary War in *Jump Ship to Freedom*.

The narrator of any work of historical fiction determines how the tension between reality and imagination is resolved. A narrator set outside the period, distant from it in terms of time and setting, will often have a stance that places the characters and plot situations into a cultural context of which the reader can never be a part. The reader remains an observer of history, not a participant. The narrator of historical fiction may also work from within that period through a first-person narrator, through a narrator who consistently maintains the protagonist's point of view, or through a narrator native to the culture, one who holds the assumptions and perspectives of that culture. Such a narrative stance allows the reader to see history from the inside through sharing the perspectives of the narrator.

Patricia Clapp seeks to resolve the narrative tension by establishing a narrator and characters who speak with authentic voices from within a culture. For Clapp, trained as an actress and playwright, it was natural to move from the theater into history. She has the trained ear that can catch the voices of those who lived in the past. In her role as a writer of historical fiction, Clapp listened to the voices of the past through reading diaries, letters, newspapers, journals, legal proceedings, military history; there she heard young female voices at important junctures in history. She began with the landing at Plymouth (*Constance, A Story of Early Plymouth*) and moved into the Revolutionary War (*I'm Deborah Sampson: A Soldier in the War of the Revolution*), the Salem witch trials (*Witches' Children*), and the Civil War (*The Tamarack Tree*). In each historical situation, it was the voice of the individual (often a young woman) that gave her the opportunity to experience history as drama.

The voice—first person, journal, or autobiography—is a means for exploring the protagonist's consciousness and bringing together reader and writer. In the process, Clapp herself comes close to assuming that consciousness because she sees and feels what her character sees and feels, speaks what her character speaks. Writer's voice and character's voice here buckle, creating a kind of collaboration in which writer and character are the same.

In *Constance*, the journal device becomes a private but dramatic form. The records Constance keeps become purgative for her and a means of access for the reader into a female voice torn by conflict over the loss of the familiar and faced with the unfamiliar. In *I'm Deborah Sampson*, an older female autobiographical narrator looks back on her life to remember and discover how that life has shaped her, or how she has shaped her life. This comes about as Deborah becomes an omniscient narrator who stands back, projects her life out onto a stage, and listens to her own voice from the past in order to understand her voice in the present.

Janet Lunn's storytelling is more affected by the cinema than the stage. She argues that her narrator works as a camera, moving in and about characters, establishing perspectives, suggesting motivations. The voices of the past are not as important for her as the stories and sensibilities of the past, all of which are mediated by an apparent or hidden narrator represented by the camera.

Although *Shadow in Hawthorn Bay* had an inception much like that of Clapp's *Constance*—both stories began to come together when the authors read actual memoirs—and though they both use narrators who consistently maintain the protagonist's point of view, Clapp and Lunn disagree on how that narrator can function. While Clapp argues that she as author can enter into the consciousness of her characters and use a narrator who comes out of the intimate relationship, Lunn argues that the writer of historical fiction can really only be a doppelgänger, a fellow traveler who shares a journey but can never really become that other traveler. A twentieth-century writer can never fully shed twentieth-century sensibilities, can never actually become a historical figure. The vitality of the narrator, Lunn writes, comes instead from the passion of the author for an imaginary figure.

Joan Blos, unlike many other writers of historical fiction, has created the historical events in which her narrator participates. What roots the text in its period is not its historicity, but the authenticity of its details and the sensibilities of its narrator. Private feelings—not to be shared in any other context—are revealed by a narrator writing for herself alone. The reader, unbeknownst to the narrator, becomes a witness to the narrator's inner life, a life not shared with anyone. Yet the journal form, Blos has discovered, has an inherent limitation. Liberating the narrator, it restricts the author. With its basic nonfictive characteristics, the form prohibits the inclusion of much that might appear in a novel. Yet it is this limitation that creates its own believability.

Muriel Whitaker claims that one way that writers can become intimate with their narrators and characters is through engaging in the child's-eye view. Examining writers of Canadian prairie fiction—W. O. Mitchell, Margaret Laurence, and Gabrielle Roy—Whitaker suggests that each uses the prairie as a stage as well as a crucible. By choosing the child as narrator, or by having the narrator focus on the consciousness of the child, the raw, uncontrolled emotion of the child in the prairie context is released. The child narrator experiences extremes of emotion with no apology. Hence the narrator brings the reader closer to the prairie experience than a controlled adult narrator might have.

Ann Donovan, in contrast, calls into question all matters of narratorial reliability in her examination of William Mayne's *Drift*. Mayne effaces his narrators, Donovan claims, so that though the story is told in third person, the effect on the reader is one of first person. Both Whitaker and Donovan point out the importance of historical and cultural setting in establishing a narrator in historical fiction; here, Donovan argues that the narrator is completely conditioned by a society. The novel *Drift* shocks by changing the gender (white male to Indian female), culture, and preconceptions of the narrator. In so doing, Mayne assaults the reader's expectations. The reader, more prone to identify with the first narrator, must go through a rite of passage with Rafe in order to assimilate the Indian culture to which Rafe has been so hostile.

Hamida Bosmajian, ranging from Hans Peter Richter's books on the Holocaust to Roland Bennewitz's novel on the post nuclear age, similarly questions the reliability of a narrator of historical fiction, though her questions arise from the distinction between the adult and the child in terms of their vision of history. Adult narrators who tell of historical atrocities must admit, in the end, to failure in attempting to stop those atrocities, or even to limit their scope. Their authority has been meaningless and impotent, and this leads the child to question, challenge, and even deny that authority in the face of historical reality. The adult voice is suspect because it is accountable. The solution to this tension comes in a narrator who disclaims narrative authority and encourages questions and challenges on the part of the child reader. Or, as Bosmajian points out, the narrator may be a child witness who, by virtue of childhood, does not bear the burden of adult responsibility. Bosmajian, in dealing with those events in history and the postnuclear age that seem beyond the child reader's comprehension, concludes that there is no cure for history, and no suitable narrator to tell these tales.

THE AUTHORIAL VOICE

27

Letting History Speak for Itself

PATRICIA CLAPP

When I was seven my parents, my brother, and I moved from Boston to New Jersey, where I was enrolled in a school for girls. I started in the second grade, continuing through the twelfth, and by and large I enjoyed it. I learned how to make paper (an ability I have never since been asked to use), discovered Latin, became acceptably proficient in French and Spanish and gathered high marks in English.

English covered a number of things, such as how to write a formal invitation and how to accept or refuse one, the study of poetry, how to fold a sheet of notepaper and insert it into an envelope properly (a lost art, judging from the wonderful, multifolded letters I receive from young readers), how to parse a sentence, and how to write innumerable essays. I still believe firmly in the restraints imposed by the essay form. You state the point, make the most of it, and quit. All those subjects I liked immensely. Unfortunately, there were also such terrifying courses as math, geography, and history, in all of which I ranked from mediocre to poor. I still count on my fingers when I try to balance my checkbook (but it balances), I have no idea where any-place in the world is located (but I travel a lot), and history was, until fairly recently, a blur of dates on which important events occurred but I could never remember which event went with which date.

In one of my history books there was a drawing of Betsy Ross, surrounded by her full skirts, her rag bag, and a number of bewigged military officers. She was looking coyly up at General Washington, her lips slightly parted, and I wanted desperately to know what she was saying. "Does this pale green suit you, George, or would you prefer a lilac shade?" But there were no words at all. It was always that way with history. Always just text. "Mistress Ross was asked to . . . ", "A decision was made to . . . ", "It was agreed that . . . ", but no word of what was *said* ever entered those pages.

In honesty I must add that I quizzed my seventh grade granddaughter about today's history classes. Combined with geography ("Confusion twice confounded!") and called social studies, she finds it acceptable. I asked her if people *spoke* in her books. "No," she said, "nobody says anything. We just read about them." So history may be acceptable, but it is still not immediate.

Along the way to becoming an adult I realized that history is not just a list of dates, but a record of what people have done, or not done, and it seemed obvious that words must have accompanied such events. Whether it was Sir Henry Stanley's anticlimactic "Dr. Livingston, I presume?" upon finding the exhausted British consul in central Africa, or Neil Armstrong's awestruck voice on the first moon landing, "That's one small step for a man, one giant leap for mankind," people speak. Whatever they do, they talk about it. The world is not silent. It is filled with audible thoughts in the form of words.

People fascinate me. I like to watch them, listen to them, wonder about them. They are exciting. And since people make history, why shouldn't history be exciting too?

The first book I wrote, quite by accident, was *Constance, A Story of Early Plymouth* (1968). It came about after a cousin of my husband's sent us an impressive manuscript of their family genealogy, with the hope that I might type it for him. Some of it dated back to the 1500s and included ancestors who were tutors to early British royalty, other ancestors who came to rather murky ends—it was all people! They wrote Wills (with a capital "W") with homely notations about which two daughters were to share ownership of a cow, who was to get the feather bed or the three silver spoons, which sons were to inherit just which section of land. They kept journals. They *spoke*. I never thought of those records as history; they were the voices of actual people, making known their desires and their opinions. When I reached the section dealing with antecedents who had boarded the little ship "Mayflower" and discovered young Constance Hopkins, fourteen years old, whisked off willy-nilly from her familiar, comfortable London home to a country inhabited by wolves and Indians, I could think of nothing but "How did she feel? Was she frightened? Did she cry at leaving home? How did she manage as she grew up?" It was a story I wanted to discover and tell.

There are, of course, infinite records of the Plymouth settlement in 1620. William Bradford's detailed journals and letters sent back to England, for example, are enthralling reading. I became so filled with the people and their accounts of the voyage, the hardships, the births and deaths, their stubborn progress—I had to put it on paper. Following Governor Bradford's lead I used the journal form for telling the story, and the words came from

Constance as I imagined her. She came to life, she and I became involved, and she spoke.

I repeated the journal, or diary, technique in both *The Tamarack Tree* (1986), a novel of the siege of Vicksburg in 1863, and *Dr. Elizabeth, The Story of the First Woman Doctor* (1974). It seems to me much more intimate than straight exposition, and gives a feeling of *knowing* what my heroine saw, thought, and felt. It may be that after long, long periods of research I became too close to stand aside. I feel that I am there, watching and listening, and I want my readers to feel the same. I can do this most effectively, I think, by climbing into my protagonist's skin. By becoming Constance, or Rosemary Leigh, or Elizabeth Blackwell, I am their voices.

Both *I'm Deborah Sampson* and *Witches' Children* (1982) are written in the first person without the journal device. The first is the true story of a young woman who disguised herself as a man and fought in the American Revolution, and the second is about the infamous witchcraft trials in Salem, Massachusetts, in 1692. All of these books are American history, and all of the heroines existed, with the exception of Rosemary Leigh in *The Tamarack Tree*. She is fictional because I wanted an outsider's viewpoint on the slavery aspect, but her experiences are real, drawn from actual accounts found in a diary kept by a young woman during that dreadful seige.

A voice is for speaking, and speech is immediate. If someone near you shouts "Fire!" you move. If someone murmurs "I love you," you listen. The mood of the speaker is in his voice and his words. It may be urgency, sentiment, fear, or triumph. The speech may be ungrammatical because the speaker is not concerned with syntax right then. Whatever the words are, whatever the tone of voice, you listen and respond accordingly because you are there and you hear what is being said. This is what I try to accomplish— to put my reader there and let the characters speak for themselves.

The opening lines of *Constance* read:

Very well then! I have seen that cold, gray, hard, bleak, unfriendly shore line that everyone is in such a twitch of excitement about. Father hung over the wooden rail gazing at it, his eyes snapping with excitement.
"Come and see, Constance," he roared. " 'Tis America! Come and see it!" (9)

The history books I encountered in school would have said, "The Mayflower first anchored off a shore of what is now Massachusetts in November of 1620."

I like it better my way. I can see, and I hope my readers can, the hard-packed silvery sand on a desolate beach. I can shiver in the November sting of cold, salt air, feel the solidity of the wooden railing as the Mayflower rocks gently at anchor, sense the hope, fear, and optimism of the passengers. I have become Constance Hopkins. My readers are seeing through Constance's eyes and hearing her thoughts. She is already becoming real to them, and what happens to her and the others in the week and months and years ahead is going to matter.

The same instantaneous absorption into a story and the "I was there" viewpoint is the beginning of *Witches' Children.*

I was a little older than most of them, old enough as John Proctor said, "to have a little sense in your head!" If I was not strong enough to resist that madness, how could children as young as Betty Parris and her cousin, Abigail Williams, withstand it? Surely they were helpless. Betty was but nine and Abigail eleven. Or were they helpless? Were any of us? Did we in fact make it happen? (9)

In each case the heroine of the book, by speaking directly, pulls the reader into her life, and the reader knows that whatever befalls that heroine is going to be a shared experience.

Perhaps part of my habit of becoming the narrator stems from having been an actress and a playwright long before I started writing books. Theater is dialogue. The audience is listening to the actual words of the characters on the stage. I want my readers to listen to the actual words of the characters in the book.

In writing historical fiction there are, of course, pitfalls in attempting to speak as people of past generations spoke. Our idioms change, as does phrasing and spelling. The latter doesn't bother me. I am *talking*, not writing, and I feel present-day readers would only be confused by outdated spelling. The essence of the early speech, its rhythms and stresses, its phrasing and elisions begin to come naturally after weeks of research reading. One cannot spend even a few hours immersed in the lengthily titled "A Relation or Journal of the English Plantation settled at Plymouth in New England by certain English adventurers, both merchants and others," written by the mysterious and still unidentified G. Mourt, or General Ulysses Grant's wordy records of the eventual surrender of Vicksburg without becoming saturated with the style. It must always be remembered, however, that in any era the style of writing differs greatly from the manner of speaking. We tend to write more carefully than we speak, especially if the written word is to be published or in any other way widely read. But the vocabulary, and the choice and usage of the words in it, can be quite quickly absorbed for whatever period I am studying.

In *The Tamarack Tree* there was an additional hazard because of the North/South confrontation. Any Southern soldier was proud to be termed a "Confederate," but the epithet "Johnny Reb" would have caused a private battle. In the South it was called the "War of Southern Independence," but in the North it was "The War of the Rebellion." As Rosemary remarks wistfully, "Same war, different names." Since my characters in that book were not only Southern and Northern, but also British, I had to be careful of who said what to whom, and how they said it.

Purely as a means of learning something of history I believe firmly that historical novels, provided they are truthful and stick to the facts, make a more lasting impression on the memory than does that kind of impersonal reporting found in the history books I tried to struggle through. To meet and know Priscilla Mullins and John Alden, as one can in the pages of *Constance*, or the indomitable Elizabeth Blackwell who emerges triumphantly as the first woman doctor in *Dr. Elizabeth*, or the confused, bedeviled Mary Warren of *Witches' Children*, or Deborah Sampson, friend of Paul Revere and a soldier in her own right—to become acquainted with these people makes their century, their problems, their victories real. They all helped to create American history, as so many of us do, every day we live. When they tell us in their own words of the houses they lived in, the food they ate, where they went, what they did, and why they did it, we believe them because they are speaking to *us*. It is not simply an account of their activities mentioned in some classroom textbook. We come to know these people, empathize with them, see why they were involved in whatever circumstances are under discussion.

A newspaper account may tell us of a divorce, a brutal street fight, an advance in science—any one of a thousand bits of information. It may mention "alleged perpetrators" and "undisclosed informants," and pussyfoot around motives, but unless we know what caused the divorce, what started the street fight, what inspired the scientific discovery, we know only the facts. If we could hear the people involved telling us what brought these events to pass, know their reasons, their personal attitudes toward what happened, it would make all the difference. People make events. For our own satisfaction it is important to know from their own words the why and the how. Speculation and guesswork belong with murder mysteries, not with history. As the narrator of historical fiction I feel it is my responsibility to remove the speculation and make the actions of my characters clear. What better way to do this than by letting my characters explain? Granted that I put words into their mouths, but only to say what history has proved.

Three of my historical novels take place in Massachusetts, *Constance*, *I'm Deborah Sampson*, and *Witches' Children*. The choice was not mine, since that is where the events took place, but my selection of those events as story material was undoubtedly influenced by personal memories of Boston and Cape Cod. It has been a great many years since I lived in New England, but I can still feel, smell, and hear it. An actual Yankee accent is not attractive—many regional United States accents are not—and in writing I ignored it.

However, in *The Tamarack Tree* I allowed the Mississippi accent to creep in from time to time, since it helped to emphasize that this was the Deep South, a fact that was important to the story. I wanted to contrast my Southerners with the Northerners and with Rosemary, an English girl. An accent, or regional ways of speaking, helped to sort them into their slots, give them local pride and their own place in the world and in the story itself. It would have been ludicrous to hear Mary Byrd, who had never stepped outside of Vicksburg, sounding like Jeff, a staunch Bostonian. These things are not consciously planned. They simply happen. The dialogue needs to carry only suggestions of regional speech, just enough flavor to make the speakers come alive.

I have never been conscious of studying any style of speech. For me that would be mechanical and I want the dialogue to flow naturally as long as work on that story exists. I spend a very long time before I start a book in research, reading everything I can find that deals with the chosen period. Books on clothes, houses, furniture, food, methods of transportation—these and other things are important for me to know. I may not use them all but the knowledge should be available. I try to find publications that were produced during the proper time and there I find the speech styles. Of course letters are the most informative, but they are not always available. Still, whatever I read gives me information on how people spoke. The flow and pace of the words start to become easy for me. The phrasing, adjectives, contractions all slip into my brain and affect the words that I put down on paper.

Writing an article such as this, an article about something I am never conscious of doing, is very strange. It has never occurred to me to wonder whether my characters should talk, or how they should speak. Of course they talk! These are not history books that I am writing; they are tales about people who unwittingly made history. And where you have people you have conversation. It doesn't matter whether the events took place three hundred years ago or yesterday—the story is about people, and people talk.

To become the spokesman for your characters, to hear in your own head the words they utter and put those words on paper, makes the people about whom you are writing come to life. Once I have made out my working calendar of the story, the historical record of what happened when, I don't think about the history, but only about what my characters say, how they react to each other and to what is going on around them. Yes, I have to ride herd on them for they do tend to take off from time to time and amaze me. Even the words they speak sometimes come as a surprise. And yet, when I read back the pages filled in a session at the desk, I find they—my characters—have remained true to their era, their place in history, and their corner of America. Their spoken words prove that every time. I may have *written* those words, but they *speak* them.

REFERENCES

Clapp, Patricia. *Constance, A Story of Early Plymouth.* New York: Dell, 1968.
———. *Dr. Elizabeth, The Story of the First Woman Doctor.* New York: Lothrop, 1974.

————. *I'm Deborah Sampson: A Soldier in the War of the Revolution*. New York: Lothrop, 1977.

————. *The Tamarack Tree*. New York: Lothrop, 1986.

————. *Witches' Children*. New York: Viking Penguin, 1987.

28

The Doppelgänger of *Shadow* in *Hawthorn Bay*

JANET LUNN

If a story is to settle into a reader's imagination, it first needs to settle into the writer's. How that happens has everything to do with how the writer tells the tale—and that has everything to do with how the writer finds a way into it.

I found my way into *Shadow in Hawthorn Bay* (1987) hand in hand with Mary Urquhart through a memoir written by an English gentleman (which memoir I no longer remember) who pioneered in Canada about a hundred and fifty years ago. In it she wrote that it pleased her greatly to see that the Scotch and Irish peasant immigrants had left their superstitions behind in their old countries. The moment I read that I knew she was right; mythology does not travel easily; it is too rooted in the land. At once I saw Mary Urquhart, a girl formed from the hills and lochs of the Scottish highlands as surely as Blodeuwedd was formed from the meadowsweet and oak flowers of Wales. And I knew things about her—that she was a seer, that she lived as deeply in the unseen world of fairies and bodachs as she did in the seen world of crofters' cottages, upland pastures, and the sheep she spent her life tending. I knew, too, the pain of her leaving the high country for the low forest world that was upper Canada in 1815.

The story began to form. It was Mary's story. I do not agree with E. M. Forster when he defines story as "a narrative of events arranged in their time sequence. . . ." The same series of events can be described from any number of perspectives—or all of them—and each will be a different story. I could have related this series of events from Luke's point of view or Henry's or even Duncan's and looked at Mary through all their eyes. I might have created a novel with a broader scope and a clearer image of the time and place in which these events occurred. But my passion was engaged by the story I'd found. Without that passion the novel's intensity would have been less clearly defined and the tone would likely have been lighter and, perhaps, more matter-of-fact.

Mary's story begins in Scotland when Duncan calls her from three thousand miles away and ends (except for its tag ends) when she stands naked in the dark, snow-cold water of Hawthorn Bay in upper Canada and tells his apparition, "I will not follow you to the grave. . . . It cannot be. I will not come."

I could not play the impartial observer to these events. I became a sort of doppelgänger attached to her as firmly as her own shadow; I could neither have moved from her point of view, nor told her story as if it were my own. What could I be but a fellow traveler, a shadow, in Mary's story? What could I really know of a fifteen-year-old living in the year 1815 whose native language was Scots Gaelic? As accurate as research—down to the last persnickety detail—of pioneer nineteenth-century life could make this story, I could never convince anyone that I was at home in that century the way Louisa Alcott or Juliana Ewing were. Alas, historical novelists can only enter the past encumbered by all our twentieth-century sensibilities, and the wonderful trick Jack Finney used in his time-travel story *Time and Again* (1986) only works inside fiction; the external world never falls away.

There is something else. Although, all my life I have been enthralled by oral and written storytelling (as a child even my daydreams were in third-person narrative with all the "he saids" and "she saids" added to the dialogue), I grew up with movies. And movies and movie techniques have affected the way I perceive and tell stories. Like Christopher Isherwood, I am and know myself to be a camera looking at a story's landscape through a lens, moving in and out of my heroine's head with voice-over monologue making itself heard as I write.

For all these reasons I've told Mary's story from her point of view but not in her voice, keeping my little distance, keeping my camera focused. How might the meaning of the story have been changed had I written it in some other way? It would have been less clear to me, certainly, but what meaning a reader takes from this, or any, story I cannot say. I'm convinced that all art is, in part, a Rorschach blot from which we derive our own meaning, meaning that may or may not have much (or anything) to do with what the artist intended. The only sure thing to be passed from the author of a story to its reader is the passion that engendered it. For me that passion in *Shadow in Hawthorn Bay* arose from a sense of loss shared with a girl who appeared in my imagination and might have lived beside me a hundred and fifty years ago. I told it the only way I could possibly have told it.

REFERENCES

Finney, Jack. *Time and Again*. New York: Simon, 1986.
Lunn, Janet. *Shadow in Hawthorn Bay*. New York: Scribner's, 1987.

29

"I, Catherine Cabot Hall...": The Journal as Historical Fiction

JOAN W. BLOS

As is true of most decisions, deciding to write my story as a journal settled a number of questions but created several more. First, having committed myself to a story set in nineteenth-century New Hampshire, I had been unable to find a tone, a manner or style of writing, that was both personally congenial and appropriate to the story. The closest I had come so far sounded sadly like Laura Ingalls Wilder at her less good moments.

Second, despite diligent research efforts (which had been pleasurable, not burdensome, so that I had halted them with regret), I had not been able to establish with certainty a number of small, specific points such as would be needed for fully developed descriptions of situation and scene. For example, would the house have been painted red or would it have been unfinished? What floor coverings, if any, would have been used in a farmer's home? There were also some questions pertinent to the story that I wasn't sure how to answer. For example, if a mother's death left a father and elder daughter responsible for all domestic tasks, which tasks would they have found essential to continue and which would they have let go?

Third, how could one be faithful to nineteenth-century New England sensibilities, sensibilities often suppressed by understatement, without boring, alienating, and probably disappointing twentieth-century readers, especially if they were children accustomed to books whose protagonists announce their feelings clearly?

When the notion of the journal struck, it seemed to solve all three problems. The voice, if not my own exactly, would at least not be Wilder's. Second, the details I was lacking were those that people generally omit in giving report of their own experience. Over and over again the reading of letters, memoirs, and contemporaneous accounts persuaded me that people then, as people now, would simply say on coming home that it was good to be warm. No one in this circumstance describes the firelight glinting off andirons whose molded ornamentation suggests the faces of lions. My floors could be floors, my houses simply there, and never mind the color. It was a great relief! Third, and finally, and probably most important, I could now be close to my protagonist without (because journals were kept then) violating her need for privacy. I would have to see clearly, and through Catherine's eyes. But then readers would know how Catherine felt by what she paid attention to, because of what she noted.

Such a parsimonious solution, attending to so many needs at once, could hardly be denied. The very first entry that I wrote appears, in somewhat extended form, in A Gathering of Days: A New England Girl's Journal, 1830–32: (1979).

Saturday, January 1, 1831
A fair day, sparkling and bright—the first of this New Year. The snow has drifted in the yard out front and sun and cold conspire together to make a glistening crust. In other years we have had more snow. But seldom is it so cold. (34)

Other entries followed soon.

The problems created by my decision as to voice lay not so much with vocabulary and diction as with point of view. For the most part they were those of any first-person narrative: nothing not directly known to the protagonist could enter the story and nothing could be told except as she would understand it (or misunderstand it). However, having read a fair number of authentic diaries in preparation for the writing, I recognized the caveats imposed by the diary form. For example, dialogue must be used sparingly as diarists tend to report the fact of a conversation, not its word-for-word content. Description would have to be limited to situations, objects, and persons of particular interest to the protagonist herself: thus the new wife of the father would be described but not the one-room school.

Mindful of these requirements, I made the first completed text reserved, and quite austere. Subsequently I expanded the text into a novel more likely to find publication. But I have always felt that the first version was closer to what might actually have been written by a nineteenth-century girl and I am glad that I left the novel's opening and closing sequences in the earlier manner. It was a way of keeping faith.

Finding the right voice is not only a means of expressing a given story. It helps to find the story; it leads the story out. This is to say that thinking (or rather writing) along with the character, the writer does not so much set down a predetermined incident as compose that very segment by the act of writing it. Although the voice is invented by the author, it has its own vitality and is formative as a result. Following the lead provided by the voice, I would find myself writing such words as *intermeddle*—words so foreign to my natural vocabulary that I would look them up in the dictionary to be sure that they existed. It was the same with the grammar. Once I had decided on the voice, its particular usages and cadence were easy to maintain. The processes of fiction are mysterious and complex. I sometimes think that only those who write fiction find them believable.

All of this matters much, much less than the extent to which the story— the fiction, the fib, the lie, the dream—is believable for the reader. It is here that the diary or journal form is particularly influential, creating a situation that both is and is not akin to that of the straight first-person account. I have noted the similarities. I believe that the differences stem from the ways in which we perceive real journals and then transfer our perceptions to their fictional counterparts. What I mean is this.

Diaries are first of all assumed to be spontaneous, accurate reports, contemporaneous with the events they describe. Thus the fact that Samuel Pepys wrote his famous account of the London fire not as the flames were licking at his door but several months thereafter is known, but often forgotten. We like it better the other way; we want to believe in it! Anne Frank's diary, we are told, was published "essentially as written." What was inessential? How did that change the whole? Mary Chestnut's Civil War diary—a work long regarded and cited as a diary—has been shown to be instead a very skillful novel written seventeen years and four attempts after the author's initial efforts to present her story. In short, it is our associations with the idea of a journal that lead to our assumption of veridicality. Put a date in front of an observation and immediately it implies authenticity. An author, it is evident, can put this to good use.

Wednesday, May 18, 1831
    Father departed this morning. Again he drove the Shipman's team, both to hasten the journey and better present himself. . . . (74)

Sunday, May 22, 1831
    On this day, in Boston, they married. I will not call her Mother. (75)

Thursday, May 26, 1831
    She is less tall than I expected—smaller, even, than Mrs. Shipman, and plainer than Aunt Lucy. (75)

To write a novel in journal form is still to write a novel. The resulting work is as much shaped, structured, and revised as any other novel and, like other works of fiction, it needs to be believed. *How* it asks to be believed is where it is different perhaps.

I learned a great deal by writing *A Gathering of Days* and I do not think I would have been as aware of the effects created by a change of voice (or the possibilities of doing so) had I not chosen to write it as a young girl's journal. It was as I worked on *Brothers of the Heart: A Story of the Old Northwest, 1837–1838* (1985), also historical fiction, that this became clear to me. In the latter book, a story set in the Old Northwest in 1837, there were times when it was necessary to be especially close to one or another of the principal characters. At such times I found it useful and stylistically possible to devise letters, notebooks, memoirs. To establish an aura of authenticity I shamelessly cited "fragments only" and solemnly noted in one instance that the remaining portion of a letter was "illegible due to water damage." I did not find it hard to improvise the different writing styles required by the different characters or types of material and, as had been the case with *A Gathering of Days*, I did not have trouble with the language.

For me the matter of readership belief, the making of a book that others will find true, is the main and sought-for prize. So the question asked by a fifth grade student remains my favorite comment on *A Gathering of Days*. It came at the end of a classroom visit, a forty-five minute session in which I had carefully explained both library and field research, had shown my notes and notebooks, and told of the writing process. The question was clearly stated and it came from the back of the room.

"Where did you find the journal and did you have to change it much?"

REFERENCES

Blos, Joan. *Brothers of the Heart: A Story of the Old Northwest, 1837–1838*. New York: Scribner's, 1985.
———. *A Gathering of Days: A New England Girl's Journal, 1830–32*. New York: Scribner's, 1979.

THE CRITICAL VOICE

30

The Innocent Eye: Perceptive Children in Canadian Prairie Fiction

MURIEL WHITAKER

Nellie McClung, Gabrielle Roy, W. O. Mitchell, and Margaret Laurence share the experience of having grown up on the Canadian prairies between the period of settlement and World War II. All have re-created that time and place through the perceptions of fictional child protagonists. McClung's family moved to Manitoba in 1880, lured by "the intoxication of being the first to plant the seed in that mellow black loam enriched by a million years of rain and sun" (McClung, *Clearing*, 31). The dialect of her Irish family and the fertility of those farmlands appear in McClung's most popular novel, *Sowing Seeds in Danny* (1908). Gabrielle Roy's story collection *Rue Des-chambault* (1957), *Street of Riches* in its English translation, takes its title from the actual street in the pioneer French-Canadian settlement, St. Boniface, where the author lived, the youngest of eight children. W. O. Mitchell was born in Weyburn, Saskatchewan, a setting that resembles the nameless small town of *Who Has Seen the Wind* (1947) and, even more, that of *How I Spent My Summer Holidays* (1981) with its Provincial Mental Hospital. Margaret Laurence's hometown was Neepawa, Manitoba, immortalized as Manawaka in several novels and the collection of stories, *A Bird in the House* (1970). It is, says Laurence, "an amalgam of many prairie towns. Most of all, I like to think it is simply itself, a town of the mind, my own private world . . . which one hopes will ultimately relate to the outer world which we share" ("Sources," 82).

These towns in the wilderness were regulated by what Northrop Frye calls a "garrison mentality" (830), which erected social, moral, and religious barriers as a defense against the unfamiliar and unregenerate. For the child, the code of respectability imposed by adults through family, church, and school included strict religious observances, social awareness—ten-year-old

Vanessa McLeod recognizes the difference between upright grandfathers and "downright" grandfathers—and the cultivation of such traits as diligence, frugality, obedience, and piety. These virtues were perpetuated by pioneer parents and grandparents who attributed to them their survival in the wilderness. The younger generations resented what Margaraet Atwood has described as "a cosmic rigidity [that] goes far beyond the strength necessary to build and sustain a pioneering community" (32–34). This difference in attitudes is a major source of family conflict, one which the child cannot win without feeling guilty.

In prairie towns, which imitated those of Ontario (Morton, 168–69) and Quebec, social status was indicated by the kind of house that a family occupied. In *Who Has Seen the Wind*, the O'Connals' three-story house with its veranda smothered in Virginia creeper and its front steps flanked by spirea and honeysuckle is an appropriate base for Brian's authoritarian grandmother whose prohibitions the boy resents. The Brick House—"the one which more than any other I carry with me," says the narrator of *A Bird in the House*—is substantial and gloomy, like "some crusader's embattled fortress in a heathen wilderness—part dwelling-place and part massive monument" (3) to Timothy Connor, pioneer. It is a house so oppressive in its silence and disapproval that the child feels her lungs are in danger of exploding. The house that Papa Edouard builds on the edge of town has a happier ambience, with its wide verandas, fruit trees, flower beds, fresh paint, and its capacity to shelter with their numerous children Maman, a creature of the day, and Papa who only emerges from his misery with the arrival of night, "so simple and sweet-smelling along our street" (142). Christine's attic room gives her a view of white clouds, rooftops, the highest branches of elms—a view that she is convinced is intended for her alone. In *Sowing Seeds in Danny*, the Watsons' improvised boxcar home romantically proves that more goodness, joy, affection, and reason can be found in the humble dwellings of the poor than in the comfortable houses of the rich.

Compensating for the town's rigidity is the nearness of the prairie, a place of adventure and freedom from adult prohibitions. The romantics' association of goodness, beauty, and transcendence with the natural world is apparent in *Sowing Seeds in Danny* and *Who Has Seen the Wind*. Pearl Watson, a paragon of unaffected goodness, is likened to

the rugged little anemone, the wind flower that lifts its head from the cheerless prairie. No kind hand softens the heat or cold, nor tempers the wind, and yet the very winds that blow upon it and the hot sun that beats upon it bring to it a grace, a hardiness, a fragrance of good cheer, that gladdens thehearts of all who pass that way.

(*Sowing Seeds*, 40)

For Brian O'Connal, images of wind, prairie, and God are inextricably fused. His experience of "the feeling" is a Wordsworthian trailing of clouds.

In addition to adopting stereotypical attitudes to nature, each author defines prairie through details that bespeak the recollected experience of a particular child. Pearl's delight in the goldenrod's plumy head, the tall gaillardia's flickering, and the radiant sunflowers is related to the author's pleasure in the flowering prairie that *Clearing in the West* reveals. Christine's perception of the grove of black oaks as a forest imbued with mystery and joy is a child's view of what the adult realizes is "merely a largish clump of trees that could not even hide the distant gable of our house" (89). When four-year-old Brian walks for the first time to the end of the street and out onto "the sudden emptiness of the prairie," it is defined by sound:

The hum of the telephone wires along the road, the ring of hidden crickets, the stitching sound of grasshoppers, the sudden relief of a meadow lark's song, were deliciously strange to him. (11)

Eleven-year-old Vanessa at the family cottage on Diamond Lake hears the plaintive cry of loons, a sound belonging to "a world separated by aeons from our neat world of summer cottages," (121) a sound lost to the adult Vanessa because civilization has driven the birds away. For twelve-year-old Hughie prairie is mosquitoes, the bark of a coyote, a prairie chicken roasted in a willow fire, a homesteader's abandoned shack, and the boys' secret cave screened by a wild rose bush. The adult Hugh on a "time return" fifty years later feels the wind, smells the wild mint and wolf willow, but finds no human traces to substantiate remembered history. Disparity between the child's perceptions and the adult's attempts at recovering them is part of the duality that the child's-eye view generates.

In *Sowing Seeds in Danny*, Nellie McClung presents a stereotypical cast of characters—a rich but stingy farm family, the Motherwells, a brilliant but alcoholic old doctor, a high-minded but impractical lady, two beautiful young women in need of husbands, several eligible bachelors (including a doctor, a minister and an English gentleman who is learning to farm), and the numerous members of the Watson clan. Puritan ethics and romantic sensibilities are combined in Pearl whose service at the Motherwells' farm constitutes the central event. She is both innocent and guileless. Unlike the other protagonists, she never uses her wiles to benefit herself. She lacks the normal child's egocentricity, relying on God to break her bedroom window so that she may enjoy the fresh air or to flatten part of the Motherwells' grain so that they will appreciate His bounty. Her goodness, her ability to perceive the truth, her sensibility, and her imagination—qualities that Jean-Jacques Rousseau and William Wordsworth attributed to children—enable her not only to comfort and encourage the adults wandering in a wilderness of greed, guilt, indecision, loneliness, and illness but also to inspire right feelings and proper actions in those who have the power of doing good. For example, Dr. Clay is persuaded to save Arthur's life by operating for the appendicitis that Pearl has diagnosed, and Mr. Francis delivers to the dying Polly the poppies she had planted as a remembrance of home. Pearl is the vehicle of McClung's didacticism, vocalizing the author's interest in temperance, politics, and ethics. She is also a vehicle for social satire, as when her response to the harvest landscape is juxtaposed to that of the rich farmer:

The billows of shadow swept over the wheat on each side of the narrow pasture; the golden flowers, the golden fields, the warm golden sunshine intoxicated Pearl with their luxurious beauty, and in that hour of delight she realized more pleasure from them than Sam Motherwell and his wife had in all their long lives of barren selfishness. Their souls were of a dull drab dryness in which no flower took root, there was no gold to them, but the gold of green and grain . . . [which] lost its golden colour and turned to lead and ashes in their hands. (127)

As this passage suggests, *Sowing Seeds in Danny* is sometimes closer to allegorical fairy tale than novel and its heroine more a fairy godmother than a credible twelve-year-old.

The theme of W. O. Mitchell's *Who Has Seen the Wind* is "the struggle of a boy to understand what still defeats mature and learned men. To him are revealed in moments of fleeting vision the realities of birth, hunger, satiety, eternity, death" (prefatory note, n.p.). The novel has two foci—the humane school principal Digby, Mitchell's social critic, and Brian O'Connal, four years old when the story begins and eleven when it ends. The antithesis between puritan ethics and romanticism is expressed through the juxtaposition of town and country. The shabby town trying to survive the Depression is a prison of bigotry and cruelty created by such authoritarian figures as Mrs. Abercrombie and the Reverend Powelly. The child escapes from the sheltered and circumscribed world (represented initially by the place under the breakfast table) to the natural world where he experiences "the feeling," a transcendental affirmation that he associates with the prairie, the wind, and God. Feelings of exhilaration are also related to the young Ben, the wild alter ego fused in Brian's imagination with the prairie: "The boy has prairie hair . . . had wind on him all the time. . . . He's the owner of the prairie. . . . he lies down on top of it" (24, 60). Ben's sharing, actively or as spectator, in the succession of deaths and burials (pigeon, dog, gopher, father) that marks the progress of Brian's education reinforces his role as bond between Brian, seeker of knowledge, and the prairie, transcendental source of reality.

Brian differs from Pearl in giving way to self-pity, anger, and fear, as when he runs away from his Uncle Sean's farm and finds himself alone on the prairie at night: "He was filled now with a feeling of nakedness and vulnerability that terrified him. As the wind mounted in intensity, so too the feeling of defenselessness rose in him" (236). In other respects, too, he is a more credible perceiver. His curiosity takes him to the steps of the Presbyterian manse in search of God, to Saint Sammy's piano box house on the prairie, to the jail where the incarcerated Ben shows the frantic unease of his caged owl—incidents that function subjectively and objectively to reveal character and develop plot.

Brian's innocence results from the protectiveness of his family, from his naivety (he thinks, for example, that the act of worshipping together can unify such disparate humans as the Bens, the Chinese, Mrs. Abercrombie, and the Minister Powelly), and from his egocentricity. His acute powers of observation produce subjective sensations, as when his examination of a dew-filled spirea leaf produces "a growing elation of such fleeting delicacy and poignancy that he dared not turn his mind to it for fear that he might spoil it" (107). The legitimacy of ascertaining reality in this way is later confirmed by Digby, who tries to explain Berkeleyan philosophy: the ice, the post office are "just a set of sensations—nothing else. They're yours, they're inside you" (293). Even when the boy's capacity for suffering has been tested by a succession of deaths, and he has concluded that "it was awful to be human. It wasn't any good" (298), the winter prairie consoles him with the exquisitely stamped tracks of a prairie chicken and the glinting ice crystals on a wild rose bush.

Thirty-four years separate the publication of *Who Has Seen the Wind* from that of *How I Spent My Summer Holidays*. Biologically Hugh is a continuation of Brian, for he is twelve years old in the summer of 1924 when the main events occur. He is a different breed of boy, extrovert, prone to use a scatalogical vocabulary, obsessed by sex, knowledgeable about local scandals, and skilled at manipulating his parents. Nevertheless, Mitchell's description of him as innocent is substantiated by his enthusiasm for the romantic adventures of Henty and Chums (he scorns his mother's Christmas gift of *Sowing Seeds in Danny*), and by his participation in such childhood rituals as the May Day basket and the pursuit of the Sunday school attendance prize. Above all, his uncritical hero worship of King Motherwell, a decorated soldier turned pool-hall operator and bootlegger, sets him apart from the adults.

The adventure-producing prairie is a sinister place populated by prostitutes, Holy Rollers, and lunatics whom the boys encounter when they swim in the Little Souris River. Such demonic elements as the stenchy cave, the nettles, thorns and bulrushes and on the riverbank, bloodsuckers, and barbed wire fences make it an appropriate setting for murder. As in Mark Twain's *Tom Sawyer*, the boys' desire for adventure entangles them in adult crime.

From the child's perspective, adults are the enemy in this "summer of defiances": "There had always been skirmishes and minor border engagements, but Bill the Sheepherder having been hidden in our prairie cave, we were now committed during those summer holidays to true war" (86). The children's weapons are lies, secretiveness, pretended illnesses, appeals to parental sympathy, an ability to take advantage of parental moods, eaves-dropping—anything that will leave them free to conduct the adventure of hiding an escaped lunatic. Only King Motherwell is accepted as being "on our side against all the adults in their upper world" (86). Nevertheless, despite their success in frustrating the authorities' recapture of Bill, the narrator admits that anxiety and fear were his most usual emotions that summer. The adventure is terminated when Hugh discovers outside the cave "a leg with only part of the foot left and the flesh gnawed off from the ankle to the knee" (138). Inside is a grizzlier memento, the head of King's wife Bella "alive with maggots, black with clotted blood, bruised like an apple and keg-swollen" (139). With this discovery, says the narrator, "I stopped being a boy" (138).

Although Hugh is in his own estimation worldly wise, his inability to perceive that King has manipulated Peter and himself into sheltering Bill and his ignorance of lesbianism limit his perspective. He can notice and report his beautiful mother's overturned tea wagon and tearful face, and visits of virile Mrs. Inspector Kydd to Bella and the women's shopping expedition, but he does not understand their significance. The irony produced by this disparity between the child's limited view and the reader's interpretation is Mitchell's most important technical achievement. The mundane title, a composition topic commonly assigned to school children in the fall term, here designates "the loss of an age of innocence."

In the two story collections, *Street of Riches* and *A Bird in the House*, the central perspective is that of a girl. Roy's heroine Christine is the youngest child of a father already so old and depressed when she is born that he dubs her Petite Misère, a nickname that she resents because it seems to pre-ordain her to suffering. The events that she reports commonly occur in any large family—companionship, illness, journeys, quarrels, unfortunate marriages, deaths. Like Brian she is subject to intense feelings—rejection and isolation when her angry father exclaims, "Oh! why did I ever have any children" (15); cupidity when she catches sight of a yellow ribbon in her sister Odette's drawer; fright and bewilderment when her sister Alicia goes mad; exhilaration when she must be transported by handcar because Dukhobors have damaged a railway bridge. Every experience analyzed retrospectively by the adult narrator leads to a better understanding of others or to a questioning of life. By accepting her father's peace offering of a leaden rhubarb pie, she perceives his "so much weightier sadness" (20). The yellow ribbon symbolizes the vivacious sister lost to the family when she becomes a nun. Alicia's madness and early death lead to a questioning of God's mercy.

She is acutely responsive to sensation—the smell of the Negro boarder's eau de cologne, the "strange and charming tinkling" of a wind bell, the motion of leaves watched from below, their nether sides "like the bellies of small animals, softer, paler, shyer than their faces" (40). Curiosity about sex and religion is fired by adult evasions and overheard conversations, for she is an unashamed eavesdropper with a child's ability to appear totally engrossed in some juvenile activity. Because she does not understand her mother's allusions to a woman's duty, the undesirability of Georgianna's proposed marriage, and the tragedy of Odette's giving up before her time "her share of the world, her youth, even her freedom" (34), her reports create that disjunction between childhood innocence and adult knowledge that is a basis for irony. As Brandon Conron points out, the immediacy of childhood experience combined with "the author's intuitive insight into the significance of the minutiae of ordinary life" effects an ambivalent perspective (x). The characters are at the same time individual and universal. Although Christine with her family loyalty, imagination, and dream of becoming a writer seems the author's alter ego, Roy warns against accepting *Street of Riches* as autobiography: "Certain events in this narrative took place in real life; but the characters and almost everything that happens to them are products of the imagination" (vii).

In contrast, Margaret Laurence admits the personal relevance of her Manawaka fictions: "I had to come back spiritually and write about my roots. . . . The return is not necessarily in the physical sense but, it really is a coming back in the mind, a coming to some kind of terms with your roots and your ancestors and, if you like, with your gods" (Kroetsch, 20–21). In *A Bird in the House* particularly, the remembered homes of the narrator are the houses of grandparents from which emanate inescapable authority, power, disapproval, and unease. Of her maternal grandfather, the fictional Timothy Connor, Laurence says: "I recall him as a man impossible to please and I recall myself rebelling desperately against this hard, harsh sort of personality. . . . And only after I had finished writing these short stories did I begin to realize that, although I had detested the old man at one time, I no longer detested him" (Thomas, 67).

Laurence's use of first-person narration and highly realistic dialogue creates a greater sense of immediacy than the other authors achieve. The voices are skillfully differentiated—Aunt Edna's thirties' slang and the wisecracks that were her shield, Grandmother Connor's gentle civility, Grandfather's ungrammatical verbs, Vanessa's indignation and sauciness. Like Christine, Vanessa is a professional listener and the houses with their vents, empty stove pipe holes, and thin walls are places where adult conversations can be overheard. Technically the device opens up plot and characterization by revealing the source of Grandmother McLeod's power over her son Ewen and Grandmother Connor's powerlessness to ameliorate her husband's behavior toward Aunt Edna's suitors; the feelings of Beth and Edna about their father; and the tragedy of Chris, who wanted to be an engineer. Vanessa's acute perceptions make her and the reader aware of the relationships between adult members of the family. Nevertheless, her understanding is limited by lack of knowledge, as the recurrent complaint, "I did not know," indicates. Why can't Grandmother McLeod be nice for a change? Why does father sound sad when he talks about his own father, the only person in Manawaka who could read Sophocles in Greek? Why does she hate the hymn that promises "Rest beyond the river"? Why can she not listen when Chris wants to talk about "the other things, the things I did not know"? Though maturity increases her capacity for interpretation, there remains, as in Roy's stories, a sense of the inexplicable *lacrimae rerum*, of which Piquette Tonnerre's death and Chris' madness are a part.

For Brian, Hugh, Christine, and Vanessa, loss of innocence is connected with their fathers' deaths, cataclysmic events that destroy their security, order, and illusions. Maggie O'Connal, by treating Brian as the head of the family, encourages him to become more responsible, considerate, and outgoing. The "old excitement" produced by contact with nature disappears; Digby sees on his face "the same expression that had puzzled him on the young Ben's—maturity in spite of the formlessness of childish features, wisdom without years" (297). The death of Hugh's father effects an epiphany. Only then does he realize not only that his hero, King Motherwell, rather than Bill the Sheepherder was Bella's murderer but also that it was he himself who provided King's motive by unwittingly revealing Bella's lesbianism. Now King's gift of a beautifully carved decoy exudes an ironic symbolism.

When Christine's father dies, she makes the most disconsolate discovery of her life: " 'For the mere fact that you live, you must pay'—all life subject to money, every dream appraised in terms of yield" (151). Her particular dream of becoming a writer must be sacrificed to the immediate necessity of earning a living by teaching. With the death of Vanessa's father (ominously foretold by a trapped sparrow in the house), the child with her mother and brother must move to the Connor house. There she learns from her mother and aunt that to survive in the house of the bear requires deception and fortitude. When her grandfather dies, "Jerico's brick battlements" tumble down; she remembers in the "ancient days" of her early childhood he had seemed not a hated tyrant but as large and admirable as God.

Nellie McClung uses the child protagonist for didactic purposes, showing how right feeling and right conduct affect the lives of others. Mitchell's child's-eye view in *Who Has Seen the Wind* is a means of examining the effect that the harsh but beautiful prairie setting, consisting of "the least common denominator of nature, the skeleton requirements, simply, of land and sky" (3) have on a child's development. In contrast, *How I Spent My Summer Holidays* seems the work of a vulgar, cynical author whose prurient language and gratuitous descriptions of violence and horror come between the boy and the reader. Gabrielle Roy uses a shifting child/adult perspective that enables her to portray the consciousness of a writer determined from childhood "to be this beloved book, these living pages held in the hands of some nameless being" (131). Margaret Laurence writes of childhood in order to come to terms with her roots, her ancestors and her gods.

The child's-eye view technique has several advantages, aesthetic and psychological. Like Jane Austen's little bit of carved ivory, the child's world is narrowly confined, a microcosm centered on home and spreading selectively into a small town and its environs where everyone knows one another. As Roy symbolically portrays in her account of a country school cut off by a blizzard, such a closed world provides great opportunities for joy and intimacy: "Often our joys are slow in coming home to us—but I was living through one of the rarest happinesses of my life. Was not all the world a child? Were we not at the day's morning?" (158). Because children do not conceal their emotions as adults do, this technique engenders powerful descriptions of rage, terror, embarrassment, happiness, sorrow, and love. When Vanessa's father dies, she cries at night in her mother's arms—"Everything seemed to have stopped, not only time but my own heart and blood as well" (107); she also hits, kicks, and scratches the maid, Noreen, in "an inexplicable fury. . . . some terrifying need to hurt, burn, destroy" (109).

The child's literalness can be a source of humor as when Brian asks the Presbyterian minister's wife, "Does God like to be all grapes and bloody?" (10) or when Vanessa classifies her grandmother as a mitigated Baptist, having overheard her father say, "At least she's not an unmitigated Baptist" (17). The literalness of Pearl Watson's spring song foreshadows the parodies of Hieberts' Sara Binks:

> The little lams are beautiful
>   There cotes are soft and nice,
> The little calves have ringworm,
>   And the 2-year olds have lice. (221)

As well, humor may be an element in the irony produced by dual perspective, that device which gives subtlety and sophistication to this kind of writing.

Since the child's sensitivity not only makes him aware of pain, oppression, and what he may see as injustice, but also provides an escape through imagination and the transcendental world of nature, the author can use the child's perspective for philosophical comment. A huge, dark lake where horses drink is Vanessa's idea of God—distant, indestructible, totally indifferent. A field of wheat asserts a benevolent deity for Pearly Watson. Brian's God, imaged as wind, is "a still and brooding spirit, a quiescent power unsmiling from everlasting to everlasting to which the coming and passing of the prairie's creatures was but incidental" (129). Christine believes that the wind of a winter storm, sorrowfully weeping, is Lucifer, cast into darkness "to whom, for a winter's night or two, belonged Manitoba" (138). Wallace Stegner calls the Canadian prairie "as good a place to be a boy and as unsatisfying a place to be a man as one could imagine," a place to discover "the beauty of the geometric earth and the enormous sky brimming with weather, and learn the passion of loneliness and the mystery of a prairie wind" (29). The "child on the prairie" theme enables the authors to recreate a historical period (generally that of their own childhoods) and to convey their own moral and religious values. Although the children on the prairie are acquainted with sorrow, their worlds also contain "the physical sweetness of a golden age" (29).

REFERENCES

Atwood, Margaret. *Survival: A Thematic Guide to Canadian Literature*. Toronto: Anansi, 1972.

Conron, Brandon. "Introduction" to *Street of Riches*. New Canadian Library No. 56. Toronto and Montreal: McClelland and Stewart, 1967.

Frye, Northrop. "Conclusion." In *Literary History of Canada*. Edited by Carl F. Klinck, et al. Toronto: University of Toronto Press, 1956.

Kroetsch, Robert. "A Conversation with Margaret Laurence." In *Trace: Prairie Writers on Writing*, edited by Birk Sproxton. Winnipeg: Turnstone Press, 1986.

Laurence, Margaret. *A Bird in the House*. Toronto and Montreal: McClelland and Stewart, 1970.

———. "Sources." *Mosaic* 3 (Spring 1970): 82.

McClung, Nellie L. *Clearing in the West: My Own Story*. Toronto: Thomas Allen, 1935.

———. *Sowing Seeds in Danny*. Toronto: Wm. Briggs, 1908.

Mitchell, W. D. *How I Spent My Summer Holidays*. Toronto: McClelland and Stewart-Bantam, 1981.

———. *Who Has Seen the Wind*. Toronto: Macmillan, 1947.

Morton, W. L. "A Century of Plain and Parkland." In *A Region of the Mind: Interpreting the Western Canadian Plains*, edited by Richard Allen. Regina: Canadian Plains Studies Centre, University of Saskatchewan, 1973.

Roy, Gabrielle. *Street of Riches*. New Canadian Library, no. 56. Toronto and Montreal: McClelland and Stewart, 1967.

Stegner, Wallace. *Wolf Willow*. New York: Viking Press, 1967.

Thomas, Clara. "A Conversation with Margaret Laurence and Irving Layton." *Journal of Canadian Fiction* 1 (Winter 1972): 67.

31

Narrative Strategy in *Drift* by William Mayne

ANN DONOVAN

William Mayne is generally considered a writer of fantasy. His novel *Drift* (1985), however, is historical fiction, a tale of Indian capture set in the days of the North American frontier. In reading this novel, one is struck by the wealth of realistic detail of Indian life and lore that enriches the action. But the novel's most interesting feature is that it is a narrative maze as devious as any Mayne has ever devised. The tension of the plot, which is considerable, is wound even tighter by the ambiguities of the narrative itself. It is this narrative, transparent and simple on the surface, that is the most notable feature of the book and upon which all its other effects and aspects depend. Because of this illusion, even language, as such, is an element of the adventure, the different and antithetical means of communication among the characters reflecting the deliberate misunderstandings Mayne has effected between reader and text. The key to this carefully arranged structure is the narrator, and it is a mark of Mayne's skill that he has subtly contrived this narration to be virtually invisible as the reader is drawn, somewhat puzzled and resistant, into its web.

The plot is basically simple. Young Rafe Considine is sitting outside his house in a frontier village watching Tawena, one of the settlement's half-assimilated Indians, trying to catch a crow. She suggests they go and look at a hibernating bear. They walk to the nearby lake but are chased out on the ice by the bear who is already awake. As they head for home, the ice breaks up in the spring thaw. They are trapped on a floe along with the bear. Luckily, they drift apart from him and land on the far shore. Unfortunately, they are on the distant side of the lake, miles from the village. Through the snow, Tawena hears something coming and flees. Rafe, left behind, is discovered by two Indian women who capture him, and, much to his bewilderment, force him to accompany them. Shortly after this, Rafe hears a horrible struggle in the forest nearby: Tawena is being torn apart by the bear that has followed them. After weeks of wandering together, during which Rafe tries and fails to escape, the Indians return him to his village, are rewarded, and depart. He misses the Indian women who have taught him much and to whom he has become attached.

This much of the novel is perfectly straightforward. But this part of the book is followed by a second, shorter section: Tawena's story. This in itself is a surprise because Tawena has been presumed dead, eaten by the bear. She can have no story. The reader assumes that some mistake has been made. Tawena's part of the tale explains this misconception, revealing Rafe's perspective, that of his white society, as limited culturally; Tawena's account shows a totally different sequence of events unfolding for the Indians, one which is based upon *their* cultural orientation.

Many authors have retold the same story from various viewpoints using different narrators' or characters' perspectives. The effectiveness of this practice depends on withholding information, juxtaposing quite different points of view, contrasting cultures or backgrounds (e.g., sex, profession, age, education, etc.) and sticking strictly to one narrator at a time. Mayne has, for the most part, been quite scrupulous in abiding by the rules he has set up for his narrative, and in doing so, has effectively drawn the reader into the story and required him to follow, project, and imagine the events related and evaluate the reliability of the characters relating them. The effect is not unlike that of Lawrence Durrell's *Alexandria Quartet* or John Fowles' *The Collector* or *The French Lieutenant's Woman*, with much of the same stunning impact.

Although the story is told in the third person, the voice of the author is effaced until it seems almost as if it is a first-person narrative. The reader is given no information at all other than what Rafe (usually) observes. Rafe's age, the location of the village, and other details of background are omitted completely, or included casually, presumably because they are known to Rafe (and Tawena) and do not pass through his mind during the narrative or require his attention. That they would be interesting or useful to the reader is unimportant to Mayne. They would dilute or distract from the unity of narrative view and therefore have no role. Such omissions make others more natural; indeed, Rafe's irrelevant thoughts, emotions, fleeting impressions are all more important in the narrative than basic information that an author might easily impart in a more conventional fiction. This is well illustrated in the opening paragraphs of the novel.

The Indian girl was trying to catch a crow that had stayed in the village by the lake all winter. The girl's name was Tawena, and she lived in the tents and cabins at the end of the village.

Rafe Considine watched her, sitting on a heap of hard snow outside his own door.

Tawena was throwing down little balls of suet from a lump of fat she had in her hand. Now and then she ate some herself. She had a fatty face, Rafe thought, and brown eyes deep in the fat. He was sure she had stolen the suet. The tent and cabin people had nothing much to live on, but some of them were well-covered. (9)

The sentences are direct, the vocabulary simple. The tense is simple past, giving an impression of present, ongoing activity. Information important to what will happen is given offhandedly, but very little else. But the novel's key, the relationship between Rafe and Tawena, is immediately established. Rafe is observant but not particularly bright or insightful; clearly he considers Tawena an unreliable savage, but he has no particular fear, aversion, or doubts about her. She is just one feature of his environment. Her ways are different; she is not his equal. Here we may note that were Tawena a male character, the entire plot would suffer, as her femaleness is merely one more aspect of her inferiority and unreliability—her otherness. In addition to their relationship, we know the time of year, a critical factor, and we see Tawena as active and Rafe as passive, modes in which they will remain, and which are an important clue to reliability.

Only the second half of the opening sentence and all of the following one could be described as coming directly from the author. The entire second paragraph is Rafe's assessment of what he can see directly or accepts as true. Even the last sentence *seems* attributable directly to Rafe, although it is only so by implication and tone: it sounds like what Rafe would think. Already we hear his unspoken voice. Soon we hear Tawena directly: "Don't move, Rayaf," she said. "Don't do ever thing. Bird for pot" (9). Tawena is clever, but she cannot speak good English. Rafe speaks, unfortunately for his future plight, not a word of any Indian language. Thus, although this implies her stupidity, Tawena has a decided intellectual advantage from the beginning.

Further, living on the edge of the settlement, scavenging on it, she has learned to *see* life there and accept it to some extent. Rafe and his family have not paid much attention to the Indians or the wilderness. When Rafe's mother hears the ice breaking up, she assumes it is the French. When Tawena invites Rafe to visit the bear, she adds, "Bear my people father," a statement that means nothing to Rafe, although he is intrigued.

Rafe thought he wanted to know what Tawena meant by looking at bear. . . . But to go and look at one is something different, even with someone you don't at all like, smelling of old fat, even if she is the bear's daughter, somehow.
Tawena was round the corner of the house. The bear was not with her, of course, and Rafe was glad of that. (11)

This explanation is entirely typical of Rafe as narrator: he is Mayne's frame for all the action, for the relationships, for the manipulation of the reader's understanding and sympathy. We are as dependent on Rafe's sensory and mental processing of events as if the narration was pure stream-of-consciousness.

Mayne does not say, "Rafe wanted to know what Tawena meant." That would give us Mayne's observation of what Rafe wanted, his omniscient certain knowledge. But the more oblique construction, "Rafe *thought* he wanted to know," tells the reader what was in Rafe's mind, and at the same time indicates Rafe's tentativeness, his lack of comprehension of Tawena's cosmology, his naivete, and even a hint of humor or irony in Rafe's thought. Similarly, landscape and action are viewed and given to the reader by Rafe:

Now the ground itself began to shake under them. All at once Rafe could not tell where he was, where he had come from, how much time had gone by, whether it was day or night, or whether he was alive or dead. . . .
. . . Something seemed to be wrong. They were still running down the lake towards the hut and the village, but the village was no longer there. It had skipped far over to the left. Rafe did not know why that could be so, but it did not matter because the fisherman's hut was straight ahead of them. . . . They went into the hut, because that was the next thing to do. (13–15)

Unfortunately, the bear has tagged along and peers in at them. We have Rafe's impression of this moment:

The bear looked back at Rafe. Rafe stood and looked at the bear. He did not know what to do. He knew there was something he could do, something simple, but he could not remember what it was. He could only remember that a brown bear was standing on all four feet just outside the door. He could smell it, and it could smell him. . . . He stood in the doorway and saw the bear walking towards him, because his eyes were still working, even if his arms would not. (16)

Occasionally, Mayne shifts to another point of view. Here, the bear's: "The bear thought about things, still deciding what to do next. . . . It did not like the way the door shook under its weight, and was not sure whether it was safe to walk on. . . . The bear had been thinking about the door lying loose on the floor and perhaps being a trap" (22). This is how the bear sees things. But even in this, it is Rafe, clearly, seeing and interpreting the bear's thoughts. This *sounds* like, has the ring of, Rafe's mind. Tawena might experience the same events, but, as the reader will learn later, she does not *hear* them in the same way. Rafe, with occasional brief variations, is the only consciousness of which the reader is aware. Like him or not, and sometimes he is not particularly likeable, however bumbling, he is our only Virgil in an unfamiliar world.

We can be sure, then, that Rafe is our narrator, but is he reliable? Wayne Booth, in discussing the "distance" of narrators from "the author, the reader, and the other characters of the story" observes that all these engage in a dialogue. He writes: "Each of the four can range, in relation to each of the others, from identification to complete opposition, on any axis of value, moral, intellectual, aesthetic, and even physical" (155) and lists some five ways these distances can be important. The first two, distance between the narrator and the implied author, and between the narrator and other characters are the two Mayne uses. Booth continues: "For practical criticism probably the most important of these kinds of distance is that between the fallible or unreliable narrator and the implied author who carries the reader with him in judging the narrator . . . "(158) and concludes, after discussing a few unreliable narrators: "All of them make stronger demands on the reader's powers of inference than do reliable narrators. . . . Sometimes it is almost impossible to infer whether or to what degree a narrator is fallible" (159).

That is our problem with Rafe.

The implied author, that is, the author created for us by the implications of his tone, style, theme, sincerity, objectivity, in short as " . . . we infer him as an ideal, literary, created version of the real man . . . *the author's second self* . . . " (159) is almost undetectable in *Drift*. Mayne is barely there, perceptible only as a pervasive, gentle irony. Booth calls Hemingway's story "The Killers" "rigorously impersonal" and remarks on the fact that his degree of distance or invisibility is unusual. Mayne has crafted his novel with this same level of impersonality.

One way this has been achieved is by simplicity. Like Hemingway, Mayne has kept his vocabulary simple, his syntax uncomplicated, his rhythms short and repetitive—all in all, much like Rafe's own interior self. This harmonious matching of the narrator's mental style with the narrative style effaces the author almost completely. It provides the added pleasure of giving the reader an unexpected delight when Rafe exhibits, after nothing but such simplicity, a flash of and then a pronounced tendency toward growth and insight. Indeed, having worked hard throughout the novel, the reader can hardly tell whether the satisfaction he feels at the end is for himself or Rafe. Our powers of inference have had an ordeal almost comparable to Rafe's.

But the second kind of distance is also at work here—that between characters—in fact, between the two major ones. Usually, the reader knows nothing about what Tawena, for example, is thinking except through Rafe's eyes:

Tawena did not think he had done well. He could tell by the way she looked at him that she thought he was an ignorant rough savage. . . . She was right. Tawena herself had made three little footprints as she came from the lake, and she still stood in two of them.

I go about breaking the world to pieces, thought Rafe. (31)

Similarly, the reader's awareness and understanding of the Indian women is based entirely on Rafe's. When the Indian women approach, Tawena disappears, taking Rafe's knife, and leaving Rafe crouched by the faltering fire he has made a mess of. Because one woman wears a cloak of deer skins and the other is in the skins of hares, Rafe thinks of them as Deerskin and Hareskin. "The Indian woman hated him. He did not hate her. But he could tell he was her worst enemy, and that at any moment she would kill him" (33).

Rafe is not killed, of course, but taken prisoner. With his capture, Rafe moves into a different and incomprehensible world, taking the reader with him. From this point on, Mayne uses Rafe's confusion to confuse the reader. The reader and Rafe are as one: nothing is known but what can be seen or felt by Rafe. For example, when the women give him food:

"Eat," she said. Rafe did not know the word in their language but he understood it. And the long black things smelled good. . . . The long black things had legs. They had eyes as well. But they were cooked, and hot, and smelled good. And most things you eat have legs and eyes, though not usually so many.
    Rafe ate his caterpillars. . . . (38)

Later, still tied, Rafe sleeps fitfully. He is awakened,

. . . because something had got hold of him. Something was on top of him, holding him down so that he could not speak. This was of course worse than a dream, and worse than real. . . . Rafe thought that there were things in the forest he had not been told about, something stronger than animals, more frightening than ghosts . . . it breathes in his ear. Where it breathes is where it keeps its teeth, thought Rafe. What is it? Can it be the mother of the caterpillars? (39)

Here Rafe plunges out of his own context and is at a loss, so disoriented that he reconstructs reality badly, based on fear, confusion, superstition, conjecture; but rather than describing this for us from an authorial per-spective, Mayne allows the reader only Rafe's perspective with all its limi-tations of age, education, experience, and character; and since the reader, therefore, is *in* Rafe's circumstances, it is impossible to evaluate this view with total objectivity. Rafe is not only the narrator of events, he is the only meeting ground between reader and reality, effecting as, Booth puts it, "a nearly complete union of the narrative and reader in a common endeavor, with the author silent and invisible" (30).

Occasionally, however, Mayne lapses. When the presence is revealed as Tawena, Mayne observes, "All his life Rafe would remember this dark night when his only friend came to visit him in the vast forest with danger close by. But at the time . . . " (39). There is no apparent narrative necessity for this interjection, and it could be omitted although it underlines in advance the poignant ending, a fact not to be guessed at this juncture. Perhaps Mayne does this to insure our trust in the narrative, which returns at once to Rafe and becomes even more *un*trustworthy, although we do not know that. Tawena tells Rafe, in several ways, to instruct the Indian women to take him home. She says she will tell the bear to tell them also, and slips away into the darkness. This sounds peculiar to Rafe, but as he wonders about it, he hears the bear attacking Tawena in the forest: "There was a fearful crunching noise now. Rafe remembered how he had eaten whole caterpillars, and at this minute the bear was eating Tawena in the same way, straight with its teeth. Tawena's plan of talking to the bear did not seem to work . . ." (40). Presently the bear snuffles and shuffles around the camp. The Indian women listen:

They were attending and obeying; they were answering quietly. After all, the bear was telling them what Tawena said it would. Rafe knew now that the only way to tell the bear anything was to let it kill and eat you, and that was how Tawena had given it the message. She had died, she had been torn apart by a wild creature, just to save him, Rafe. He knew it must be so though he did not understand a word the bear said. (41)

And here, the reader takes the bait along with Rafe. The natural egoism of white dominant culture, hope, and all previous experience/reading, suggest that Rafe's understanding of what is going on in the forest is true. Rafe and the reader are told to believe something and they do believe it: Tawena has spoken to the bear, Tawena has been killed by the bear, and the bear has conveyed a message to the Indian women. Mayne's entire narrative hangs on the reader's *believing* this preposterous sequence. But so cleverly has he entwined us with Rafe, who has crunched up his caterpillars and sensed the supernatural abroad in the forest, that we *do* believe what Rafe does, even though we sense that Rafe is not a particularly sagacious or insightful hero (like many to whom we are accustomed in fiction). Mayne, as author, has told us *nothing*, only what Rafe believes. Foolish Rafe, gullible reader, clever author.

Having maneuvered us to this point, Mayne continues the basic tale of Rafe in the wilderness. Rafe is clumsy and stupid from the Indian point of view. The women find him a sore trial and treat him with disdain while taking care of him. He cannot understand their instructions; he cannot do simple tasks such as building a fire with sticks; he lumbers noisily along in the forest. In short, he is uncivilized. They punish him for his apparent laziness and obvious incompetence. Once in a while he hears the bear in the forest, and once, after falling asleep when he should have been building a fire, he awakens to discover a small fire in a bit of moss and thinks perhaps the women have been secretly nice and built it for him: "He thought it could not be a mystery, because there are no such things. He thought that Deerskin or Hareskin had come back and been secretly kind to him. Rafe was all at once very happy, because one of them must like him . . . " (52).

However, he deceives himself and the reader by reasoning thus; and although the phrase "he thought it could not be a mystery," a syntactically peculiar one, cries aloud for the reader to *notice* this mystery, while the following ironical "because there are no mysteries" declares that there certainly is one here, in perfect harmony and trust with this demonstrably unreliable narrator, the reader hardly pauses in rushing to agree.

But the women are not pleased with him, thumping him and twisting his face in vexation. He tries not to cry and sets himself to learn. They teach him simple skills until finally, "All at once the little group of them round the fire felt like a family. Rafe felt he belonged to them and they belonged to him. He was full of tough bird and woody parsnip, and they had been kind to him, and they were all three alone in the wild places. What nice faces they had, he thought, when they were not cross" (53).

So things go better, the women teaching, Rafe learning. Rafe, convinced in spite of Tawena's whispered message (to say nothing of the bear's) that they are taking him with them into slavery, decides to escape; he craftily makes a bid for freedom. Unfortunately, he gets lost in the forest and panics. His situation becomes more desperate when he realizes something else is with him in the forest: "Behind him something moved among those trees. Not fast, not perhaps following him. But maybe following him; always there, not coming any closer, and not being seen . . . always he heard behind him the thing that followed, followed, with never a breath of voice, never a glimpse, merely breaking its way through the forest after him" (61).

In terror he flees; it continues after, now snarling, growling, even touching him in the darkness—a dream? No, no dream; it is laughing and seizing him. It is Deerskin. Rafe " . . . was so glad to be rescued that he clung on to Deerskin, hugging her, holding her, as if she were the only safe place in the whole world. She and Hareskin had followed and saved his life" (65).

Although she twists his face to chastise him for running away, it does not hurt his face so much as his feelings:

. . . he knew how badly he had behaved, how he had been so ill-mannered, so ungrateful, he had insulted the people who had kept him alive, how he had scorned their feelings, wasted their time and annoyed them. What they had done was follow him patiently, creep up on him in the dark, and give him a very great fright. They thought it was funny, and somehow so did Rafe. (65)

Rafe is changing, becoming different, and after this they work more amiably together. In fact, when Hareskin is shot and nearly dies, Rafe saves her by making a poultice for the wound from moss as he has seen his mother do.

Once more, Rafe encounters the bear when he is gathering wood in the forest. He hears it coughing and growling in the mist, first in one direction, then in another. When he regains camp and tells Deerskin, she listens and then "she made it quite plain to Rafe that there was no bear near, had not been, and would not be, and that he was to stop being silly and fetch more wood," (74) which he does. At last, crossing a narrow ledge under a waterfall, they come face to face with the bear, crossing in the opposite direction. Deerskin, Hareskin, Rafe, and the bear consider what to do.

He had another feeling about it too, because there had been bears all round them, right from the day he and Tawena went to look at one. That bear had only wanted a lump of bacon to eat; in the forest a bear had looked at him without harming him. . . . Rafe began to feel there was something different about bears, as Tawena had said. (87)

As the little quartet ponders, noises from below float up, bearlike noises; not the shadowy gray wolf that has been skulking nearby, but another bear, which the first one lumbers off to investigate.

Shortly after this, the Indian women march with Rafe into his village. By now Rafe and the women can communicate, and Deerskin says, " 'We will take you in. . . . That will be safe for us. And you are dressed like Indian so be careful.' . . . when Rafe came close, he found that his own people had a strange strong smell he did not much like. He led the way through, and no one knew him" (94).

Rafe goes to his house and enters. "It was like going into a box, a trap." Rafe has come home. At last he understands:

He understood too that he was not going to be sold as a slave. . . . All that Hareskin and Deerskin wanted for him was a reward, some return for their trouble or kindness. That was what the bear had told them on the night that Tawena had visited him. That was what they had told him but he had not understood, that night in the forest. They had brought him back to gain a present, not because they liked him. But he was sure that at the end they had liked him. (95)

Had they? We can only conclude that this is so because we also like Rafe now. We like him and the Indian women, and so it must be true. And this is the end: the women receive a pony and travois, and they leave; Rafe resumes his life as it was. He wonders about Tawena, knowing now how she felt.

He saw, as if it was happening again, that Tawena had despised him when they reached the shore again [for his clumsiness]. . . . She will have hated me, he thought. But she did her best to save me, and she did.

But if she had lived, how would it have been? (103)

With Rafe safely back at the village and the story complete, the reader's feeling of satisfying closure receives a rude shock to discover that Tawena's story follows. How anticlimactic! And how can this be, inasmuch as she is dead?

In the retelling with Tawena as narrator, the reader hears quite a different voice indeed. Tawena's version begins on the shore after they have drifted across the lake. She is exasperated with Rafe's noisiness, his helplessness. " 'The white people do not think,' said Tawena to herself. 'Their faces are

pale and their hearts do not work. He is, moreover, dancing like a bear' "
(107).

Tawena thinks conversationally to herself and views things in her own
way. Rafe is a liability in the wild. She cannot depend on him.

He is worse than a bear, she thought. In fact, a bear would have more sense than
to make such noise. A bear is a wise creature. . . . It was no use talking to [Rafe] in
her own language, and she did not know enough of his to explain. And how could
I explain, she thought, to people who know nothing? And I have no breath now I
am blowing on the fire to make it burn. (109)

She fears they cannot get home unless they work together, a doubtful
prospect considering Rafe's uselessness. He does, however, have a good
knife, which she has borrowed to strike sparks from a rock. Rafe watches
with interest, but without comprehension. While she is thinking and working
on the fire, she hears two Indian women approaching. They will kill her if
they find her because her family has broken tribal law: her cheeks are
unmarked with the scars of acceptance. She hopes the women, obviously a
mother and daughter on a foraging expedition, will pass, but they smell the
smoke and turn toward Rafe and Tawena. She tells Rafe they are coming,
that she must not be discovered, and slips away. Rafe understands none of
this and flounders about, then tries to keep the fire going. The women come
upon him as Tawena watches from hiding.

They came up to Rafe as he knelt over the fire. . . . Tawena could not understand
how Rafe did not know, how he could not have heard. But he did not know. When
he did look up his action was pathetic and ridiculous. He behaved like some sim-
pleminded animal, smiling at the Indian women, thinking he had been rescued,
saved, set on his way home.
    The smile soon went away. (112)

Tawena follows the trio, safe because of the noise and blundering of Rafe's
passage, and conceives a plan she hopes will take them all back to the village
eventually. She observes Rafe and the women, and disparages Rafe's lack
of politeness.

"Bear," said Tawena to herself.
    She loved Bear, real Bear, because Bear was the animal of her people. She loved
him for his strength and pride, for his greed and anger, for his ferocity and his way
of doing all he wanted. But she, and all her people, would laugh at him too, for the
way he walked (not caring about his track) . . . for the way he would eat (not minding
how sticky his jaws got). Now Rafe was eating like Bear. (117)

She discusses her plan with Maneto and visits Rafe in the camp to tell him
what she will do. Then she disguises the tracks to look like a white boy,

followed by a bear: "Now anyone looking would see how a white boy had come here, a bear had come after him, and only a bear had gone away." Then,

She started the next thing she had to do. She began a great noise. She ran about, stamping her foot into the frosty ground. She tore off a strip of the brown village dress she wore. She shook and broke branches, throwing herself down among them and against them, making them snap and whip. She was acting out a child being caught by a bear, and eaten.

The worst part came at the end . . . she lifted the bright blade and cut herself deep the length of her forearm, the sudden burning pain, the hot and cold of the blade and the blood, made her scream the loudest scream. And that was all from her, because she was not meant to be dead. She had to be dead. Rafe had to think she was dead. (120)

Rafe does. The reader does, or rather, did. At this point, awakening to what has happened, *really* happened, the reader, instead of being relieved at Tawena's escape (like Rafe, we felt sad at her terrible end, her great sacrifice), feels anger, admiration, and deep chagrin. Tricked! No better than clumsy Rafe—ignominious!

Here Tawena's voice, *her* narration, can take on any aspect. The reader can be told directly by the author, by the narrator, or by his own surmises whatever Mayne chooses. We *know* Tawena's story already; the entire sequence lies before us in a new light, seen for the first time in its true meaning. Authenticity is clear; we were duped by Rafe's blindness, blinded ourselves in turn. Out of curiosity, seeking to fill the now deeply suspicious gaps of Rafe's original story, we follow Tawena's feet, Indian feet. In great pain and weakness, she assures that Rafe will be taken home, even building a fire he is supposed to manage:

He is going to sleep again and has made no fire, and that is very foolish. White men are like this. No doubt they think of something, but what it is they do not know. They talk so much all the wisdom runs out of their mouths. But I know there should be a fire, and if there is not there will be something worse for him.

While Rafe slept Tawena made fire. . . . (128)

And when Rafe makes his break for freedom, Tawena discovers this: "She went to look for him, because it was not right for him to wander alone, by night or by day. She heard him easily. 'It is Rayaf or a bear,' she said to herself. 'He goes as quietly as he can, like a tree walking' " (140).

She follows, leaving a Rafe-like trail for the women to read since Rafe has learned under their stern tutelage to hide his tracks. Uncertain if they will pursue him, leave him, or kill him, Tawena watches them encircle Rafe, and she sees that they will not kill him, that they have become fond of him. Sadly, feeling alone and lonely, she sees Hareskin shot near the whiteman's camp. But the bullet had been meant for her, had glanced from a tree and struck Hareskin. It is Maneto's expression of displeasure with Tawena: " 'I have done this,' said Tawena. 'In spite of all, if one of them dies the other will not take the white boy to his own village . . .' and she followed slowly. . . . 'If she should fall . . . I shall bring the other woman to her, and they will kill me . . .' " (144).

Instead she helps Hareskin back nearly to camp, where she is found by Deerskin, then trails the trio as they struggle on. She sees Rafe helping the women, saving the wounded one, being gratefully treated. Her loneliness is acute: "She went away into the forest alone, very much alone. 'I am alive,' she said to the bird with blue wings, 'but not as I want to be. I cannot say who I am, and no one cares for me' " (150).

By now, Tawena's story is no longer Rafe's retold. It is truly Tawena's, the Indian story. The mother and daughter and Tawena form their own unit, at one with the place they are and the spirits that move there. Tawena's narrative is that of Bigfoot, Maneto, and Wendagoo, of wolves and the bird with blue wings, and the bear.

Rejoining her own mother a day before Rafe arrives in the village, she observes his return with the Indian women. She shows herself to them in the crowd: "The daughter [Hareskin] looked at her, touched her own cheeks, and said nothing. Tawena touched her own left shoulder. That, for them, was a long conversation, with much meaning" (163).

By now the reader, too, can understand this conversation and its full meaning. What a distance he has come under Mayne's relentless shepherding: from a very limited and somewhat confusing perception of events, given by an unreliable narrator, through a more straightforward, open narrator explaining an unknown world, to a clear understandable story. The dim twilight of Rafe's narrative, darkening the reader's understanding and dogging Tawena's version so long, has disappeared. Were the reader to return to the beginning and read again, he would find a third version, the one hidden from him the first time around, and which he has himself now constructed. The plot, such as it is, has become relatively unimportant. That is, "what *really* happened," now known through Tawena's story, has no significance per se. Perspective is what is important, what creates the tension and opens up before the reader's gaze an undetected world.

In the story itself, Rafe, at this point, has lagged behind the reader. *He* has no idea what has happened to Tawena and is unaware of her presence still. She approaches him, after the Indian women leave, to return his knife as she has intended to do all along, as she has promised Maneto. He does not recognize her; she speaks, calls him by name,

Then she began an extraordinary thing. She leaned forward, pointed her elbows out, and took a deep breath. . . . She made a noise like a bear snuffling and hunting.

Somehow she made the noise of claws on wood. She took another breath and screamed.

Rafe had heard a scream like that in the woods. . . . (164)

At last the two narratives become one. Rafe has joined the reader in the new perspective. But even though Tawena, to his amazement and enlightenment, reenacts all the events for him, he cannot know everything. Rafe knows more, but far from everything. The author knew all from the first; now the reader does, too, achieving what Booth calls "a secret communion of the author and reader behind the narrator's back" (300). He has finally escaped any narrator.

The effect of Mayne's novel, as Booth warns and as we can observe, is to make unusual demands upon the reader. But to what purpose? Wayne Booth and Wolfgang Iser have in turn given critical attention and approval to narrative opaqueness. Booth speaks of the "[t]hree general pleasures that are in some degree present whenever the reader is called upon to infer the author's position through the semitransparent screen erected by the narrator."[1] And Iser describes "[spurring] the reader on to build up the syntheses which eventually individualize the aesthetic object" (118). In short, the reader who creates the text for himself has thereby a greater stake in both the events and the narrator/narrative. A happy ending, closure, growth of and identification with the characters, plausibility of plot, and similar narrative conventions all bow to the satisfactory participation of the reader in the process itself.

Few novels for intermediate readers make these demands. Young readers are usually served up a transparent narrative that relies on one or two appealing features to capture their involvement. Creativity is almost all on the author's part. By his masterful use of the narrator's voice, Mayne, in *Drift*, offers the reader not only a rousing tale, but a hand in making it and thereby a greater response to its rich and multileveled diversity.

NOTES

1. Booth, p. 301. ("the pleasure of deciphering, the pleasure of collaboration, and secret communion, collusion, and collaboration") which leads to participation on a moral level, "one of the most rewarding of all reading experiences." p. 307.

REFERENCES

Booth, Wayne C. *The Rhetoric of Fiction*. Chicago: University of Chicago Press, 1961.

Iser, Wolfgang. *The Act of Reading*. Baltimore: Johns Hopkins University Press, 1978.

Mayne, William. *Drift*. New York: Delacorte Press, 1985.

32

Narrative Voice in Young Readers' Fictions about Nazism, the Holocaust, and Nuclear War

HAMIDA BOSMAJIAN

What motivates an adult to address young readers in narratives about the history of Nazism and the holocaust or the future possibility of global nuclear war? In reading such narratives adults become aware of crises in memory and anxieties over the child's past, present and future. Memory and anxiety are screened by seemingly judicious and deliberative choices from historical experience expressed through rhetorical strategies suitable for the mode called "young adult literature." Narratives about Nazism, the holocaust and nuclear war are by definition in the "ironic mode" (Frye, 1957) of a cruel, life-denying world. However, the implied reader of such fictions is imagined as needing an enabling pedagogy that retains life-affirming trust in a future and avoids the compulsive repetitions of the punitive pedagogy experienced in historical time. Children died in the Nazi holocaust, some survived, almost all children will die in a nuclear holocaust, but somehow the adult writer implies that the child will fulfill a promise the writer's generation could not keep.

The failure of adults to prevent historical trauma delimits the credibility of the adult voice in serious narratives about such topics. We suspect and find in these narratives an anxiousness on the part of the "implied author" (Booth, 1983) to be accountable by addressing the historical issues that contribute to the young generation's ambivalent heritage and threatening future. Young people's questions as well as their occasionally open hostility in the texts of these narratives challenge narrators and implied authors to generate text-intrinsic dialogue as well as "reader-text interaction" (Iser, 203). This is usually accomplished through "blanks in the text" (Iser) that disclaim narrative authority and encourage reader participation. Thus the implied authors of narratives about Nazism, the holocaust, and nuclear war avoid authoritative attitudes so that the young reader can question and explore life-threatening myths, paradigms, and emotions by which humanity has led itself to disastrous dead-ends. As a result, definitive closure is replaced by insistence on irony and open-endedness that encourage participatory and dialogical interactions within the text and between reader and text. Irony, negation of closure, textual blanks, and author-narrator ambivalence toward revealing specifics of historical trauma and compensating for it with enabling pedagogy contribute to the "meta-irony" of these fictions: by presuming to offer new strategies for living, the texts intrinsically deconstruct themselves and maintain thereby the patterns through which we compulsively repeat.

Narrative voice and its reliability are the most important rhetorical strategies in reader-text interaction, even when the narrator is in a situation that the reader's desires and values reject. We find in young people's narratives about historical trauma the first-person narrator contemporary with the age of the intended reader as well as the first-person narrator who, for therapeutic and pedagogic reasons, recalls the past from the vantage point of the present. Horst Burger's *Why Were You in the Hitler Youth? Four Questions for My Father*, (1978) Hans Peter Richter's *Friedrich* (1970), and Ruth Minsky Sender's *The Cage* (1986) re-collect and re-figure the time between 1933 and 1945 through various uses of first-person narration, while Gudrun Pausewang uses the first-person main character to envision and pre-figure a time to come in *The Last Children of Schewenborn* (1983). Whitley Strieber in *Wolf of Shadows* (1985) and Louise Lawrence in *Children of the Dust* (1985) depict the postnuclear world through "third person center of consciousness" (Booth, 153). First-person narration about personal experiences in historical trauma gives the illusion of high reliability because of the great number of facts and experiences absorbed by the narrator. Actually, however, the narrator's psyche is overwhelmed by the facticity of trauma and is unable to come to terms with it except through noninterpretive factual iteration. We may get a deceptive sense of clarity because of factual material, but the narrators are simply unable to gather meaning and significance from their experiences. The use of third person is an attempt to avoid this dilemma, but that point of view has its own problematics in this context.

NAZI HOLOCAUST NARRATIVES

The voice in narratives about Nazism and the holocaust is a public and critical consciousness that shows how the energies of persons gather themselves in relation to external events, often out of survival demands. Yet, the background of the deeply personal and private also deprives or sustains the person imprisoned in historical trauma. Fear and personal deprivations lead the narrators of Burger's and Richter's novels to lose themselves in the group structures of Nazism, while the mere memory of a loving and accepting parent sustains Minsky Sender's Riva in the camp and helps her survive.

The painful relation between public and private self gives the narrative point of view of Burger's *Why Were You in the Hitler Youth? Four Questions for My Father* its unusual complexity. The novel alternates between the first-person discussions of Walter Jendrich and his son and the third-person center of consciousness when Walter recalls his childhood and teen years during the Nazi era. Each of the father-son dialogues moves to one of four questions: Tell me about the Jews? How was it at school and in the Hitler Youth? Why did you volunteer to go to war? How were the last days of the war and how was it afterward?

The first name of young Jendrich is never mentioned, a subtle omission, for not only does it suggest that all young Germans should ask his questions, but also that he is still an unproved self, is still able to address the father and the young reader with arrogant innocence: "I don't know, for some the word Father is like a chewed out piece of gum before you spit it out. . . . Many simply say 'my old man' or such. . . . You won't have to think of Fatherland, Father in Heaven or 'honor the Father and Mother' " (5). He himself has no problem saying "Father," though he shows himself unreliable when he wishes there would be another Hitler "only to prove to you that we, the younger generation, would not fall for him. We could handle the Nazis." Walter replies, "Just this kind of attitude scares me. It shows that people learn nothing from history, especially not if they didn't experience it" (70). In spite of the father's self-critical honesty, the question of how much the son "learns" remains open.

In answering the first question Walter tries to get to the radicals of his memory by describing, in third person, how he as a five-year-old shoved a Jewish boy into a ditch where he drowned. But he taps the deeper root, his loveless and rigid family life, only tentatively just before he describes his crime. "At the end of the war I was sixteen, as old as you." His father returned in good health from the American POW camp declaring "that he was a National socialist and would always be one" (7). Hearing this, Walter awakens as "from a deep sleep" and realizes that "in the dark [I] had crept into the wrong dwelling. Suddenly I smelled the stench all around. My God, did I ever think that way? . . . How far back would I have to go to discover the origin of the lie?" He uses the metaphor of the stinking dark dwelling to explain and at the same time block his full comprehension of the Nazi era and his loveless dead family life.

Walter avoids discussing his home life, but mentions it often enough so that the adult reader becomes aware of his problem. Through third-person narration he creates critical distance to his past, depersonalizes and universalizes it, thus making it bearable. The lack of love in his family is so painful that he prefers to implicate himself in history rather than confront that lack. At the same time, Walter always was and is a person of conscience, even as a five-year-old: "If I shove him now...The thought was quite suddenly there and could not be repressed. Walter felt his heart beat in his throat. The fear 'you can't do this,' the image of what would be when it happened grew smaller and smaller. The urge to do it became more and more powerful. He closed his eyes and breathed deeply; he didn't even hear the splash. When he opened his eyes, Gerhard Wandres had disappeared" (11). Pale and frail Gerhard is a threat to Walter's own sense of helplessness even as he feels sorry for him (10). When the police arrive, Walter gets hysterical, cries and pleads, refusing "to pull himself together as he was always told to do." Suddenly, a man, dressed in S.A. and SS attire pushes through the crowd and licenses the incident:

"A German boy doesn't cry," he said firmly but not unkindly. "And you are a German boy, aren't you?" Walter nodded and, winking at him, the man continued: "I know your father. He's all right. Go home now and don't be afraid. We'll fix this.". . . As he passed through the crowd [Walter] overheard the SS officer saying to the police "bookbinder . . . Wandres . . . Jews." Then he was alone. . . . A strange depressing idea rose in him. Did they let him go because the matter wasn't important, because Gerhard Wandres and his mother were Jews? (14)

Burger shows here that the potential to victimize is already in the child, but also that the child knows that this is wrong. Victimization is licensed in the family and, by extension, in the public life of the culture, making the child and young adult an accomplice in and perpetrator of murder motives. This license has a price: Walter must neither confess nor cry, he must deny his feelings and eventually even the therapeutics of the first-person narration. As a small child he committed a crime and afterward split his inner awareness from the events of the world around him. Walter continues to tell about the increasing and hysterical violence in a world licensed by "total war," but at the end he decides for life: "What idiots they were to join that murderous adventure! For what?" (96). Through honest communication with his son, he tries to avoid the behavior patterns that brought him to his own impasse: he speaks without heroics, without slogans and with great effort to discover words that are still meaningful.

Burger's narrative communicates not only an authentic assessment of the Nazi period and its atrocities, but also a father's attempt to avoid repetition by changing the mode of familial communication. The son senses that his father never has been allowed to grieve: "There was no one with whom they could cry. . . . They were expected to function. Finally, even we, the younger generation attacked them . . . we forgot that the word 'understanding' wasn't in the vocabulary they were taught. They had received and given so many beatings that they were no longer capable of the gentle touch" (154). At the deepest level the narrative urges that change will only come if familial and public punitive pedagogy is transformed. That possibility is left open. Father and son do not find an ideal relationship, but the contemplative insight that while we can never fully comprehend another's experience we are capable of enabling that blank through understanding.

The anonymous first-person witness narrator in Richter's *Friedrich* has no dialogical partner, nor does he posit an external listener. His witness monologue informs accurately and clearly about the years 1929 to 1942 and indirectly memorializes his friend and implicates himself, but he confesses without confessor and without raising consciousness and conscience. The narrator exemplifies the *unbewaltigte Vergangenheit*, the "unmastered past" of postwar Germany. He does not comment on or interpret how he felt about the persecution and eventual death of his childhood friend Friedrich, nor is he able to grieve over his losses, not because they were too traumatic, but because grieving them would entail a critique of the world he has chosen to accept and is too afraid to abandon. Thus the sense of distance and control in the narrative, even when highly emotional and traumatic incidents are depicted, is due to the narrator's personal restraint.

Both Friedrich and the narrator were born in 1925 and grew up in the same apartment house. Each early chapter ends with a reference to Jewishness, always accentuating differences, so that the narrator is ready to accept Nazi myths when he joins the Hitler Youth. After Friedrich's close-knit family is destroyed, Friedrich moves from hiding place to hiding place, occasionally seeking and finding refuge with the narrator's family who are never capable of making a serious commitment to him and abandon him when he seeks entrance to the shelter during an air raid. A piece of shrapnel kills Friedrich that night.

The narrator's family members are "bystanders" who have values but are too timid to realize them and too concerned with the comforts of their family unit. Potentially good people, they submit anxiously to an aggressively hierarchical social structure symbolized by the grandfather who announces during a visit: "I do not wish the boy to associate with this Jew" (22). Father and mother look frightened and the narrator takes his cue from their timidity. When Friedrich's Jewishness is discovered in 1938 at a municipal swimming pool, he observes the harassment from a distance, though they played and swam together all afternoon. Friedrich is oblivious to such betrayals. After the persecutions intensify, he still invites his friend to his bar mitzvah where the narrator witnesses a depth of spiritual life totally lacking in his own family.

Without the contrast of the Schneider family, the narrator's parents would come across as conventionally good and caring parents; nevertheless, they demonstrate conventional "good behavior" in an authoritarian society before and during the Hitler years. For example, when it snows Frau Schneider plays with Friedrich outside, but the narrator's mother insists on her housework, saying "work comes first, my boy" (13). When they are finally ready to join the Schneiders, they hear the landlord yell from his window: " 'Will you leave my roses alone, you dirty Jewboy you.' My mother stepped back. 'Come,' she said, 'come away from the window' " (12). Even after he joins the Nazi party, the father advises Herr Schneider to leave Germany where anti-Semitism is public policy, but Herr Schneider, caught in the illusion of reprieve, insists that he, too, is German and that this anti-Semitism is temporary. Yet, he requests: "If something should happen to me . . . please look after my wife and son." The father agrees nonverbally; articulation would be too much of a commitment.

The narrator perceives choices between right and wrong, perceives denial of commitment and action. No court of law would try him and his parents; Herr Schneider himself would testify to their "decency," but they have failed. Each could have been the safely anonymous narrator, yet they all witnessed. In *Friedrich* the everyman narrator testifies to words said and heard, to deeds done and observed but without interpretations and discovery of meaning for himself and the society he lives in; therefore, he cannot redeem himself. The pathos of Friedrich's tragedy is complemented by the narrator's tragedy of arrested development signaled at the very end when the family sees Friedrich dead: "Mother cried against Father's shoulder. 'Do pull yourself together!' begged Father. 'You'll endanger us all otherwise.' " He himself has no response. The text of his narrative hints at choked grief, but there is no letting go and no liberation for this witness.

The first-person narration of the memoir-autobiography of the concentration camp survivor focuses on shaping some "version of survival" (Langer, 1982) in a world that constantly threatened to consume all dimensions of being human and traumatized him or her with tremendous physical and psychological pressures compared to which family tensions and personal identity crises appear minor. After the ordeal, the survivor has to cope with the fact of survival, with guilt and with a feeling of being less than those who died, for in attempting to survive the inmate had to see and not see the atrocities of the camp world, had to face a condition of powerlessness that often led to unthinkable temptations (Bosmajian, chap. 2).

Can the holocaust experience be adapted to the maturity level of the young reader? Actually, all survivor memoirs are adaptations of experience, all show the limits of language, all are selective and self-censoring. Ruth Minsky Sender's *The Cage* is one of the most explicit holocaust narratives for young readers. Again, the adult is motivated to recall the past because of a child's questions: Why did the Nazis kill my grandparents? Why did people let them do it? It couldn't happen here (4). Nancy is still a small child, but when she says " . . . it couldn't happen here. Our neighbors, our friends, they would help," Sender begins to address an external audience as "suddenly it is 1939 again for her." From the beginning, *The Cage* is written in the present tense, for the past is always present to the narrator. In the last chapter she answers Nancy's concerns: "We must learn from those horrors. We must learn what happens when people remain silent while others are persecuted. . . . We must learn, my child, not to ignore the ugly signs, as my family—as the people of my generation—did." She assures her: "As long as there is life there is hope." These directives are but words to cling to, whereas the text of the autobiography reveals why the writer only rarely sleeps without nightmares. Moreover she says, "we must learn," implying that so far we have not yet learned.

Minsky Sender's witnessing of the holocaust follows the pattern well established in narratives for adult readers: there is the caring environment before the Nazis, followed by the brutality of the invasion, ghettoization of the Jews, their deportation, arrival in the camp, the struggle for survival until liberation. The motive for writing springs not only from the need to confess what one saw or to instruct new generations, but also to speak and bear witness for those who have been silenced, in Sender's case her three younger brothers and her mother.

The Cage projects the ethos of the good mother in a dangerous world. She loves, works, and cares, but ultimately she cannot protect her children from the trauma of history. Riva, the narrator, tries to be such a mother. Her mother was a widow left with seven children she supported by managing a tailoring factory: "She gives us the best she can in a home filled with love. We are all happy surrounded by friends we can trust and count on" (8). In September 1939 the idyll is shattered. Now Riva realizes that "the bravest person I have ever known is Mama" (17) who, free of the myth that families must stay together, sent her three oldest children across the border to Russia, where they survived the war and were eventually united with Riva.

But Mama cannot stay the horrors of the Lodz ghetto—the yellow star, the searches, the slave labor, the deportation: "September 1942. The ghetto walls are closing in. Terror and panic fill every home" (32). "Mama's face has lost all trace of liveliness" (34). She is seized for transport and Riva becomes a mother to her brothers at the age of sixteen (36). "For days the four of us hardly eat or sleep. We huddle together on Mama's bed and cry. Outside the days are warm and sunny. I look at the sky and wonder, How can the sun still shine?" (36) She takes on the burden of a mother while herself in need of maternal comfort (mother's bed) and cosmic protection; neither are given.

After her mother's deportation, time is a dateless struggle, but the image of her life-affirming mother does sustain her. Riva becomes officially her brothers' mother, but can not keep them from death in this traumatic world and time. She writes letters to her mother but never mails them. When she wants to stop this seemingly futile activity, a friend counsels: "We may forget what happened today, but your letters will remember" (85). The need to communicate with her mother becomes Riva's way of surviving. In the camp she will write poetry for her absent mother, who thus continues to be a presence for the narrator.

Riva is first transported to Auschwitz where she stays a week and learns

"You'll end up in smoke. You'll end up in smoke. Those words spin around and around in my head" (141). She is then transferred to the labor camp Mittelsteine where Madame Commandant becomes the bad mother who licenses child abuse. One day she starts whipping a girl for stealing potatoes and when the girl's sister pleads, "we are hungry. Please forgive us," the commandant forces the intercessor to beat her sibling. She obeys, but, unable to bear this ordeal, escapes into madness: "Mama, can you see me, Mama? I did not let them hurt Chanele. Let's go home." Triumphantly the commandant as evil mother announces: "I did not beat her. Her sister did" (172–75). The good mother is beyond hearing while the daughter was forced to act the abusive parent. The narrator tells the incident without commentary, but how profoundly it affected her is evident from her subsequent behavior.

Sender's voice throughout the present tense narrative is that of the sensitive and intelligent teenager talking to a somewhat younger sister. She does not analyze herself or interpret her experience; she simply presents it, though the reader familiar with holocaust literature always senses the implied author's careful choice and omission of detail. This limits the narrative point of view, but also enables the narrator to swerve from the profound self-implications often found in survivor autobiographies. The plain "I felt guilty, guilty that I had survived" (243) suffices for Riva. She survived because of her special gift to express herself in writing poetry by which she helps maintain the morale of her fellow inmates so well that the commandant is persuaded to get Riva professional medical care when she is dangerously sick with blood poisoning.

The chapter where her gift is recognized follows immediately after the description of the traumatic beating. Inadvertently Riva does what most children do in abusive parent relationships—she aims to please, though the implied author does not seem to be aware of this. When she recovers from her illness, she pleases the commandant during a Christmas celebration by reciting her poem "Message for Mama," a poem of longing, not for maternal love, but to shelter and comfort the mother, to "feel her pain, feel her sorrow" for having failed to protect her child: "We will find you, dear Mama, please do not despair." The commandant allows Riva to continue to write and admits to her "You remind me that I, too, have a mother." The irony is that the commandant says this to a motherless child who is so desperate that she momentarily wants to see the good mother as well as the good child in the commandant: "There is something human in that woman, something that can be moved by a poem" (217).

Minsky Sender's "version of survival," shows the victim in a situation unusual for most survivors of the holocaust; few had her privileges, but her understatement of atrocity foregrounds the yearning of the child abandoned in the trauma of history: Riva yearns to be mothered, wants to mother and aches with the realization that even the best mother cannot protect her child

in a historical trauma such as the holocaust. In this her two voices join—
the voice of the mother she is to Nancy telling of the child-mother who
mourned at her brother-son's grave at the end of the war (245). She ends
by promising Nancy "as long as there is life, there is hope," reiterating in
this profound platitude her own victimized mother's futile assurance.

NUCLEAR HOLOCAUST NARRATIVES

The reality, structures, and symbols of Nazism and the holocaust are
frequently perceived as analogous to those that may lead to global nuclear
war (Markusen & Harris, 1985), the bombing of Hiroshima proving that
humans are capable of using such weapons. If the writer's motive for recalling
the death world of Nazism and the holocaust is "lest we forget," the motive
for nuclear war narratives is the indefinite postponement of our "sense of
an ending" (Kermode, 1967). Holocaust literature always experiences that
failure of language to contain the horror of historical time in a book; nuclear
literature hopes that the alien, homeless, and futureless time can be contained between the covers of a book. In comparison to the paucity of explicit
narratives about nuclear war for adults (Schwenger, 1986), the number of
narratives for young people is surprising. One may surmise that the young
reader is the privileged reader for narrators and authors in a world that
denies the death world of nuclear war through illusions of reprieve or through
fantasies of the terrible sublime where the elect have the blessed assurance
of the ultimate rescuer or the bliss of ecstatic dissolution (Mojtabai, 1986).

None of such fantasies are in nuclear fictions for young readers, but neither
do we find political or social causes for nuclear confrontation in Pausewang's,
Strieber's or Lawrence's fictions. Instead, ordinary people have a sense of
helpless foreboding until the bomb is dropped one day. After that comes
the struggle for survival. The apocalypse is in the past; the future has already
happened. The punitive and aggressive power structure of Western civilization is life-destroying and, while some maintain that attitude after the
devastation, cooperative and nurturant community values are foregrounded
as the only way to survive or die humanly. Family structures are also either
destroyed or must be relinquished for the sake of the greater good. But,
while the community-minded survivor becomes the moral norm and the
individual who greedily appropriates food and shelter for his sole survival
is the deviant, both groups are doomed in the three narratives under discussion—*Homo sapiens* will become extinct. Survival is only a matter of
time, for each novel communicates that nuclear war is truly the end of
humankind as we know it.

In the last chapter of *The Last Children of Schewenborn*, the first-person
narrator, Roland Bennewitz, speaks to the reader in the present tense. At
the age of seventeen, his calling is to be the teacher of the last and doomed
children of Schewenborn. Because of his maturity in the postnuclear world,

he is a reliable narrator in the context of personal and community experience and yet is powerless to provide lasting remedies for his world. He was almost thirteen when the nuclear flash occurred just as his family was on the way to visit his grandparents in Schewenborn. At the end, only Roland and his father survive and Roland, once the middle child as *Dümmling* of the family, emerges as a fulcrum of support to his father and the community. Herr Bennewitz, too, becomes a teacher, but loses confidence when one of the students calls him a murderer. After that he no longer sleeps well. Roland, however, does not accuse him in spite of the fact that there is no future: "Hardly any newborn in and around Schewenborn is normal. Almost all, if they were born alive, are crippled or blind, deaf-mute or mentally handicapped. They negate all hope. For no matter how hard the people of Schewenborn try to survive, they will become extinct. It is only a matter of time" (123). Roland has only a choice of attitude with which to face the end; there will be no internal audience for his memoir. Thus he speaks from the future that has been to the present that is. It is the implied author who intends to shock the reader into awareness of what could be and she uses Roland to be the youthful teacher for the youthful reader.

The screens of denial and the images of hope are two illusions of reprieve that keep humans from seeing and acting. Even Roland struggles with this by losing consciousness when reality is too unbearable for him. He faints the first time when he visits the hospital and sees the images of suffering culminating in the image of a dead baby taken away from its screaming mother: "They took the child away from the screaming woman by force and laid it across the chest of the dead young man. I saw how the bandage slipped from his stump and exposed the torn bloody flesh. I passed out" (40). He falls in and out of consciousness when he, along with his parents, succumbs to typhoid, the second wave of death that ravages the community and destroys all remnants of order. For two weeks he hovers between life and death, as if subconsciously making up his mind. He decides to live, at least for the time being.

Frau Bennewitz's denials and desperate need for hope in a future become understandable to Roland when his father tells him after the typhoid crisis that she became pregnant two days before the bomb was dropped. Roland inadvertently is prepared for the trauma of this birth by a series of increasingly constricting horrors, which he describes precisely and without commentary or feeling, letting the images speak for themselves: "And everywhere, especially under the trees, I stepped upon tiny bird skeletons. . . . in the pale yellow willows hung a few corpses locked into each other—small black skeletons with shrunken flesh" (73). Among the wild, desperate, and abusively treated children around Schewenborn is Andreas, a legless boy who sits in his excrement in a baby carriage and wishes for death. He begs Roland to hang him. Roland, still capable of love for his family, asks Andreas a final impossible question: do we meet our family again after death?

Andreas curses his parents: "The devil take them and their whole generation. . . . They saw it coming. They saw without acting. . . . Why did they bring us into the world if they cared so little for us ?" (88) Again, he begs Roland to kick the baby carriage. Roland complies: "I swallowed. Then I kicked the carriage with all my strength so that it shot forward; I ran away. Only at the end of the park I turned around. Andreas was still swinging" (88). A few hours later he takes him down, buries him in a cave, and takes the baby carriage home for his mother who "fixes it up" for her unborn child: " 'Isn't it sweet?' she asked repeatedly, wanting to be praised" (89). The stark images speak for themselves; Roland cannot afford analysis or interpretation.

Shortly before the birth, Frau Bennewitz demands that the family walk to their home town; she cannot believe that it no longer exists. Giving up their home in Schewenborn, the family goes on a useless quest during which the mother finally surrenders all hope. When they return, the house is no longer theirs and they join the homeless. During the night Roland's mother gives birth in a ruined castle. Roland takes baby Jessica Marta in the dark and warms her. Hope and love surge up in him and he actually allows himself to express feelings: "Every time it made a sound or moved I got warm with happiness. I was filled with tenderness and wanted to do everything to make it survive" (113). The next morning reveals to him how devastating it is to feel: "My little sister Jessica Marta had no eyes. Where they were supposed to be was nothing but skin, ordinary skin. There was only a nose, and a mouth rooting at my chest, ready to suckle." His emotional and ethical need to care and nurture reaches here its grotesque nadir.

As he tries to draw his father's attention to the newborn, the father misunderstands and instead indicates to Roland that mother died during the night: "I began to scream. I screamed and screamed until, bathed in sweat, I lost consciousness." As he regains it, he sees his father preparing to expose the newborn. Father and son communicate intimately through the blanks of their pain and despair:

"Where are you carrying her?" I asked filled with fear.
"Go to sleep," he said.
I noticed that he avoided my eyes.
"You can't do that," I whispered.
Tears ran down his face.
"What is more merciful—this or that?" he asked.
I staggered to him and stroked the carton.
"Listen, don't hurt her," I sobbed.
Father shook his head.
"Stay here," he said. "Stay with mother."
He left me alone for a short while, but it seemed forever. When I finally heard him on the steps, I met him. He still held the carton in his hands. But now nothing cried or rustled in it. (115)

Out of context, these are the most ordinary of sentences, their plainness proves both expressive of the horror and insufficient to the momentousness of grief. Roland's fear of abandonment—he has just lost his mother and sees his father abandoning the newborn—the father's merciful denial of parenting, their unspoken refusal to touch the infant in the styrofoam box, the choked need to care, the father's meaningless, in another context so comforting "stay with mother," communicate a world where nothing is "normal." When he returns nothing cried or rustled in the box. The next day they bury mother and daughter. There is a hiatus on the page, a blank that speaks louder than words. Then, Roland moves to his teaching of the last children of Schewenborn, a static futureless present.

Whitley Strieber chose a third-person center of consciousness for *Wolf of Shadows*, a limited choice as far as exploration of historical causes or human motivation are concerned, but enabling because the perceptions of the intelligent wolf make the reader aware of other than anthropocentric consequences of nuclear war. By choosing the wolf, a conventional projection of human ferociousness and inverting it to an image of restraint and care for community, Strieber implies that if a wolf can be thus, *Homo sapiens* could be so much more. The wolf's humane heart is the center of the novel where humans have unleashed a wilderness incomprehensible to the animal: "The cloud boiled in fury. It was hate unbound—not the struggling rage of an animal trapped by the human hunter's agony-jaws, nor the anguish of the mouse wriggling on a hungry tongue, but something else, a steaming clotted malevolence that killed all and killed indifferently, humbling everything from mayfly to man" (13).

During the devastating nuclear winter that starts in June, two women, an animal ethnologist and her daughter, are adopted by the wolf pack. On their trek south they come upon "the traffic jam of the dead" who tried to escape Minneapolis (56) where Wolf of Shadows notices the shadows of humans on the walls and human skulls, teeth, and charred bones beneath the ice under his feet. Man's brutality has not ceased: farm houses are looted and their owners brutally murdered. When two armed men try to strip the women of their padded clothes, the wolf protects them. A profound bond is established between the woman, free of wolfish egocentricity, and the humane wolf to whom Strieber gives an indirect voice while maintaining the boundaries between animal and human as the following values-oriented passage reveals:

Wolf of Shadows had become very close to the mother. He considered that he now had two mates, the beautiful wolf he shared with the gray, and this one, who was a mate of the heart.

He licked her forepaws and she put her face close to his. He was used to her growling ritual, which he endured patiently, sometimes making sense of the emotions she conveyed, sometimes not. "You know what the difference is between wolves and men? Each of you is all of you. And you know it, and take your love of one another from it. Before the war people became so separate from one another we were like leaves in the sea. We were alone." (91)

While the wolf's limited center of consciousness indirectly indicts Western civilization's ruthlessness and denial of kinship with nature, now globally abused, Strieber offers alternatives in his afterword and in the epigraphs to his chapters by citing native Americans whose life worlds European presumptions of superiority and conquest destroyed. They are perceived as antecedents to twentieth-century mass deaths. The voices of these now silent people speak in Strieber's book. Chief Luther Standing Bear: "He [the wise man] knew that man's heart away from nature becomes hard; he knew that lack of respect for living, growing things soon led to lack of respect for humans too." Alienation, homeless, futurelessness—the fate of white people in *Wolf of Shadows*, was already experienced by the Nez Perce: "Husband dead, friends dead . . . strong men, well women, and little children killed. . . . They had not done wrong to be so killed. . . . Our going was with heavy hearts, broken spirits . . . all lost, we walked silently into the wintry night." Black Elk is the voice of muted hope in the last chapter's epigraph: "It may be that some little root of the sacred tree still lives. Nourish it, then, that it may leaf and bloom with singing birds."

In the afterword Strieber abolishes distance between reader and implied author as he responds to two questions the reader may have: Is such a bonding between human and animal possible? Why aren't we told about the pack's arrival in the southern valley where the waters flow? He answers that he has no scientific evidence for such bonding, but his fiction urges us to discover radical new ways of thinking to solve our impasses, among them the assumption that "animals are lower beings because they cannot manipulate nature as we do." He cannot say if Wolf of Shadows and his pack ever found the warm valley because "the true end of the story comes when we decide, as a species, to dismantle the machine and use our great intelligence on behalf of the earth that bears us, instead of against her."

The narrative advocates the values of intelligence, nurturance, and community. Strieber juxtaposes the consciousness of a male animal, embodying those values, with an aggressive "phallocentric" civilization, implying that our shadow is not the wolf but the paradigms we live by. The positive human energies are with the intelligent and empathetic scientist and mother, her natural counterpart being the earth as abused maternal sustainer. This tale with strong thematic emphasis is close to allegory or fable, while the third-person point of view, the ancestral voices of the American earth, and the direct commentary of the implied author enable the reader to go beyond the trauma of the first-person voice and consider alternatives to nuclear winter.

Though there is hardly any distance between the values of the implied author and the third-person center of consciousness in *Wolf of Shadows*, the narrative remains in the ironic mode because of the obvious limits of the animal's perceptions and the bondage of a nuclear winter. Third-person center of consciousness is, however, a very empowering point of view in *Children of the Dust*, enabling the authorial voice of Louise Lawrence to move from the death-world of a global nuclear war to a narrative that finally transcends the mode of irony and moves into the countermode—romance.

In romance the cosmos is not indifferent to human destiny. From the beginning, the implied argument in *Children of the Dust* is that a divine plan exists for the world and for humans, even though humans make choices that will eventually annihilate *Homo sapiens*. Evolution continues as humans immediately adapt with radical mutations to the radiation ravaged earth and give way to *Homo superior*, a process supported through the center of consciousness of four characters, each being more or less distant from the norms of the implied author who functions in the context of the narrative much like a divine cosmic designer.

This is by no means an ironic and pessimistic narrative in spite of the fact that humans will be replaced by white furred and pinhead-eyed mutants. While alienation and loss are experienced by the old world, there is also the discovery of new values and new ways of living, as well as the evolution of human intelligence and psychic energies hitherto untapped. Those centers of consciousness, which are close to the implied author, are future directed, either intuitively or intellectually. Futurity is also enhanced by the almost biblical pattern of descent with its paradigm of continuity and order in spite of radical change.

Nuclear war occurs in part one to Sarah, the daughter of Professor Bill Harnden who is away from home when the bomb drops. His second wife—Veronica—, her stepdaughter Sarah and her own children, Catherine (Kate) and William, try to survive as best as they can. Catherine chooses intuitively to be the survivor, not by appropriating life-support material, but by practicing restraint so as to avoid contamination. Sarah intuits that Catherine is the chosen child for the future and, shortly before she resigns herself to her death, she takes Catherine to Johnson, another survivor. Sarah "knew it was all for a purpose, that she had to go on. Something in the future was dependent on her" (32). When she reaches her early teens, Catherine will produce a new human community with Johnson. Her parent, Bill Harnden, also fathers Ophelia, the child of the bunker society of part two. She is the fragile product of a hierarchical and aggressive male society whose dependence on technology and the pre-war paradigms makes them "extinct as dinosaurs." While Ophelia rejects the opportunity to join the agrarian, communal, mutant world of Catherine and Johnson, her son Simon will, after initial resistance, join it and unite with the mutant Laura, granddaughter of Kate.

The implied author weaves the genealogy of the characters so close to the development and discovery of the plot that the reader is hardly aware that along with the de-structuring of hierarchical orders occurs the abolition of the nuclear family, its individualistic privatism and therewith the neuroses we associate with the dense family unit, exemplified in this novel by Sarah's stepmother Veronica and her son William. Females are foregrounded along with the values of intuition and imagination as well as practical wisdom, exemplified in the *magna mater* figure of Catherine-Kate. Bill Harnden teaches the constructive values of the old world to the bunker children but cannot make the adjustment to the new, even when he admires it. Ophelia remains the unconverted human while Simon becomes the convert who will attempt to synthesize the skills of the old ways with the needs and virtues of the new. Thus the highly directional implied author constructs a dialectic that communicates a strong sense of order and pattern and therewith, by definition, purposefulness and meaning.

Nevertheless, there is a price for transcending the ironic mode of "Sarah," for the narrative succumbs to the myths of rebirth through apocalypse and links the theory of evolution with the myth of progress. The end—nuclear war and the ending of the book—implies that life will steadily get better as humans empower themselves in mind and spirit and achieve moral goodness. This suggests that nuclear war is but the inferno we must endure so that we can purge ourselves in the struggle for survival and eventually reach paradise projected by the vision of Timberley to which Laura leads Simon: "Simon caught his breath. . . . El Dorado out of human legends . . . the celestial city become reality. . . . It seemed to flow into the land around it, melt with the greenwhite sheen of wooded hills and water meadows until the whole valley glowed and the glory stunned him" (174). In this context nuclear war, though human made, is part of the far flung plan of a benign universe. It is a rhetoric reinforced by the directional voice of the narrative, in the end so much more reassuring than the ambiguous openendedness of *Wolf of Shadows* and certainly more so than the tragic insight of the narrator ending his days with the last children of Schewenborn. Politically Lawrence's narrative is far removed from that of Strieber and Pausewang in spite of the fact that all three authors advocate community over privatism. Pausewang and Strieber hope to "scare straight" through their narratives; Lawrence sees everything, including nuclear war, in a grand and ultimately consoling design.

These six narratives project six versions of survival in actual and imagined historical time; all of them, even Lawrence's, are desperate attempts to justify and make sense out of experience. Nowhere is that struggle more evident than in first-person narration, especially when the individual has no analytical and interpretive distance from subjective experience, as is the case with the unnamed narrator in *Friedrich* and the way Roland records events that traumatized him so profoundly. The first-person voice of Minsky Sender always has the past present, even as she selects details suitable to the young listener-reader. Walter Jendrich cannot bear the first person and objectifies his traumas through the third-person center of consciousness, empowering himself with interpretation and analysis. Even the limited third-person center of the wolf allows Strieber to immediately make his reader aware that nuclear war affects all of nature, not just humans. Lawrence uses the third person to project eventually a world that gratifies human desire, while the others define, through narrative voice, a world that desire rejects. All these rhetorical strategies aim to instruct, to judge historical trauma on ethical terms, and to somehow create meaning.

"It is not enough to cover the ground with leaves. We must be cured of it by a cure of the ground," advised Wallace Stevens in "The Rock." The ground is not cured in and through these narratives. None of the narrators in the first three novels can risk to relive primal losses, pain, anger, and grief in the trauma of personalized historical time. The narrator of *Friedrich* remains caught in his chosen bondage. Jendrich's message to his son— vigilance, engagement, learning from experience—have all the limitations of the reasonable man's solution and fail not only to cure the ground of familial deprivation, but also neglect to take into account that historical analogies quickly break down as each traumatic event encroaches in different disguises. Similarly, Riva's hope and advice that we recognize the signs of recurrence are no cure but an assignment, for the Holocaust will not be repeated the way it was and Riva, the grieving child yearning to be a good mother, will not necessarily read the signs and protect her daughter.

The three postnuclear war fictions extol the values of community over individual and familial needs. The idea of community has a long history and continues to be a fantasy in our civilization, but the iteration "if only we cared more for each other," does not take into account the deprivations and resulting needs of alienated individuals in mass societies. Thus these narratives offer as a cure a truism that remains as unexamined as "where there's life, there's hope." Our six stories about holocausts offer but leaves that cover the ground; their implied authors and narrators maintain us as we are. The cure remains undiscovered, even where the young reader is supposedly given an answer. This is no criticism by this reader-interpreter; it is the realization that these storytellers have covered the ground with leaves gathered in a book.

REFERENCES

Booth, Wayne. *The Rhetoric of Fiction.* 2d ed. Chicago: University of Chicago Press, 1983.

Bosmajian, Hamida. *Metaphors of Evil: Contemporary German Literature and the Shadow of Nazism.* Iowa City: University of Iowa Press, 1979.

Burger, Horst. *Warum warst du in der Hitler-Jugend? Vier Fragen an meinen Vater.*

(Why Were You in the Hitler Youth? Four Questions for My Father). Hamburg: Rowohlt, 1978.

Frye, Northrop. *Anatomy of Criticism*. Princeton: Princeton University Press, 1957.

Iser, Wolfgang. *The Act of Reading*. Baltimore: Johns Hopkins University Press, 1978.

Kermode, Frank. *The Sense of an Ending*. New York: Oxford University Press, 1967.

Langer, Lawrence. *Versions of Survival*. Albany: State University of New York Press, 1982.

Lawrence, Louise. *Children of the Dust*. New York: Harper and Row, 1985.

Markusen, Eric and John B. Harris. "The Role of Education in Preventing Nuclear War." In *Education and the Threat of Nuclear War*, edited by Belle Zars, et al., 33–54. *Harvard Educational Review*. (August, 1984). Reprint Series #18, 1985.

Mojtabai, A. G. *Blessed Assurance. At Home with the Bomb in Amarillo, Texas*. Boston: Houghton Mifflin, 1986.

Pausewang, Gudrun. *Die letzen Kinder von Schewenborn oder . . . sieht so unsere Zukunft aus?* (The Last Children of Schewenborn). Ravensburg: Otto Maier Verlag, 1983.

Richter, Hans Peter. *Friedrich*. Translated by Edite Kroll. New York: Holt Rinehart and Winston, 1970.

Schwenger, Peter. "Writing the Unthinkable." *Critical Inquiry*, 13 (Autumn, 1986): 33–48.

Sender, Ruth Minsky. *The Cage*. New York: Collier Macmillan, 1986.

Strieber, Whitley. *Wolf of Shadows*. New York: Alfred A. Knopf, 1985.

PART VII
Biography

Introduction

GARY D. SCHMIDT

Biography, like historical fiction, is a re-creation of the past, yet it has the additional constraints of nonfiction. The biographer is obligated to chronicle actual events, record motives, capture the essence of diaries, letters, and private conversations. Selecting from among these events, motives, and accounts, the biographer exercises the imagination in a manner similar to the fictive ways of the historical novelist. Nevertheless, the biographer is bound by certain events that exist outside of the imagination, which are the stuff of history.

Though those events are in some senses restricting, they may at the same time suggest a design that brings order to a life. It is this design that the biographer must discover and impose upon the material that research on the subject has yielded. For the writers in this section, that design is mediated principally through the narrator. The narrator's voice both shapes the design and is shaped by it, the two being interdependent.

As a biographer, Milton Meltzer casts himself in the guise of a designer, one who looks over an entire life, picks out specific moments, and arranges those moments in such a manner that together they become a design that gives order to a life, an order that is perceptible to the reader. Many of his works focus on groups that have been oppressed and figures who have been ignored or misjudged. *Tongue of Flame: The Life of Lydia Maria Child* brings to light an almost forgotten champion in the fight against slavery. *Thaddeus Stevens* reevaluates a character seen historically as a raving and somewhat mindless reformer.

In other works, Meltzer uses primary voices, the voices of those who lived through the experience, not the reconstructed voices of a biographer. In *Bread and Roses*, Meltzer recounts the grim story of the labor movement through citing and arranging contemporary documents. Instead of choosing public documents, he chooses works that were never meant to be published—letters, journals, narrative accounts. Meltzer uses a similar technique in *Bound for the Rio Grande: The Mexican Struggle, 1854–1860*; *Brother, Can You Spare a Dime*, dealing with the Great Depression; *The Jewish Americans: A History in Their Own Words: 1650–1950*; and *The Black Americans: A History in Their Own Words.*

Certainly the biographer as designer is present in these works, but his voice is a subdued one, represented only in the short, objective introductions to the pieces. The voices that come most vividly are those of the speakers themselves. The reader hears tales of lynchings from those who have seen them, learns of early attempts of Jewish settlers to become part of the young American community by those who struggled for that acceptance, rediscovers the pain of the Great Depression by listening to those who cry out from it. Whether focusing on an individual life or communal lives, Meltzer has given voices dulled by misconception and the passage of time a new hearing in the reader's consciousness.

For Jean Fritz, the design of biography is based upon the sense of incredulity she herself feels, an incredulity that is shared by her narrators. The details of history itself are so extraordinary, she argues, that a biographer need not reconstruct dialogue, or establish fictive links between real events. Fritz's voice, like Meltzer's, is selective in determining which events will be recounted.

Most of the titles of Fritz's biographies suggest narrators who take viewpoints more common to the narrators of historical fiction: *Can't You Make Them Behave, King George?* sounding like the petulant voice of an irritated member of Parliament; *Where Was Patrick Henry on the 29th of May?* recalling the pointed accusations of a lawyer; *Who's That Stepping on Plymouth Rock?* re-creating the puzzled wonder of those witnessing the Plymouth landing. The titles indicate a narrator who holds a novel vantage point of the historical events. Gently satiric, prodding, challenging, the narrator speaks directly to those characters, assuming the stance of a narrator of historical fiction. The narrator and the reader (who takes up a similar stance) force the biographical figure to answer the title's challenge. When the actual text begins, the narrator has moved the reader out of the genre of historical fiction and into that of biography, where the distance between the narrator, the reader, and the biographer disappears. By making the reader participate in the challenge, Fritz allows the reader to enter into the heart and mind and times of the biographee.

Although Jean Fritz recognizes the boundaries of biography, her autobiography, *Homesick: My Own Story*, has a distinctly fictive quality. In the foreword she writes, "Since my childhood feels like a story, I decided to tell it that way, letting the events fall as they would into the shape of a story, lacing them together with fictional bits, adding a piece here and there when memory didn't give me all I needed" (7). Fiction and nonfiction are fused in story.

For Robert Quackenbush, design comes through humor. Quackenbush chooses to subvert the seriousness of his subjects by including humorous details and asides. The result is a biography that seems to participate in a number of genres: folklore, fantasy, historical fiction, nonfiction informational books. The narration itself is fragmented, so that though one narrative voice dominates, it is itself at times supplemented and at times subverted by figures out of another genre who insert themselves into biography in order to comment upon the subject. So pigeons discuss wing construction in *Take Me Out to the Airfield*, Goodyear's children complain about the dreadful rubber smells in *Oh, What an Awful Mess!*, and teddy bears comment on Theodore Roosevelt's childhood in *Don't You Dare Shoot That Bear!* The titles themselves suggest a union of narrator and character (much like the titles of many of Jean Fritz's biographies.)

Humor is also a device of James Playsted Wood's narrators, as Marilyn Jurich observes. Wood suggests that the biographer must be a participant and observer. As a kind of Everyman, the biographer becomes an extension of his subject, so that the biographer and the subject merge. As Wood tells the stories of literary figures, he becomes extensions of those figures. At the same time, he establishes a narrator who is a trickster, using humor and irony to subvert the reader's expectations.

Jurich argues that this design works for those figures for whom Wood feels sympathy. He includes nonsense in his biography of Lewis Carroll, humor in his biography of Twain, close observations of the natural world in his biography of Thoreau. But this design is not effective when Wood deals with authors for whom he has little sympathy; unable to become an extension of these figures, he sets himself against them and sometimes misunderstands them. Wood, suggests Jurich, is in this sense inseparable from the narrator.

Janice Alberghene explores the tension between fiction and nonfiction in Jean Fritz's *Homesick: My Own Story*, arguing that the autobiography comes as much from art as from memory. Alberghene claims that Fritz participates in both male and female autobiographical traditions, using a straightforward narrative progression based on a single character's point of view at the same time that she delineates an incomplete character, one who is homesick. Alberghene shows that Fritz is aware of the tension she creates by introducing fictive links into autobiography. But the order of the work arises out of that tension.

THE AUTHORIAL VOICE

33

The Designing Narrator

MILTON MELTZER

The biographer's image is not reality itself. The reality is the ceaseless flux of that life, with its billions of moments of experience. That reality is the raw material from which the biographer works. In that reality countless events succeeded each other in the order of time. But the subject's own consciousness of those events is not the biographer's. The subject could not know, as the biographer knows, what lay in the future. Here is where imagination comes into play. The mind of the biographer must be free to seek some arrangement or pattern in the life he or she has studied. He makes connections, holds back some facts, foreshadows others, decides on juxtapositions, attempts to balance this element against that. Using documentary evidence in imaginative ways without ever departing from its truth, the biographer tries to give a form to flux, to impose a design upon chronology.

How does the biographer go about discovering the design for the work? I will use my biography of Langston Hughes as an example. Early in the 1950s Hughes and I had collaborated on a book about black history. Strangers at the beginning, we became friends during the course of the work. Years later, we collaborated on a second book, about blacks in the performing arts. As this was entering proof, a publisher asked me to write some short sketches of various people for a project designed to appeal to young readers in black communities. One of the sketches I did was of Langston Hughes' life. When he saw it, he called to say how much he liked it. Then it occurred to me, why not try to do a biography of Hughes for young adults? "What would you think of it," I asked him hesitantly, because of course he could easily do it himself. (He had already published two volumes of his autobiography for adults.) "Go right ahead," he said, and "I'll try to help you however I can." So with a contract from Crowell I set to work.

Since this was to be a book about a writer, the most important source of information was his own work. I knew that my audience was young people, that they were primarily interested in Hughes for his poems, stories, and plays, and that the role of his blackness in his work was of paramount importance. So I began research with very detailed analysis of the Hughes autobiography—*The Big Sea* (1963) and *I Wonder As I Wander* (1964). These volumes carried his life story only up to the age of forty, by the way, and now he was sixty-five. In a book for young readers I was constrained to keep the text down to some 40,000 words, not necessarily a handicap. One had to leave out a lot in writing about so richly varied a life. That necessity can be a blessing.

Some biographies are enormous compendia of facts, full of the clutter of daily life, with the subject's every ticket stub and laundry bill thrown in. It is important, however, to remember that the biographer does not imagine the facts. He selects them. His imaginative powers come into play when he creates the form into which the facts will go.

As I made notes on Hughes' writing I built a list of things to do to clarify, corroborate, or extend what his work suggested to me. Hughes also gave me certain materials from his own files, and he answered the many questions I asked him. In addition, I got help from more than fifty people who had known him, some from as far back as his early school days, some from college years, and some way on up through decades of his long professional career as the first black American to seek to make a living entirely from his writing. Other writers, editors, publishers, agents, actors, directors, singers, dancers, composers who had played some part in his multifaceted work gave me interviews or answered my queries by letter and phone. Some lent me letters, papers, photographs, or clippings. Much material on Hughes is held at Yale University, the Schomburg Center for Research in Black Culture in New York, and Lincoln University in Pennsylvania. Among the liveliest sources were newspapers and periodicals. They carried news stories about him and articles by him, as well as editorial comments on him. And then there were the fat files of his own newspaper columns, which appeared weekly for over twenty years, first in the Chicago *Defender* and then also in the New York *Post*.

Beyond his autobiography were Hughes' other writings, of course. It is an incredibly long bibliography. I read every one of these publications, for they voiced what he taught and felt and dreamed and feared and hoped. The biographer must be constantly sensitive to what he finds that characterizes his subject. Not any fact, but this *particular* fact or phrase or word is what is wanted to represent a fact of the reader to see. Anything that is vivid and human will help the biographer to discover the configurations of a life.

So I began writing, shuttling from one document to another, trying to form in my mind an image of my subject. Since I was writing about someone I knew, an image was already there, though it may have been modified by what my research had unearthed. My personal relationship with my subject was only one of many such relationships in his life. I saw him from my perspective. Now that perspective was altered, perhaps, by what I had learned from the views of many others. To the testimony of my own eyes I added the testimony of others, which may or may not have been corroborative.

One of the biographer's biggest problems is identification with his subject. It can lead to triumphs or disasters. The biographer seeks to understand a life by coming as close as he or she can to that person. Yet biographers must be careful not to reshape the subject in their own image. When writing about Hughes, of course, the inward and spiritual life was reflected in his work—his poems, songs, plays, stories, novels, autobiography, columns about that most delicious of creations, Jesse B. Semple. It is easier, when your subject is a writer, to take part in his inner life.

But to convey that inner life, while always difficult, is only part of the task. The biographer is interested in every aspect of the subject's history—the physical as well as the psychic, the public as well as the private. The economic and social circumstances that helped shape him are part of the story. The world of his life-span, as he experienced it, must be considered. In the case of Hughes, I started out with the fact that he was an American, and black. And for the Afro-American, life in the land where "white is right" has always been difficult. It is this that Hughes' poetry and his life illuminate. Before he was twenty-five he had made himself the poet laureate of his people. Their life was his life. So it was that complex life that I had to try to clarify.

When biographers try to do more than compile the facts they are taking all the risks of the narrative art without the full freedom novelists enjoy. Novelists can summon up all the resources of their imagination alone. Novelists have the liberty to invent anything they choose to carry out their purpose. Biographers, however, must work within that mass of gathered facts. They must use to the full their freedom to select, to arrange, to depict. Like novelists, biographers seek to capture character in action, personality in performance. Unlike novelists, they owe the reader historical truth. If they succeed, it is because they have found the right design.

There are times, however, when the biographer's designing involves quite a different process, when the historical situation demands that the subjects speak for themselves. I have let them speak like this in several books. One of them, *The Black Americans: A History in Their Own Words* (1984), tries to help the reader understand what American blacks felt, thought, did, suffered, and enjoyed from 1619 to the 1980s. What blacks have had done to them, how they have lived through it, and how they have fought back is the living stuff of their history. In this book they tell the story in their own words—through letters, journals, speakers, autobiographies, proclamations, newspapers, pamphlets. These records reveal what happened to living men, women, and children of the past because they speak with their own voices, recording their experiences from the time the first slave ship landed in Virginia, to the present.

Another kind of book, again drawing on living history as reflected in people's own words, is *Brother, Can You Spare a Dime?* (1969). My narrative weaves together a collective memory. For many those grim years of the Great Depression is a past unknown, dim, forgotten. In my history of that tragic time, the unemployed, the poor, the homeless tell about their own lives, in their own words. What they say is not a substitute for history. It is only a part of it, but one sorely neglected. Their voices speak of personal experience, so that we come to feel what it was like to be alive in their time and place. Their voices enrich the group memory and help us recover from the past what still lives.

Both of these books—and many of my others—make use of documentary history, but not in the usual sense of collections of official papers—constitutions, laws, treaties, judicial decisions. Important as those are, they are rarely readable and never personal. Here we have another kind of document, the intimate voices of people who, in their own writing never intended for a public audience, reveal their joys, fears, expectations, griefs, protests, achievements. In the process, the designing narrator crafts the ordering of the narratives, so that readers are caught up in the violence of a mob, the hunger of a child, or the struggle for a job as told in the words of those who lived those experiences.

In both these processes—whether the writer speaks or the subject speaks—the truth comes through the ordering. The biographer's image, the historian's image, although they are not reality itself, take on their own reality, which the reader perceives through the design. Structure and design are meaning. The writer, then, does more than impose an arbitrary order on a single life or the collective life. Whether the writer is the narrator (as in *Langston Hughes*) or the subjects are narrators (as in *The Black Americans* or *Brother, Can You Spare a Dime?*), the writer has collaborated with his subjects and discovered a design which the subjects, bound by their own time, might not have recognized.

REFERENCES

Hughes, Langston. *The Big Sea*. New York: Hill and Wang, 1963.
———. *I Wonder as I Wander*. New York: Hill and Wang, 1964.
Meltzer, Milton. *The Black Americans: A History in Their Own Words*. New York: Crowell, 1984.
———. *Brother, Can You Spare a Dime?* New York: Knopf, 1969.
———. *Langston Hughes*. New York: Crowell, 1968.

34

The Voice of One Biographer

JEAN FRITZ

As a young, beginning writer, I once took a publicity tour with my editor. We shared the same hotel room—a female editor, I may add—and one evening I sat down at the desk to write a letter home to my husband. When I finished, my editor remarked, "Do you know that when you write, you move your lips?"

I didn't know. I felt a bit embarrassed like a slow reader who has silently to mouth every word. I doubt if I still do this; still, I don't think it's a bad idea. I suppose I had developed the habit of listening as I wrote, testing the rhythm of the sentences, fitting the punctuation into my voice.

It is hard for a writer to comment on his or her voice. Once one has struggled through those awful preliminary stages of stilted, textbook-like writing, and has begun to feel at home with written words, a writer's voice seems as natural as his walk. The voice is not always the same; it adapts itself to the subject at hand but it is the writer's *own* voice. Of course sometimes the voice doesn't ring true and has to be worked over again and perhaps again. Trying out words, I often feel as if I am throwing coins down on a counter as we did when I was a child in China to determine by the sound if the coin is genuine or counterfeit. The voice I have developed, I realize, is the voice of a narrator. Indeed, I feel lucky to have written fiction before tackling biography, for *story* is what I look for and *people* are what I hunt down. Real people. It is the truth of biography that attracts me. It is so much more dramatic, more bizarre, stranger than anything I could ever dream up. Even in telling a dinner table story, I love to hear people say, "Isn't that incredible!" I love to say it myself. So biography seemed to suit my voice, for throughout my books I suspect you can hear me whispering, "Yes, it really happened that way. Can you believe it?"

I remember reading with my children the popular orange Bobbs Merrill biographies about the childhood of famous Americans. The theory was then that children could identify best (and perhaps only) with other children. Preferably children like themselves. Moreover, children wouldn't read a biography that didn't contain a fictionalized dialogue. Educators went further. Children shouldn't be bothered with explanations of the motives of characters. Deeds alone were enough.

Well, I knew my voice would never fit such a pattern. Besides, I had enough confidence in children to believe that they would react as I did to the surprises in history, to the extraordinary nature of people of whatever age and they would be curious, as I am, about what leads people to do what they do. I had equal confidence in the startling quality of pure fact and in the wealth of specific and sometimes out-of-the-way details that can be depended upon to bring events to life. I would make up nothing. I would include conversations only when I had a documented source for it.

I think because my childhood took place in China in a very different world, I have always hung on to memory consciously and tenaciously for fear it might slip away altogether. As a consequence, I feel the child in me is still alive and well and I expect that in real life as well as in print you can hear that the child persists in my voice. As I write, I am aware that my audience is children and I don't want to lose them. I hope for their undivided attention, so I talk informally, conversationally, often in simple declarative sentences—not so much for the sake of simplicity but because I believe in the strength of my material and want to present it without distraction.

Not that I am against long sentences. I am delighted to be able to string a long series of explicit facts together. "In 1735," I write in *And Then What Happened, Paul Revere?* (1973), "there were in Boston 42 streets, 36 lanes, 122 alleys, 1,000 brick houses, 2,000 wooden houses, 12 churches, 4 schools, 418 horses (at last count) and so many dogs that a law was passed prohibiting people from having dogs that were more than 10 inches high." Children love to know numbers; they like lists, and for much of this information I am indebted to a secondhand copy of Justin Winsor's wonderful two-volume history of Boston—one of the most useful purchases I've ever made. For dramatic effect I often isolate separate words or phrases and let them stand alone.

To focus attention and quicken the pace, I often use questions. In my book *Where Do You Think You're Going, Christopher Columbus?* (1980), for instance, I am describing how frustrated Columbus was when in effect he was grounded between his third and fourth journeys.

"Indeed, it wasn't easy to stay quietly at home in Spain while other men were exploring his Indies. . . . At least five men were leading their own expeditions. . . .

"And what was Columbus doing?"
"Sitting on dry land, twiddling his thumbs." (62)

In this passage I am indirectly getting inside Columbus' mind, and by asking the question and answering it as I have, I have quickly demonstrated his impatience. With humor, I hope. I never consciously think, "Now I must work humor into this." Humor is simply indispensable to me, not just as a writer; and if it didn't crop up frequently in my work, it wouldn't be my natural voice.

So although it is my voice I use, I adapt that voice and in the long books for older young people, I take a more leisurely approach and follow the time sequence more closely. When I have extra information that is helpful to know but doesn't quite fit into the rhythm of the writing, I enclose it in brackets as if it were an aside. Without fictionalizing, it is possible to look at the world through someone else's eyes and to experience that person's emotions. I still maintain the voice of the narrator and if nothing else, I must show understanding. I don't excuse and obviously don't approve of Benedict Arnold's becoming a traitor, but a narrator must not be didactic or judge. It is clear that he acted wrongly, but given the kind of person he was and given the particular set of circumstances in his life, I show how he rationalized his behavior. There is plenty of documentation for this. Few people, I think, commit such a crime (or perhaps any crime) without finding some way to justify themselves.

I had a harder time entering the mind of Pocahontas because of course she, herself, left no written records. Fortunately, the settlers, especially John Smith, left full accounts. John even left a word-for-word record of his unhappy conversation with Pocahontas in England and for this I am very grateful. This one conversation substantiates much of what I suspected of her feelings as a younger girl and also her feelings as a married woman in England. Yet time and again in order to give the Pocahontas story the emotional intensity it deserved, I had to resort to such qualifying words as "perhaps," "she must have," "she may have," "probably." I did feel that I was filling the gaps with reasonable assumptions based on wide research, yet I didn't like to compromise my voice in this way. At the same time, it seemed to me that Pocahontas, who has only been a myth as far as school children are concerned, needed to be rescued. Actually, of all the characters I've written about, I feel closest to Pocahontas. Since the main facts of her life are recorded, I am not uneasy. Still, I wish my voice could have been more certain at all times.

I have often said that I don't pick subjects; they pick me. I hear their voices and I suddenly have an intense desire to record them. If these voices in turn have to be filtered through my voice, there is no help for it. All biographers accept this. It is the only way that the past can speak.

REFERENCES

Fritz, Jean. *And Then What Happened, Paul Revere?* New York: Coward, 1973.

————. *The Double Life of Pocahontas.* New York: Putnam, 1983.

————. *Traitor: The Case of Benedict Arnold.* New York: Putnam, 1981.

————. *Where Do You Think You're Going, Christopher Columbus?* New York: Putnam, 1980.

35

Laughter in Biography: Narrating for Today's Children

ROBERT QUACKENBUSH

Writing and illustrating for today's children is not easy. Nor is teaching. Writers and artists and teachers know that. Just ask them. And there is much in the news about how reading and art in schools is on an accelerated decline and that we are faced with being an illiterate nation. Television has been pointed to as the culprit. So has the rise in broken homes. Not to mention writers, artists, and teachers. All looks pretty hopeless and on the brink of going out of control—not helped by the fact that we are living in chaotic times.

If I were to make a book about this sad state of affairs, you can be sure I would have a couple of animals to the side of the gloomy text making some hilarious comment. Those little characters would be the only light shining in the mire, who, like the child pointing out that the emperor is not wearing clothes, point to a truth—that on the dark side of life, humor can sustain us.

I recall my first introduction to this way of working when I was in high school and studying the classics. The plays of Shakespeare stand out in my mind. He often used a moment of comic relief in his tragedies. The porter struggling to open the door in the middle of the night in *Macbeth* is one of my favorite examples. The works of Oscar Wilde were another influence. What could be funny about a baby being abandoned in a railroad station? Wilde made it so in *The Importance of Being Earnest*.

Humor became my guiding light when I began writing and illustrating my first books for young readers. It has stayed with me ever since. Within the framework of humor is another element that I often employ, which I call "off the cuff, or Greek chorus support." I've used this element since my first books. It appears as a letter a little boy is writing to his cousin about a disastrous party given for his sister Lou in the illustrated songbook of *Skip to My Lou* (1975). It is the chorus of animals gathered at the window sill making comments about Henry the Duck's worsening condition as he follows his doctor's advice to eat a lot of lollipops to cure his accumulating ailments in *Too Many Lollipops* (1975). Most often it has become the focus of my humorous biographies for children.

My first biography for children was written and illustrated at the time our son, Piet, took his first steps in 1975. He must have thought that if he could do that he could also fly because he climbed up on the sofa shortly after walking and started flapping his arms. Before my wife, Margery, and I could stop him, he fell off the sofa and landed smack on his nose. Realizing that this was an archaic instinct in the works, I decided that it was time to tell Piet about the Wright brothers and the first human flight in a heavier-than-air craft in a picture book called *Take Me Out to the Airfield!* (1976), subtitled *How the Wright Brothers Invented the Airplane*.

From the moment I began the book, I knew the kind of book that I didn't want it to be. I didn't want it to be the kind of book about inventors and other famous people that I had read as a child. They were usually very dry accounts of how the people suffered and had to do without before they realized their achievements. So many of them, it seemed, lived in log cabins, chopped wood, studied by firelight, walked miles to school, and sold the family linens for a crust of bread in order to achieve their goals. "Who wants any part of that?" I remember thinking at the time. What was missing from these accounts, I knew, was something that had led my childhood family and me and a great many others through a depression and world war—the sound of laughter. And that became my voice.

Therefore, I wanted to include humor in my first biography as an enticement to Piet and children everywhere to want to read about the two famous brothers and how they invented their airplane. I did this by offering a straightforward telling of the story and added at the bottom of each page of text two modern children asking questions of a pilot at an airport to further explain the complicated details of the brothers' invention. Next to these characters two pigeons make funny comments to one another about what is being said. For example, the pilot on one page explains to the children that it is the curve of the wing—called the camber—that helps to lift a plane in the air. In response to this, the pigeons say to one another: "I never noticed my curves before," says one. "Nor I," says the other.

The success of *Take Me Out to the Airfield* launched me on more biographies in a similar format. When Piet got interested as a child in toy cars, I told the story of Henry Ford in *Along Came the Model T* (1978), with aside remarks being made by two children and a garage mechanic talking about cars. When Piet became intrigued with the space movie and toy figures, I told a story of Robert H. Goddard, the inventor of the first liquid fuel rocket, in *The Boy Who Dreamed of Rockets* (1978) with aside comments being made by two children talking with an astronaut at a launching pad. Then as he got older the subjects became broader and the humor more outrageous. First, among the new editions was a story of Charles Goodyear called *Oh, What an Awful Mess!* (1983).

The Goodyear book has probably the shortest text of any of my biographies and it lent itself to some of the funniest illustrations. When I researched Goodyear's life, I had the feeling that his wife was not too sympathetic about his messing up her kitchen over a ten-year period making rubber experiments. What wife would be? Consequently, her reactions and their children's reactions to his experiments became the focus of the book. During one of the experiments, one of the children asks, "Mama, why does our house always smell so bad?" In this book, the cartoonlike illustrations outweigh the text, making the story, based on true facts, seem fictitious.

A much more complicated subject followed with the invention of the telephone and a story of Alexander Graham Bell's life in *Ahoy! Ahoy! Are You There?* (1981). The title came from the fact that the standard answer Bell wanted when answering a telephone was a jolly "Ahoy!" which was abandoned, to his regret, for the commonplace "Hello." Cartoonlike illustrations are again featured in this book. One illustration shows a mangled mess of telephone lines that was attached to poles along the streets and avenues of New York City. The following page shows the blizzard of 1888, which tore down the poles and lines, and a little boy outside shouting up to his mother's window, "Hey, Mom! Clear skies!"

The stories of James Watt and Robert Fulton were put together in one book called *Watt Got You Started, Mr. Fulton?* (1982). Although these two great inventors had lived in different times, my reason for putting them together was because Fulton had used a Watt engine in his first successful steamboat, the Clermont. The aside humor in the book is based on a famous burlesque routine of twisted word meanings. On one page a reporter is shown interviewing Robert Fulton. The interview goes like this:

"Mr. Fulton, who invented the engine for your steamboat?"
"Watt."
"I said, 'Who invented your steam engine?' "
"Watt."
"Mr. Fulton, excuse me for asking, but are you hard of hearing?"
"What?"

Many more biographies followed. In a story of Thomas Alva Edison called *What Has Wild Tom Done Now?!!!* (1981) the book is divided into one-page chapters (in answer to the request of a child who wrote and asked, "Do you ever write chapter books?") and given titles like those used in early silent movies. Chapter two, titled "Tom's Narrow Escapes," tells how Edison as a boy got butted by a ram while exploring a bee's nest and was nearly buried in grain when he fell into a bin while exploring how wheat was stored.

For a story of Samuel F. F. Morse and the invention of the telegraph called *Quick, Annie, Give Me a Catchy Line!* (1983) the title and the comic asides came from the fact that Annie Ellsworth, the daughter of a friend, chose the first message that was sent over Morse's invention. Several of the spots show Annie offering suggestions to Morse. In one she says, "How about: Let them eat cake?" And Morse responds, "No! No! No! That will never do for the first message on my telegraph. Besides, it's been done before."

Here a Plant, There a Plant, Everywhere a Plant, Plant! A Story of Luther Burbank (1982), the life story of the famous plant breeder, provided me with an opportunity for some aside "crossing" jokes for children. For one aside a farmer is passing by Burbank who is attending to a tomato plant. "Hey, Luther!" shouts the farmer laughing. "What do you get when you cross a lawn mower with a tomato?" Burbank responds coolly as he works, "I know, I know. Sliced tomatoes." Or another: "Hey, Luther!" says the farmer, "What do you get when you cross a cactus with a buttered roll?" And Burbank responds, "I know, I know. A sticky bun."

Cats provide the aside humor in *Mark Twain? What Kind of Name Is That? A Story of Samuel Langhorne Clemens* (1984). At one time Twain's mother had nineteen of them. And Twain, himself, kept cats around him all his life. In his last years in his house called Stormfield at Redding, Connecticut, he had a cat in every room. His favorites were named Beelzebub, Blatherskite, Apollinaris, and Buffalo Bill. I discovered this little-known fact about the beloved humorist by accident in a newspaper clipping in the picture collection at the New York Public Library. In one of the asides in the book a cat is pointing to a frog and saying to his feline companions, "You mean *that* made Mark Twain famous?" The aside, of course, refers to Twain's story "The Celebrated Jumping Frog of Calaveras County."

Color plays a comical aside in a story of Charles Darwin called *The Beagle and Mr. Flycatcher* (1983). The book follows the course of his five-year voyage around the world aboard the HMS Beagle. Darwin was seasick the whole time. So is it any wonder that I selected a sickening green for the main color of the illustrations?

Teddy bears are the aside focus in a story of Theodore Roosevelt called *Don't You Dare Shoot That Bear!* (1984). The bears have a marvelous time with their comments such as this from the opening page:

"What was TR called as a child?" asks one bear.

" 'Teedie,' answers a second. And his older sister Anna was called 'Bamie.' His younger brother Elliott and his younger sister Corinne were called 'Ellie' and 'Conie.' "

A third bear asks, "Was anyone in the family called 'Mittie'? I always liked that name."

"As a matter of fact," answers a fourth bear, "that was the nickname of TR's mother."
(9)

It was pure joy to write and illustrate *Once Upon a Time! A Story of the Brothers Grimm* (1985). So much of what happened to the brothers in their lifetime was amusing as they sought to preserve fairy tales and folk tales for all time. They bartered for a number of their stories. People came from all over to trade them for whatever the brothers had to offer—usually coffee and rolls—until along came an old soldier who would settle for nothing short of the brothers' old trousers. What fun I had illustrating that! And the brothers' changing of a fur slipper to a glass slipper prompted me to do a comical illustration of Prince Charming discovering Cinderella's *bunny slipper* on the staircase of the palace.

In a story of Peter Stuyvesant called *Old Silver Leg Takes Over!* (1986), pigs dominate the aside jokes that complement the text. When Stuyvesant arrived to govern New Amsterdam he set about to transform a ramshackle fort and a village of muddy footpaths into a well-organized city that was to become New York. He thought it was a disgrace the way pigs were allowed to roam, and he ordered them to be kept in pens. Throughout the book, the pigs make remarks about their new governor and the state of things. "Remember the good old days?" one pig says to another behind the picket fence that has been placed around them.

A personal favorite was working on the life of Jules Verne for *Who Said There's No Man on the Moon?* (1985). So much of his life is unknown because he kept to himself. But finding unknown facts about him at some of our important library sources in California and New York made this an especially interesting project. The aside comments to the text are made by a reporter and Verne during an interview—the only one that Verne gave in his life. The rest of the asides included questions that children ask me about my writing and illustrating. I figured that it would be the same for Verne. The actual interview went this way:

> "You have traveled a great deal, of course, Monsieur Verne."
> "Mais non, just a tourist in the Channel and in the Mediterranean."
> "Is that all? So you never met any cannibals?"
> "I knew better than that."
> "Nor any Chinese?"
> "Never."
> "And you didn't circumnavigate the globe?"
> "Not even that." (32)

Another great president I chose for my biography series was Andrew Jackson in the book *Who Let Muddy Boots Into the White House?* (1986). The aside remarks in this one are made by two children talking with Jackson's pet parrot named Old Poll. But my favorite frontier hero is Davy Crockett. To tell his story in *Quit Pulling My Leg!* (1987), I employed two raccoons to separate fact from fiction to find a great man behind a legend.

My most recent biography for young readers, I am happy to say, is about a woman. It is a story of Annie Oakley, a true representative of the American spirit. Titled *Who's That Girl with the Gun?* (1988), it tells the story of a child who overcame great hardship and abuse and grew up to achieve international fame as a crack shot. After her success, she shared her wealth and talents to help others. The aside remarks in this story of courage are made by a poodle, who was part of Annie's traveling act. Two puppies ask the poodle what it is like working with Annie. "In a word: Wonderful!" answers the poodle.

A lot of biographies. And there are many more I want to do. Every time a letter comes from a child asking me to do a book about a current favorite hero I think about what I craved as a child. I say aloud, "Well, yes, why not!" and the process begins again.

REFERENCES

Quackenbush, Robert. *Ahoy! Ahoy! Are You There?* Englewood Cliffs, N.J.: Prentice-Hall, 1981.

———. *Along Came the Model T.* New York: Parents Magazine, 1978.

———. *The Beagle and Mr. Flycatcher.* Englewood Cliffs, N.J.: Prentice-Hall, 1983.

———. *The Boy Who Dreamed of Rockets.* New York: Parents Magazine, 1978.

———. *Don't You Dare Shoot That Bear!* Englewood Cliffs, N.J.: Prentice-Hall, 1984.

———. *Here a Plant, There a Plant, Everywhere a Plant, Plant!* Englewood Cliffs, N.J.: Prentice-Hall, 1982.

———. *Mark Twain? What Kind of Name Is That?* Englewood Cliffs, N.J.: Prentice-Hall, 1984.

———. *Oh, What an Awful Mess!* Englewood Cliffs, N.J.: Prentice-Hall, 1983.

———. *Old Silver Leg Takes Over!* Englewood Cliffs, N.J.: Prentice-Hall, 1986.

———. *Once Upon a Time! A Story of the Brothers Grimm.* Englewood Cliffs, N.J.: Prentice-Hall, 1985.

———. *Quick, Annie, Give Me a Catchy Line!* Englewood Cliffs, N.J.: Prentice-Hall, 1983.

———. *Quit Pulling My Leg.* Englewood Cliffs, N.J.: Prentice-Hall, 1987.

———. *Skip to My Lou.* Philadelphia: Lippincott, 1975.

———. *Take Me Out to the Airfield! How the Wright Brothers Invented the Airplane.* New York: Parents Magazine, 1976.

———. *Too Many Lollipops.* New York: Parents Magazine, 1975.

———. *Watt Got You Started, Mr. Fulton?* Englewood Cliffs, N.J.: Prentice-Hall, 1982.

———. *What Has Wild Tom Done Now?!!!* Englewood Cliffs, N.J.: Prentice-Hall, 1981.

———. *Who Let Muddy Boots into the White House?* Englewood Cliffs, N.J.: Prentice-Hall, 1986.

———. *Who Said There's No Man on the Moon?* Englewood Cliffs, N.J.: Prentice-Hall, 1985.

———. *Who's That Girl with the Gun?* Englewood Cliffs, N.J.: Prentice-Hall, 1988.

THE CRITICAL VOICE

36

The Applauded Jigsaw: Patterns of Lives Contoured by Voices: The Literary Lives of James Playsted Wood

MARILYN JURICH

Now that television, computers, and other "high" technologies, along with aggressive investigative reporting, have made privacy and secrets obsolete, our "heroes" and public figures appear to be creatures of media and public relations hype, all apparently clothed as emperors and empresses but actually naked. If biographies written for adults tell us of their subjects' flaws, frustrations, frailties and of their idiosyncratic, unemulatable selves, what stance, then, in biographies for the younger readers? Shall youth's biographer, as of old, be something of a preacher or teacher presenting an inspiring role model for young readers to live (or die) by, evading any embarrassing blemishes while emphasizing applaudable public achievements and cautiously ignoring "the inner drive and motives" (Goff, 214)? Geoffrey Trease, an English children's writer, justifies offering younger children only the outer layer of the onion while adroitly suggesting "the inner layers" for older readers (149–50). The extent to which a biographer can respect and protect his young reader's sensitivity and inexperience, yet at the same time trust the young reader's understanding and sense, may be a difficult determination. How can the "authentic person" be revealed unless the subject is depicted "warts and all," with all his fears, yearnings, contradictions, limitations? Shall the biographer protect and console the young (as well as himself, parents, teachers) by diminishing the disagreeable to feature the admirable?

Every biographer has problems in "seeing" the subject. "Entering into" another person, by empathy, can be a danger to truth and to the art of biography, for as with the "tagged life" approach that categorizes the subject according to some instructional or inspirational scheme, the "entered life" may yet be another form of "the art of trespass" (Fisher, 299–300). Thus, before he can approach his subject, the biographer must be the most reasonable of writers, must recognize the very few moments when he is privileged to commune with another's psyche—when letters, diaries, dreams, reflections provide access. The biographer needs to be the sanest of writers, knowing himself fully, or he will be seeking and finding only himself in his subject, mistaking his own mind and fantasies for those of "the other." Leon Edel points out that "the mind and inner world of the subject is unique and cannot be fashioned by anyone else" (64).

James Playsted Wood, writer of twelve literary biographies for young people, suggests that the biographer "must seize on the salient and most representative actions and characteristics of his subject" ("Writers Do Not Exist," 696). Applying "negative capability" to the writing of biography, Wood argues that in order to find the essential person, the biographer must become everybody by remaining nobody, and that through absorbing his subject, the biographer can recognize all the possible roles and personal qualities of that subject. If the subject of the biography is also a writer, the biographer has really been that person all along.

When Wood made these revealing statements, his biographies for young readers included those of Thoreau (1963), Emerson (1964), Stevenson (1965), Conan Doyle (1965), and Lewis Carroll (1966). The biographer's relationship with these writers, so Wood asserts with whimsical perversity, does not emerge out of the biography's being an extension of the biographer; rather the biographer becomes the extension of his or her subject. For Wood, the biographer is a medium capable of tapping into the spiritual potential of a subject; further intensification, through the accumulation of data, may even cause the identities of biographer/subject to become inseparable. So Wood once recognized that he had begun unconsciously taking on the eccentricities of Lewis Carroll ("Writers Do Not Exist," 694–95).

Yet Wood, whose middle name is Playsted, is always tempted "to play instead of" presenting a strictly accurate report. "In theory I approve of honesty," he confesses ("The Honest Audience," 612). Elsewhere, Wood acknowledges that he will include details only when he is convinced that they are factually, philosophically, and emotionally true for his subject ("Writers Do Not Exist," 612). Is he twitting us? A biographer cannot both be an extension of his subjects (or they of him) and also remain external to his subjects, both participant-observer and recipient-reflector.

In his "critical" year, 1966, when Wood suggested that biographers need to be mediums, he may have been influenced by personal affinities for his subjects to 1966: Thoreau, Emerson, Stevenson, Conan Doyle, Lewis Carroll. But if the biographer is a medium imbued with his or her subject, how can he or she give a balanced view of the life and the works of that subject? Wood does not explain. Nor does he address the temptations of the biographer for the young to sidestep the sorry or the sordid in the subjects' lives, the temptation to instruct, indoctrinate, or inspire. By looking at Wood's biographies we can see how he "solved" these problems, and we can consider whether his practice of biography underwent changes in approach after 1966.

Wood, so we glean from his discourse on writing biography, is a trickster—often ironic, proposing the preposterous and declaring the devious. This combination of humor and irony affects his view and the reader's view of the subject, threatening and subverting expectations. His biography of Thoreau, *A Hound, A Bay Horse and A Turtle Dove* (1963), opens with an ironic challenge to conventional wisdom given the young:

Henry David Thoreau defied the economic system, the government, and the social pieties of early nineteenth-century New England, in which he lived. He refused even to take them seriously. As a result, he neither starved, nor was struck by lightning. Instead, he spent one night in jail, and all the rest of his life, as nearly as any man can, doing exactly what he wished. (xi)

Wood uses irony to expose his subject as well as to startle the reader. After recognizing Thoreau's scorn for society, after revealing the pride Thoreau expressed in his "loneliness" at Walden, Wood remarks, "Only a man as rich in friends as Thoreau was throughout his life could afford to affect such scorn for companionship" (63).

The delightful paradox in the title *The Man Who Hated Sherlock Holmes* (1965) is that Conan Doyle could not do away with Holmes, of whom he had wearied, because of public outcry that Holmes be resurrected. But the most effective irony is that which Wood finds in the contradictory characteristics of his subjects. *The Lantern Bearer: A Life of Robert Louis Stevenson* (1965) opens: "Robert Louis Stevenson was one of the most romantic and entrancing men who ever lived—or else he was not. He was gifted, brilliant, fascinating, a courageous and intrepid soul who was more spirited and sprite than body and substance. So his friends saw him" (3). The next paragraph begins, "Stevenson was vain, a poseur and something of a hypocrite . . . a self-indulgent nomad . . . self-consciously parading . . . so some others saw him" (3). The biography continues with Wood's gentle derision of Stevenson, a perpetual child who liked to upstage all other contenders for the attention and admiration he craved.

For no other of Wood's subjects is the paradox in personality so pronounced as it is for Charles Lutwidge Dodgson/Lewis Carroll, the two names suggesting polarities in character—the fastidious, too sensible, dignified reverend, mathematician, and college don fending with the frivolous, insensible, irreverent writer of children's fantasies. Wood seems to enjoy himself best in this biography for having to make the game work, for fitting together the parts of an impossible but wonderfully colored Rubik's cube.

Wood's trickster voice dominates the opening. "Charles Lutwidge Dodgson, who was born in Daresbury, Cheshire in 1832, had only one head.

Though he was to be two people, he had only two hands, two feet, and on most days the usual number of noses, fingers, and toes" (3). This explosion of nonsense, appropriate both to the subject and the subject's writing, is also the free-flowing folderol approach that Wood most cherishes in his own voice as a writer. Young readers like this sort of silliness. For no other subject (including Stevenson and, later, Twain, also "dual" in name and temperament), does Wood better sustain the contrarieties, make them more credible and ultimately joyous. For Wood himself—as his Lewis Carroll reveals him—combines audacity and authority, and seems eager to at once reveal and conceal his own identity.

Among the five early biographies, *Trust Thyself: A Life of Ralph Waldo Emerson* (1964) is least convincing, perhaps because Emerson's life allows Wood too little controversy, puzzle, or jest. There are a few humorous asides. After Emerson's Aunt, Mary Moody Emerson, disavows her nephew for the apostasy he expressed in "The Harvard Divinity School Address" (1838), Wood comments, "Like most people, she tolerated only her own kind of nonsense" (74). Mostly, though, the biography is bland because the biographer is remote from his subject, possibly because Emerson himself is remote as a person. Like Hawthorne, to whom Wood's *The Unpardonable Sin* (1970) also ascribes a lack of energy and high spirits, Emerson seems to reveal that Puritan disposition for self-examination and self-discipline that may well have led to a successful career and a significant life, but does not lead a biographer to an intimate portrayal of character.

Wood ascribes to Emerson an egotism natural to most great men and all serious writers (34); Emerson was ambitious yet aware of limitations, becoming a minister so he could have a pulpit from which to demonstrate his talent for eloquence and literary expression. Emerson disliked most men as being lesser. Still, Wood attempts intimacy. Perhaps believing he can reach the great man at a less lofty time in life, he depicts Emerson at twelve, imagining the boy walking the Boston streets, all the while thinking about the deeds of heroic men, of "his family's proud history, of feeling apart— he was after all Ralph Waldo Emerson—yet feeling related not only to those other people on the street, but to the budding United States, the whole Universe" (17). In trying to come close to Emerson as a boy, Wood only comes out further away.

Yet he succeeds better at Emerson the writer: "Emerson could not begin with A and progress methodically through B, C, and D to a firm conclusion at Z. He saw in sudden flashes of insight . . . or longer moods of quiet communion with the thoughts of writers" (55). Wood admires Emerson's aphorisms, his "hard-hitting" words (90–91), but overlooks his poetry except for "Threnody."

Wood is interesting in recognizing Emerson as a satirist of "save-the-world" reformers. Emerson's individualism is Wood's—the view that the individual, not the masses, accounts for American values. Trust thyself is what Wood believes, and what he would like to instill in his young readers. Trust not in groups or governments that promise to provide for mass well-being is the corollary that follows and a message that Wood, in various forms, reinforces in several biographies. In his first biography on Thoreau, *A Hound, A Bay Horse and A Turtle Dove* (1963), Wood reveals a clear political motive. Insisting that "government exerts a far greater control over the private life of the individual than it did in Thoreau's time," Wood examines the "absolute control" imposed in communist and fascist systems and warns the reader that such "control" is increasing in socialized democracies. Advertising and public opinion, Wood perceives, exert subtler influences than government, numbing people into conformity.

Wood's proselytizing in his Thoreau biography is less objectionable than elsewhere, largely because he separates his views from the overall biography (mostly in the preface and conclusion) and because his views are, in effect, expansions of his subject's. Less acceptable is Wood's intrusion into the mind of the younger Thoreau, sometimes made to explain his subject's actions. In portraying how Thoreau felt at Harvard among fashionable classmates, Wood explains that this village boy from a poor family knew only "wood-chucks and foxes, how to make pencils, how to sail a homemade boat on the Concord River. His uncle had taught him how to swallow his nose" (16). Wood too coyly observes that such accomplishments would not impress Harvard. And Wood is unconvincing in his absolute dismissal of Thoreau's romantic attachment to Ellen Sewall, writing that in 1839 Thoreau "was in love with his hero, Emerson" (41), no one else. But, at least, Wood has touched upon such matters for his young readers.

Wood more acceptably "becomes" the older Thoreau, able to participate in Thoreau's hopes for sale of *A Week on the Concord and Merrimack Rivers* (1849) and able to share Thoreau's disappointment when it failed to sell, incurring debt. Often Wood is so close to the spirit of Thoreau that Wood/Thoreau is/are interfused. For example, Wood relates how Thoreau had once virtually hypnotized a woodchuck and then reflected that the woodchuck was more naturalized than he, the woodchuck's ancestors having lived in Concord so much longer than his; Wood, catching the spirit, adds, "It would be illuminating to read what the woodchuck wrote in his journal that night about Henry Thoreau" (90). The biographer joins his subject in writing of *The Maine Woods*: "You can feel the wet, smell the sharp cold air, shiver with the forest cold, and see the moonlight on the silent water of the lake . . . " (110). Wood seems to hike with Thoreau, undaunted by angry waters and thick woods, and to have like Thoreau, the wild—"the eagle and the fox"—in him.

Yet, Wood is also the teacher and the literary critic here, defining tran-scendentalism, appreciating the textural quality in Thoreau's sentences, re-cognizing Thoreau's trenchant statements, his tenderness and his savage humor. What Wood best accomplishes, however, is to help us understand the essential Thoreau through an unrelenting investigation of character that depends on contrasting the myth and the man, a method he later uses to excellent effect in his biographies of Jonathan Edwards (1968) and Cotton Mather (1971). Rather than simply rescue Thoreau from stereotype and oversimplification, Wood agrees that, indeed, Thoreau was standoffish, impatient, often sharp and bullheaded, especially with his equals. But Thoreau had his reasons. More significantly, Thoreau had attributes far more appealing than the ones often cited, for example, he admired those who lived honestly, showed kindness to children (for whom he had enormous sympathy), and displayed a mystical sense for music. Wood makes the wry-necked Henry more endearing by explaining his "failures" as successes, realizing those "failures" as commentaries on the greater failures in society, of social hypocrisy. Unlike those who practice sham—pretend admiration to advance ambition—and those who elevate their egos—show disdain to "inferiors"—Thoreau refused such power by shunning the game of success. Since he would not be "a player," he did not lose his self. For this reason Wood sees Thoreau as ever youthful. Uncompromising in his honesty, Thoreau could remain "clear-eyed, questioning, and independent..." (xvi). Such youthful idealism Wood gives voice to for his young readers.

But a major shift in approach comes when Wood chooses to write *I Told You So!: A Life of H. G. Wells* (1969). Has Wood, three years after his proclamation of 1966, chosen another rationale for telling a life? Surely of all the literary lives Wood depicts (up through 1972), this life for Wood seems the most disagreeable. Although Wells was an idealist, as were Thoreau and Emerson, sharing with them a confidence in a better life, Wood finds Wells objectionably "adolescent" (167). It is that Wood admires the individualism of Emerson and Thoreau but not Wells' belief in world government, Wells offending by "trying to save the world single-handedly."

At the start Wood assaults his subject, likening him to Alexander the Great or Caesar in his ambition to remake the entire world for all time (3). Yet Wood the trickster admires the circus feats, the astounding legerdemain of H. G. Wells who "trailed backward and forward in time as he wished... made a man invisible. Thirty-one years before it was dropped on Hiroshima, he predicted the atom bomb. He rewrote the world's history as he thought it should be written and outlines the world's future as he demanded it be lived" (4). Along with Wood, we are breathless at Wells' numerous roles—teacher, seer, socialist, world planner, novelist, scientist, sociologist, propagandist, political prophet—and then we realize that Wood is breathless with disdain for Wells who did *too much*, was undeservedly egocentric, self-promoting, irresponsible, insipid, or, at best, overgeneral and vague. Seemingly Wood believes he has tricked his young readers into seeing the real sham behind Wells' spectacular circus feats.

Unlike Wood's other subjects, Wells rose from the lower classes, was self-educated, depended on his own ingenuity to gain recognition. While Wood is often flabbergasted at the means Wells devised "to rise above his circumstances," Wood sees these circumstances as necessarily limiting, negative in the influence they had on Wells' temperament, mind, and writings. Having such an attitude toward Wells, the biographer can never sympathize or empathize with his subject. At best, then, Wood remains an objective commentator while at worst, a propagandist deriding Wells' ideas or dispensing with them. It is revealing that Wood never tries to enter the mind of Wells, nor do we ever sense the subject's emotions. The only personal knowledge we derive concerns Wells' marriage, and there is one quick mention of Wells' extramarital affairs.

The question that remains is how fair Wood can be to the literary works of a man who constantly irritates him. He finds Wells' science fiction pessimistic, gruesome, and more interested in biology than humanity. The philosophical books present theories that Wood generally scorns, although he acknowledges that *Anticipations* (1902) prophesied accurately many modern inventions and conditions. Wells' more sober prophecy—total wars in the twentieth century that are finally resolved by the formation of the World State—is derided by Wood as Wells' "sanitized and computerized Holy Grail" (69). Wood responds to Wells' attack on universities as being "mere cram schools" by questioning how Wells would know this, not having attended one (70). And Wood does not comment on such crucial reforms as Wells' suggestion that world religions be studied in schools to give children a larger moral sense (160–61), nor does he make comment on the "Declaration of the Rights of Man" in *The New World Order* (1940)—rights of all humans to food, medical care, education, work of choice, equal protection under law, the right to be conscientious objectors (163).

By contrast, in *The Man Who Hated Sherlock Holmes* (1965), Wood enthuses over Doyle who "was not out to change the world," rather to describe it entertainingly. While Wood admits that the Holmes stories are "simple" thrillers, without real subtleties, he finds them marvelous games, convincing recreations of 1890s gaslit London, satisfyingly consistent in their portrayal of the Holmes-Watson relationship. For all of Doyle's wish to lay the character of Holmes to rest, despite public demand, Wood is caught up by Holmes as a man of heart and humor, an intellectual of wide-ranging understanding and unswervable moral code.

Conan Doyle is certainly the most rugged and versatile of Wood's subjects: athlete, seaman, doctor, correspondent, military man, student of spiritualism, public-spirited champion of good causes, and so forth. He is Wood's hero as man and writer. Wood enjoys explaining how Doyle based Holmes on the great Edinburgh surgeon and diagnostician Dr. Joseph Bell, under whom Doyle had served as an assistant. For his young readers Wood patiently explains how Doyle used research skills especially in his historical novels, "wonderful tales of battles, duels, secret missions, fiery escapades, and miraculous escapes" (86).

Perhaps of all his subjects, Wood saw himself most as an extension of

Mark Twain, who "wanted golden wealth . . . in the large economy size" (65).
Mark Twain, Wood makes clear, responded to life with exaggerated feelings,
extreme reactions. *Spunkwater, Spunkwater! A Life of Mark Twain* (1968)
begins with an animated mingling of opposites (as several of Wood's biographies do): "Mark Twain loved cats. He loved his wife almost beyond his
ability to express the depth and breathlessness of his adoration. . . . ", and
he loved "daughters, money, cigars and exploding in a temper. . . . Mark
Twain hated as intensely as he loved" (1–2). Here Wood is careful to add
that Twain hated mostly what is loathesome—cruelty, hypocrisy, dullness,
cheating. Twain's quickness in jumping to judgment and his fondness for
the outrageous and eagerness for attention make him the perfect subject for
Wood, who prefers the subject who allows the biographer to perform stunts
and balancing acts to convey the character. A humorist, Wood is teased by
Twain's mischief and madcap schemes, enjoys the "trickery" of Twain, his
rollicking travels to Eastern cities, on the Mississippi, to Lake Tahoe and
Virginia City. Admitting Twain's confidence, vitality, incorrigible certainty
about just everything, Wood is even buoyed by Twain's peevishness, intem-
perance, and inveterate lying. Of course, "lying" is the basis for the American
tall tale, for example, "The Celebrated Jumping Frog" (1867), and the basis
for humor in Twain's writings and public performances. Wood is the perfect
audience for Twain's more constructive "lies," as when he "stretches the
truth" by way of drawing dramatic attention to the real lies in life—sham,
fraud, deceit; so lying is raised to an art form.

Wood, who seldom discusses his subject's methods of writing, is plainly
fascinated by Twain's having no method at all, writing whenever and wherever, ever sure of himself. Whereas Wood found Dodgson/Carroll an odd
couple, he finds Clemens/Twain perfectly merged. Perhaps he oversimplifies
when he claims that Twain's pessimism about the "damned human race"
was not authentic, on the ground that Twain was a self-dramatizer who felt
bursts of emotion *at the moment* and who was so good humored that he
enjoyed his "pessimism." This despite "The Man Who Corrupted Hadley-
burg," *Joan of Arc, What Is Man?* Perhaps Wood prefers cheerful interpretations for his young reader, for himself.

It is more difficult for him to find a positive sense of life in Nathaniel
Hawthorne, and in *The Unpardonable Sin . . .* (1970), Wood. Wood admits
to Hawthorne's not being a happy man by nature, and concurs with Emerson
that Hawthorne died of "inner loneliness" (170). Yet, Wood, uncomfortable
with dismality, scrapes up some pleasant facts by dispelling some myths.
Hawthorne's mother was not, as alleged, an invalid recluse, but an active
and sociable widow who enjoyed family outings. Wood manages to find
snatches of humor in Hawthorne: in an 1821 letter to his mother Hawthorne
writes, "What do you think of my becoming an author and relying for support
on my pen. Indeed, I think the illegibility of my hand-writing is very author-
like . . . " (17). Wood makes a point that Hawthorne at Bowdoin was not a

puritanic hermit but the sociable collegian, who played cards, smoked, drank, was popular. Even after his graduation, Wood insists, Hawthorne did not go into mysterious isolation in an upstairs room of his family's house to learn his craft while avoiding the world, but that during these years of apprenticeship Hawthorne went to dances and the theater and on frequent trips with his uncles (30). Always the pointer of paradox, Wood discovers a happy Hawthorne (especially after his marriage) who writes melancholy tales, but there is no place here for the nimble-witted teasing that Wood so enjoys and is so skilled at; for he sees a tragic undertone in Hawthorne: "As part of the heritage of his earliest years Hawthorne had a feminine sensitivity and refinement, but he was as strongly masculine. There were many tensions in Nathaniel Hawthorne. He observed the present minutely but felt part of the past. He sought solitude but needed society. He hated politics but sought political jobs . . . " (19). Hawthorne recognized the unpardonable sin of self-absorption but could not escape it.

This is the most psychological of Wood's biographies, more so than his Mather, Edwards, or Dickinson. Hawthorne could write only in protected circumstances; this frailty was joined to his fierce devotion to truth. If his unpardonable sin was, as he said of himself, that he had "ice in his blood," Hawthorne is pardoned by Wood, for, paradoxically, the sin of isolation was the source of his great portrayals of people detached, withdrawn from their fellows.

Two biographies that would, so it appears, thrill few and scarcely appeal to young readers are *Mr. Jonathan Edwards* (1968) and *The Admirable Cotton Mather* (1971). Wood's motive for writing both soon becomes apparent—to vindicate each of these Protestant ministers from the opprobrium and accusation given them falsely by those of more "enlightened" modern times. By revealing them accurately within their own times, Wood hopes to sweep away the negative myths. He says of Cotton Mather: "No man of the American past has been more consistently derided" (vi). Mather, scorned by some in his own day as a self-aggrandizing "poseur" despite his professions of contrition, in our own day is often the harsh theologian, bogus historian, pseudo-scientist, persecutor of witches during the Salem hysteria of 1692. Wood aims to clear his defendant of a number of charges.

In both biographies Wood is defender and judge, historian and tourist guide, investigative reporter, examining their diaries as well as the socio-political matrix of the New England town. As a biographer, he is a distant admirer, sympathetic but not intimately engaged. He is not the personal extension of either man, but the examiner of his subject's values and our instructor in clarifying those values for moderns. What is surprising is that this narrative voice of the devoted teacher who seeks to restore his subjects works well, for both puritan divines are given an exciting relevance.

The vindication of Mather for contributing to the witchcraft hysteria is predicated on Mather's essential tolerance, generous sympathies, and lucidity of mind. Mather and his father had urged moderation and Mather had wanted to "cure" the accused rather than condemn them. To further persuade his readers, Wood calls to witness James Russell Lowell, Hawthorne, Longfellow, and Vernon Louis Parrington (*Main Currents in American Thought*), all of whom believed in Mather's innocence (61–62).

Like Mather, Edwards has been indicted for contributing to religious mania, the spiritual disasters that occurred during the great revivals of 1740 and 1741. Wood's refutation here is simpler, not as dramatic. He finds in Edwards a temperament of an ascetic nature given sometimes to ecstatic devotion, a person scrupulously honest, conscientious, and caring, though with a formidable exterior. Puritans do not allow a biographer to "come up close," and so the biographer is hard pressed to find the natural man within the theological man of God. Wood defends Edwards as trying "to help overwrought men and women distinguish between what seemed truly spiritual emotion and false symptoms of mere excitement or envious aping" (63). He suspected as well as sanctioned an emotional climate of overpowering religious energy. Wood successfully shows that Edwards' dismissal from his church was basically the result of a political faction. Edwards' spirituality, Wood concludes, was authentic, poetic, and despite its elements of repressive Calvinism, a precursor of Unitarianism and Transcendentalism (151).

Emily Elizabeth Dickinson (1972) also aims to reconstruct a life generally misunderstood by the public because mythologized or misunderstood by biographers. Wood intends to free her biography from the melodrama and "pedantic dessication" so frequently imposed on it, to free it from "legend, rumor, gossip and fantasy" (13). He will concentrate on facts, not embroider mystery upon enigma. The difficulty here is, of course, that expressed by Sewall in his essay, "In Search of Emily Dickinson," when he asks how a biographer can tell the story of a life that has no story (74).

Wood paints nineteenth-century Amherst as a Grandma Moses bustling New England community, where young Elizabeth experiences sleigh rides in winter, cattle shows in summer, parties and family gatherings, and readings at the Shakespeare Club at Amherst Academy. Emily, brother Austin, and sister Lavinia are dominated by their father, Edward Dickinson, chief lawyer, trustee of Amherst Academy, state senator, Whig congressman, "River God" of the whole community.

Most at ease with strong, outgoing, and ambitious subjects, Wood responds to Edward Dickinson's sense of civic pride, interest in politics and the railroad, sense of family and religion, and to his determined, strong, ambitious daughter Emily. But Emily does not emerge in Wood's biography. Trying to avoid being trapped in the enigma of a life "without a story," Wood creates traps of his own. He tries to individualize the younger Emily, and just as he relieves Hawthorne from the image of gloomy recluse, he attempts to demythologize Emily by inviting the young reader to participate in her youthful experiences. She is an active and sociable student at the South

Hadley Female Seminary in 1847; she and Lavinia take an exciting jaunt to Washington, D.C., in 1854; she plays hostess to eminent guests at the Dickinson household. Yet Wood cannot revise Dickinson's later retreat from town and friends; he cannot get a clear focus on "the later Emily" (after 1860), and the problem may not simply be with Emily's baffling eccentricity.

Plainly Wood is uncomfortable with certain subjects—disliking Wells for his political beliefs, his vulgarity and shrillness, shunning Hawthorne the detached man though admiring his writing. Emily is like Hawthorne, although Wood does not draw a comparison, in being preoccupied with religious matters, with the soul, death; she has a painful sense of existence, is intense, introspective, detached from the ordinary. Wood's problem is compounded by his subject's being a woman, and he seems too removed from her in temperament and values, perhaps too removed from the female imagination to perceive Emily's essential spirit.

What primarily absorbs Wood in Emily the woman is the question of her having been attracted to certain men and who these might be, a topic especially relevant to female consciousness in the nineteenth century when women's identities were defined by men and marriage, but Wood pursues the question like a detective searching out a missing person. After analyzing the "facts" associated with such possible romantic interests as Benjamin Franklin Newton, a young law student in her father's office who encouraged her poetry, and the older men Emily was reputedly attracted to—Samuel Bowles II, publisher of the *Springfield Herald*, Dr. Josia Gilbert Holland, writer for the same, Otis Phillips Lord, lawyer and political figure, the family gardener who is not named—Wood finds no conclusive evidence, nor does he subscribe to the scholars' candidate, the Reverend Charles Wadsworth. Whimsically he concludes that Emily may have loved none of them, all of them, some of them, or an imaginary man of her own fantasy. Exulting in paradox and playfulness, as ever, Wood mentions another possibility: Mabel Loomis Todd, Emily's editor, concludes that Emily Dickinson "loved poetry better than she loved any man" (78).

Wood's judgment of Emily's writing is eccentric. He misses completely the humor and irony in her poems, noting only the obvious "pain." Her poems are too intense; "No one could live at this pitch of emotion and retain his sanity. Emily Dickinson could not" (103). She had a desire "to be a complete woman" while at the same time "she tried to remain a child" (118). That she saved all her poems suggests that she could not tell the better from the worse (173). None of Wood's statements about the poems are based on substance and developed through the analysis required to comprehend poetic intention. His judgment of Emily Dickinson the poet is without merit, just as his sense of Emily Dickinson the person is without that "extension of sympathy" that makes his other subjects breathe, act, become.

Yet it is in this biography that, for the first time, Wood clearly recognizes the difficulty or even the inability of the biographer who cannot show causality, or suggest the relationship of emotion and thought to incident. Thus, Wood grasps the intimacy of his subject and recognizes his own distance from her psyche. In this last biography, Wood has been challenged by a woman, a poet. The prankster who enjoys the game of biography, which he has played so well with others, is tricked into discovering what he cannot do.

As a biographer for young people, Wood has recognized abilities. Though he admires and is sometimes amazed by the accomplishments of his subjects, he never deifies, and he does not set them up as role models. Closest to adulation in his life of Conan Doyle, Wood levels the subject by reporting on the profit motive that determined many of Doyle's artistic decisions and by dismissing Doyle's interest in mysticism. In the lives of Stevenson, Thoreau, and particularly Carroll, Wood enters the essential man. He comprehends, without approving, Stevenson's need for attention; Thoreau's need to express abrasive truths; Carroll's affection for and attraction to little girls (Wood does not flinch from this unconscious need of Carroll to satisfy sexual need in a way that was "safe" to both photographer and model, although Wood does not discuss the sexual intrigues of H. G. Wells with adult women). In his Wells, Mather, and Edwards, Wood comes close to sermonizing, negatively on Wells, especially his ideas on world federalism, positively in redeeming Mather and Edwards, whom he commendably restores without sanctifying. Wood gives us only the muffled voices of Emerson and Hawthorne as men, though he gives us their clear voices as writers. He succeeds with Twain's humor and moral outrage, if minimizing his pessimism. He looked for Emily Elizabeth Dickinson, but perhaps found only the Elizabeth in this complex woman.

What narrative voice dominates, what voice is appropriate for different stages of a subject's life is difficult for a biographer to determine. Like a fictional character, the subject of a biography may force certain decisions on his or her "creator." The inattentive biographer will hear voices other than the natural ones, which will give his work "life." If the biographer is too attentive to each breath and syllable the subject insists on, the design of narrative voices needed to give the life a pattern will be lost. Perhaps the biographer will choose too many voices and, rather than achieve a resonance of character, will only cause static, distortion.

In a chronological life-and-writings approach, the narrative voices that tune into the character must be carefully orchestrated. Wood plays at many voices: trickster-entertainer, teacher-literary critic, commentator-investigative reporter, historian-judge, sympathetic-empathetic participant. Most of Wood's voices are well chosen, a few too timid or too strident. One notable exception, the biography of Emily Dickinson, is too silent, though the silence, also, provides discovery. As critics of Wood the biographer, we seek the contours of these voices to solve the jigsaw he has so adroitly constructed.

REFERENCES

Edel, Leon. *Writing Lives*. New York: W. W. Norton, 1984.

Fisher, Margery. "Biography." In *Matters of Fact: Aspects of Non-Fiction for Children*, edited by Margery Fisher, 299–405. New York: Thomas Y. Crowell, 1972.

Goff, Patrick. "Biography: The Bad or the Bountiful?" *Top of the News* 29:3 (April 1973): 210–20.

Trease, Geoffrey. "Old Writers and Young Readers." In *The Cool Web: The Pattern of Children's Reading*, edited by Margaret Meek, et al., 145–56. London: Bodley Head, 1974.

Wood, James Playstead. *The Admirable Cotton Mather*. New York: Seabury Press, 1971.

———. *Emily Elizabeth Dickinson*. Nashville, Tenn.: Thomas Nelson, 1972.

———. "The Honest Audience." *Horn Book* (October 1967): 612–16.

———. *A Hound, a Bay Horse, and a Turtle-Dove*. New York: Pantheon, 1963.

———. *I Told You So! A Life of H. G. Wells*. New York: Pantheon, 1969.

———. *The Lantern Bearer: A Life of Robert Louis Stevenson*. New York: Pantheon, 1965.

———. *The Man Who Hated Sherlock Holmes*. New York: Pantheon, 1965.

———. *Mr. Jonathan Edwards*. New York: Seabury Press, 1968.

———. *The Snark Was a Boojum: A Life of Lewis Carroll*. New York: Pantheon, 1966.

———. *Spunkwater! Spunkwater! A Life of Mark Twain*. New York: Pantheon, 1968.

———. *Trust Thyself: A Life of Ralph Waldo Emerson for the Young Reader*. New York: Pantheon, 1964.

———. *The Unpardonable Sin: A Life of Nathaniel Hawthorne*. New York: Pantheon, 1970.

———. "Writers Do Not Exist." *Horn Book* (December 1966): 694–98.

37

Artful Memory: Jean Fritz, Autobiography, and the Child Reader

JANICE ALBERGHENE

Although most autobiographers of childhood write for an adult audience, the past ten years have seen an increasing number of authors who speak intimately to young readers in autobiographical narratives directed toward a child audience. Virtually all of these authors are known primarily as writers for children and therefore might be expected to be especially in touch with their former child selves. Indeed, many writers for children make just such a claim when explaining the sources or inspiration for their stories. A close look at their autobiographies suggests, however, that these texts owe at least as much, if not more, to art as to memory. At the same time, this is not to imply that "art" is synonymous with "fiction," and that "memory" is synonymous with "truth." Memory fails and memory often lies, even if facts about one's life are what one's after.

In this context, the candor of Jean Fritz's autobiography comes as something of a shock. Fritz begins *Homesick: My Own Story* (1984) with a discussion of method:

When I started to write about my childhood in China, I found that my memory came out in lumps . . . my preoccupation with time and literal accuracy was squeezing the life out of what I had to say. . . .

Since my childhood feels like a story, I decided to tell it that way, letting the events fall as they would into the shape of a story, lacing them together with fictional bits, adding a piece here and there when memory didn't give me all I needed. (7)

Fritz's candor indicates that *Homesick* is less a paradigmatic autobiographical text than an extraordinary one, but its very extraordinariness is what makes the book so useful a focus for pointing out two considerations to have in mind when thinking about the narrative art of autobiography for children.

The first of these considerations takes its cue from Domna Stanton's reflection that

the specific texture of an autobiography also represents the mediation of numerous contextual factors . . . [such as a particular intertext or set of intertexts]. More broadly, every autobiography assumes and reworks literary conventions for writing and reading. And its texture is ultimately determined by the way in which meaning can be signified in a particular discursive context, an (ideo)-logical boundary that always already confines the speaking subject. (10–11)

Intertext or set of intertexts, literary conventions, particular discursive context—can *Homesick* bear such detailed scrutiny? Quite simply, yes. On a practical level, *Homesick* can bear the scrutiny because of the volume of related autobiographical and biographical material,[1] but in this present essay, as in an earlier study of *Homesick's* relationship to American literature, my interests are broadly contextual rather than specifically intertextual.[2] I want to explore the intersection in *Homesick* of two additional and equally relevant contexts: that of writing for children and that of being a female autobiographer.

The context of writing for children immediately raises that perennial bogey of children's literature: Does the book in question provide good "role models" for its child readers? Fritz's uneasiness with the question highlights both its freight of prescriptive assumptions (not to mention its condescension to child readers) and its essential irrelevance to her own concerns. Consider, for example, these remarks from her acceptance speech for winning the Boston Globe–Horn Book Award for *The Double Life of Pocahontas*:

But actually I was writing for my own sake because I wanted to learn. . . . Although on the whole I was very much pleased with how students and teachers worked with my biographies in the Jean Fritz contest, I was saddened by the entry that required students to list the attributes necessary for the perfect person—as if my books were being used subversively in a lesson on character building. Well, this is not what I'm after. ("Turning History Inside Out," 30)

Wanting to learn—to learn about and make sense of the self—is one of the chief reasons for writing an autobiography. But the "self" that makes it to the page is a persona, a crafting of the self that blends memory and desire. I am not saying anything new here in terms of contemporary theory about autobiography; my position rephrases the implications of the title of Paul John Eakin's recent *Fictions in Autobiography: Studies in the Art of Self-Invention* (1985), a book Estelle Jelinek summarizes as "claim[ing] that autobiographical truth is not a fixed but an evolving constant in a process of self-creation" (*The Tradition of Women's Autobiography: From Antiquity to the Present* [1986], 4).

Critics such as Jelinek and Eakin theorize about autobiographies intended for an adult audience. But I want to do more than suggest that we ought to accord texts intended for children the same serious critical consideration. We are accustomed to the idea that biography and autobiography for children are only relatively truthful in that they delete material thought to be inappropriate for tender sensibilities. In this sense, the children's texts limit exploration of character. And I have to confess that my original intention in writing about *Homesick* was to look at what Fritz left out, speculate why, chastise her mildly, explore the implications of her omissions, and then conclude that *Homesick* is a good book despite its shortcomings. What I want to suggest instead is that far from being a limitation, writing for a child audience can be an enabling situation in which the writer, in particular the woman writer, can explore or create a self and find a voice that writing for an adult audience may preclude.[3]

To follow this line of thought we need to return to the foreword of *Homesick*, where Fritz mentions including "fictional bits" in her "lacing" the story together. This leads to her concluding, "Strictly speaking, I have to call this book *fiction*, but it does not feel like fiction to me. It is my story, told as truly as I can tell it" (7). Here the book's nature as autobiography could be called into question, my earlier references to autobiography's fictionalizing notwithstanding. If the book is "fiction," not autobiography, what I attribute to the enabling situation of writing for a child audience could be ascribed instead to the fiction writer's license to create. Fritz's avowal "It is my story, told as truly as I can tell it" provides, however, a good reason for seeing the book as an autobiography. Any lingering doubts can be put to rest by turning to Jelinek's definition in *The Tradition of Women's Autobiography*: "I consider an autobiography as that work each autobiographer writes with the intention of its being her life story—whatever form, content, or style it takes" (xii).

This is an expansive definition. It is one that admits many works into what Jelinek calls the tradition of women's autobiography, a tradition she outlined several years ago in "Introduction: Women's Autobiography and the Male Tradition." What is fascinating about *Homesick* are the ways in which it does and does not belong to the women's tradition of disjunctive, decentered, domestic, fragmentedly selved self-imaging. *Homesick* is, for example, matrilinear in that China-born (and China-situated) Jean longs for the day she and her missionary parents will go home to the America she has never seen. Jean focuses her longings by writing to and thinking about her grandmother back in Washington, Pennsylvania. In contrast to the ferment of China, Jean's grandmother's world is undeniably domestic. One evening during the seige of Wuchang (the city across the river—the time is the mid–1920s, and the nationalists and the communists are battling each other), Jean tries to alleviate her anxiety by asking her parents what people back home consider to be news. The answer is whether or not it will frost and if the tomatoes ought to be covered up (89). Jean's view of America is so domestic that her best friend exclaims, " 'Your trouble is that you think America is [i.e., equals] just feeding your grandmother's chickens' " (116).

Yet *Homesick* is "masculine" in many ways. Unlike the decentered, disjunctive narrative typical of women's autobiographies, Fritz's autobiography has a single point of view—young Jean's—that is so central and consistent that she sometimes sounds very naive. She is *focused*, however, as is the narrative, which moves determinedly forward to Jean's reunion with her grandmother. Like other women autobiographers, Fritz includes journal-like entries in her story, but these entries—italicized passages in which Jean thinks about her grandmother—are used to advance the "plot" and punctuate its underlying theme of going home. (In contrast to *Homesick*, its sequel, *China Homecoming* [1985], seems to speak more to the adult reader than to the child. *China Homecoming* is decentered, disjunctive, anecdotal; it matches Jelinek's description of texts in the female tradition.)

The paradox is that Fritz uses "masculine" formal elements in a work progressively masculine in movement but feminine in that it presents a fragmented or incomplete self: Fritz feels that she is not "American" enough. This is a central issue in the text, one that makes it impossible to write off Fritz's sense of incompleteness as a concomitant to her being a child and therefore unfinished. The fragmented self is so characteristic of women's autobiographies that the significance of *Homesick*'s formal structures might be seen to pale were it not for the book's detailing the emergence of another sense of self, one in marked contrast to the incomplete self. This self feels whole because it is a "self-at-home." The second half of *Homesick* is an accretion of self-at-home episodes, only two of which we have space to look at here.

In the first we see Jean on deck as the *President Taft*, the ship bringing her from China to America, approaches the Golden Gate. Fritz portrays herself in the "heroic or exceptional terms" Jelinek associates with the male tradition in autobiography ("Introduction," 5):

Dressed in my navy skirt, white blouse, and silk stockings, I felt every bit as neat as Columbus or Balboa and every bit as heroic when I finally spotted America in the distance. . . .

Then the ship entered the narrow stretch of the Golden Gate and I could see American hills on my left and American houses on my right, and I took a deep breath of American air.

" 'Breathes there the man with soul so dead,' " I cried,
" 'Who never to himself hath said,
This is my own, my native land!' "
I forgot that there were people behind and around me until I heard a few snickers and a scattering of claps, but I didn't care. I wasn't reciting for anyone's benefit but my own. (128–31)

The second episode is mythopoeic in its autochthonous answer to the question of origins and home. Jean and her family have sailed the breadth of the Pacific and traveled by car cross-country to Pennsylvania. As they approach Jean's grandmother's home on Shirls Avenue, Jean's mother worries that the street will be "one big sea of mud . . . 'worth your life to drive through' " (137). And so it is. Jean's father puts his hand on the horn, the car in low gear, and they careen through mud hubcap-deep to arrive triumphantly, up out of the very earth. Jean runs into her grandmother's arms and hears her cry, " 'Welcome home! Oh, welcome home!' " (138).

I haven't done this reading of *Homesick* to undermine Jelinek's delineation of male and female traditions in autobiography, but rather to underline the importance of intended audience: Jelinek's authors did not write for children. But then, on one level, neither does Fritz, as Elaine Edelman reported in an interview in 1981:

> When asked why she hadn't yet written for children about a woman, her whole body whips around on the couch. "I'm not a sociologist," she answers. "I'm not trying to provide role models. I'm exploring for my own good. If it 'helps' children, fine." Later, she amends that. "I can't say the audience has no effect at all. With Columbus, for instance. He'd been so wrongly portrayed to children—just a blah figure, a persistent man. No one had told any of these really rotten things he did. A character isn't just good or bad—it's both. Everyone." (77)

The date of this interview is important; it was conducted when Fritz was beginning to write *Homesick*, a book she called "a kind of autobiography" and which Edelman characterized as "another stage in her on-going dialogue between child and adult" (77). That the dialogue between child and adult was no simple chat is revealed by Fritz's reference to Columbus, the subject of one of her biographies for children. He was soon to become a metaphor for Fritz herself in *Homesick*'s description of her feeling "every bit as heroic" as Columbus as when she "finally spotted America" from the deck of the *President Taft* (128).

Reaching this stage in the dialogue between child and adult prompts some writers for children to leave the child behind and write books for adults. Fritz certainly had the option; not only had she previously written biography for adults (*Cast for a Revolution: Some American Friends and Enemies, 1728–1814* [1972]), she would have been joining in a hundred-and-fifty-year-old tradition of writing about one's childhood and adolescence.

A person who is homesick, however, does better to turn to the conventions and impulses of children's literature. So too does a person looking for a pattern with which to construct a unified sense of self. As critics Christopher Clausen, Virginia Wolf, and others have shown, children's literature does its best to bring both the stories' protagonists and child readers home. The protagonists return with a more integrated sense of self, not one that is more diffuse. And perhaps in writing the returns, the authors who create them feel their own real selves experience that integration too. At least that seems to be the case with Fritz, who responded to the question, "How were you particularly attracted to writing for children?" like this: "I wonder sometimes whether it was the fact that my childhood was so cut off from the rest of my life, and that I had the feeling I should hang on to it very strongly in my memory or else I would lose a whole big chunk of life itself" (*Contemporary Authors*, 16: 127).

NOTES

1. *Homesick* was preceded by *The Cabin Faced West*, an early novel Fritz now sees as a "companion book" to *Homesick* ("There Once Was," 435) and has been followed by another autobiography, *China Homecoming*. In addition to writing biography for children and for adults, Fritz has commented extensively on her practices as a writer, contributed to the *SATA* autobiography series, and based several short stories on her early days in China.

2. *Homesick* revises the mainstream (adult) autobiographical tradition of presenting the passage through time as the psychic equivalent of expulsion from the Edenic paradise of childhood; Jean's journey is from being a "foreign devil" in China to being an inhabitant of an America where Edenic moments are possible. American literature typically presents the New World as a new Eden; in Fritz's very American book, the conventions of American literature partially pre-empt some of the conventions of autobiography ("Paradise Regained in *Homesick: My Own Story*").

3. My view of writing for the child audience parallels that of the following critics who have explored the implied contract between the writer and reader of autobiography: Elizabeth W. Bruss, *Autobiographical Acts: The Changing Situation of a Literary Genre* (Baltimore: Johns Hopkins University Press, 1976); Philippe Lejeune, *Le Pacte Autobiographique* (Paris: Seuil, 1975); Paul de Man, "Autobiography as De-Facement" in *The Rhetoric of Romanticism* (New York: Columbia University Press, 1984); and William Leake Andrews, "The Identity of (Not in) Autobiography," Discussion Group on Autobiography and Biography, MLA Convention (San Francisco, 28 December 1967).

REFERENCES

Alberghene, Janice M. "Paradise Regained in *Homesick: My Own Story*." Panel on the Autobiography of Childhood, Twelfth Annual Conference of the Children's Literature Association. Ann Arbor, Mich., May 17, 1985.

Clausen, Christopher. "Home and Away in Children's Literature." *Children's Literature* 10 (1982): 141–52.

Eakin, Paul J. *Fictions in Autobiography: Studies in the Art of Self-Invention*. Princeton: Princeton University Press, 1985.

Edelman, Elaine. "Jean Fritz." *Publisher's Weekly* 220, no. 4 (1981): 76–77.

Fritz, Jean. *The Cabin Faced West*. Illustrated by Feodor Rojankovsky. New York: Coward, 1959.

———. *Cast for a Revolution: Some American Friends and Enemies, 1728–1814*. Boston: Houghton Mifflin, 1972.

———. *China Homecoming*. New York: G. P. Putnam's Sons, 1985.

————. *Homesick: My Own Story.* Illustrated by Margot Tomes. New York: Dell, 1984.

————. "Jean Fritz." *Something About the Author Autobiography Series*, 2, 99–109.

————. "There Once Was." *Horn Book* 62, no. 4 (1986): 432–435.

————. "Turning History Inside Out." *Horn Book* 61, no. 1 (1985): 29–34.

————. *Where Do You Think You're Going, Christopher Columbus?* Illustrated by Margot Tomes. New York: G. P. Putnam's Sons, 1980.

"Jean Fritz." *Contemporary Authors*, New Revision Series, 16, 127.

Jelinek, Estelle C. "Introduction: Women's Autobiography and the Male Tradition." In *Women's Autobiography: Essays in Criticism.* Bloomington: Indiana University Press, 1980.

————. *The Tradition of Women's Autobiography: From Antiquity to the Present.* Boston: Twayne, 1986.

Stanton, Domna C. "Autogynography: Is the Subject Different?" In *The Female Autograph*, 5–22. New York Literary Forum 12–13. New York: New York Literary Forum, 1984.

Wolf, Virginia. "Paradise Lost? The Displacement of Myth in Children's Novels." *Studies in the Literary Imagination* 18, no. 2 (1985): 47–63.

PART VIII
Informational Books

Introduction

GARY D. SCHMIDT

Like the writer of biography, the writer of informational books is constrained by events that lie outside the fictive imagination. Such a writer is concerned with presenting a body of material that is factually based. Yet also like the biographer, the writer of informational books uses the imagination to craft a design that will gather that information and give it greater import and meaning than that generated by facts alone.

Many now-forgotten informational books in the first half of the twentieth century used a narrator who spoke with the enormous authority of the encyclopedia. Omniscient, confident, rational, distant, such a narrator took the stance of one whose purpose was to impart fact—a not-so-distant descendant of Mr. Gradgrind. But informational books in the last three decades have rejected this approach, which never received universal acceptance. Instead, the narrators of these books speak with a great range of voices; they feel free to be bitter, exultant, humorous, technical, hortatory. In each case, the narrator's voice is suited to the material, structuring it and being structured by it.

Laurence Pringle goes so far as to reject "informational books" as a term suitable for his work, principally because of the connotations which that term suggests for the narrator. Instead, he argues that his works are infused with his personal voice, a voice that questions, probes, and provides hope. This is revealed not only in his selection of subjects, but in his challenging of accepted truth about subjects, particularly subjects in the natural sciences. The result is a rejection of the notion that pure objectivity is essential in nonfiction. Pringle would argue that, even if it were attainable, complete objectivity is not desirable.

Fascinated by the interconnections of living and non-living things, Pringle uses a narrator to reflect his own sense of wonder at the natural world. And in his explanations Pringle finds that facts cannot be isolated; instead, they contribute to the development of a sense of values. The narrator's conclusions in Pringle's works express such values and establish a sense of real hope for the reader. In the end, facts lead if not to moral growth in the reader, at least to a greater awareness of the position and responsibilities of the individual in an ecological community.

In *The Philharmonic Gets Dressed* and *The Dallas Titans Get Ready for Bed*, Karla Kuskin plays with the encyclopedic voice and the humorous voice. In each book she deals with characters who are engaged in a serious business, and yet these characters also "play." It is this juxtaposition of the serious with the potentially humorous that establishes the focus for both books. Kuskin claims that her narrators—particularly the narrator of *The Philharmonic Gets Dressed*—never try to be humorous. Their stance is formal and serious; yet the reality they deal with has an inherent humorous quality. Classical musicians do ordinary, mundane things like put on socks and soak in bubble baths; football players act like disgruntled children being sent off to bed. The two work together to provide a picture of a complete life, as well as bring the child reader closer to adult occupations that may seem distant and inaccessible.

Marc Simont's illustrations for these books are similar in stance and purpose to those of the text; they also combine the serious business of an occupation with its underlying comic humanity. Writing of his vision of illustration, Simont suggests

I like to take a text and make it my own—pretend it is something I wrote. I'm sure all artists feel that way. It's the only way the illustrator can be free to make the sort of contribution that can give the work added breadth. A good text, in my opinion, is one which, with a minimum of words, can open up the maximum vistas. I like to be able to say to an author, Thanks for the push-off, leave the rest to me. (Personal letter to Gary D. Schmidt, May 4, 1988)

Simont expands the text by scattering figures over the page, all set in various poses, all dressing or undressing, all succumbing to the humorous vision of the artist. Text and illustration work to close the distance between a child reader and a philharmonic orchestra or a professional football team.

Ellen Tremper argues that an author's involvement and interaction with a text is revealed principally through narrative voice. This necessitates that an author suit the narrative tone to the subject. Aliki, for example, chooses a first-person narrator to depict the wonder a child feels in the presence of dinosaur fossils in *Digging for Dinosaurs*. The first-person narration eliminates distance between the narrator and the child reader, establishing a human perspective through a personal voice. As the narrator's voice expresses wonder, both characters and the reader share that wonder. In *Mummies Made in Egypt*, the narrator uses a strange, otherworldly tone appropriate to the mysterious rites of ancient Egypt. Tremper claims that by manipulating rhythms and sentence lengths, Aliki creates a "petrified" tone, a distant, eerie voice.

Jean George, Tremper suggests, also annihilates the narrator, but not through Aliki's mode of distance. Instead, the narrator seems to be absorbed into the natural world, and it is that very absorption that allows the narrator to gain a unique vantage point. In *The Moon of the Winter Bird*, George has eliminated the human narrator and used one that speaks from within nature itself. Thus the information in the book comes by way of the story itself; story and information are integrated in the narrator's perspective.

Each of these authors has found a design that shapes the manner in which the information is presented. Meredith Klaus warns, however, that the design itself must be subject to scrutiny in that it can reflect an author's bias. Narrative voice reflects authorial predisposition. Both Anno and Isaac Asimov, Klaus suggests, seek to force onto medieval history a narrator who distorts that history and suggests the authors' own distaste. For Anno in *Anno's Medieval World*, the design is a movement from the barbarian, superstitious world of the Middle Ages to one of rationality and knowledge in the Renaissance. For Asimov in *The Dark Ages*, the design is a struggle between light and darkness. The inflexibility of these designs comes from a lack of empathy by the authors for the period, and, Klaus argues, distorts their presentation of the Middle Ages.

By contrast, Klaus shows that Richard Lyttle's *Land Beyond the River*, Aliki's *A Medieval Feast*, and Sheila Sancha's *The Luttrell Village* avoid inflexible patterns and use narrators that express enthusiasm and delight in things medieval. Lyttle denies the barbarism of the age, arguing that history represents a continuous flux between movements of high culture and moments of chaos. Aliki delights in the art, the food, the music, the gardens, the world of the Middle Ages, and expresses that delight through a narrator who revels in simple skills and pleasant companionship. Sancha depicts the everyday life of a small medieval village with no sense of the condescension that marks Anno's work.

THE AUTHORIAL VOICE

38

A Voice for Nature

LAURENCE PRINGLE

First, let's get one thing clear: I don't write informational books, whatever they are. Sounds like something having to do with data, statistics, factoids, and answers to crossword puzzles.

I write nonfiction, which differs from fiction mainly by having no or few invented characters, situations, or dialogue. I do not write in order to jam a lot of jargon and facts into some poor reader's head but to express my feelings, values, my vision of the world—my voice.

My voice is first revealed in my choice to write nonfiction rather than fiction. Some authors write both; most don't. I began to write nonfiction articles for magazines while in college. Maybe fiction seemed too intimate, but more likely the writing assignments in my many science courses—I was a wildlife biology major—simply primed my nonfiction pump. In any event, the publication of a few articles opened a path that became the path of least resistance. My nonfiction voice grew in confidence while my fiction voice remained largely untested and unsure.

Having chosen to write nonfiction, a writer further reveals his or her voice in choice of subjects. For me it is the life sciences, in a broad sense, from cockroaches to the effects of nuclear war. At times I must venture into physics and chemistry, but feel more at home in woods and swamps, and I am happy that we have people like Roy Gallant, a key mentor in my writing career, who feels more at home in astronomy and the earth sciences.

I am a skeptic (*not* a cynic) and tend to challenge authority and accepted truths. This has influenced my choice of subjects, as I have questioned popular but incorrect notions about forest fires, dinosaurs, vampire bats, wolves, coyotes, and killer bees. Part of my goal is to show that the process of science aims for a better understanding of the world. As long as we keep asking questions, that understanding can change.

Skepticism, I feel, should also be directed at new technologies and at the vested interests that come into play with such issues as nuclear power, environmental health, biocides, and acid rain. There are usually extremists on both sides whose motivations bear a close look. My voice is not a bland, neutral one, with equal space and weight given to opposing interests, and I avoid any claims of strict objectivity in jacket blurbs.

I am fascinated by the complex interconnections between living and non-living things, and this aspect of my voice seems to be present in virtually everything I write. It seems especially rich (loud?) in such titles as *Animals and Their Niches* (1977) and *Frost Hollows and Other Microclimates* (1981). It certainly affected the content of *Throwing Things Away: From Middens to Resource Recovery* (1986). This book could have been tightly focused on the contemporary problem of solid waste management: What shall we do with all this stuff we throw away? As the subtitle suggests, however, I roamed further, including ideas about archeology (which is based largely on past trash), on dumps and landfills as cultural institutions, and on the variety of wildlife (including polar bears and wolves) that scavenge at dumps and land-fills. I took pleasure in bringing in the voice of Wallace Stegner, with quotations from his essay "The Town Dump," and in writing about how our garbage has caused increases in gull populations, which then led to increasing numbers of costly collisions of gulls and aircraft. Lots of interconnections!

I promote the idea of kinship between humans and other living things— a sort of "we're all in this together" attitude. A few years ago I proposed to an editor a book that I wanted to call, simply, *Home*. As I envisioned it, *Home* would be a picture book of only a few hundred words, about home in its broadest sense. It would include both humans and other animals. It would even include homeless people who live in cardboard boxes and bus stations. It would emphasize the similarities of basic needs among all sorts of creatures.

The editor didn't share my enthusiasm. She wanted a book focused on animal homes. "Leave the people out." I needed money from a contract advance and couldn't afford the time needed to find a more amenable editor. I am fond of the book that I wrote, *Home: How Animals Find Comfort and Safety* (1987), but feel that my voice was muffled somewhat by an editor (whose judgment was based in part on the marketplace; more about this below).

The book does include a few instances in which I tried to link humans with other living things. An example occurs where I describe worker honey-bees "filling in gaps and cracks, especially in early autumn when cold nights reveal where chilly drafts enter the nest. Like many a human family, ho-neybees caulk and cover the places where precious heat escapes. This re-duces their energy cost and provides a more comfortable home in winter."

One of the many reasons I like *Wolfman* (1983) is its title, so I decided to write a similar book about a man who had devoted decades to the study of spiders, and call it *Spiderman*. The editor's initial interest vanished when she talked to the publisher's sales people, who believed they could not sell enough copies of a book about spiders. In essence they said, "Give us a book about something with fur and brown eyes," so I now have a contract for a book about a man who has devoted his life to the study of black bears. The economics of bookselling has at least temporarily stilled my voice on the subject of *Spiderman*.

To return to the idea of fostering kinship with all living things, and an appreciation of nature and its diversity, here is my ending for *Vampire Bats* (1987): "The vampire bat, after all, is not a mythical monster. It is a fascinating real creature that happens to need blood in order to fly, to raise its young, to live."

Sharks are other creatures that so many of us have been taught to fear. In *Sevengill: The Shark and Me* (1986), Don Reed writes: "The shark was a force of nature, like a mountain or a storm. My perception of her had changed, but she herself had not changed, except perhaps in learning to associate me with the availability of food because I fed her. She was neither my friend nor my enemy. She was like the sea itself, a positive part of the natural world, to be respected."

The beginnings and ends of books, as well as those of chapters, are places where nonfiction writers often express their voice most directly. My feelings led me to name *Home*'s last chapter "No Place Like Home," and to conclude:

The hermit crab's plight shows once more that all of animals' homes can be matters of life and death. It also brings to mind that old saying, "There's no place like home." People say that to express appreciation for the warmth and security of home, but the words can have another meaning. What happens to an animal when it finds "there's no place like home"—no place remaining that is like the snail shell or nesting site it needs for life?

Anyone who cares about saving the earth's rich variety of animal life must also care about all of the diverse places that are animal homes.

I didn't know the book would end that way. The facts and my values led me there. In 1987 James Cross Giblin made a similar observation about the ending of his *Walls: Defenses Through History* (1984). "Sometimes," he said, "the material leads you to a conclusion you did not expect." Here are most of his last two paragraphs:

None of the walls was ever entirely successful. If an enemy was determined enough, he usually found some way to get over, around, under, or through the wall. In spite of this, nations and states continued to build defensive walls. . . .

Today, in the atomic age, some leaders and scientists are still seeking the ultimate defensive wall. But perhaps the time has finally come to admit that no such wall is possible. Confronted by nuclear weapons, any nation that wants to feel secure in the future will have to reach some sort of understanding with its enemies. It can't hope to achieve security by building a wall. (106)

Thus a writer's fascination with the history of walls led him to make a political statement. Individual readers may interpret it differently; my interpretation is "Don't fall for the futile fantasy of Ronald Reagan's so-called Strategic Defense Initiative."

Today, listening to a radio call-in show, I heard a father tell a psychologist of finding a will written by his thirteen-year-old daughter—perhaps a cry for help from someone considering suicide. I recall the wretchedness of my own early teens, when no one told me that for most people life gets better. Today I believe strongly that writers of both fiction and nonfiction must offer hope to young readers.

Most of my books for teenagers deal with tough issues. I don't minimize the difficulties of accomplishing social and political change, but usually conclude with the thought that people have the ability and power to effect change. Thus, the last lines of *Living in a Risky World* (1989) read, "People accept the inevitability of risk. In a democracy they have the right to participate in the dialogue about how hazardous life should be."

In *Nuclear War: From Hiroshima to Nuclear Winter* (1985), I focused on the likely outcomes of nuclear war and did not write about the politics of the arms race and disarmament efforts. I was upset when one reviewer found it lacking in hope. Perhaps he needed a strong dose of hope on the day he read the book, or perhaps he missed parts of the book, including its ending: "What we have learned, together with our unproved assumptions, strongly suggests that the nation that starts nuclear war will be making a murder-suicide pact with its opponent and threatening every living thing on earth. That is knowledge enough, and a powerful incentive for people to work to ensure that all of the rest remains forever a mystery."

The voice of a nonfiction writer can sometimes be detected in specific details, in his or her choice of anecdotes, quotations, and even illustrations. Nonfiction authors usually have a great deal to say about the illustrations of their books. They may provide artists with reference material on key ideas that need illustrating; they locate or take photographs themselves. Within budget constraints I try to illustrate my books with a rich variety of images, including—when appropriate—political cartoons, which can eloquently express wisdom about a controversy.

You can also hear my voice in my selection of words from others. In three of my books for young adults, you will find reference to people "finding wormholes in the fruits of technology." I don't know who coined this phrase—was it Senator Joe Biden?—but I think it wonderfully sums up the risk consciousness and the healthy skepticism toward technology that has grown in the past three decades. My books about land use choices and about restoring environments, among others, include quotations from Aldo Leopold, the ecologist-philosopher whose wisdom about the relationship between humans and nature is part of the foundation on which the environmental movement is based.

Part of the writing process is being alert for those nuggets of wisdom, pithy quotes, and anecdotes about situations and individuals that help convey ideas. The lives of specific people and their words can add greatly to the appeal of nonfiction. Finding these people to write about can be a challenge in scientific fields where many definitions and long explanations are needed to explain what investigators are studying. In my research I am delighted to come upon scientists whose studies can be clearly described, with a minimum of jargon, to young readers, and whose questions—how do vines find objects to climb, why do insects rest overnight within the blossoms of some spring wildflowers—are matters that anyone might observe and wonder about.

One of the unfortunate realities about writing nonfiction is that few readers write to an author to tell of their reaction to a book. Fiction writers are sometimes told how their stories and characters have touched the lives of their readers. Nonfiction authors get much less of this; many letters have a "this week we will write to authors" class assignment taint to them.

Sometimes teachers or librarians tell me how they have used a book of mine, and about how it affected their lives and the lives of specific children. Beyond this extraordinary feedback, and the praise of reviewers, I am left with raw hope—that somewhere out there, young people hear my voice.

REFERENCES

Giblin, James Cross. *Walls: Defenses Through History.* Boston: Little, Brown, 1984.

Pringle, Laurence. *Animals and Their Niches.* New York: William Morrow and Company, 1977.

———. *Frost Hollows and Other Microclimates.* New York: William Morrow and Company, 1981.

———. *Home: How Animals Find Comfort and Safety.* New York: Scribner's, 1987.

———. *Living in a Risky World.* New York: William Morrow and Company, 1989.

———. *Nuclear War: From Hiroshima to Nuclear Winter.* Hillsdale, N.J.: Enslow Publishers, 1985.

———. *Throwing Things Away: From Middens to Resource Recovery.* New York: Crowell, 1986.

———. *Vampire Bats.* New York: William Morrow and Company, 1982; Hillsdale, N.J.: Enslow Publishers, 1987.

———. *Wolfman.* New York: Scribner's, 1983.

Reed, Donald. *Sevengill: The Shark and Me*. San Francisco: Sierra Club/Knopf, 1986.

Stegner, Wallace. "The Town Dump" from *Wolf Willow*. 1959. Reprint. Lincoln: University of Nebraska Press, 1980.

39

Removing the Distance

KARLA KUSKIN

Details are fascinating. They teach us how the world works, button by buttonhole. *The Philharmonic Gets Dressed* (1982) grew from a few details that have caught my eye at various times and held it. As a child, whenever I was given a new doll, I would immediately examine the layers of doll clothes to determine what lay under what. Years later I saw the attention with which my own children watched their musician father dress for a formal concert. "Dad's putting on his tail" my daughter Julia would announce on these occasions. To these memories add that magical word "underwear." Simply saying it can induce instant and hilarious laughter in a room of seven to ten year olds. I made this discovery years ago when I wrote a poem about a big bug eating a little bug. The last lines are: "That big bug ate that little bug / because that little bug was there. / He also ate his underwear."

Sometimes when I am asked what *The Philharmonic Gets Dressed* is about I give the short answer: music and underwear. It sounds like an incongruous pairing and usually elicits smiles. But beneath the funny incongruity there is a slim, serious thought about people and their work. The men and women in my story are quite ordinary. They live very much the way we all do, they dress in usual ways (except their clothing is all black and white), but the work they do is really quite special. It is the work of art.

The narrator's voice in *The Philharmonic Gets Dressed* never tries to be funny. It just presents facts, quietly at first, to draw the reader into the rhythm of the telling. "It is almost Friday night. Outside, the dark is getting darker and the cold is getting colder. Inside, lights are coming on in houses and apartment buildings. And here and there, uptown and downtown and across the bridges of the city, one hundred and five people are getting dressed to go to work." The voice continues, describing the process step by step. It is straightforward and precise. It uses numbers the way they would be used in a serious study, detailing how many people shower, bathe, shave, sit down or stand up to put on their pants—the statistics of dressing. And it is this deliberate, almost formal tone contrasted with the subject matter (socks, bubble bath, suspenders) that makes for humor.

Another element that may add to the fun, while leading the reader on, is the slight note of mystery. Many young readers who do not know the meaning of the word philharmonic will wonder just what these people are preparing to do. The narrator, dropping hints along the way, is coming to that. "When all the men and women are completely dressed in black and white, they get ready to go out." Details of their outer wear and modes of travel follow and we learn just where they are going and their time of arrival. It is then revealed (for those who have not already guessed) that these are musicians. At this point the narrator's voice takes on a certain, almost musical, urgency. The rhythms of the prose speed up, the sentences grow a little longer and more complex and when the conductor enters and gives his downbeat the narrator discusses the instruments of the orchestra in a solo, a brief verbal overture. The very last lines of the story, referring to the musicians, are "their work is to play. Beautifully." The pun stresses that serious thought mentioned earlier. People like us can do wonderful work, work that is a pleasure.

While the idea and the form of *The Dallas Titans Get Ready for Bed* (1986) is similar to *The Philharmonic Gets Dressed*, there are some not so subtle differences between the two books. From the opening line of *The Titans* there is never any question about what this group of people do because they have just finished doing it. Instead of watching them dress for their work (which also is play), we watch them undress. Here the narrator's voice does communicate some humor, but it is still just in its role of reporting facts. For example, the players have funny names (Trample, Thud, etc.) and from the descriptions of their talk and behavior we can see that, big and tough as they are, they often sound like kids. When Coach Scorch tells them it is time to go home and go to bed the grown up and enormous Jones says "Rats" and the equally old and large Bones says "It isn't fair" and kicks the door to his locker. Sounds familiar.

Details of clothing, padding, and the like are recorded with the same kind of precision used in *The Philharmonic Gets Dressed*, but in this case the narrator's figures add up to the fact that the players are making a terrible mess of the locker room. Any young reader who has ever been admonished to "Clean up your room!" will be pleased to find a room obviously and outrageously messier.

In both these books I think one of the keys to the humor is the juxtaposition of awe-inspiring adult work with the homely details underlying it. Examining the mundane mechanics of musicians dressing or fullbacks undressing brings these heroes down to a child's-eye level where the shortest reader can smile in recognition of that which is familiar and, at times, a little absurd.

REFERENCES

Kuskin, Karla. *The Dallas Titans Get Ready for Bed.* New York: Harper and Row, 1986.
————. *The Philharmonic Gets Dressed.* New York: Harper and Row, 1982.

THE CRITICAL VOICE

40

Felt Presence: Narrative Tone in Informational Books for Children

ELLEN TREMPER

The text of an informational book has to be one that enables the reader to access and decode its information. This metonymic relationship, in which the container is taken for the thing contained, is most successfully realized in those books for children—whether straight nonfiction or fiction—in which the author's involvement in the subject matter is revealed through the quality of the narrative voice. Its tone, of which children are very aware—the quality akin to someone else's infectious laughter—is what makes children read on, absorbed in the story and learning, willy-nilly. And of course, their finding out about the world is the ultimate desideratum.

There must be some imaginative involvement of the author with the subject—in the best case, even empathy—which carries the young reader along. This "empathic" relation of author to text is aptly described by John Keats in a letter to Richard Woodhouse of 1818: "As to the poetical Character. . . . it has no self. . . it lives in gusto. . . . A poet is the most unpoetical of anything in existence; because he has no Identity—he is continually in for—and filling some other body—The Sun, the Moon, the Sea and Men and Women who . . . have about them an unchangeable attribute—the poet has none" (226–27).

The ability of the author to become one with or enter the subject is extremely crucial in the writing of children's books since children will turn off or even stop reading what bores them. Of course, there is no simple prescription, nor would we want there to be one, for the achievement of imaginative engagement. But it can be recognized when it does exist and ought to be described so that others can make available to children the most interesting reading fare possible.

One more thing must be said before beginning a more specific analysis of the characteristics of narrative tone in children's informational books. Such literature ranges along a fiction-nonfiction continuum with almost imperceptible differences between the genres. Similar techniques may be employed by authors in all these kinds of narratives. It should be obvious that information can be passed along to the reader no matter the vehicle, and that often the books most successful in communicating information rely on a careful blending of fantasy and fact that draws the young reader in unawares.

Such is the case in the "science" books of Aliki and Jean Craighead George. Two of Aliki's books, *Digging for Dinosaurs* (1981) and *Mummies Made in Egypt* (1979), illustrate her extraordinary ability to suit narrative tone to subject. Both of these are picture books with an artful adjustment of tone to the accompanying illustrations as well. *Digging for Dinosaurs* is for children of, perhaps, three or four to eight or nine, depending on the level of interest and sophistication. It is a very funny book, amusing to adults as well, the humor of which is obvious from the title page. On it is a picture of a fossil digger leaning on his spade, contemplating the skull of a dinosaur, with a word bubble as in comic books issuing from his mouth. Enclosed is the text "Alas, poor Brontosaurus." The literary allusion, of course, is lost on the young readers or listeners, but there is humor for them merely in the disparity between the high solemnity of the tone and the ridiculousness of addressing any words to an inanimate, long-dead dinosaur skull. The picture, too, a charming, black line drawing shaded with a gray wash, suggests the humorous, almost twinkling-eyed, vision of the illustrator-author. The reader is, after this introductory page, prepared for the tone of the text that follows.

There are two kinds of type in this book, and each has its own tone. There is the straight narrative given us in the traditional font of the printer. Aliki uses the first person "I" for her narrative voice, which immediately supplies her human perspective and dimensions to the "story" that follows. Something as enormous or even as terrifying to a child as a dinosaur is more easily comprehended through this very human, personal voice. Her tone, in other words, verifies the wonder and the fears of her audience; children are not alone in their response. And, occasionally, there is humor, albeit fairly tame, in this part of the narrative. For example, at the beginning of the book, Aliki says: "TYRRANOSAURUS used to scare me. I still can't believe how big it is. Just its head is almost twice my size. I'm not afraid of dinosaurs anymore. Sometimes I call them 'you bag of bones' under my breath" (4). The author registers her wonder at these creatures before launching into the story of what they were, how they were discovered, and how they are dug up and carried to museums where the bones are reassembled like a huge, three-dimensional puzzle.

Then there is a second kind of printing, actually that in Aliki's hand-lettered word balloons, which provides the comic (in both senses of the word) continuity. Little figure drawings of all kinds of people crowd onto the pages, permitting us to see the great lizards in their proper size relationship to human beings. The words of these people suggest various possible responses to the dinosaurs. Aliki's empathic connection with her audience, whose awe is, in fact, her subject, verifies here as well the child's various feelings. These little people interact amongst themselves as they take in the colossal apatosaurus (brontosaurus) before them. They say: "Wow!" "It weighed 90,000 pounds!" "Eee" (This last said by a little girl being scared by a bigger boy.) "Stop that, you bully!" (Said by a man to that bigger boy.) "Imagine putting it together." "Like a jigsaw puzzle" (1). There is a figure, a little bigger and somewhat separated from the others, who carries a sketch pad and appears on successive pages. She seems to be a childlike stand-in for Aliki herself, who provides a running commentary and continuity from page to page.

It is, then, in the word bubbles that Aliki's humor is most obvious, and it is through them, as well, that she manages to humanize her subject and make it come alive. On a later page, she categorizes the different kinds of workers who are all necessary to the job of finding and preparing the giant fossils for museums. These include paleontologists, geologists, draftsmen, workers who dig the fossils, photographers and so on. One digger says to the photographer whose job it is to take pictures of the fossil find but who here is taking the workers' picture, "We're not the fossils." "Oh, yeah?" says another worker. This kind of witty repartee is truly delightful to sophisticated young readers and cannot fail to engage their attention to the end of the book. By this time, they have learned an enormous amount about dinosaurs.

Mummies Made in Egypt, by virtue of its subject alone, is for older children. For the most part, the syntax is extremely simple with virtually no subordination or even compound structures. The effect, stylistically and tonally, is one of austerity and coldness—quite the opposite of what Aliki achieves in *Digging for Dinosaurs*. But this effect is very intentional. Again, Aliki brilliantly suits narrative tone to her subject and to her illustrations, which are colored line drawings in the archaic, stylized Egyptian manner.

Practically all of the sentences are only one line of print so that an almost hypnotic trance is induced as one reads, repeatedly, sentences of the same length. For example, in defining a mummy, she writes:

> A mummy is a corpse that has been dried out so it will not decay.
> The earliest Egyptians were mummified naturally.
> The corpse was buried in the ground.
> The hot dry sand of Egypt dried out the body.
> The preserved body turned hard as stone, into a
>   fossil.

As time went on, burials became more elaborate.
The dead were wrapped in a shroud of cloth or skin.
They were buried in pits lined with wood or stone,
   or in caves.
Bodies not buried directly in the sand became exposed
   to dampness, air, and bacteria.
They decayed. (5–6)

There is, of course, method to this otherwise stylistic madness. Aliki achieves the same sort of imaginative empathy with her subject that she does by another route in *Digging for Dinosaurs*. Her tone is, as it were, petrified or mummified, attracting us by its strange, almost otherworldliness, just as the subject does.

As in *Digging for Dinosaurs*, there is also a text in Aliki's own printing that accompanies the illustrations. But unlike the hand-lettered text in the word balloons of that book, the tone of this commentary reaffirms the austere mummified quality of the narrative in the printer's font. Aliki surely achieves the kind of self-annihilation that Keats described in his letter to Woodhouse. Even the last sentence, "Many of the illustrations in this book were adapted from paintings and sculptures found in ancient Egyptian tombs," completes this authorial annihilation through its passive construction.

We also feel ourselves in the presence of poetry in *The Moon of the Winter Bird* (1969) by Jean Craighead George. Self-annihilation or, in other words, George's absorption into the natural world about which she writes, is felt from the first paragraph. She pulls the reader into the landscape: "The December moonlight fell on drizzling clouds that blanketed America from the great plains to the Atlantic Ocean. . . . Beasts slept, birds sat still on their perches, weeds and grasses slumped against the earth. The sun was at the winter solstice and the longest night of the year was upon the Northern Hemisphere. The land, responding to the sun-short days, was cold" (1). Even before she introduces the protagonist, a song sparrow whose "inner signal" has not functioned, and who has failed to fly south with the onset of colder weather and shorter days, George's use of the rhetorical device of personification reveals her empathic connection with nature. Even the grasses are fatigued by their fight against the cold and "slump" against the earth. The land "responds" to the winter solstice, the longest night of the year, by being cold. Everything in this landscape appears to have given up, to have succumbed to the cold and dark.

George's extended metaphor—the blankets and sheets of the sky's linen closet—serves to dampen readers' spirits, quite intentionally, so that they will be heartened all the more when the song sparrow makes his appearance. This he does at the end of the introductory and general section of the "story." The bird is depicted heroically; separated from his kind, he struggles to survive in the northern landscape that has, itself, given in to the cold. He is a tiny node of heat and energy who warms, by his example, the hearts of men as well as his own small body.

Jean George's empathic approach to her subject becomes more pronounced as the story of the song sparrow's fight for survival on the longest night of the year develops. Her narrative tone manages, at the same time, to be both matter-of-fact and poetic. It is as if she achieves a double vision: she sees her subject as would a nature documentarist, equipped with a telescopic lens, yet also sees the world quite literally from a bird's-eye view, humanizing through personification—watching, studying, and dreaming. Through this double perspective, the child can both observe and become the bird as the sparrow views the cold, unyielding world.

What is so extraordinary about George's narrative is that she manages to merge the many discrete "facts" about the song sparrow's existence with the particular story of this heroic bird into a single seamless narrative. Its miraculously neutral yet empathic tone is a perfect vehicle. An excellent example of the faultlessly woven strands of fact and fiction is the following description of the parasitic cowbird's attempt to lay her eggs in the nest of the song sparrow. "A few minutes later the cowbird took the second egg away and left hers. The next day the song sparrow's mate once again recognized the cowbird egg, covered it, laid her own, and flew away. The impostor came at daybreak to take the third egg. Slipping snakelike toward the bush, she did not see the stalking cat. One pounce and the sparrows were free . . . " (21).

All the time that George is communicating these facts about the life of the song sparrow, she is also committing the reader emotionally to the bird. Here we actually rejoice that the "evil" and "snakelike" cowbird is destroyed by the cat. At the end of the story, this very cat almost kills the song sparrow, and our sympathies are quite withdrawn. In fact, the tension is quite unbearable. The cat is mistakenly locked out of the house by its unwitting owner and seeks shelter under the very tree our song sparrow is roosting in for the night.

His fear, however, protected him. . . . Unable to move, he did not attract the attention of the cat who relied on movement to see her prey. . . . Fear used up the song sparrow's energy, and by two in the morning he had lost considerable weight. . . . at last the alarm clock went off in the house, and the song sparrow relaxed slightly in anticipation of the coming rituals of dawn. . . . Footsteps came down the stairs. . . . The cat rotated her ears. These sounds she knew. Coming wide awake, she scanned her environment in the manner of the predator. Presently she looked up. One snow-covered cone on the tree was fuzzy. Rising slowly, she stared as it trembled ever so slightly. The cone was breathing. She crouched to spring. The bird listened and waited in terror.

The door of the house opened. The song sparrow flew from the spruce. The cat shot off the sill and through the doorway as the man leaned down to get his paper. The winter bird was safe. (35–37)

Readers are drained by anxiety over the bird's hazardous ordeal. George's ordinarily complex syntax, her usual medium for information, gives way in the detailing of this frightening experience to short staccato bursts that increase the pressure and suspense. Kazue Mizumura's brilliant accompanying illustrations on these pages are a minimalist interpretation of cat's paw prints, ominous in their simplicity.

The same kind of empathic connection George achieves with this sparrow is created by her in a science mystery book called *Snow Tracks* (1966). The ostensible purpose of the book is to teach children how to be good observers and logicians by reading correctly the animal messages left in the snow. But in it the disappearance of Chief Half-an-Ear, an anthropomorphized mouse, is of increasing concern to the young reader. "Little niceties like looking before he rushed had made Chief Half-an-Ear the oldest mouse in the woodland—two and a half years old" (15). The reader is finally very relieved to learn that the sudden mysterious disappearance of the mouse's tracks actually means that Chief Half-an-Ear is safe, in the cage-trap of a young snow hunter who wants him for a pet. And the mouse (George's moment of compromise between fact and fiction) is quite happy to grow old in his new soft, warm nest, safe from predators and with a lifetime supply of peanut butter.

When we consider informational books for older children and teenagers, we can see that George's or Aliki's reliance on illustrations is not necessary to the same extent. For example, Don Lawson's series on America's wars or his *The Long March: Red China Under Chairman Mao* (1983) is illustrated with a few photographs, but the power of these texts depends on the exciting events he relates and his colorful prose. In describing a part of the Long March, Lawson writes:

A forced march was difficult under the best of conditons. At night. . . . To light their way the Long Marchers lit torches made of dry reeds from the riverbank tied together in bundles and soaked in kerosene. . . . Often afterward those who had taken part . . . recalled the beauty of the light flickering from the thousands of torches . . . making the moving column resemble a fiery dragon in the night.
But soon it began to rain, extinguishing all the torches. Some marchers lost their way and fell silently to their deaths off the steep cliffs into the surrounding darkness. (70)

This is a compelling narrative, by turns stirring or depressing, but always interesting. There is a recognizable voice behind these words, energized by and committed to the subject so that it is alive for the reader as well. Yet the truth is that the audience for whom this book was intended will not exist if children are not "hooked" on reading at a much earlier age. Certainly we care about the quality of the informational literature available for older readers, but most probably what is more important is upgrading the quality of books for younger children.

Fortunately, there are many new and wonderful informational books being published. On the other hand, it is dismaying to discover that so many fine books in this category, among them some of Jean George's, are no longer in print. Publishers should be encouraged to reissue them. And equally important, parents, teachers, and other adults should be spending more time reading them aloud. The human voice, further dramatizing implied authorial tone, cannot fail to go unnoticed by small children. Their uncanny ability to decode nuance may be the key to turning them into better informed, more literate adults.

REFERENCES

Aliki. *Digging for Dinosaurs*. New York: Harper and Row, 1981.

————. *Mummies Made in Egypt*. New York: Thomas Y. Crowell, 1979.

George, Jean Craighead. *The Moon of the Winter Bird*. New York: Thomas Y. Crowell, 1969.

————. *Snow Tracks*. New York: E. P. Dutton and Company, 1966.

Keats, John. *The Letters of John Keats*. Edited by Maurice Buxton Forman. London: Oxford University Press, 1960.

Lawson, Don. *The Long March: Red China Under Chairman Mao*. New York: Thomas Y. Crowell, 1983.

41

Narrative Voice in Books for Young People on Medieval History and Culture

MEREDITH KLAUS

Children's books on the history of the Middle Ages reflect the prejudices and predispositions of adult histories and historians. Some retain the traditional view of the Middle Ages, an aesthetic point of view demanding a beginning (the collapse of the Roman Empire), a middle (barbarian darkness), and an end (return of light). Such histories suppose a steady climb up the steps of progress from that time to our present position on the top step. But, since history is not a clear progression, the historian must recognize the welter of confusion that history is.

One book, with a narrator's voice that is strictly aesthetic, is *Anno's Medieval World* (1979). Anno is an artist, not an historian, and the emphasis in the title should perhaps be *ANNO'S Medieval World*. In several of his books, such as *Anno's Journey*, Anno uses a cinematic technique, flashing from one historical period to another with the flick of a page, never focusing on a specific historical period. A similar technique appears in this book, which is more of an historical tour de force than an accurate account of medieval life.

Anno sets his story in a mythical kingdom, supposed to be a composite of Europe existing in barbarian darkness: "At night they saw the moon in the sky and could not understand why it waxed and waned, or where it came from or where it went. But this they did know—that if they walked far enough, they would reach the sea, and that if they sailed far enough, they would reach the edge of the world where the ocean flowed over the rim in an endless waterfall" (unpaged). The accompanying illustration shows a seashore, with fisherfolk pulling a boat ashore and spreading their nets to dry. The upper right hand corner shows their imaginary world picture, with ocean falling off the edge of the world and a boat teetering precariously, about to pitch off the edge.

It is obvious at first glance that Anno has no intention of writing a history of medieval life. To begin with, the people of his "small country" (hardly an apt description of the European continent, which seems to be the actual topic of his book) pray to "the gods." Two pages later, when a cathedral occupies the center of the illustration we find " . . . it is God who moves the spheres." It is apparent that Anno's story actually begins in neolithic (hunting-gathering) times, acquires some classical costumery and architecture, and then moves abruptly to the Renaissance, with its incongruous fascination with both science and witchcraft.

Anno, in his concern in this book with scientific progress, and with, primarily, the formulation of the heliocentric theory, mistakenly places the witchcraft hysteria that plagued Europe from the fourteenth to the seventeenth century back into his "medieval world." Actually, the concern with witchcraft as a religious and legal problem did not become serious until, at the earliest, the publication of the *Malleus Malleficarum* in 1453. The hunt for witches and scientific truth were pursued with equal vigor contemporaneously. A greater concern with scientific evidence and rapidly increasing scientific technology did not immediately (or perhaps ever) affect a world searching for scapegoats. However, in Anno's book, two pages out of twenty-two pages on life in the Middle Ages are concerned with an obsessive fear of witchcraft:

People believed that God lived in heaven and that the devil lived in hell. They believed that witches were the devil's servants, flying hither and thither through the air, plotting evil against the world. Whenever the crops failed or the cattle died or there were floods or drought, it was obviously the work of witches. And when the plague swept the land and people died like flies in the winter, it was the witches who were to blame. (unpaged)

In this way, throughout the book, Anno's narrative voice keeps telling us of the dichotomy between enlightened modernism and the pathetic ignorance of medievalism: "There were no microscopes then so no one knew that bacteria existed, much less that they caused the plague. People blamed the witches for this and other misfortunes and determined to put an end to their evil . . . " (unpaged).

At the end of the book the adult reader finds the author's note, explaining the purpose of Anno's book. He was, it appears, enthusiastically absorbed by two events in the history of ideas—the discovery that the earth was round (actually an idea not unfamiliar in earlier times) and the replacement of the Ptolemaic theory with the Copernican. This concern is reflected in the whole series of illustrations in the text. In the background of the first illustration the landscape appears perfectly flat, as the little people in the illustration believed their world to be. As the story progresses, the landscape changes from flat to round, first appearing as a hill or mound, gradually becoming a semicircle, then an almost complete circle and finally, in the last illustration, a complete circle, pictured as a globe complete with wooden stand. He is enthusiastic about the discoveries of Copernicus and Galileo and the scientific revolution they began. He is not enthusiastic about medieval life, and the voice with which he speaks about that life is entirely negative.

For some the book is irreparably marred by such misrepresentations, and they certainly would preclude its use in teaching medieval history. However, the art work, with its medieval flavor, perhaps reminiscent of the Utrecht Psalter, is charming enough to be retained for its own value. Each page is a marvelously complex and fascinating scene, with a cast of characters from serfs to sovereigns. On one page miners wheel a cart full of ore on tracks leading out of a mine, a blacksmith works at an anvil with a group of onlookers, a Hansel and Gretel cottage nestles under a gnarled and twisted tree, straight out of a Japanese painting, a tree that bears tropical blue foliage and a parakeet. An angel watches us from one corner of the decorative border, while an aged Pan pipes from another. In the bottom corners are small cupid figures. On each page, marvelous little human figures dance in circles or labor at their tasks, or simply watch the others in fascinated curiosity.

The melange of iconography reflects the incongruities of the history, and whatever the value of the illustrations as works of art, the voice of the narrator speaks to us more loudly of his admiration of the virtues of the modern world and his bias against the benighted past. But history is too much of a piece to have glowing light coming from absolute darkness.

Like Anno's linear and progressive mode, Isaac Asimov's *The Dark Ages* forces history into an aesthetic form more appropriate to literature than to history. Perhaps it is not entirely coincidental that Asimov's early Foundation Trilogy followed exactly the same pattern as does his history of the Middle Ages. Asimov devotes the first five chapters of his book to the conflicts of the Roman Empire with the Germanic tribes, from the first appearance of the Germans in Europe, about 1000 B.C., until the final collapse of the empire. This conflict is clearly stated in terms of civilization versus barbarism, light against dark—there is nothing of the failures of the Romans themselves, other than their failure to combat and overcome the German tribes.

Roman rule was not entirely beneficent and those ruled by them, as the Germans would have been, were as likely to think of them as exploiters and tax gatherers as they were to see them as the bearers of the light of civilization. The Romans surpassed the Germans in their attainment of literacy, in the superb governmental administration, and in their plumbing and heating systems—our modern American devotion to this sort of thing predisposes us to support emotionally those who so excel and to look down on those who do not. (Much the same kind of prejudice can be found in many American history textbooks and their treatment of the native American culture.) "Rome made no further attempt to conquer and civilize the Germans, something which turned out, in the end, to be bad for the Romans, and for the Germans too, and perhaps for the whole world" (69).

The body of the book is devoted to the rise and fall of the various Frankish kingdoms, but the last chapters emphasize the overriding tenor of the author's voice. Section ten is entitled "The Darkness Begins to Lift" and is concerned with certain tenth-century developments Asimov sees as lightening the barbarian darkness, among them the combination of the moldboard plow and the horse collar: "The horse-drawn moldboard plow meant that agricultural productivity began to show a steady rise and this meant that there was an increasing food surplus available to support armed men . . . " (228).

It cannot be argued that the time between 500 and 1000 A.D. was a comfortable and secure time to live in Europe for the bulk of the population. But how many years since then has it been? The light that comes and goes during the long years lights a very small part of human life.

Countering the major theme of the book—light versus darkness—is the eminently civilized voice of Asimov himself—intelligent, witty, controlled, always looking sceptically at warfare, always conscious of the real "advances." The plow and the horse collar provide more food for the peasant farmers of Europe as well as for their masters, the knights.

Unlike Anno in his vision of life in the Middle Ages, Asimov is never historically inaccurate. His attention to historical detail is both pervasive and unremittingly impeccable, as is his attention to accuracy in all his writing. He is also capable of using an ironic narrative voice in speaking of the Romans as well as barbarians. One example, for the reign of Justinian: "The thing to do, as he [Justinian] saw it, was to send a second capable general who, for one reason or another, wouldn't be a threat to the Emperor under any circumstance. As it happened, he had the perfect candidate (Things always seemed to break right for Justinian)" (69). And he goes on: "It is an odd fact that anyone who wishes to start a war must always make it appear that he is fighting in a just cause, even if the real motive is naked aggression. Fortunately for the would-be aggressor, a 'just cause' is very easy to find" (69). With this method of ironic characterization, Asimov skillfully involves the reader in the complex personalities and politics, the waves of invasion and migration, the building and dissolving of kingdoms in the early Middle Ages. We become acquainted, in thumbnail characterizations, with Theodoric and Attila, with all the Dagoberts and Childeberts, their wives, their children and their poor relations, their friends and enemies. There are even occasional glimpses of what all this meant to the ordinary people of the time.

Yet Asimov always has in view of his major theme, the struggle of light and dark, the slow movement of history toward the light of reason. Every barbarian gloom is the threat of evil and "The Dark," every gleam of progress is "Light." The body of the book is devoted to the rise and fall of the various Gothic and Frankish kingdoms, but in the last chapters "The Darkness Begins to Lift."

As the darkness fades, the power of the barbarian rulers is replaced by that of another elite—the Renaissance aristocrat.

This slow dawn between 950 and 1000 was not a change, like Charlemagne's, destined to fade—rather it was to be followed by many other changes, one after another, in quicker and quicker succession, until the accumulation of them exploded into an almost unbearably brilliant civilization that (with all its faults as well as its virtues) spread far in western Europe through all the world.

And the end of which—we can only hope—is not yet. (234)

Some books, however, particularly more recent ones, consider history as a current, flowing in fluid curves, rather than a linear and ascending progression. Since he or she no longer has to prove that history is moving toward some dramatic climax, the author may speak in a sympathetic tone to allow a greater degree of empathy with the persons and events of the narrative. The author speaks of them not as if they are moved by the impersonal forces of history but as reflecting the needs and wants of a particular group of people or of individual human beings. Such a book is Richard B. Lyttle's *Land Beyond the River* (1986), on the urge that moves a man or moves a whole tribe to extend horizons, to explore the land beyond the river.

Lyttle begins his history in Fort Ross, the Russian Fort on the north coast of California, reaches back to the last days of the Roman Empire, talks about the Huns, the Goths, the Vandals and the Saxons, gradually moves eastward to the Moslem conquest, stops for breath with Genghis Khan and the Mongol migrations, and ends neatly with the Russian migration into Siberia, Alaska, and the California coast. It is a more global pattern than the narrow focus on the darkness passing across Europe.

Rather than a geometric form or an evolutionary process, Lyttle as speaker develops a narrative mode that enables him to relate historic events as process itself, as a current, flowing in fluid curves. Lyttle sees history as an endless succession of sweeping waves, each one both destroying and building anew. Both speaker and sympathetic listener, Lyttle takes an objective, perhaps even a sympathetic look at the various migrations generally referred to as "the Scourge of God" or "the Golden Horde"—the Huns, Mongols, and Vikings—some of them pirates and raiders, but many of them simply peaceful farmers, traders, and restless explorers.

Rather than speaking of the people and events of the Middle Ages in an ironic and condescending tone, as does Asimov, or in the negative manner of Anno, Lyttle is effervescent and enthusiastic. The positive quality of his narrative voice is important in stirring in young readers a love of and enthusiasm for the reading of history. Lyttle celebrates the strivings of the human spirit. As he relates the story of the fall of the Roman Empire and of the Germanic migrations, he tells us of the consistency of human wants and needs. Empires do not live and die like people. Rather people meet the conditions of their time and make of them what they can.

The narrator, viewing history as an ongoing event rather than a geometric form, can attain the global perspective lacking in many histories of the Middle Ages. For young readers this may be the most valuable attribute of *Land Beyond the River*. Chapters on the Moslems, Vikings, and Mongols give us an insight into the development of the vast Eurasian continent. The author's voice speaking of these distant lands and peoples tells us of their accomplishments. He tells us of the high cultural achievements of the Islamic culture (during the "dark ages"): "Arabs had time to study, think, and create. They built a culture far in advance of any society that could be found in Medieval Europe. They delighted in stories and poetry. They pioneered in the study of astronomy, medicine, philosophy, chemistry and mathematics . . . " (90).

Turning from the global perspective and the extensive text of Lyttle's history to a picture book that focuses on a single aspect of life in the Middle Ages, we find an example in Aliki's *A Medieval Feast* (1983). Here the author-illustrator speaks in a quiet, explanatory voice, but one that delights in an abundance of detail. Gone is the dark tone of witchcraft fears and barbarian darkness. Instead Aliki delights in the sunshine of a medieval garden.

The medieval feast is a single incident in the round of events in a medieval manor. There is to be a royal progress, wherein the royal court will visit Camdenton Manor, its Lord and Lady:

> It was announced
> from the palace that the King
> would soon make a long journey.
>
> On the way to his destination, the King and
> his party would spend a few nights at Camdenton
> Manor. The lord of the manor knew what this
> meant. The king traveled with his Queen, his
> knights, squires, and other members of his
> court.
>
> There would be a hundred mouths to feed! (unpaged)

The author speaks here first with the commanding voice of the king, then with the concerned and apprehensive voice of the lord of Camdenton. But the illustration, with the rich complexity of a medieval manuscript, counterpoints both command and apprehension. The title page itself, with a picture of a gleaming white swan swimming on a clear blue pond, a miniature castle peering at it from a distance, is bordered by an arabesque of patterned leaves, the linear border contrasting with the tension of the curling leaves, which both reach toward the center and pull back to the border. Tiny tendrils and seed pods punctuate the leaf pattern. Later in the book this leafy border will be varied with bunches of grapes, singing birds, and flowers.

Aliki's illustrations provide a detailed account of life on the manor. Although the tale is framed by the king's announcement and his departure, Aliki emphasizes throughout the people who are doing the work—men building stockades for horses and erecting tents for people; women gathering vegetables, tending bees, and snaring birds and fish; children carrying stacks of firewood, and, of course, battalions of cooks and kitchen boys preparing food in the vast and cathedral-like kitchen.

Aliki's feeling of joy and festivity pervades the labors. The lord of the castle may be worried about bankruptcy—"There would be a hundred mouths to feed!"—but his retainers work with calm and quiet intensity. The faces of the tiny human figures have a classic repose and serenity in the midst of their labors. Only an occasional emotion surfaces—the look of consternation on the lord's face when he reads the announcement of the four and twenty blackbirds baked in a pie. There may be hard work for all, in addition to their no doubt sufficient daily chores, but there is an absorption in the task and a feeling of its importance in the scheme of things.

In a picture of two women gathering vegetables, the garden itself is a rich and luxuriant green, fruitful and full of life. The vegetables are tiny but lovingly detailed. One woman picks a cabbage and holds it carefully as a holy relic. The other woman, her blue gown mirroring the sky, holds an overflowing basket. On a small stream, a family of swans swims by, while on the opposite bank hives of bees hum contentedly near an orchard. Lazy ducks drift between clouds and sky. Bordering the picture a panel with a background of rich golden yellow illustrates the various fruits and vegetables and herbs mentioned in the text—peas and radishes, leeks and sage, apples, plums and melons, parsley, mint and thyme (with a bee between the mint and the thyme). The enclosed feeling contributed by the panel, the balance of the two women facing each other as they bend to their task, and the glowing color of sunshine reflect the joy of skillfully performing a needed task.

A book similar in tone but with a contrasting narrative voice is Sheila Sancha's *The Luttrell Village: Country Life in the Middle Ages* (1982). Although Sancha echoes the joy and enthusiasm of Aliki and the empathy of Richard Lyttle, her major concern is accuracy in portraying each detail of village life. The book is a description of the village of Gerneham and is based, in part, on some of the illustrations in the Luttrell Psalter, commissioned around 1330 by Sir Geoffrey Luttrell, who "wanted to include pictures of himself and the familiar faces surrounding him in an elaborate prayer book." Sancha used contour maps, archeological reports and historical resources to "put the people of the psalter back into their hills."

Much like the *A Medieval Feast, The Luttrell Village* shows the villagers at their daily tasks, tracing the course of the year in a fourteenth-century English village. The loving accumulation of detail combines with the nostalgic voice of the modern historian, looking at a past of firmly fixed rule and order. Sancha's pervasive tone speaks of strict attention to the facts of medieval life, but both text and illustration convey a quiet content in the midst of some privation: "[A]n ordinary house in the village of Gerneham on a cold winter's morning in the year 1328. The cobbled ground on which the house and sheds were built was called a *toft*, while the long stretch of land where vegetables grew in summer and where sheep, goats, and pigs were kept in pens, was called a *croft*" (unpaged).

The accompanying illustration shows the thatch-roofed, wattle and daub house of the farmer; the outbuildings, including poultry house, sheepfold and pigsty; even, beyond the vegetable gardens, the family's beehives. On the opposite page a cross-section of the house shows the family huddled around the central fire, the smoke rising through the two smoke-holes in the roof, while cattle browse in the adjacent manger:

An entire family lived, ate and slept in the room in the middle of the house. . . . Ovens were either built outside in the toft or indoors behind a partition. The housewife would burn a bundle of wood inside the oven and, when the flames had died down, bake her bread on the ashes. The villager's two oxen were stabled beyond the passage. They were the pride of his life and he groomed them each day with a wisp of hay. After a breakfast of bread, cheese and thin ale, he and his son yoked them together, ready for the plow. (unpaged)

Spring comes to the village, and the following pages show the entire village at work, plowing the fields. It is a lively scene, with dogs scampering across the plowed furrows, barking enthusiastically at the hordes of birds that have descended on the sown fields:

Pigeons from Sir Geoffrey's and the priest's dovecotes followed the carts, while rooks and crows rose cawing from the nearby wood, swooped down and fought over the grain as soon as it was out of the sacks. Some boys did their best to hit the crows with sling-stones, but they were forbidden to kill pigeons because they belonged to their lord and to the church. One man scattered the seed, while another followed with a horse-drawn harrow, covering the seed as quickly as possible. It was always a battle with the birds. (unpaged)

Here Sancha does not avoid speaking of the difficulties and oppressions the villagers suffer from the constant demands of overlord and church and the hovering presence of a threatening nature. But both text and illustration sing to us across the ages of the settled security of a life in which everything, even a boy's slingshot, had its function and its place.

REFERENCES

Aliki. *A Medieval Feast*. New York: Thomas Y. Crowell, 1983.

Anno, Mitsumasa. *Anno's Medieval World*. Adapted from the translation by Ursula Synge. New York: Philomel Books, 1979.

Asimov, Isaac. *The Dark Ages*. Boston: Houghton Mifflin, 1968.

Lyttle, Richard B. *Land Beyond the River: Europe in the Age of Migration*. New York: Atheneum, 1986.

Sancha, Sheila. *The Luttrell Village: Country Life in the Middle Ages*. New York: Thomas Y. Crowell, 1982.

Index

Contributors

RICHARD ADAMS, author of *Watership Down*, *The Plague Dogs*, ballads, a collection of folktales; winner of the Carnegie Medal (1972).

JANICE ALBERGHENE, associate professor of English, Fitchburg State College, Fitchburg, Massachusetts.

LLOYD ALEXANDER, author of the *Westmark Trilogy*, the *Chronicles of Prydain*, and many other titles; winner of the Newbery Award (1969).

LIONEL BASNEY, professor of English, Calvin College, Grand Rapids, Michigan.

JOAN BLOS, author of historical fiction, including *Brothers of the Heart* and *A Gathering of Days*; winner of the Newbery Award (1980).

HAMIDA BOSMAJIAN, professor of English and Pigott-McCone Chair of Humanities, Seattle University, Seattle, Washington.

RAY BRADBURY, author of science fiction and fantasy, including *The Martian Chronicles*, *Fahrenheit Four Fifty-One*, *Dandelion Wine*.

PATRICIA CLAPP, author of historical fiction, including *Constance: A Story of Early Plymouth*, *I'm Deborah Sampson: A Soldier in the War of the Revolution*, *Witches' Children: A Story of Salem*; playwright.

BARBARA COONEY, illustrator of *Chanticleer and the Fox*, *Ox-Cart Man*, author-illustrator of *Miss Rumphius*, *Island Boy*; twice winner of the Caldecott Award (1959, 1980).

PETER DICKINSON, author of a trilogy about England, *Tulku*, *City of Gold*; twice winner of the Carnegie Medal (1979, 1980).

ANN DONOVAN, curriculum librarian, Central Washington University, Ellensburg, Washington.

W. D. EMRYS EVANS, lecturer in education (English), The University of Birmingham, Birmingham, United Kingdom.

LEONARD EVERETT FISHER, painter, illustrator, author of many titles, including a series on colonial Americans and colonial American craftsmen, *The Seven Days of Creation*; winner of the Pulitzer Award for painting (1950).

JEAN FRITZ, author of historical fiction, biography, and autobiography, including *The Cabin Faced West*, *Brady*, *What's the Big Idea, Ben Franklin?*, *Homesick: My Own Story*.

ANN GRIFALCONI, illustrator of *The Jazz Man*, poems by Langston Hughes, author-illustrator of West African stories, including *The Village of Round and Square Houses*.

JAMES HIGGINS, professor of education, Queens College, Flushing, New York.

MALCOLM JONES, co-author of *Jump! The Adventures of Brer Rabbit*; book review editor of the *St. Petersburg Times*.

MARILYN JURICH, professor of English, Suffolk University, Boston, Massachusetts.

JEAN KARL, Founder and director of Children's Book Department at Atheneum; author of a book on publishing, *From Childhood to Childhood: Children's Books and Their Creators*, and of science fiction novels for children.

MEREDITH KLAUS, associate professor of English, Eastern Michigan University, Ypsilanti, Michigan.

KARLA KUSKIN, poet, author of information books, including *The Dallas*

Titans Get Ready for Bed, A Space Story; winner of the NCTE Award for Excellence in Poetry for Children (1979).

LOIS KUZNETS, associate professor of English and comparative literature, San Diego State University, San Diego, California.

JULIUS LESTER, author of *To Be a Slave*; reteller of folktales, including *Long Journey Home: Stories from Black History, The Knee-High Man and Other Tales.*

JOANNE LEWIS, professor of English and comparative literature at California State University, Fullerton, California.

MYRA COHN LIVINGSTON, poet, author of *A Circle of Seasons*; a book on writing poetry, *The Child as Poet: Myth or Reality?*; anthologist; winner of the NCTE Award for Excellence in Poetry for Children (1980).

LOIS LOWRY, author of the Anastasia Krupnik books, *Autumn Street, A Summer to Die.*

JANET LUNN, author of *Double Spell, Larger Than Life, The Root Cellar*; winner of the Canadian Library Award (1982).

RUTH MACDONALD, professor of English at Purdue University, Calumet, Indiana.

RODERICK MCGILLIS, professor of English, University of Calgary, Calgary, Alberta, Canada.

MILTON MELTZER, author of biographies on Langston Hughes, Winnie Mandela and of informational books on the holocaust, including *Never to Forget: The Jews of the Holocaust*; editor of primary materials in American Black history and the American Revolution.

EVE MERRIAM, poet, author of *Catch a Little Rhyme, Fresh Paint, You Be Good and I'll Be Night*; winner of the Yale Series of Younger Poets prize and the NCTE Award for Excellence in Poetry for Children (1981).

ALICE MILLS, lecturer in myth and fantasy at Ballarat College of Advanced Education, Victoria, Australia.

PATRICIA MORLEY, author of *Kurelek: A Biography*; professor of English and Canadian Studies, Concordia University, Montreal, Canada.

LAURENCE PRINGLE, former editor of *Nature and Science*; wildlife biologist; author of informational books, including *Frost Hollows and Other Microclimates*, *Feral: Tame Animals Gone Wild*.

ROBERT QUACKENBUSH, author-illustrator of biographies, picture songbooks, mysteries, including *Mark Twain? What Kind of a Name Is That?*, *She'll Be Comin' 'Round the Mountain*, *Gondola to Danger: A Miss Mallard Mystery*.

MAURICE SENDAK, author-illustrator of *Where the Wild Things Are*, *In the Night Kitchen*, *Outside Over There*; winner of the Caldecott Award (1964) and the Hans Christian Andersen Award (1970).

ELLEN TREMPER, professor of English, Brooklyn College of CUNY, Brooklyn, New York.

NICHOLAS TUCKER, lecturer in developmental psychology, School of Cultural and Community Studies, The University of Sussex, Sussex, United Kingdom.

JILL PATON WALSH, author of realistic fiction and fantasy, including *Goldengrove*, *Unleaving*, *A Chance Child*, *The Green Book*.

MURIEL WHITAKER, professor of English, University of Alberta, Edmonton, Alberta.

NANCY WILLARD, poet, author of *A Visit to William Blake's Inn: Poems for Innocent and Experienced Travelers*, *The Island of the Grass King*, the Anatole Trilogy Series; winner of the Newbery Award (1982).

About the Editors

CHARLOTTE F. OTTEN is Professor of English at Calvin College in Grand Rapids, Michigan. She is the author of *A Lycanthropy Reader: Werewolves in Western Culture* and *Environ'd with Eternity* and has contributed articles to *Shakespeare Quarterly*, *Milton Studies*, *Notes & Queries*, and *ELR*.

GARY D. SCHMIDT is Associate Professor of English at Calvin College. He wrote *The Art of Robert McCloskey* and *Classic Models of Rhetoric*. His articles have been published in *Journal of the Rocky Mountain Medieval and Renaissance Association*, *Mediavalia*, *Medieval Connections*, and the *Children's Literature Association Quarterly*.